EXILE

EXILE

The Captive Years of Mary, Queen of Scots

ROSEMARY GORING

BIRLINN

First published in 2025 by
Birlinn Limited
West Newington House
10 Newington Road
Edinburgh
EH9 1QS

www.birlinn.co.uk

Copyright © Rosemary Goring 2025

The right of Rosemary Goring to be identified as Author of this work has been asserted by her in accordance with the Copyright, Designs and Patents Act 1988.

All rights reserved. No part of this publication may be reproduced, stored or transmitted in any form without the express written permission of the publisher.

ISBN: 978 1 78027 838 4

British Library Cataloguing-in-Publication Data
A catalogue record for this book is available from the British Library.

Designed and typeset by Hewer Text UK Ltd, Edinburgh
Papers used by Birlinn are from well-managed forests and other responsible sources.
Printed and bound by Bell & Bain, Glasgow

Contents

Acknowledgements — vii
Family Trees — x
Map — xiv
Introduction — xv

1. 'They have robbed me of every thing I had in the world' — 1
2. 'This detention which I think rather harsh and strange' — 13
3. 'I have made great wars in Scotland . . .' — 21
4. 'I am no enchanter' — 32
5. 'I never wrote anything concerning that matter to any creature' — 43
6. 'Bound hand and foot' — 53
7. 'It is ill with me now I fear worse to come' — 64
8. 'My trembling hand here will write no more' — 72
9. 'If the vessel was ever so little stirred' — 82
10. 'Smite him to pieces' — 87
11. 'A waste and howling wilderness' — 99
12. 'Esteemed by you as an enemy instead of a friend' — 112
13. 'It is full of blood' — 122
14. 'Unless she could transform herself into a mouse or a flea . . .' — 129
15. 'The bath has soothed my nerves' — 138
16. 'I immediately burn the draughts of the ciphers' — 152
17. 'I am very fond of my little dogs' — 161

18	'She cannot do ill while she is with my husband'	176
19	'Being in constant dread . . .'	186
20	'Tribulation has been to them as a furnace to fine gold'	201
21	'I look this day for no kingdom but that of my God'	214
22	'I know my duty to you, as much as any son in the world towards his mother'	222
23	'I seek the quiet with all my heart'	232
24	'One of the most whimsical and austere persons whom I have ever known'	244
25	'Eated in the face with small pocks'	253
26	'Her Majesty might have her body, but her heart she should never have'	268
27	'Look to your consciences'	275
28	'I pray God grant you as much happiness in this world as I expect in leaving it'	286
29	'Laughing with the angels'	297
	Aftermath	309
	Further Reading	319
	Index	327

Acknowledgements

First acknowledgement, with a book like this, must go to all the historians and translators who have written about Mary, Queen of Scots or edited her voluminous correspondence. Their work is the bedrock on which *Exile* rests. I must also record my thanks to the staff at the National Library of Scotland and at Edinburgh Central Library, not just for their existence in a time when cuts are threatening libraries across the country, but for their eagerness to assist whenever required.

George Lasry, one of the team of cryptographers at the DECRYPT project, was a great help before I even began writing this book. As a result of his team's remarkable powers of sleuthing, interest in Mary's years of imprisonment in England has been revivified. Claudia Bolling of The Abbotsford Trust, and James Holloway, provided very useful information and thoughts on the provenance of Amias Cawood's 'Head of Mary, Queen of Scots after decollation', which is held at Abbotsford.

Friends and family have all been on the case during *Exile*'s gestation, and their encouragement has urged me on. Particular appreciation is owed to my granddaughter Imogen, for her indefatigable promotion of its predecessor, *Homecoming*, asking staff in every bookshop we visit if it is in stock, and then posing with a copy for a photo. I do hope she is training her brother Oliver to follow in her footsteps. Another great supporter has been Allan Hunter, who never grew bored asking how Mary was faring, even when it was obvious there was no glimmer of light at the end of the tunnel.

I am, as always, immensely grateful to the staff at Birlinn, all of whom are a pleasure to work with. Andrew Simmons is the best editor a writer could wish for: engaged, encouraging and clear-eyed, while publicist Jan Rutherford is unfailingly supportive and enthusiastic. Many thanks, too, to Steven Veerapen for casting an expert eye over the text, and to copy-editor Sarah Ream, who did an excellent job in fine-tuning the text. Any errors that remain are entirely mine. As for artist Patrizio Belcampo, his evocative image of Mary perfectly complements his cover for *Homecoming*.

Above all, I am indebted to my husband, Alan Taylor, for whom 'long-suffering' does not begin to describe his role. When I first introduced Mary into our household, neither of us could have imagined we'd still be living with her five years later, and, most likely, for a great deal longer. As well as enduring countless conversations about Stuart and Tudor politics, he has been valiant in accompanying me on trips around England, keeping my spirits up as I wrote and making invaluable suggestions on the final manuscript. There is not space here to acknowledge his contribution fully, so I simply thank him with all my heart for his help with *Exile*, and so much else down the years.

Family Tress

STEWART/STUART, HAMILTON and LENNOX

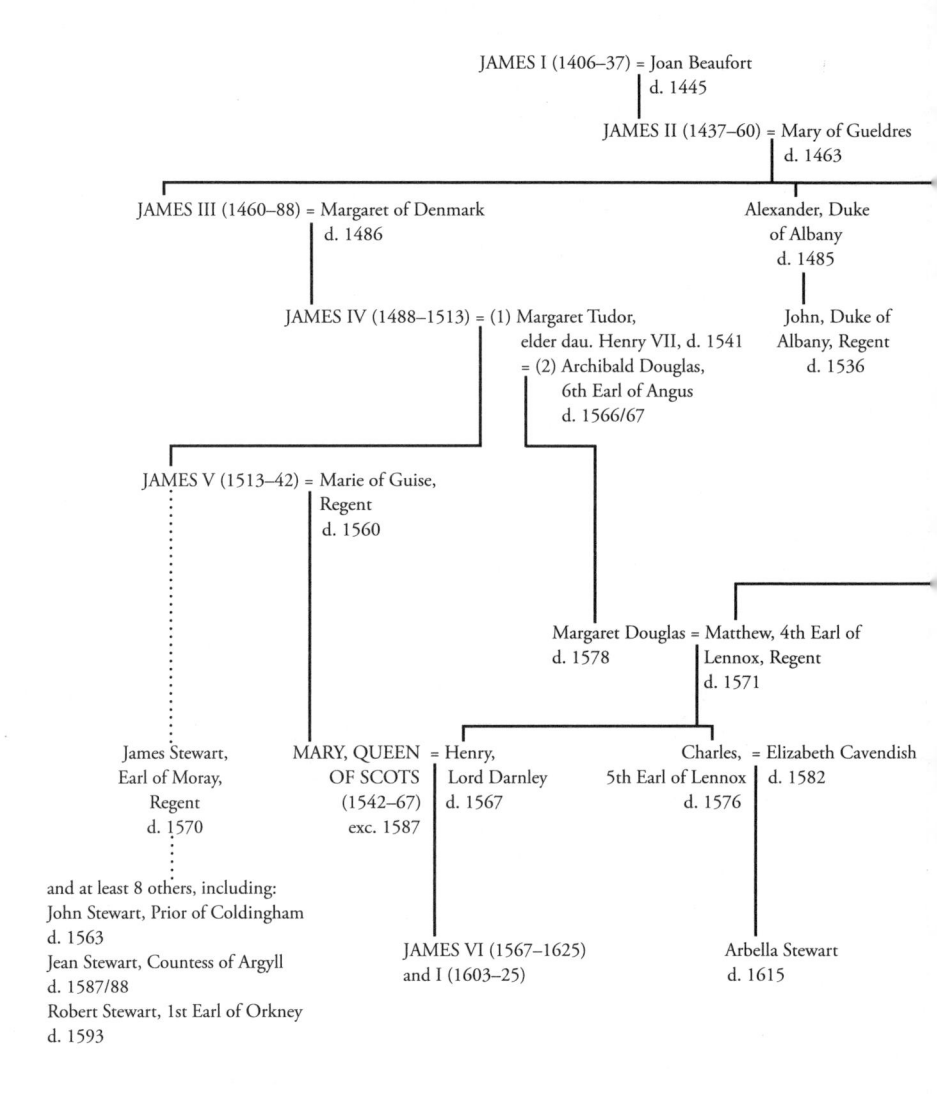

JAMES I (1406–37) = Joan Beaufort
d. 1445

JAMES II (1437–60) = Mary of Gueldres
d. 1463

JAMES III (1460–88) = Margaret of Denmark
d. 1486

Alexander, Duke of Albany
d. 1485

JAMES IV (1488–1513) = (1) Margaret Tudor, elder dau. Henry VII, d. 1541
= (2) Archibald Douglas, 6th Earl of Angus
d. 1566/67

John, Duke of Albany, Regent
d. 1536

JAMES V (1513–42) = Marie of Guise, Regent
d. 1560

Margaret Douglas = Matthew, 4th Earl of Lennox, Regent
d. 1578
d. 1571

James Stewart, Earl of Moray, Regent
d. 1570

MARY, QUEEN OF SCOTS (1542–67) exc. 1587
= Henry, Lord Darnley
d. 1567

Charles, 5th Earl of Lennox
d. 1576
= Elizabeth Cavendish
d. 1582

and at least 8 others, including:
John Stewart, Prior of Coldingham
d. 1563
Jean Stewart, Countess of Argyll
d. 1587/88
Robert Stewart, 1st Earl of Orkney
d. 1593

JAMES VI (1567–1625) and I (1603–25)

Arbella Stewart
d. 1615

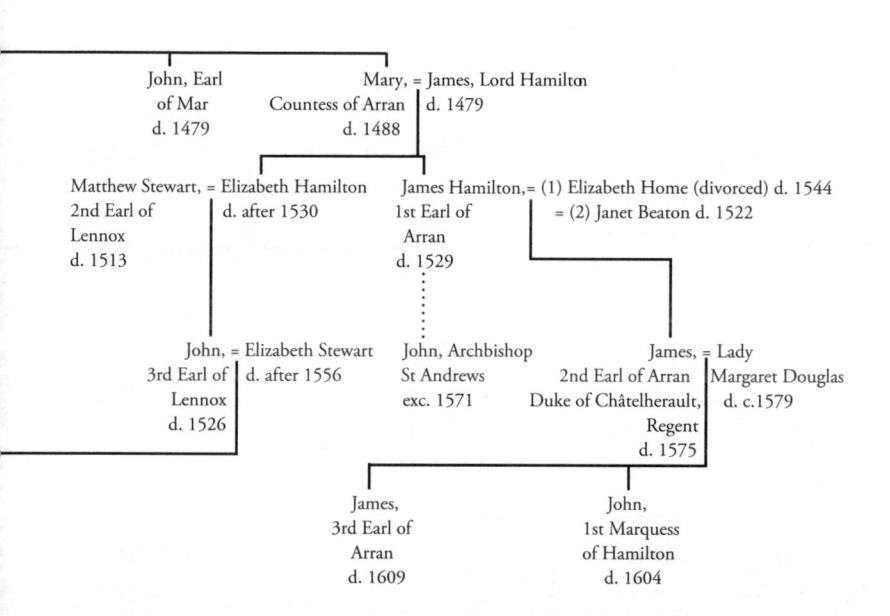

```
John, Earl            Mary,      = James, Lord Hamilton
 of Mar         Countess of Arran   d. 1479
 d. 1479           d. 1488
```

Matthew Stewart, = Elizabeth Hamilton   James Hamilton, = (1) Elizabeth Home (divorced) d. 1544
2nd Earl of   d. after 1530   1st Earl of   = (2) Janet Beaton d. 1522
Lennox   Arran
d. 1513   d. 1529

              John,   = Elizabeth Stewart   John, Archbishop   James,   = Lady
           3rd Earl of   d. after 1556   St Andrews   2nd Earl of Arran Margaret Douglas
            Lennox   exc. 1571   Duke of Châtelherault, d. c.1579
            d. 1526   Regent
                                                                      d. 1575

                                              James,   John,
                                           3rd Earl of   1st Marquess
                                              Arran   of Hamilton
                                             d. 1609   d. 1604

⋮ illegitimate descent

= married
exc. executed
d. died

GUISE

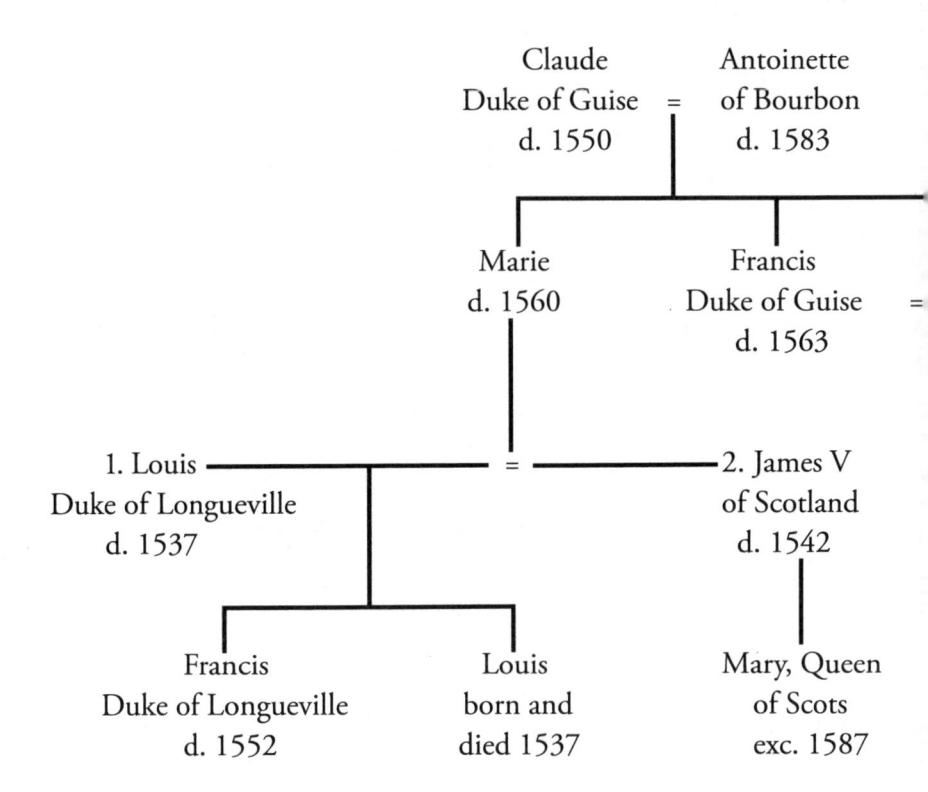

```
                    Claude                Antoinette
                 Duke of Guise    =       of Bourbon
                    d. 1550                 d. 1583
                        |
         ┌──────────────┴──────────────┐
                  Marie                   Francis
                 d. 1560               Duke of Guise    =
                                          d. 1563
     1. Louis ─────────── = ─────────── 2. James V
  Duke of Longueville                   of Scotland
       d. 1537                            d. 1542
         |                                   |
   ┌─────┴─────┐                              |
   Francis       Louis                   Mary, Queen
Duke of Longueville   born and           of Scots
   d. 1552      died 1537                exc. 1587
```

Anne d'Este	Charles	and seven more
d. 1607	Cardinal of Lorraine	who lived beyond infancy
	d. 1574	

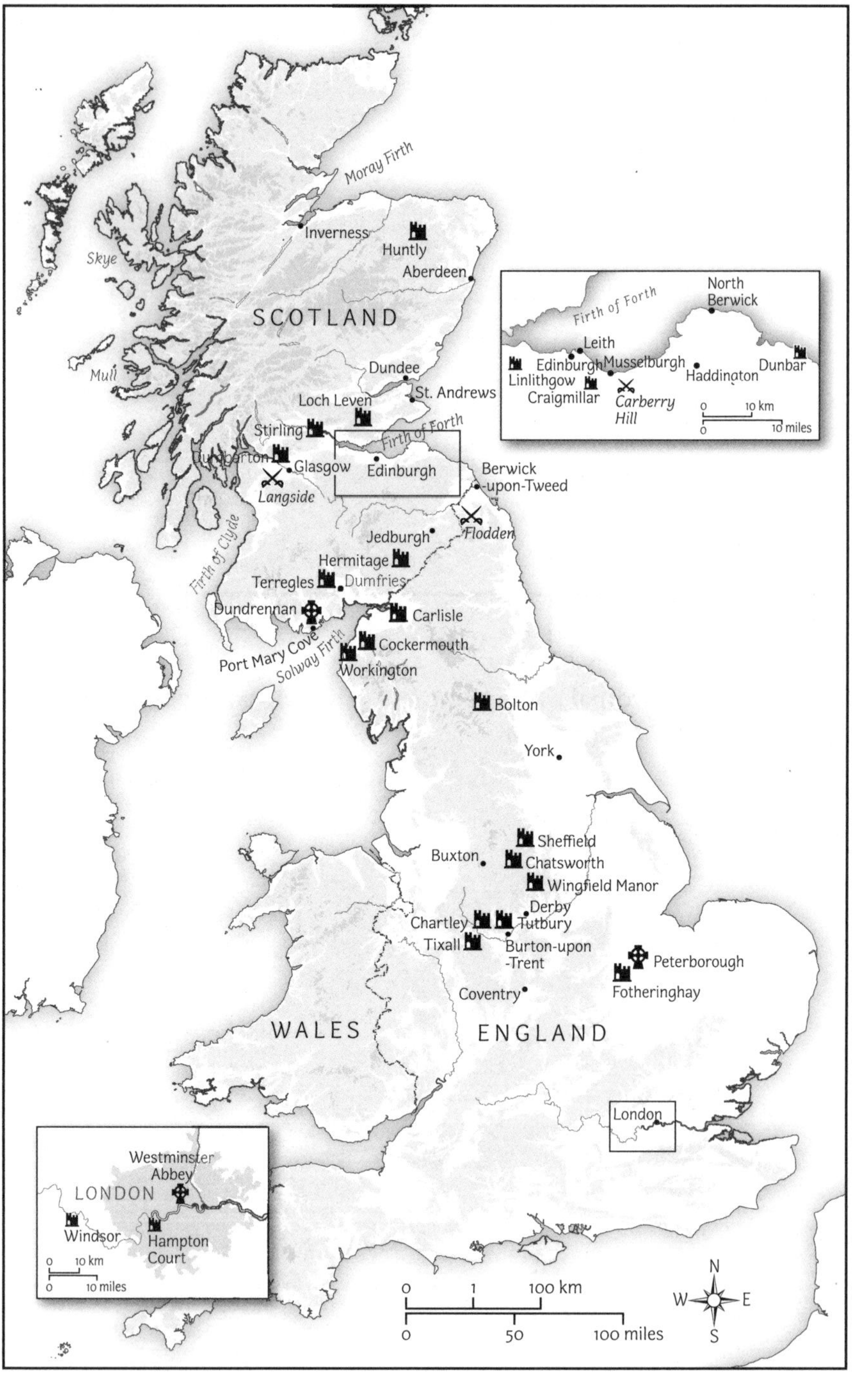
Moray Firth
Inverness
Huntly
Aberdeen
Skye
SCOTLAND
Mull
Dundee
St. Andrews
Loch Leven
Stirling
Firth of Forth
Dumbarton
Glasgow
Edinburgh
Langside
Berwick
-upon-Tweed
Flodden
Firth of Clyde
Jedburgh
Hermitage
Terregles
Dumfries
Dundrennan
Carlisle
Port Mary Cove
Solway Firth
Cockermouth
Workington
Bolton
York
Sheffield
Buxton
Chatsworth
Wingfield Manor
Derby
Chartley
Tutbury
Tixall
Burton-upon
-Trent
Peterborough
Fotheringhay
Coventry
WALES
ENGLAND
London
North
Berwick
Firth of Forth
Leith
Edinburgh
Musselburgh
Haddington
Dunbar
Linlithgow
Craigmillar
Carberry
Hill
0 10 km
0 10 miles
Westminster
Abbey
LONDON
Windsor
Hampton
Court
0 10 km
0 10 miles
0 1 100 km
0 50 100 miles
N
W
E
S

Introduction

If this book were a novel, nobody could predict its ending. With the story of Mary, Queen of Scots, however, the final chapter is well known: the ailing queen, dressed in russet, with a small dog hidden beneath her skirts, places her head on the block, and awaits the executioner's blow, still believing herself to be the rightful Queen of Scotland. This book is an account of how she reached that point and of the ways in which, on many occasions, her bloody beheading might have been averted for a happier conclusion to her story.

In hindsight, Mary's flight across the Solway Firth to England sealed her fate. Even had things worked out better, she made a calamitous misjudgement in expecting her cousin Elizabeth I to help her quell the Scottish rebels and regain her throne. This was an error she was understandably reluctant to recognise, only slowly acknowledging that she was not a guest of the English state but its prisoner.

Perhaps because the outcome of her terrible choice is so familiar, many historians have devoted most of their energies to the first half of Mary's life, galloping through the latter period, when she was held in captivity, as if it were a codicil. Yet Mary's almost nineteen perilous and eventful years as a prisoner were anything but a footnote. Between her arrival in England in 1568 and her execution in 1587, she lived in an almost perpetual state of agitation, with an ongoing series of intrigues and dramas – from armed rebellions and daring plans for escape to the opportunity to marry – keeping hopes alive that she might regain her liberty. There was even the possibility of her being restored to her throne with Elizabeth's blessing.

All of this is fascinating. As is the fact that fascination with Mary never seems to dim. Do we really need another account of her often-told tale? And why, as I have done, write one book on her years in Scotland – *Homecoming* – and another on those she spent locked up in England? I asked these questions myself, wondering what new can be said, before realising that there is no definitive biography of Mary Stuart, no comprehensive narrative, and that each account comes from a particular perspective, bringing a different set of assumptions to bear on the facts, which inevitably influence that version.

On a prosaic level, *Exile* picks up events where *Homecoming* ends, bringing the story to its tragic conclusion by way, on Mary's part, of almost two decades of wrangling, disillusionment and despair, and mounting anxiety on the English side. To have stopped at the Scottish border would have felt like abandoning Mary when her situation became most vulnerable but also, to my mind, most interesting.

As with its predecessor, *Exile* is told through the locations where Mary lived and history unfolded. Approaching it in this way offers an extra dimension to our understanding of what she experienced, the ruinous or restored castles and houses in which she stayed adding context and colour to her tale. It is one thing to know that after arriving in England she was constantly shuttled between residences, quite another to visit these buildings and stand where she stood. To gaze over the same countryside or streets as she once did is to share something of her experience, to make the connection between her age and ours. At times this is largely an exercise of the imagination, as at Chartley or Fotheringhay, where so few traces remain. At others, such as Bolton Castle in Yorkshire or St Mary's Guildhall in Coventry, the sixteenth century and its Machiavellian politics can almost be tasted in the air.

Finding a fresh angle from which to view Mary's downfall is reason enough to revisit her life, but as libraries show, history's most pivotal figures are constantly reappraised, the shelves filled with updated interpretations and retellings, each relevant for a new generation. This abundance confirms what every writer knows: that history is not static. The past does not lie mothballed behind us. It is there to be grasped and evaluated in light of our own times and preoccupations. Reinterpretation and reassessment are the lifeblood of what Tom Devine calls 'the Queen of disciplines', and they are what make history sing. So too is groundbreaking research. In the case of Mary, the recent discovery by a team of international cryptographers of a cache of letters written in cipher during the years 1578 to 1584 has rekindled interest. These furtive missives shed further light on the queen's ceaseless diplomatic manoeuvring and reveal the issues that consumed her as she attempted to plot a way out of her predicament.

The day-to-day detail of Mary's imprisonment, as shown in these newly found letters and in many other sources, is enthralling. The documents offer an insight into the functioning of her household under extreme duress. We see the nature of her friendships and alliances within her entourage, among her far-flung supporters and, most vividly, with her captors, especially the melancholy Earl of Shrewsbury and his shrewd, opportunistic wife, Bess of Hardwick.

Equally interesting is the gradual change in Mary's personality in captivity as the gravity of her position became clear. Suffering chronic ill health and, on several occasions, coming close to death, Mary subtly changed from the headstrong, vivacious, open-hearted young woman who rode at the head of her army and danced the night away at the Palace of Holyrood into a far more cunning and calculating individual. Prematurely aged by her afflictions and the often unhealthy quarters in which she was held, she lost her youthful beauty and grace. In their place she gained a richness of personality and a gravitas that in part explains her continuing allure. She grew more thoughtful, pious and determined when faced with conditions over which she had almost no control. And as her disillusionment increased and she learned to be less trusting, she became formidable.

Exile traces these shifts in character, witnessed by those around her and in her own writing, as her focus narrowed to self-preservation and she learned to place her faith in God alone. Although this part of her tale is cloistered compared with the adventurous activity of her life in Scotland – more *Tinker, Tailor, Soldier, Spy* than *The Three Musketeers* – it is arguably even more compelling. She might not have been conducting her affairs from the centre of power or on the wing on horseback, but even as the deposed queen attempted to bargain from a position of weakness, she refused to become a victim. Instead, she insisted on seeing herself as an active and powerful agent and never for a moment lost sight of her status as a sovereign queen.

Not that Mary's life had hitherto been easy. The woman of twenty-five who landed at Workington in Cumbria in the late spring of 1568 was already versed in hardship and heartache. When only five years old, she had been sent by her mother Marie of Guise to her relatives in France for safety. Married young to the Dauphin, Francis, she was for a brief period Queen of France, one of the most illustrious titles in Europe. On the death of her husband, when he was a mere youth, she returned to Scotland in 1561 as an eighteen-year-old widow. She took up her throne as a devout Catholic, despite Scotland's year-old Reformation, in which the country had turned against Rome and embraced the Protestant faith.

At that point, the auspices were not propitious, Mary knowing too little of her homeland to understand fully its politics and personality, and mistrusted for her adherence to the now proscribed religion. Yet with remarkable foresight and tolerance in one so young and isolated, she accepted her country's change of heart and gathered Protestant councillors around her. After what she had seen of the Huguenots' persecution in France, it seems she had no stomach for religious conflict at home. As a result, for several promising years she held the competing forces of her fractious court together, earning the admiration and affection of the people.

It was on her marriage to the venal Henry Stuart, Lord Darnley, that her reign began to spiral into chaos. His murder, at Kirk o' Field in Edinburgh, in 1567, caused uproar, and Mary was soon implicated. By marrying James Hepburn, Earl of Bothwell, who was the prime suspect in Darnley's death, she lost all respect and honour. After defeat by the Confederate Lords at the Battle of Carberry Hill, she was taken prisoner and incarcerated for almost a year in Lochleven Castle. During this time her half-brother James Stewart, Earl of Moray, became Regent and ruled the country while her infant son James was kept under the care of John Erskine, Earl of Mar, at Stirling Castle. Despite the allegations of the Confederate Lords that the queen represented a threat to the country, her draconian and humiliating treatment was seen in many quarters as unacceptable, as was her forced abdication. This was a politically disastrous period for Mary, but it was also a time of private sorrow, since shortly before abdicating she miscarried twins.

When Mary landed in England, charged with adrenaline from her precipitous flight, she had only recently escaped from her rebels. A few days earlier her army had been routed by the Regent Moray's troops at Langside, near Glasgow, and as she abandoned the field, terrified he might capture her, she made the panic-stricken decision to cross into England. From there, she reasoned, she could muster support from Elizabeth; she might also call on help from France, where she was dowager queen and retained a degree of influence and wealth.

Throughout her reign Mary made a number of catastrophic decisions, for which she must be held accountable: marrying Lord Darnley, then marrying the man believed to have murdered him and, worst of all, fleeing to England. Yet throughout these events, Moray emerges as an increasingly daunting figure whose manipulation of events throughout her reign, and after her escape to England, was designed to ruin her. Even had she been wiser, she could have done nothing to change his zealotry or ambition. If Mary's abduction to Lochleven were not evidence enough, Moray's testimony before the York and Westminster conferences in 1568, at which he produced the dubious Casket Letters to incriminate Mary in Darnley's murder, indicate what sort of a man he was. His assassination, in 1570, greatly cheered her.

As the walls of England's prisons closed around her, and hopes of returning to Scotland became increasingly forlorn, Mary faced a far more redoubtable, life-long enemy. Elizabeth I, who was thirty-four when Mary became her captive, was more intellectually gifted and considerably more cautious than her cousin. She was also blessed with advisors who counselled and steered her, sometimes deviously, in the direction that best served England's interests. Although she could be emotional and quixotic, her consigliere William Cecil, Lord Burghley, was steadfast in protecting her from the snares, as he saw it, of the Scottish queen.

That Elizabeth never met Mary shows her awareness of her cousin's ability to beguile. Yet despite Mary's protestations of friendship and love, nothing could make her presence palatable. As a potential figurehead for Catholic rebellion, she represented a mortal threat to Elizabeth personally, and to the country at large. Devout Catholics, who still held to the old religion despite the Reformation, believed Mary had a stronger claim to the English throne than their queen. She was descended from her grandfather James IV and his wife Margaret Tudor, the older sister of Henry VIII, and thus in direct line of succession. By comparison, Elizabeth was a usurper. She was the only child of Henry by his second wife, Anne Boleyn, whose marriage, which took place following Henry's divorce from Catherine of Aragon, was not recognised by the Catholic Church. Elizabeth's position, as technically illegitimate, was therefore precarious. During the short reign of her Catholic half-sister Mary Tudor, she had been imprisoned. Her narrow escape was due in large part to her keeping a cool head and saying as little as possible that could be deemed incriminating. That traumatic incident was to shape the rest of her life, and the manner in which she treated her sister queen.

Many of the issues that perturbed the English and Scottish governments, and kept Mary in a barely endurable limbo, carry an echo or resonance for us today. Among Elizabeth's greatest fears was invasion or war with one of Europe's great Catholic powers, allied to a rising of Catholics at home. At the same time as keeping Mary under her watch, and trying to prevent her colluding with Philip II in Spain or the kings of France, much of Elizabeth's diplomatic energy was spent holding at bay the potentially contagious religious conflicts in France and the Low Countries. It was no easy task to maintain good relations with potential allies such as France while keeping Spain's vaulting territorial ambitions in check.

In Scotland, meanwhile, the youthful James VI was playing a delicate game, dancing between subservience to Elizabeth and the pro-English clique at court – in the hope that he would eventually inherit the English throne – and indulging in flashes of rebellion, as he tried to assert himself as an independent ruler, rather than the Queen's puppet. The tension between both countries did not erupt into aggression, but there were moments when it came close. After Mary's execution it was the Scottish people, rather than their king, who would gladly have marched against England in protest.

Enduring periods when she received no news or letters, the imprisoned Mary was aware of some but not all of what was going on in Scotland, at Westminster, and in Europe. Information reached her slowly and intermittently, which was particularly vexing where her son was concerned. A refrain of her voluminous correspondence, on which *Exile* draws heavily, was the request for information concerning his welfare. Among the cruellest aspects of her time in England is her separation from him, and his guardians' deliberate policy of poisoning him against her. By the time he was old enough to reign, James and Mary were strangers. Had their bond been close, he might have been able to negotiate her release, even if not, as she would have liked, as joint ruler of Scotland. Their estrangement, however, made this impossible. To that extent, you might say that Mary's life lay in her son's hands, and that he can be accused of being careless with it. In the end, though, he was not as careless as she was.

The thread that runs through Mary's prison years is her duel with Elizabeth. Each was devoured by suspicion of the other, and the consequence of so much mistrust was an atmosphere of secrecy and deception, in which treachery flourished. The antics of Elizabeth's spymaster, Francis Walsingham, saw the English state conduct a campaign of undercover espionage unrivalled until the Cold War. With the full force of the English secret state acting against her, what chance did Mary have?

For her part, Mary revelled in the chance to contact her supporters covertly by means of coded letters, and was happy to use anyone, be it a laundry maid or a passing aristocrat, to convey her messages to the outside world. Despite being an essentially kind-hearted and frank individual, she proved herself a natural when it came to the black arts of subterfuge and dissemblance. In letters smuggled out to friends and fellow conspirators, she was direct and to the point, showing admirable pragmatism. Impulsive she could be – and even in maturity she retained some of the recklessness that had blighted her youth – but for the most part, when it came to outwitting her captors, she was clear-headed and calm.

Beneath the dramas and the diplomatic jousting that enliven these years runs a constant undercurrent of duplicity. No matter in which of the grim fortresses or grand houses she was confined, Mary spent much of her time at her desk writing, petitioning, demanding, imploring. Countless candles were burned as she wrote into the early hours, the flickering light in her chamber visible evidence of her unquenchable spirit. Some of these letters are bread and butter, repetitive in their pleas and requests, but many bring her into the room with us. On her forty-second birthday, 8 December 1584, Mary wrote to Elizabeth: 'may god give you as many happy years as I have had of sorrow these last 20 years!'

To the last, she retained her wit, and her dignity. Is it any wonder, then, that she has intrigued every generation since? Whether revered as a Catholic martyr or reviled as a 'monstrous dragon', whether viewed as a woman unequal to the demands of the throne or as a ruler crushed by forces beyond her control, she remains, in any reading, a tragic figure. As well as being the subject of countless biographies, she has fired the imagination of novelists the world over, beginning with Walter Scott's all-forgiving portrayal in *The Abbot*. Plays and operas have brought her back to life, as have poets and songwriters to this day. Robert Burns captures the sadness of her cruel end in his 'Lament of Mary Queen of Scots on the Approach of Spring'.

> O! soon, to me, may summer suns
> Nae mair light up the morn!
> Nae mair to me the autumn winds
> Wave o'er the yellow corn!
> And in the narrow house o' death
> Let winter round me rave;
> And the next flowers that deck the spring
> Bloom on my peaceful grave.

Liz Lochhead's play *Mary Queen of Scots Got Her Head Chopped Off* takes its title from the heartless Scottish rhyme, chanted as children picked the heads off daisies and dandelions. Unsentimental and modern, it frames the story as a contest between the two queens: 'Poor Elizabeth,' says Mary, 'tonight you dance in my dream. Tomorrow and ever after I will dance in yours.' Even Bob Dylan is said to have written about her in 'It's All Over Now, Baby Blue', supposedly a reference to the sky-blue stockings she wore on the scaffold. I can't find her in his lyrics, but the musician Richard Thompson makes a persuasive case that this is Dylan's homage, relocating events to Greenwich Village. If nothing else, 'It's All Over Now, Baby Blue' would make a good title for the last chapter of her life.

Exile is one more stone on the ever-growing cairn, a depiction of the ominous but captivating years in which Mary shaped not just her own destiny but also that of her homeland and the British Isles. Perhaps one aspect of what makes her perennially interesting is that she remains forever beyond our reach, never entirely understood or knowable. Whatever the reason, it is safe to say that fascination with this exceptional woman, whose beguiling personality was riven with fatal flaws, will long outlive us all.

Chapter 1

'They have robbed me of every thing I had in the world'

WORKINGTON HALL AND COCKERMOUTH CASTLE

Seagulls patrolling the Solway Firth on the afternoon of Sunday, 16 May 1568, would have spied a small fishing boat slip out of Port Mary Cove, near Dundrennan in Galloway, and begin the four-hour crossing to England. Even from a height it would have been obvious that this was no ordinary fishing trip. On deck was a group of around twenty passengers, none of them in fishermen's garb. Among them was a tall young woman with shorn auburn hair and shabby, cast-off clothes, whom the others treated with deference. They were better dressed than she was, but despite her outward appearance, her demeanour was regal.

As the boat crossed the invisible border between Scotland and England, history was made. This was Mary, Queen of Scots's escape from the country where she had been forced illegally to abdicate. As she watched the Galloway hills and coastline fade into the blue distance, she did not consider herself to be turning her back on her homeland. Dread of her half-brother James Stewart, Earl of Moray, whose army had recently routed hers, was the impulse behind her flight; but she fully intended to be back home within a few months, along with an army to help win back her throne. With the sea air in her face, and no sign of her enemies in pursuit, she must have allowed herself to hope that her fortunes were on the turn.

Although the passage to Cumbria was swift, speeded by the strength of the treacherous tide, it was to prove the most fateful of the many journeys Mary had undertaken in her twenty-five years. As a child of five, she had been sent from Scotland by the hazardous west-coast sea route to France for safety. Her return, in 1561, as an eighteen-year-old widow, had also been fraught, dogged by the risk of capture by the English before she could take up her throne. Yet this May-time crossing, while calm and uneventful, was the most risky of all.

It was a fact of which Mary appeared oblivious, despite the advice of her closest advisors. It was also a decision she would live to regret deeply. Towards the end of her life she admitted that those who had urged her not to leave for England 'would not accompany me until I gave them an attestation and certificate in my handwriting that it was against their wish, and in spite of them, that I came to England'.

In her wake, she left her toddler son James, and a country in uproar, torn between support for her and for the Earl of Moray, her half-brother. As Regent, Moray had presided over Parliament when, in 1567, it passed an Act declaring Mary guilty of the murder of her husband Darnley, thus justifying his usurping of his queen. A few days before she reached England, Mary's army had been roundly defeated by Moray's at the Battle of Langside, near Glasgow, since when she had been fleeing in fear of her life.

Moray, who was leader of the Confederate Lords, the Protestant clique who had imprisoned the queen in Lochleven Castle and forced her into abdicating, had been appointed Regent in her place. Mary's terror of him was such that she had travelled by night and rested by day while making for Dundrennan Abbey in Galloway, from where she planned to escape to England. There she expected to be helped to regain her throne by her cousin Elizabeth I, who had been one of the few to offer support during her incarceration in Lochleven.

The fishing boat drew closer to the English coast, and Mary must surely have reflected on her final minutes in Scotland. As her horse plunged into the creek at Port Mary Cove, where the fishing boat had been anchored, Archbishop Hamilton had grabbed the bridle and begged her to reconsider. 'Do not trust your person in England,' he counselled. She ignored his pleas and instead placed her faith in a woman who had every reason to mistrust her, and whose own advisors saw Mary as England's greatest threat.

The queen, who was intent on avoiding capture, had already proved herself to be a most redoubtable and unfathomable individual. Headlong flight did not suit her, being more the behaviour of desperation, and possible defeat. As previous events had shown, she was no coward. Whatever else could be said of Mary, she had experienced misfortune and calamity, not always of her own making. Two of her husbands had suffered dreadful deaths. The youthful Francis, King of France, had died in agony from what is thought to have been an abscess behind his ear, while Henry Stuart, Lord Darnley, had been murdered in one of the most sensational Scottish crimes. At the time of Mary's escape, her third husband, James Hepburn, Lord Bothwell, widely suspected to be the author of Darnley's death, was being held hostage by the King of Denmark and Norway, to be used as a political pawn. Instead of mustering an army to rescue her from Lochleven Castle, as he had planned, he had been forced to flee, making an electrifyingly narrow escape from Moray's forces as he sailed from Scotland for Norway. As Mary headed unwittingly towards captivity, he was already behind bars in Denmark. Like his wife, he would die, in 1578, without ever regaining his liberty. Unlike Mary, he seems also to have lost his sanity.

Around seven in the evening, the fishing boat reached the English coast, and Mary likely disembarked at the village of Siddick, on the mouth of the River Derwent, not far from the town of Workington. Among the small party who accompanied her were the lords John Fleming, Alexander Livingston, John Maxwell Herries and Claud Hamilton, who were doubtless trepidatious about what lay ahead. Not so their queen. On disembarking, Mary stumbled. A bad omen, you might say, but she and her followers decided to interpret it as a sign that she would take possession of England. News had yet to reach the English court of her arrival, but the Scottish party's hopes spelled anxiety for the English crown.

Two centuries later, William Wordsworth imagined the scene in his poem 'Mary Queen of Scots – Landing at the Mouth of the Derwent, Workington', in which he paints a romantic picture of Mary's arrival – 'Her landing hailed, how touchingly she bowed!' – but concludes in a melancholy tone,

> but Time, the old Saturnian seer,
> Sighed on the wing as her foot pressed the strand,
> With step prelusive to a long array
> Of woes and degradations hand in hand –
> Weeping captivity, and shuddering fear
> Stilled by the ensanguined block of Fotheringay!

In the excitement of reaching her destination, Mary probably never cast a glance backwards over the firth. She had no reason to suspect that this was the last time she would be within touching distance of home. But in the weeks, months and years that lay ahead, she was to be held in a succession of castles and stately homes that were increasingly far from the border, making rescue or escape harder.

Although she was now in a foreign land, Mary anticipated returning home triumphantly in the middle of August, having raised an English or French army. She held the moral high ground, her abdication under duress being illegal. This fact alone had brought around many of her citizens and courtiers who had previously been outraged at her marriage to Bothwell – not only was he tainted by his role in Darnley's demise, but many believed Mary had been his lover before Darnley's killing and had been privy to the murder plot.

During Mary's eleven months of captivity at Lochleven Castle, where she suffered a miscarriage of twins and was at times harshly treated, the public mood towards her had subtly shifted. The underhand behaviour of Moray and his supporters caused great unease, and gradually opinion was turning back in her favour. This was a good reason not to leave the country but to stay, gather support, and make another bid to oust her usurper. At the very least, she should have sailed for France rather than England, where she had a private income and, as dowager queen, could hope to rally help. Yet Mary seemed hell-bent on placing her future in Elizabeth's hands. The pair had never met, and never would. Despite the formal flowery effusions of their correspondence in recent years, there was no genuine affection between them. This was not only a matter of different temperaments: Mary warm, impulsive, charismatic and intelligent; Elizabeth intellectual, cool and, while she too could be playful and spontaneous, by nature far more cautious and stately.

In Mary, she recognised a sovereign queen who had been wronged, and with whom she sympathised. Forcible abdication was not an act she could condone. She also recognised a woman whose claim to the English throne was both legitimate and strong. Elizabeth's own position, as the Protestant daughter of Anne Boleyn and Henry VIII, and declared illegitimate as an infant by Parliament in 1536, left her vulnerable should there be an uprising of Catholics. Few better understood the vagaries of political life, and the fine line between power and, quite literally, political death.

If Mary did not recognise that her claim to the English throne might make her a focal point for a Catholic rebellion if she entered the country, and that she therefore would be seen as a deadly rival, then she was naive and foolish. Since she was neither, her determination to cross the border and seek refuge there is – like so many of her actions – difficult to comprehend. Mary's biographer Antonia Fraser writes perceptively of her decision to enter England: 'it was a brave one, a romantic one even, but under the circumstances it was certainly not a wise one'. When Mary was in France as a young woman, she had been declared not merely the heir to the English throne, but its rightful incumbent. There were many in England who thought that she, rather than Elizabeth, should be their queen.

Once they were all ashore, Mary and her entourage were conveyed from Siddick to Workington, where rumours spread of the Scottish queen's arrival. As they rested after their journey, Lord Herries, one of her most devoted and sensible allies, sent a message to Henry Curwen, of Workington Hall, saying he had arrived with an heiress, whom he thought to marry off to Curwen's son. The Curwens were an old family, whose service to the crown – including a decisive role in defeating William Wallace during the wars of Scottish Independence – had won them royal favour. The family motto suggests they knew their worth: *Si je n'estoy*: 'If I had not been there.' Even though Henry Curwen was away, the party was immediately invited to stay. Mary's identity was easily guessed, not least by one of his French servants, who recognised her from a previous encounter 'in better days'.

In 1568, as today, there was nothing particularly remarkable about where the boat landed, nor the town where Mary stayed for the first night of her almost nineteen-year captivity. At first glance, the area around Workington is almost a mirror image of Dumfries and Galloway: tussocky fields grazed by dairy cattle, beneath an expanse of cloud-washed sky. By appearance alone, Mary could not have imagined the political and cultural gulf that lay between the two countries, and the depth of enmity she would soon encounter.

In Roman times there had been a robust coastal defence system along the Solway, to counter attack from north and west. By 1568, however, Workington was beginning to show the first signs of the industrial town it was to become. Two years earlier, Elizabeth had encouraged mining for metal ores in the area around Keswick, twenty miles to the south-east. Since iron ore was badly needed to boost England's military arsenal, Workington soon developed as a port handling timber for iron-smelting. By the nineteenth century, it had become a thriving industrial town, based on coal, steel and high-quality iron ore. Today, despite the herds of cattle, there is a tired, post-industrial feel in places along this coastline. Less than twenty miles south is Sellafield, site of the former nuclear power station known as Windscale. No longer operational, it is in the process of being decommissioned. Nevertheless, its reputation as the most hazardous nuclear site in western Europe casts a pall over the region.

From the north, reaching Siddick involves driving through a series of villages so close they almost run into each other. Towards

Siddick a field of wind turbines stretches into the distance. Some stand sentry over the traffic, and passing beneath them feels like being at the feet of giants. Because of the railway line that hugs the coast, the Solway Firth is only fleetingly visible from the road. To get a better view, I pulled onto the verge at Siddick and climbed a fence by the railway embankment. Beyond, pale blue water stretched mistily, revealing another line of wind turbines where sky met sea. Even this close, Scotland was not visible.

Two miles away is Workington, with its large industrial port a short distance from the town. A typically northern town, with streets of compact nineteenth- and twentieth-century terraced houses, Workington's town centre features high-rise parking lots and four shopping malls, designed on the principle of a hot cross bun. Where the malls intersect is a circular canopy, like a space ship or outsized dentist's lamp, from which music pumps out. A plaque informs readers that the Hub is 'the world's first permanent outdoor 3D soundfield performance and promotional space'.

On a warm Sunday morning in September, business in the malls was steady. One shop advertised 'Buy Three Get Three Free', but there was no stampede. When I asked directions in a café for Workington Hall, the staff showed me on Google Maps, but within a couple of minutes I had lost my bearings. I approached a young woman, who took out her earbuds. The name Workington Hall left her blank. 'Do you mean Curwen Castle?', and she pointed up the steep street.

If the shopping centre of Workington is dominated by uninspiring late twentieth-century architecture, its crown is a warren of characterful Georgian townhouses arranged around narrow, winding streets and a cobbled square garlanded with hanging baskets. Many properties are brightly painted and spruced up; a few are in need of a facelift. In a backstreet, a group of woebegone men, possibly homeless, were lounging, enjoying the sunshine and troubling no one, although passers-by noted them and hurried on.

Beyond the Georgian district, at the very top of the town, lies a park of mature trees. In its heart stands Workington Hall, aka

Curwen Castle or Curwen Hall. A cavernous ruin, its grilled gateway and walls are plastered in signs: 'Danger! Keep Out!' 'Warning: anti climb paint'. 'There is no lead on this roof. NON-LEAD FLASHING HAS BEEN USED THROUGHOUT.' A substantial rectangular structure, it gives off a military air, although today it is clearly embattled by vandals and thieves rather than marauders. Despite the decay, you can still imagine the gates opening and horsemen pouring out, armed with swords or guns.

In the mid fourteenth century, Gilbert de Culwen (Curwen) III built a peel tower here, but the present building, constructed on the site of the original tower, dates to around 1404, when a heavily fortified house with a gatehouse was built around a courtyard. For easy defence, it stands on a steep hill, which falls away into woodland towards the rear. Peering through the windows revealed a rich undergrowth of weeds, saplings and mounds of fallen masonry blanketed in moss. With its massive walls and graceful arched windows and entrance, its dereliction does not detract from its authority, and its presence suggests a slumbering guardian keeping watch over the town.

When Mary visited, she was given a room in the west wing of the Hall. Thereafter the Curwens named it Queen Mary's Room, although its royal guest spent just one night there. During her visit, she wrote her second letter to Elizabeth since fleeing the Battle of Langside, asking for protection and for an urgent meeting. 'I entreat you to send to fetch me as soon as you possibly can,' she wrote, 'for I am in a pitiable condition, not only for a queen but for a gentlewoman, for I have nothing in the world but what I had on my person when I made my escape, travelling sixty miles across the country the first day, and not having since ever ventured to proceed except by night, as I hope to declare before you if it pleases you to have pity, as I trust you will, upon my extreme misfortune.'

Going on to describe the behaviour of the Confederate Lords, whom she accused of Darnley's murder, she continued: 'They have robbed me of every thing I had in the world, not permitting me either to write or speak, in order that I might not contradict their false inventions.' Her previous letter, written from Dundrennan Abbey, where she had spent her last night in Scotland, had explained her predicament: 'I am now forced out of my kingdom, and driven to such straits that, next to God, I have no hope but in your goodness.' In this latest missive, she expressed her confidence in Elizabeth, 'not only for the safety of my life, but also to aid and assist me in my just quarrel'.

Signing off 'your most faithful and affectionate good sister, and cousin, and escaped prisoner', she despatched her servant John Beaton to London with this letter, in which she enclosed the heart-shaped diamond Elizabeth had once sent her as 'a pledge of amity and good will'. The meaning of the diamond was clear: she was calling on Elizabeth to honour her pledge. Meanwhile, reluctantly obeying the queen's wishes, Lord Herries had written from Dundrennan to Richard Lowther, the deputy governor of Carlisle, seeking permission for Mary to enter the country. She sailed before receiving either permission or invitation.

As a thank you for the Curwens' hospitality, Mary gave them a tiny agate communion cup – two inches by two inches – which may have been the one she used when travelling. Given her recent travails, the uncertainty of what lay ahead and how reliant Mary had become on her devotions, it was a generous gift. Since then the cup has been known as the 'Luck of Workington', and is now on display in the museum across the road from Workington Hall. It is often said that while it brought the town good fortune, Mary left her luck behind when she handed it over.

How significant is a one-night stay in a life that would span forty-four years? In this case, it matters. Workington Hall represents one of the many imponderable and poignant what-ifs in Mary's career. That night, she was treated as an honoured guest, not a national threat. As she lay awake, unable to sleep because her fear of Moray catching her had not abated, she could nonetheless allow herself to hope that she had outwitted her enemies. Although the net would soon be drawn around her, these were among her final hours of freedom. Had she listened to reason it would still have been possible to recross the Solway Firth, or sail for France, where she had family and friends. There is a sense of a fast-emptying hourglass in Mary's first days in England, when Elizabeth did not reply to her letters, and captivity drew closer. Escape and a change of plan were still possible. But as the sand trickled through the hourglass, Mary's options narrowed.

The next day, Mary left Workington for the town of Cockermouth, six miles away, where she was to be met by Lowther. There, she spent the night at Cockermouth Castle as a guest of the merchant tailor Master Henry Fletcher, who earns a footnote in history for his kindness to the queen. Seeing how poorly she was dressed, with no clothes except what she wore, he is said to have given her thirteen yards of crimson velvet for a gown, and had a dress made up for her, albeit on credit.

Cockermouth, which retains its medieval layout, was a textile centre by the early Middle Ages. It is the gateway to the Lake District, an elegant Georgian town whose rivers – the Derwent and the Cocker – have been both a commercial blessing and a curse. In recent years, the town has suffered devastating flooding, as indicated by plaques on buildings indicating how high the waters rose in 2009 – 2.5 metres. Photos show cars bobbing in the street and the RNLI rescuing townsfolk from their half-submerged homes.

Cockermouth Castle, like Workington Hall, sits at the top of the town, far from risk of flood waters. It is screened by a lush canopy of trees, and only a glimpse of turrets is visible from the pedestrian bridge crossing the Derwent that leads to the town centre. The castle stands apart beyond a quaint, narrow street of townhouses, called Castlegate. This leads away from the airy boulevard of the main street, where upmarket shops and cafés offer an appealing flavour of the Lake District: Kendal Mint Cake, hiking and cycling gear, hearty pub fare. The castle, sadly, is a private dwelling, and only occasionally open to the public. Its attractive wrought-iron gates allow a glimpse of medieval masonry at its entrance, and of manicured lawns and well-tended flowerbeds. Too much peering is discouraged by willow fencing atop the iron fences. On the gatepost is an entry panel, with a buzzer for a housekeeper.

The high, mossy wall continues several hundred metres up the street, inset with a couple of doors, but the castle essentially lies hidden from view. Aerial photos are more helpful, showing a roughly triangular medieval layout, arranged around a large courtyard. The first castle on this site was built by the Normans in about 1130, but the present ruin is what remains of the castle that replaced this, constructed between 1370 and the early fifteenth century. A noticeboard behind the gateway explains that new building work took place in the Outer Bailey in the 1800s, creating a residence, with stable and offices, which, one assumes, is where the present-day owners live. Perhaps understandably, given the number of tourists that flock to the Lake District, there is a strong sense of privacy being carefully guarded.

Master Fletcher's generosity and concern meant Mary's stay at the castle would have been comfortable, a balm to her frayed nerves after the anxiety of recent days. Even so, she spent the night seated rather than in bed, still fearing Moray's arrival. By the time morning arrived, and with it her departure for Carlisle, she must have been exhausted. Lowther, who was to escort Mary to Carlisle, was accompanied by 400 soldiers, a menacing presence that ought to have put Mary on her guard. He too was struck by her sorry state – 'her attire was very mean' – and as well as asking that her expenses at the castle be defrayed, provided her with horses to take her and her party to Carlisle. Unsurprisingly, then, despite the small army surrounding her, Mary viewed her move to Carlisle as more like a royal progress than the taking of a prisoner.

She would not have felt so complacent had she known that not only had Lowther immediately written to Queen Elizabeth to inform her of Mary's arrival – promising to make sure she could not escape until he was informed of Elizabeth's wishes – but had also alerted the county 'by beacon'. This was telling, since beacons, or bonfires, were used to warn of impending invasion or other dire emergencies. Such was the light in which her arrival, and what it signified for the country, was viewed. Until he heard from Elizabeth, however, Lowther remained uncertain as to how he should treat the royal visitor. Playing safe, he welcomed her as a distinguished guest while discreetly maintaining a guard that made escape impossible.

Chapter 2

'This detention which I think rather harsh and strange'

CARLISLE CASTLE

The sight of Carlisle Castle should have alerted Mary to the reality of her situation. Such was her confidence that she had made the right decision in coming to England, however, it was several days before she recognised that she was a captive. On 18 May 1568, as she and her party approached the castle's menacing walls, the signal it gave was very different from the two grand residences where she had just been a guest. Although Workington Hall and Cockermouth Castle were fortified, they were more akin to dolls' houses than military outposts when compared to the defensive strength of Carlisle Castle.

Lowther and his army would have cleared a path through the streets of this medieval market town as they made their way towards the castle drawbridge. The sight of the beautiful, tall woman on horseback, who had the unmistakeable grandeur of high estate, would have set gossips alight. Who else could this be other than the bloodied but unbowed Queen of Scotland? Sadly, what Mary made of Carlisle we will never know. It was nothing like Edinburgh, but given her dislike of the Scottish capital, this might have commended it to her.

Only ten miles from the border, Carlisle was enclosed by unbroken walls, within which the populace and those in the region could take shelter in times of trouble, and from which it could be robustly defended. A map from around 1560 shows the castle dominating the city, looking down on it from its elevated position above the river Eden. It stood at the top of a wide central thoroughfare, off which ran narrower streets and passages and neatly laid out rows of shops, houses, gardens and orchards. A handful of gateways, or ports, which could be guarded, allowed entry through the walls. In terms of layout, if Carlisle Cathedral represented the city's heart, the castle was its head.

Today, as in Mary's time, despite being built in pinkish-red sandstone, the castle has a brooding, menacing presence – 'a dour and pugnacious look', says the official guidebook. Low-lying, apart from its imposing medieval keep, it gives the impression of a crouching beast ready to spring. This is fitting, given the role it has played down the centuries, in perilous proximity to a warring and covetous neighbour. By the sixteenth century, when Mary arrived, the castle was the headquarters of the march wardens, high-ranking officials charged with the unenviable task of keeping marauding Scottish reivers, and their equally violent English counterparts, in check. Mary's third husband, Bothwell, was Lieutenant of the Scottish Marches, and in one encounter with the notorious Elliot clan in Liddesdale, not far from Carlisle, was so gravely wounded it was initially thought he would die. Earlier in the century, the appointment of the Frenchman Anthony Darcy as Warden of all the Scottish Marches so incensed the Hume family that they ambushed and beheaded him, carrying his head home as a trophy. Such was the violent mayhem in the borderlands throughout the century that events that elsewhere might have precipitated international crises were considered business as usual and hastily dealt with.

For hundreds of years, Carlisle Castle was the principal English stronghold along a border strung with castles, roughly following the line of Hadrian's Wall. This massive, intimidating structure, stretching from the Solway Firth in the west to Newcastle in the east, was designed to protect the country from attack from the north. A large Roman fort once lay on the site of the present-day castle, and supplying its soldiers was in part the reason for Carlisle's early growth and prosperity.

Much of Carlisle Castle, which was begun in the twelfth century, was constructed with stone from the ruinous Roman wall, thereby knitting one era's defences into another. A third-century Roman altar, dedicated to the gods by a soldier from the Danube frontier, once served as a door lintel in the warden's apartments. It is now displayed beside the door, reinforcing the memory of military occupation and shared trepidation of trouble from the north.

The first castle, on or close to this site, was the work of the English king William Rufus, and was probably built of wood, within a stockade on an earth mound. In 1122, as the threat from Scotland intensified, William Rufus's brother Henry I initiated the building of a stone castle with towers, as well as stone defences for the town. Within a few years, the castle had fallen into the hands of King David I of Scotland, who died here in 1153. When finally the Scots left Carlisle, in 1157, Henry had the fortress further strengthened.

In the years that followed, the castle endured attack and siege, playing a pivotal role in the country's defence against Scotland, particularly during the wars of Scottish Independence. The tower that Mary, Queen of Scots was later to occupy was built by Edward I, whose wife Margaret lived in the palace within the castle's inner ward (where the luxury of a bath was provided). If the castle's raison d'être was to subdue Scotland, now, with Mary's appearance, a dangerous northerner was in their midst. Although she did not yet recognise her predicament, her presence represented trouble to a degree England had rarely if ever experienced.

The crenellated outer gateway, through which Mary's party would have entered, is severe, like almost everything about this place. The modern visitor might find it atmospheric, fascinating, perhaps even charming, in a minatory sort of way. But for those in bygone times who were not required to buy a ticket, crossing the drawbridge over the deep, murky moat and passing beneath the portcullis, with its wicked teeth, must have sent a shiver up their spines.

On the summer's morning when I visited – Bastille Day, as it happens – I arrived by way of Liddesdale. This was the lawless district in which Bothwell had been savagely attacked by the Elliots, and where Mary had fallen off her horse on her return to Jedburgh from Hermitage Castle, where her lieutenant and future husband lay recovering in bed. The consequences of that fall had nearly proved fatal, and it is tempting to wonder if, in light of what she was later to endure, she did not sometimes wish it had all ended there, in the peace and comfort of her home country.

On the narrow, winding roads through Liddesdale, torrential rain that put the windscreen wipers into a frenzy was followed by sunshine. As I passed Hermitage Castle, a smoky mist covered the hills, which were grazed by sheep that looked more like goats. There is a sense of isolation about Liddesdale, with its rugged, bleak, beautiful terrain. Leaving such sparsely populated countryside behind and crossing the border involves a change of gear, both geographical and mental.

The city of Carlisle is a workaday, bustling place, much of its centre built in red brick that has darkened with age. While it does not exude the metropolitan pizzazz and brass neck of its sister city Newcastle, for many borderers Carlisle is their preferred city for partying. Beneath its sombre exterior lies – I am told – a sense of fun and joie de vivre. Neither term is applicable to the castle. Set high on a mound, its front walls are skirted by a busy dual carriageway. What is visible of the castle and its precincts from the pavement outside is squat and sturdy, with a very no-nonsense demeanour. Although there is no longer a moat, given the steepness of the ditches beneath, it is easy to imagine how effective this ring of water would have been. Added to the ditches were a drawbridge and portcullis, making the castle almost impregnable.

In the outer gatehouse, through which you enter the castle, the ticket office occupies a small, dark chamber that was once probably used by an officer serving those in the apartments overhead. As I stood in the queue, in the gift shop an American tourist was trying to dissuade his daughter from buying a very realistic, lethal-looking sword. He did not look relieved when the man behind the till assured him it would be possible to take it home if packed in the hold of the plane.

The upper floor of the gatehouse holds the warden's apartments, which have been reconstructed as they might have looked in the sixteenth century: firedogs, logs and tongs by the capacious kitchen hearth, a four-poster bed in the warden's bedroom, and a mezzanine chamber, possibly for servants, with a wall of wooden shutters that look down into the main hall with its long dining table and stately chairs. This might have been the domain of the famous Thomas Dacre, Warden-general of the English Marches. It was Dacre who found the Scottish king's body on the battlefield at Flodden where he and thousands of Scotland's nobility died in 1513. The rancour between England and Scotland long predates this dreadful event, but by the late sixteenth century tensions along the border were as bad as they had ever been. When Mary was in residence, the Warden of the Western March and Governor of Carlisle was Henry, Lord Scrope, whose wife was to play an important part in her unfolding drama. Comfortable though these rooms are, the guidebook's author suggests they were not grand enough for a warden, and might instead have been used by the sheriff.

Beyond the gatehouse lies an expanse of parade ground, ringed by nineteenth- and twentieth-century barracks, each block named after a famous battle: Ypres, Arnhem, Alma, Gallipoli and Arroyo. The significance of the castle in the story of Mary, Queen of Scots may have been fleeting, but the castle's military story has continued into recent times. It served not only as a stronghold in the fight against the Scots but also as a bulwark against civil unrest in the nineteenth century, and as the training and departure point for many soldiers in the First World War. An anti-aircraft gun was positioned on the roof of the keep during the Second World War. The castle is still in use today as a centre for the Army Reserve and the Cumbria Army Cadet Force, and houses Cumbria's Museum of Military Life.

Because of the castle's constantly evolving purpose, its layout and architecture have been repeatedly altered and added to as circumstances have dictated. Even so, those hoping to catch a glimpse of the castle as Mary knew it will not be disappointed. Across the parade ground stands the inner gatehouse, beneath which is an elegant half-moon battery, which, in Mary's day, was built high enough for guns to be fired across the outer walls. It was lowered in the 1830s, but descending into its gloomy, verdigrised depths gives a flavour of what its sixteenth-century gunners would have faced.

Passing through the inner gatehouse brings you to what feels like a miniature walled town or a stage set. Described by the guidebook as the castle's 'nerve centre', and encircled by high red sandstone walls and walkway, it contains a collection of well-kept buildings in a cobbled yard. A relatively modern powder magazine and militia store occupy the site of the former medieval royal palace, alongside the shell of the Great Chamber.

Casting a long shadow over them all is the keep, with its sheer walls, narrow windows, outside staircase and vertiginously high roof. It was once even higher, but was lowered and reinforced in the sixteenth century to bear the weight of artillery. At various points along the wall-top walkway stand glossy black cannons, giving some idea of why additional structural support was needed. Today these guns are decorative, but in an earlier age they were the equivalent of weapons of mass destruction.

Looming over the courtyard, the keep draws the eye and captures the spirit and meaning of Carlisle Castle, both of which could be grisly. Also known as the Great Tower, the keep has fulfilled many functions in its 900-year lifetime. It was constructed on the principle of the French-style *donjons* – practical but intended to parade the owner's power and status – and has been knocked about constantly since its early days.

Seeing me staring upwards as I took in its scale, a guide at a loose end offered to show me what he considered one of the Great Tower's most notable features. We entered, and he took me past a barrel-vaulted cellar used to store food and provisions into a second, similarly vaulted room. Using his mobile phone to light the way, he led me through this room and down a ramp into another chamber beyond. At its far wall he swept his torch over the stonework. By the light of the pale beam it was possible to see that the stones had been eroded into strange scoop-shaped patterns, as if subjected to centuries of scouring sea and wind.

These, he explained, were the licking stones. Prisoners thrown into this cellar, with nothing to drink, resorted to licking the walls for the moisture that ran down them. The thought of those parched tongues, and how desperately they searched for water, was horrible. As many as ninety prisoners could be packed in here, the guide said, for as long as three months. Given the dimensions of the room, it is doubtful that even half of them would have survived. It might have been my imagination, but there was a dank feeling to the room, as if the walls were running still with damp. It was a relief to leave and head upstairs into the light.

Holding prisoners in this miserable ground-floor chamber was relatively rare. Most were kept on the second floor, where a series of striking carvings in the stonework are thought possibly to be their work. Some of these carvings – of knights in battle, animals, and one of a naked woman surrounded by spears – have been dated to around 1480, on the basis of the armour depicted. A few are elementary, but others are so good they might be the work of a stonemason. The guidebook questions whether prisoners would have had access to the lobby where the wall is covered in carvings, suggesting instead that they were the pastime of bored guards or a resident priest. On the same floor as the carvings is the room where David I is thought to have died. With floors connected by narrow spiral staircases, the keep is a warren of rooms with fireplaces, deeply recessed windows and out-of-sight latrines. It is a castle unto itself. Was Mary aware of its close – and ferocious – links with her homeland? Was she ever shown the carvings, or the vault where the unluckiest prisoners were confined?

As deputy governor, Lowther would have taken Mary directly to her quarters, in what was then called the New Tower or the Warden's Tower. (Thereafter it was renamed Queen Mary's Tower.) It stood in the south-east corner of the inner ward, with a view on one side towards the city, and on the other across the river Eden and northwards to Scotland. Unfortunately, after falling into disrepair it was demolished in 1835, and all that remains is the octagonal stair turret – part of the royal palace – that led from the Great Chamber to her rooms.

The walkway on this part of the walls offers views over the dual carriageway to the BBC Cumbria offices, the cathedral, and the redbrick town. One can also stare down on the unfilled gap where Mary once lived. Fortunately, J. M. W. Turner and others immortalised it in paint before it was destroyed. Turner's delicate wash drawing shows a low tower protruding from the walls, enclosing a spiral staircase. Two windows in the upper floor are thought to be the room where Mary stayed. The ground falls away steeply beneath its walls, although had she been so minded, Mary might nevertheless have eluded Lowther and his meticulous watch.

That haunting thought follows you around the castle. Little more than a week after arriving, Mary was writing of 'this detention which . . . I think rather harsh and strange'. Two days later, when corresponding with Lord Fleming, whom she had despatched to London, she said that she was being well treated, 'but nevertheless as a prisoner'. Now that she understood her predicament, why did she make no attempt to escape? On horseback, it was less than an hour's gallop over the border to relative safety, from where she could have sailed for France. As the weeks of her captivity in Carlisle ticked by, there is a tantalising awareness that at no point in her life hereafter would she be so close to home and rescue. Yet while Mary took no steps to free herself, awareness of her proximity to Scotland was foremost in the minds of her captors.

Chapter 3

'I have made great wars in Scotland, and I pray God I make no troubles in other realms also'

BEHIND BARS

News of Mary's arrival in England reached Westminster on 20 May, two days after she reached Carlisle. What was the expression on Queen Elizabeth's face, on learning that her rival for the crown was expecting her help? Perhaps more importantly, how did Elizabeth's chief counsellor, William Cecil, react? Images of a cat with a long-hunted mouse come to mind. He might not have purred, but to have the person he viewed as the biggest challenge to his queen enter his lair of her own volition must have ranked as one of the most triumphant days of his career.

At a hastily convened meeting of the Privy Council, Elizabeth and Cecil disagreed about how best to proceed. Cecil wanted Mary immediately returned to Scotland, where Moray would deal with her. Elizabeth, recognising this would be a death sentence, wished to find a way to restore her to her throne and to settle the matter of her alleged complicity in her husband's murder. In the end, they compromised by deciding to treat her as a guest until these issues could be resolved.

Accordingly, Elizabeth sent two envoys to pass on her condolences about what had happened to Mary in Scotland. One was Francis Knollys, her vice-chamberlain, who was to be Mary's first 'keeper', and the other was Lord Scrope. Although Mary had her own people around her, Lady Scrope was appointed as her attendant. Her brother was the Duke of Norfolk, who would one day die because of his association with Mary and his ill-judged hope of marrying her. His sister may have introduced him to the queen.

Mary had crossed into England with around twenty attendants. On arriving in Carlisle, Knollys noted that she had six ladies in waiting, although he later referred only to three or four, and these 'not of the finest sort'. By some accounts, no more than three or four of her party were allowed to stay with her in the castle, the rest being boarded in the town.

In the following weeks, her household grew to thirty or forty as her old staff and supporters joined her from north of the border. As well as her courtiers already mentioned – including Fleming's and Livingston's wives – there was her loyal supporter, sixteen-year-old Willie Douglas, who had helped her flee her captors at Lochleven Castle, and George Douglas, who had also aided her escape, and was in love with her. There was her servant Bastian Pages and his wife, whose wedding she had attended the night of Darnley's murder, John Leslie, Bishop of Ross, and John Beaton, Master of the Household. There was also the closest and most devoted of her companions, Mary Seton, who would remain at her side for the following fifteen years, until ill health forced her to retire to a convent in France. On arrival, Seton distinguished herself by her skill in dressing her mistress's hair, using hairpieces (called periwigs or perukes) while Mary's hair, which had been shaved off during her flight to Dundrennan, regrew. Unfortunately, the queen's hair never regained its former glory, and such artifices were necessary for the rest of her life. Alongside these very close attendants was added a posse of workaday domestic staff who cooked and skivvied for her.

Like almost all those who came into contact with Mary Stuart, regardless of their allegiance, Knollys and Scrope were immediately taken with her. In a joint report to Elizabeth, they did not try to hide the favourable impression she had made, saying that she possessed 'an eloquent tongue, and a discreet head, and it seemeth by her doings she hath stout courage and a liberal heart adjoined thereunto'. Knollys's assessment of her continued in a letter to Elizabeth's consigliere Cecil: 'And yet this lady and princess is a notable woman . . . She showeth a disposition to speak much, to be bold, to be pleasant and to be very familiar. She showeth a great desire to be avenged of her enemies . . . The thing she most thirsteth after is victory . . . whether a princess and lady to be nourished in one's bosom, or whether it be good to halt and dissemble with such a lady, I refer to your judgement.'

That even an evangelical Puritan such as Knollys was charmed by the Scottish queen gives a sense of her charisma. Indeed, during the months Knollys was charged with her custody, he seems to have grown fond of her, and possibly enamoured. In his mid fifties, with a large family, he was married to Catherine Grey, who was related to Elizabeth, with whom she was a very close friend. A portrait shows a man with currants for eyes and a bushy grey moustache and beard, neatly trimmed, as befitted a courtier of his standing.

Despite his evident regard for the Scottish queen, Knollys was frustrated by Elizabeth refusing to make clear whether Mary was a prisoner or to be treated as a guest. The Queen of England was vacillating, as if she dreaded confirming her fears about her cousin, preferring instead to allow her to languish in limbo, along with all those charged with her care. Uncomfortable at keeping another queen against her will, she swithered, playing for time. At this point it seems she intended eventually to restore Mary to Scotland. Just not yet.

Although he awaited guidance, Knollys evidently guessed how things stood, hence his anxiety over the risk of Mary's slipping out of his grasp. In a letter to Cecil, written after he had left the castle, he described the shifts of guards keeping watch on her day and night, and their overseers. He also gave a detailed account of her accommodation and its potential weak points. After mentioning two postern doors that might have allowed her to flee, and the ways in which this eventuality had been prevented, he continued: 'This queen's chamber at Carlisle had a window looking out towards Scotland.' If its bars were to be sawn off, he said, 'she might have been let down, and then she had plain grounds before her to pass into Scotland . . . there was another window of her chamber for passing into an orchard within the town wall, and so to have slipped over the town wall, that was very dangerous'.

Dozens of armed soldiers were stationed in the outer rooms in Mary's tower, and Lord Scrope occupied the chamber next to hers. Whenever she went outside, as when attending services at Carlisle Cathedral, or for a walk or a ride, a large guard of soldiers accompanied her. Despite Knollys's insistence on tight security, she was allowed astonishing leeway. Knollys described the scene where Mary, guarded by twenty-four halberdiers, watched the male members of her retinue play football 'the space of two hours, very strongly, nimbly and skilfully, without any foul play offered, the smallness of their ball occasioning their fair play'. Momentarily diverted, the nature of the game seems to have interested him more than the possibility of Mary taking to the hills. He was not so relaxed when Mary went 'a hunting the hare'. You can feel Knollys's alarm as he writes of her 'galloping so fast upon every occasion, and her whole retinue being so well horsed' that he became acutely aware that 'some of her friends out of Scotland might invade and assault us upon the sudden, for to rescue and take her from us'.

Mary might have represented a threat to the country, but she was also seen as a prize. Lowther had claimed her as his, since she had arrived in the district without a passport, but he was challenged for the right to hold her by the Earl of Northumberland. As Lord Warden of the Marches, the earl arrived in Carlisle demanding she be handed over to him. An unseemly spat erupted between the two men, who were like foxes competing over roadkill. Northumberland, a staunch Catholic, was so incensed that a man of Lowther's inferior status should defy him, let alone stake his claim to the queen, that he called him a 'varlet'. This was a grave insult, but Lowther won the confrontation, with the help of his soldiers. Seeking to justify himself, he wrote to Cecil complaining that very few of the gentlemen and sheriffs of Cumberland and Westmorland had responded to the beacons alerting them to the Queen of Scotland's arrival. Fear of Mary's presence igniting a civil war within England was uppermost in Elizabeth's mind in these unsettling weeks. Since placing

Mary in the care of a Catholic in a part of the country where the old faith still held sway would not have been wise, she gave her backing to Lowther, who retained his trophy.

In their first meeting with Mary, Knollys and Scrope tried to soothe her tearful bewilderment over why Elizabeth had not yet sent for her. The Queen sympathised with her, they said, and was keen to meet, but could not do so until Mary's name had been cleared of involvement in Darnley's murder. Their attempts to placate her were not helped by the cast-off dresses Elizabeth had sent with them as presents. These garments were so low-grade that even they recognised the insult. In the words of Mary's biographer Jane Dunn, 'Elizabeth's gift of her inferior gowns was more a reminder of their relative power than solely an expression of lack of sisterly generosity.'

Such a shabby gesture sent a message Mary could not fail to understand. Poorly dressed, she would command less respect and begin to feel her condition as a humble fugitive. It was also a reminder – or a portent – that even her royal status could not protect her from the indignities of a captive whose fortunes lay in another's hands. Mary, however, was not to be so easily tamed. When she refused to wear any clothes but her own, Knollys had to send to Scotland for her wardrobe. Few pickings were left in Holyrood, as seen by the pathetic delivery sent by Moray, to Mary's disgust. She complained to Knollys that the three coffers he had despatched contained only one gown, of taffeta, and the rest 'is but cloaks and coverings for saddles and sleeves, and partlettes [a sleeveless top worn over throat and shoulders] and qweyffes [coifs, or caps], and such like trinkets'. He had again to write to Moray, requesting that the queen's belongings at Lochleven Castle be forwarded. This duly happened, her clothing filling five carts and so many panniers it required four horses to carry them. This was only the start. Once Mary was in receipt of her income from France as dowager queen, her outfits and accessories multiplied. Soon, there was no question of her looking like anything other than one of the best-dressed and best-looking of European royalty.

That first fortnight in Carlisle was revelatory. Even while disappointed at Elizabeth's coldness, Mary recognised that the person whose favour would do her most good was Cecil, since he could bend the Queen to his will. Thus her letter to him, written either in May or June, was an exercise in sycophancy:

> Master Cecile, the character which you have of being a friend to equity, and the sincere and faithful service which you render to the queen madam my good sister, and consequently to all those who are of her blood and like dignity, induce me in my just cause to address myself to you above all others in this time of my trouble, to obtain the benefit of your good counsel, which I have commanded my lord Herries, the bearer of this, to explain to you at length. So referring to him, after commending myself to your wife and you, I will pray God to have you in his holy keeping,
> Your very good friend,
> Mary R

Mary had despatched Herries and Fleming to speak to the Queen and Cecil. In a letter sent shortly afterwards, addressing Elizabeth as 'my nearest kinswoman and perfect friend', she claimed that she understood Elizabeth's hesitation to help her, but 'as my affairs require such great haste, let me see if the other princes will act in the same manner, and then you cannot be blamed'. A note of bitterness then crept in: 'you have admitted into your presence a bastard brother of mine [Moray] . . . and you refuse me that favour'. There was no mistaking Mary's discontent, nor her determination not to be bested.

In a subsequent letter, she also requested a passport be given to Herries, so that he could go to France. Not surprisingly, Elizabeth would not allow him to leave London. Although she was perplexed as to how to deal with her cousin's plea for help without jeopardising her own position, the idea of Mary raising Catholic support from France, Spain or elsewhere was alarming. Bad enough the possibility of a national revolt of Catholics in Mary's favour; far worse a foreign power helping her regain her Scottish throne, and invading England at the same time.

As the weeks passed in Carlisle, and the conditions of Mary's imprisonment grew more stringent under Scrope, she did not hide her growing resentment. Reporting back to Cecil, Knollys said it would be 'vanity' not to expect Mary to bring the French into Scotland 'to satisfy her bloody appetite to shed the blood of her enemies'. By this time Mary was not mincing her words. Knollys reported her as telling him and Scrope that she would seek help from the kings of France and Spain, 'whatsoever come of me, because I have promised my people to give them aid by August'. Her tone then grew threatening: 'I have made great wars in Scotland, and I pray God I make no troubles in other realms also.' Unsettled, Knollys added that, 'parting from us, she said, that if we did detain her as a prisoner, we would have much ado with her'.

Knollys's position was unenviable. Mary was chafing under the restraints put upon her, and galled by Elizabeth's refusal to meet. She railed against her rebels in Scotland, which gave him the chance to press her on the need for an inquiry into her role in Darnley's murder, in order to clear her name. Elizabeth added to his efforts, writing to promise that Mary would be restored to Scotland if she allowed the commission to determine her innocence. She also wrote to Moray, asking him to refrain from harassing Mary's supporters and outlining Mary's accusations of high treason against him and his men. Observing the way Elizabeth carefully played each side, the Spanish ambassador, Diego Guzmán de Silva, agreed with one of Mary's party that 'the Queen of England uses towards his mistress fair words and foul deeds'. By late June, Mary's envoy, Lord Herries, had come to the same conclusion: 'For whatever the Queen of England might pretend, her real intentions towards her cousin were clearly proclaimed by her actions. She has been boasting in private of the great captive she has made without having incurred the expenses of a war.'

It is little surprise that Mary was reluctant to agree to a trial – not that this word was ever used, since England had no authority to try her as a foreign sovereign whose alleged crime had been committed in another country. Not only did England have no jurisdiction over her, but it was in Elizabeth's best interests to favour the Protestant ruler of Scotland, whose friendship bolstered England's security against potential threat from Catholic France or Spain. Mary could also imagine how Moray would twist the truth to her disadvantage. Although she was unaware of this, she would not have been surprised to learn that immediately on hearing that Mary was in England, Moray had sent his secretary, John Wood, to the English court, to clarify the Regent's position and underline Mary's catalogue of wrongdoing. Alison Weir, in her life of Mary, writes that her secretary Claude Nau said that 'after Elizabeth had heard what he had to say, her kindness to Mary diminished somewhat'. While Wood was at court, he received from Scotland translations of some of Mary's private letters, which allowed him to hint that there were more scurrilous ones available. Thus Mary's cause was further undermined.

Even so, Moray and his party were aware that she had a justifiable grievance against them, and their panic was tangible when the Regent wrote to Elizabeth on 22 June. In this revealing letter, he sought assurance that, if he produced incriminating letters from Mary and could prove they were genuine, Elizabeth would not allow Mary back to Scotland: 'it were most reasonable we understood what we should look to follow thereupon, in case we prove all that we allege . . . For when we have manifested and shown all, and yet shall have no assurance that it we send shall satisfy for probation, for what purpose shall we either accuse, or take care how to prove, when we are not assured what to prove, or, when we have proved, what shall succeed.' Whatever other talents Moray had, clarity of prose was not one of them. Yet his agitation was understandable. The only way to safeguard against Mary's vengeful return was to ensure her lifelong incarceration. This was what he wanted Elizabeth to guarantee.

By now, the forces against Mary were gathering pace. Under Cecil's instruction, Darnley's father, the Earl of Lennox, composed an accusatory *Narrative*, drawing on various witnesses to damn

Mary, and citing one of the so-called Casket Letters, in which Mary appeared to be writing to Bothwell as a lover while still married to Darnley. In this, he wrote, she named the date of Darnley's murder – 'the night of Bastian's marriage' – and reminded him that he must get rid of his wife by poison, as they had already agreed.

The previous month, Moray had commissioned Mary's former tutor George Buchanan to outline the events surrounding Darnley's murder and at the same time implicate Mary. Buchanan set to work with such enthusiasm that his *Book of Articles* was ready the following month. The scholar, who had once been an admirer of Mary, was now to become her nemesis. Drawing on his *Book of Articles*, which was expressly composed to result in a guilty verdict at the inquiry, he later wrote *Ane Detectioun of the Duinges of Marie Quene of Scottes*; *De Jure Regni apud Scotos, or, A Dialogue, Concerning the Due Priviledge of Government in the Kingdom of Scotland*; and a history of Scotland, *Rerum Scoticarum Historia*, all of which scurrilously blackened her name. Though a learned man and respected scholar, he showed few qualms about turning malicious gossip and unfounded speculation into so-called history. Thanks to his twisting of facts, Mary was for centuries viewed as conniving, cunning and weak.

It was an agenda that worked to Moray's advantage, and it seems that while John Wood was at Westminster, Cecil privately gave some sort of assurance that whatever the outcome of the inquiry, Mary would not be restored to the crown. At this point, Moray agreed to submit to the trial, at which he and his men would stand as the accused. He must have taken comfort from the fact that, as the historian Jenny Wormald writes, Elizabeth 'obviously much preferred [him] as the person controlling events in Scotland'.

A grim foreboding is felt when reading the various letters from and to Mary, and between Moray and Elizabeth's court at this juncture. Elizabeth professed herself willing to restore her cousin to Scotland, once she had been declared innocent: 'Oh, Madam, there is no creature living who wishes to hear such a declaration more than I. But I cannot sacrifice my reputation on your account. To tell you the truth, I am already thought to be more willing to defend your cause than to open my eyes to see the things of which your subjects accuse you.'

Knowing what we do of Cecil's views, Mary's chances of release were slimmer than even the Queen of England was aware. He based his argument for detaining Mary on her perceived immorality: that she had been part of or aware of the plot against Darnley, and that her participation was confirmed when she married the chief suspect in his murder. Although she was a sovereign queen who had been illegally forced to abdicate and had never been given a chance to answer the charges levelled against her, and although she had freely come to England to seek Elizabeth's help, he believed the moral charge against her was sufficient to imprison her indefinitely.

The sudden reappearance of Mary's 'privy letters', intended to show her guilt, was suspicious. As Antonia Fraser writes, the letters, which had not been mentioned since the previous year, 'seemed not only to swell in importance, but also actually to grow in number as the campaign mounted in fervour'. Referred to as the Casket Letters, because of the silver casket in which they had allegedly been discovered, they were considered to be the smoking gun. Moray planned to produce them as irrefutable proof of Mary's depravity. When Mary learned about them, she became ill with worry.

Meanwhile, as her time in Carlisle drew to a close, she was writing ceaselessly. It was a habit that was to continue for the rest of her life, her need to communicate with the outside world a way of retaining a measure of control and dignity, possibly even sanity. Agnes Strickland, Mary's biographer and the editor of a three-volume collection of her letters published in the mid nineteenth century, was impressed by her style, as will be anyone who immerses themselves in her correspondence. Mary's letters, Strickland wrote, 'very far surpass those of her most accomplished contemporaries – not even excepting those of Bacon and Philip Sydney. It is a positive refreshment to turn from the laborious, pedantic and mystified compositions of Queen Elizabeth to the easy, unaffected, perspicuous letters of Mary Stuart.'

Mary had a directness of tone and clarity of expression that mark her out as an excellent writer. Even more importantly, for those attempting to understand her at this distance, is that her personality infuses every line. Other than in diplomatic correspondence, where formality was required, or in the standard conventional greetings and sign-offs, there was no barrier between who she was and how she wrote. The result is an extraordinary treasure house of information about almost every aspect of her life and on which this account, like so many others, is based.

From Carlisle, in a mood of imperious frustration, Mary wrote to Lord Fleming in London, instructing him, on reaching France, to ask the king for money and soldiers so she could recover her strongholds taken by Moray. He was also to tell the king that her trinkets and jewels had 'been sent out of the kingdom by the rebels for sale'. She wrote a forlorn letter to her uncle, the Cardinal of Lorraine, saying that if he did not take pity on her, it was 'all over with my son, my country and myself'. Describing the situation in Scotland, she reported that Moray and his men 'demolish all the houses of my servants and I cannot aid them; and hang their owners and I cannot compensate them, and yet they all remain faithful to me, abominating these cruel traitors. When I parted from my people in Scotland I promised to send them assistance at the end of August. For God's sake let them not be denied and deceived . . . It is all one for myself, but let not my subjects be deceived and ruined, for I have a son, whom it would be a pity to leave in the hands of these traitors.'

She wrote to her mother-in-law Catherine de' Medici in France, saying she had 'not a penny' and was without the means even to purchase a chemise. And she wrote several letters to Elizabeth, repeatedly asking for her assistance, outlining her grounds for restoration to her throne, and requesting to leave England. To her chagrin, she soon discovered that far from being allowed out of the country, she was to be sent to the wilds of Yorkshire.

Chapter 4

'I am no enchanter'

BOLTON CASTLE

When Mary first heard that she was to be moved deeper into England, she baulked, saying she would have to be carried there. 'I will not stir,' she told Elizabeth. 'I am confined here as in a prison, my servants are treated with severity, and my hands, as it were, completely tied, not having the requisite intelligence, while they [Moray's party] are seeking favour with your council.' In one particular letter to Elizabeth, on 5 July, she appears like a bird fluttering at the bars of its cage: 'suffer me to go into France, where I have a dowry to maintain me, or at the least to go into Scotland. . . . permit me, if you please, to depart hence without delay – anywhere, so that it is out of this country.' She also hints that she suspects poison is being dropped into Elizabeth's ear: 'Do not as the serpent that stoppest his hearing, for I am no enchanter but your sister and natural cousin.'

Setting her free was not on Elizabeth's agenda. Growing awareness of the vulnerability of Carlisle Castle to Scottish attack made the Queen less rather than more willing to release her. The risk of rescue grew greater as opinion in Scotland warmed towards Mary's return. Evidence of the tide turning in her favour, among Protestants as well as Catholics, was seen in Kirkcaldy of Grange's change of allegiance. The staunch Protestant soldier and Governor of Edinburgh Castle, who had led the queen in disarray off the battlefield at Carberry, had now switched sides and was holding the castle for her. Maitland of Lethington, her slippery secretary, also reaffirmed his loyalty. Like Kirkcaldy, he would later suffer grievously for his change of heart.

To prevent the risk of Mary's adherents thundering south and carrying her off, she had to be moved somewhere secluded, at a safe distance from the border. Nottingham and Fotheringhay castles were discussed, but it was Bolton, Lord Scrope's ancestral home, that was settled upon as fit for that purpose. Officially, Mary was not a prisoner, even though the conditions of her stay were severely restricted, and the presence at all times of armed guards was hardly conducive to the fiction that she was a free agent. Elizabeth did not declare her a captive, yet neither would she allow her to depart the country. The contradictions of Mary's situation gave a hint of the dragging years of confinement that were to follow.

When it became clear that her removal from Carlisle was not a matter of choice, Mary had little option but to agree. It is a measure of Knollys's diplomatic skills, and Mary's confidence in him, that he eventually won her over. Perhaps she also recognised that behaving amenably might serve her purpose better. However, when Knollys said the reason for the move was that Elizabeth wanted Mary to be closer to her, she was not fooled. She commented drily that the Queen could have her removed anywhere she liked. Bolton was, if anything, more remote from London than Carlisle, since it was not on a main route. By now, her powerlessness was becoming all too clear.

Since arriving in England, Mary's household had greatly expanded and on the day of her departure from Carlisle on 13 July, four carriages, twenty packhorses and twenty-three riding horses were required, costing more than Knollys had expected. The first night of this seventy-mile journey was spent at Lowther Hall, as a guest of Richard Lowther, who, as in Carlisle, treated her with deference. Dread of a rescue attempt was so intense that it was not until Lowther met her party on the road to accompany them to his home that she learned Bolton was her destination.

On 15 July, after a second night at Wharton, in Cumbria, they reached Bolton Castle. It was an hour after sunset, but in the lingering evening light, the castle would have been visible long before they rode up to its gates. A massive four-cornered medieval fortress, dating from the fourteenth century, it is like an emblem of the Middle Ages. Once there, Mary and her retinue were given the best rooms, ousting Lord and Lady Scrope from their bedchambers and living quarters.

From the Scottish Borders, where I live, the drive to Bolton Castle passes through a landscape rich in violent history. The route took me through Jedburgh, Otterburn, Corbridge. Around the military base in Catterick, north Yorkshire, an expanse of army huts and barbed wire was a reminder equally of the twenty-first century's ongoing conflicts and tensions, and of the early modern era, where trouble was closer to home. Road signs warning of crossing tanks felt appropriate as I made my way towards one of the best fortified – and best built – castles in England.

After I reached the bustling market town of Leyburn, in the Yorkshire Dales National Park, it was only a few minutes before Bolton Castle came into view on a hillside. On a dazzlingly sunny June day, I left the car knowing it would turn into a slow cooker in my absence. My eyes watered as I gazed up at the castle's battlements. The heat was baking, and the indoor cool promised by the castle's thick walls was unusually appealing.

Although Bolton was badly damaged by Cromwell's army following a siege in 1645, more than enough of it remains intact to evoke its former authority. Constructed on an imposing scale, in another location it would look implacable. Its position, however, is delightful, overlooking a shallow soup bowl of lush meadows and fields, fringed by the low, rolling Wensleydale hills. In summer, beneath a cloudless, azure sky, the prospect is so tranquil it is hard to imagine there was ever the need in these parts for a stronghold this imposing. First impressions, of course, can be misleading. Even as Mary was being led to her chambers, Lord Scrope and his men were preparing against possible attack. Given the castle's defences, it would have been a ferocious foe that attempted to breach its high walls. The greater danger was her slipping out of their grasp and getting away before they noticed.

Entering the castle on the first floor, visitors pass through the café, situated in a dark, high-beamed room, formerly one of the castle's eight halls, where an enormous fireplace is occupied by a wood-burning stove. The ticket office lies beyond in a vaulted chamber, redolent of the tantalising smell of cold stone, woodsmoke and the dampness peculiar to places this old. Beneath the first floor lies the engine-room of the castle: a honeycomb of stone-flagged, low-beamed or stone-vaulted chambers dedicated to provisioning and upkeep. There is a brew house, which would have worked overtime, fresh water being deemed unsafe in the Middle Ages. Everyone who could drank small beer, which had a low alcohol content and antiseptic properties. Alongside are a bake house and meal house, and a room dedicated to kneading and proving bread. A wine cellar stands next to the Well Chamber, the well of which was probably that used for the manor house that pre-dated the castle.

There are storerooms, stables with space for eight to ten horses, and a provender house, where horse feed was stored. This wing also accommodates an armourer's workshop and an archers' garrison. Perhaps most impressive of all is the stone-flagged and cobbled threshing floor and mill, where flour was ground for bread. Its size indicates the number of mouths that needed to be fed.

On the first floor is a malting house and granary, where grain passed via a chute down into the bake house and meal house. This is also the floor containing two kitchens, alongside butteries, where great quantities of dry and preserved foods could be stored to last through the lean winter months. In short, the castle contained within its walls everything necessary for the smooth running of a substantial military and domestic operation. Less pleasing to contemplate is the pit dungeon, known as the oubliette. Its presence is a reminder of how grim Mary's and earlier times could be. Prisoners were lowered – or perhaps simply pitched – into this windowless recess through a trapdoor, to be forgotten forever, as its name suggests; the French verb *oublier* means to forget. The guidebook reassures visitors that few prisoners would have ended up here, but notes that an arm bone was found manacled to the wall.

Overhead, away from the baking, malting, brewing, stabling and making of weaponry, the atmosphere is elegant and relaxed. Fronds of foliage decorate windowsills and fireplaces, echoing the medieval practice of strewing rooms and burning fires with herbs and potpourri, to fragrance and refresh the air. A child's idea of a castle, Bolton has a tower at each corner (only the north-east tower and much of the east wing have not survived), and a network of tight spiral staircases burrows through the walls like woodworm. It is arranged around a forbiddingly dark central courtyard, entered by the double-portcullised gateway. With sheer, high walls, this is a gloomy place, although useful: when Scottish marauders approached, livestock could be corralled in here for protection.

The best view of the courtyard is from the castle roof, although visitors who, like me, are leery of heights, will find the drop unsettling. Taking photos with one hand gripping the rail does not produce great results. On the day I visited there was to be an archery demonstration, and at one end of the courtyard an enormous target, like a giant's dartboard, was ready for use. If this medieval pastime did not appeal, you could instead watch the castle's wild boar being fed.

It was in the palatial south-west tower that Mary and her entourage were housed. This had been renovated after Henry VIII's army set the castle on fire, in 1536, in response to John Scrope's involvement in the Pilgrimage of Grace. This was a serious popular revolt in the north, fuelled by grievances including Henry VIII's dissolution of the monasteries, increasing governmental control of the area and the enclosure of land for pasture. Fortunately for the Scropes, they were back in royal favour by Mary's day.

Accompanied by a train of fifty-one attendants, Mary put the castle under considerable pressure. Although only thirty-five of her retinue lived in, the rest finding rooms in the locality (where her horses were also stabled), this was a large group to accommodate. After reaching Bolton Castle, Knollys wrote to Cecil with a list of searching questions for the Privy Council: 'Whether she [Mary, Queen of Scots] shall be served as a Queen with assays [tasting of her food], etc? What number of men and women attendants, and their diet, if allowed? What order to the Master of the Jewel-house for plate, etc? . . . Whether the charge of the Stable shall be in the household or not?' To help furnish the place in the manner to which Mary was accustomed, rugs, furniture and tapestries had been borrowed from neighbours. Queen Elizabeth sent pewter vessels and a copper kettle for boiling beef, but so stretched were the royal finances (or her generosity of spirit) that these were only offered on loan.

Taking it as their due, Mary and her party colonised the finest living quarters. There was a sun-filled living room called the Solar – only on the upper levels of a castle was it safe to have larger windows to let in the light – and a Great Chamber, where today boars' heads, armour and weaponry adorn the whitewashed walls. Lady Scrope's bedchamber, where Mary is said to have slept, has been furnished with a small (reputedly haunted) four-poster bed, strewn with rumpled bedding and clothes, and a chair on which more clothes are draped. On entering, it feels as if the queen has just stepped out. A spinning wheel and a basket of wool and knitting needles hint at her occupations, Mary being an accomplished needle-woman. A wide ruff sits on a dressing table, and in one of the two deep window embrasures is a *prie dieu*, with candles, crucifix and prayer desk at which to kneel. Dressed like this, the bed chamber feels like a stage set.

Above it lies the grander apartment of Lord Scrope. This room was first occupied 600 years ago by Richard le Scrope, Lord Chancellor to Richard II. He was the castle's founder, and a formidable, impressive figure. A soldier of great stamina, he fought at the Battle of Crécy and countless other conflicts over a thirty-year period. Knighted at the Battle of Durham, he is thought to have been the model for Geoffrey Chaucer's 'truly perfect, gentle knight' in *The Canterbury Tales*. To look from the windows of his room is to feel a faint tug of the past on your sleeve.

Not for the first time a guidebook contradicts the information offered in the property. This, it says, is more likely the room where Mary and her attendants slept. Given its grandeur, this seems plausible. With light pouring in from its deep-set windows, a massive fireplace and a private privy or garderobe, Mary's time in residence would have been more physically comfortable than the lives of the vast majority of people in England and Scotland. The same could be said for all her abodes in the dreary years that were to follow, even when she was obliged to endure draughts and damp. Ordinary mortals could only dream of luxuries such as a bed, a pillow and indoor sanitation. Whether they would have envied Mary is another matter.

A list of the Scottish household at Bolton Castle adds to the impression of luxury and indulgence. This small army included a secretary, Mary's master of the house and her master of the horse. There were three stable grooms, three laundresses, four grooms of her chamber, two yeomen of her pantry, two yeomen of her warder (guards), two cooks, a pastelar (pastry chef), four turnbroches (to rotate the roasting spit), a physician, reader, apothecary, surgeon, embroiderer, and more.

While at Bolton, Mary was treated like an honoured guest, able to hunt and see friends. On one memorable occasion she joined a gathering of local Catholic worthies in the Great Chamber, where she spoke about her faith, putting to rest unsettling rumours that she was being converted to Protestantism by Knollys. When news of this reached London, Knollys and Scrope were severely chastised. Nor was Westminster paranoid. Among those who met the Scottish queen at Bolton were rebels who would later be involved in the Northern Rising.

A strict eye was kept on Mary throughout her long years of imprisonment, to ensure she was not practising her Catholic faith, although considerable lenience was often shown. Complaining about this prohibition to Elizabeth while at Bolton Castle, she added: 'I begged to be, at least, allowed to exercise it in the same manner as the ambassador of a foreign prince is permitted to do; but was told that I was a kinswoman of the queen's, and should never obtain that indulgence.'

This being summer, Mary would have enjoyed roaming the castle gardens, despite the presence of guards at every step. Falling away beneath the southern wall, today's gardens attempt to recreate those from medieval times. There's a small plot filled with plants used in medicines, cooking and for adding fragrance to rooms, linen and clothes – bugloss, yarrow, thyme, comfrey and lovage; there's a dyer's garden growing plants used to dye clothes – dyer's chamomile, foxglove, purple loosestrife, and many others. In Mary's day, there might have been fruit trees in abundance – apples, pears, plums – but what you were less likely to find was a vegetable plot filled with broccoli or kale. The Elizabethans disliked green vegetables, thinking they upset the 'humours' – the four bodily fluids believed to determine a person's temperament – phlegm, blood, yellow and black bile – which, if they got out of balance, would lead to illness. Despite this risk, they would grudgingly use green vegetables in stews.

At the bottom of the garden is a bee house in a tiny white-washed outhouse where, beyond a peephole, bees are busy at work. Their Tudor counterparts would have been useful not just for honey but also for providing wax for candles. As I was about to leave, I spotted a swallow on the rafters, so close it was within touching distance. Although it seemed unperturbed by company, I tiptoed out.

After an hour exploring the castle interior, it was pleasant to sit outside, soaking up the warmth, albeit in the shade. My bench beneath the south-west tower overlooked an immaculately clipped maze, which shimmered under the afternoon sun. Two teenage girls, previously sighted using their phones in the great hall, made their way listlessly around, too tall to suffer a moment's anxiety about finding their way out and, to all appearances, killing time until their parents had explored every corner of the castle.

With its beds of lavender and roses, the gardens soften the aspect of the castle. Less cosy is the aviary at the foot of the laid-out terrace, where birds of prey slumber or gaze bright-eyed, depending on species. Rows of cages with falcons, hawks, buzzards, eagles and a raven are a direct link to Mary's love of hawking, and of all things outdoors. In 1562, in an early attempt to win over her cousin to the idea of a meeting, she had sent Elizabeth a gift of falcons. Few enticements would have been more meaningful. The majesty of these birds would not have gone unnoticed by royalty, nor their fiercely independent nature.

Looking into each of the cages, I saw a barn owl trying, in vain, to sleep. In another, a tawny European eagle sat on the ground by its door, following my movements as if I were prey. With every step, I could feel eyes trained upon me. That these magnificent creatures were behind bars, allowed out only under strict supervision and for short periods, seemed another nod to Mary's house arrest.

Like an employee ahead of his annual appraisal hoping for approval, Knollys sent a map showing security arrangements to Elizabeth. Moray wrote, warning that he had heard Mary was to make her escape with the help of English supporters, led by 'your friend George Heron', who was Deputy Keeper of Tyndale. According to legend, despite being closely watched, Mary did indeed evade her guards. Climbing from a window by rope, she only made it a few miles to a place now known as the 'Queen's Gap' before being captured. There is a version of this story, or perhaps it refers to another attempt entirely, in which her attendant fell while climbing out of a window, the noise alerting the guards.

But even this might be apocryphal. Although Mary had expressed frustration at her constraint, she still trusted her cousin and probably felt no need to risk her neck falling from a rope. Not until early October, when perhaps she began to sense what lay ahead, did she warn Knollys that her attitude might change: 'If I shall be holden here perforce, you may be sure that being as a desperate person I will use any attempts that may serve my purpose either by myself or my friends.'

To Mary's delight, her envoy Lord Herries finally returned from London, bringing with him Elizabeth's promise to restore her to her throne, regardless of the verdict, albeit under stringent conditions. Greatly encouraged at what appeared to be a guarantee that she would shortly be on her way from England, Mary at last agreed to the commission, which was to take place in York in October. Among the conditions imposed on her return to Scotland was that, if innocent, she renounce her claim to the English throne during Elizabeth's lifetime. She must also cease her alliance with France. Most troubling, from Mary's perspective, was that Mass was to be abandoned in Scotland entirely. Yet the fact that terms were imposed on the restoration did at least suggest the end of her ordeal was fast approaching. Choosing to be optimistic, Mary decided, against the advice of her closest friends, to place her future in Elizabeth's hands. It would not be the first time that her advisors despaired.

Riding a wave of confidence in her cousin's word, she now told her supporters in Scotland to cease fighting, so long as Moray's men did likewise. A cooler head would have been less precipitous, but Mary seems either to have been deluded or gullible. Her faith in Elizabeth had already been knocked, and yet she persisted in the expectation of being delivered back to her homeland. A letter on 1 September shows both her anxiety at her predicament, and her belief in Elizabeth: 'like a vessel driven by all the winds, so am I, not knowing where to find a haven, unless, taking into your kind consideration my long journey, you bring me into a safe harbour'. Yet stormy seas lay ahead.

Before the inquiry opened, Cecil told Moray that 'It is not meant, if the Queen of Scots shall be proved guilty of murder, to restore her to Scotland, howsoever her friends may brag to the contrary, nor yet shall there be any haste made of her delivery.' Thus, before any evidence had been heard, Elizabeth was already reneging on her promise. Mary could not have known this, but equally, in light of the ambiguous reception she had so far received, she should have been sceptical about the assurances she had been given.

For Moray, the pressure was on to prove Mary's part in her husband's murder. Suddenly, the significance of the Casket Letters became paramount. Meanwhile, at the news that Moray was to produce them before the commission, Mary's party, who had gathered in Dumbarton Castle, immediately declared them forgeries. Even so, they dreaded what their appearance might lead to.

Chapter 5

'I never wrote anything concerning that matter to any creature'

THE CASKET LETTERS

While waiting for the inquiry to begin, Mary allowed herself to be taught to write in English by Knollys, whom she now dubbed 'the schoolmaster'. 'Excuse my evil writing this first time,' she wrote in the postscript to her first letter to him ('Excus my ivel vreitin thes furst tym'). It was during their amicable meetings that he tried also to instil in her an interest in Protestantism. He prided himself that he had succeeded to some degree, but Mary appears simply to have been attempting to win Elizabeth's favour, knowing Knollys would report back to her. It would take more than a smitten English courtier to change Mary's convictions, although, as evidenced by her speech to local Catholics in the castle chapel, she clearly felt the need to refute any appearance of converting.

It is poignant to think that these weeks at Bolton, in the early autumn of 1568, were the last relatively happy days of Mary's life. Expecting her situation to be soon resolved, allowing her to overturn her enemies and regain her throne, she had no inkling of what lay ahead. Other, less vital, matters were on her mind.

She seems to have made a friend in Lady Scrope, and debate continues, four and a half centuries later, as to whether Mary and Lady Scrope's brother Norfolk, the foremost nobleman in England, met at Bolton. Certainly, Lord Scrope believed his wife was becoming dangerously close to the Scottish queen, and in September insisted she cease all contact with her and take up residence in a house two miles away.

The York conference opened on 4 October, and for Mary the omens were good. Elizabeth had expressed the hope that this gathering would produce a 'good end to the differences, debates and contentions grown and continued between her dear sister and cousin Mary Queen of Scots and her subjects'. A panel of three English commissioners comprised Thomas Howard, Duke of Norfolk, who was the commission's chairman, Thomas Radcliffe, Earl of Sussex, and Ralph Sadler, a soldier and diplomat well known to the Scots. Among the commissioners on Mary's side were the group's spokesman John Leslie, Bishop of Ross, and her lords Livingston, Herries and Robert Boyd. Representatives of the Scottish rebels included Moray, Mary's implacable enemies Patrick Lindsay and James Douglas, Earl of Morton, and Maitland of Lethington, whom Moray described as that 'necessary evil', now that he was moving towards Mary's side. Not that she trusted Maitland either, even though his wife was her once devoted attendant, Mary Fleming.

In the opening days of the inquiry, Mary's representatives charged the rebels with taking up arms against her, holding her prisoner at Lochleven and forcing her to abdicate. It was a daunting array of accusations, all of them – one would have thought – irrefutable. She had also instructed her commissioners how to respond to the Casket Letters if they were produced: 'ye shall desire that the principals be produced, and that I myself may have inspection thereof, and make answer thereto; for ye shall affirm in my name I never wrote anything concerning that matter to any creature, and if any such writings be, they are false and feigned, forged and invent by themselves, only to my dishonour and slander; and there are divers in Scotland, both men and women, that can counterfeit my handwriting'.

Mary's handwriting was bold and clear and, as she indicated, known to many around her, including her attendants, privy councillors and courtiers. High among the possible suspects as a forger is Mary's secretary, Maitland, who admitted he could copy her writing. The prime suspect, however, is Morton's relative, Archibald Douglas. It was he who had most probably smothered Darnley in the gardens at Kirk o' Field, giving him a strong motive for casting the blame onto the queen. Years later, he was charged with forgery in another case. His fingerprints, one could say, were all over the Casket Letters.

In the annals of Scottish history few subjects have caused as much debate and uncertainty as the Casket Letters. Books have been devoted to analysing and interpreting them, with historians coming down on either side of the question of Mary's culpability, or feebly (perhaps forgivably) sitting on the fence. Found in a small tooled silver and gilt box in Bothwell's rooms at Edinburgh Castle, this seemingly astonishing discovery comprised eight letters purportedly from Mary to Bothwell, a long love sonnet to Bothwell and two marriage contracts between her and Bothwell. The originals, written in French, were destroyed in 1584, almost certainly by James VI. The question that remains over their interpretation, and on which Mary's reputation hangs, is whether they were forgeries, authentic or a combination of both. In the words of her biographer John Guy, 'The sole evidence that she [Mary] was a party to the murder plot comes from them. There is no other proof.'

Only Casket Letter I, which is known as the Short Glasgow Letter, is dated, and none is either addressed to anyone by name or signed. The love sonnet, which is poor in quality, has been completely discredited, so need not bother us. Guy describes the extent to which genuine letters have been tampered with to make them appear incriminating. Most of the letters are in Mary's hand, but were probably written to Darnley rather than Bothwell, or written after the events they are claimed to point to. With minor forged additions, or by altering their context, or splicing letters together, their meaning could be made to fit a different narrative.

By far the most troublesome of the letters is Casket Letter II, or the Long Glasgow letter. Along with the Short Glasgow letter, it was allegedly written from Glasgow while Mary was in attendance on Darnley, who was suffering from smallpox (more likely syphilis). In it, the writer refers disparagingly to her husband – 'Cursed be this pocky fellow that troublith me thus muche' – and talks of his reluctant admission of conspiring against her, then appears to make reference to murder: 'Think also if you will not find some invention more secret by physick, for he is to take physick at Craigmillar and the baths also. And shall not come forth of long time.'

If the letter is wholly genuine, then by suggesting he be killed by 'physick' – i.e. poison – there is no doubt that Mary was eager for Darnley's death. But Darnley did not die by poison. Nor did the Confederate Lords produce this document as evidence when they rebelled and forced their queen to abdicate, even though being able to prove her murderous intent would have helped justify their actions. It is telling, in fact, that they did not mention the existence of the Casket Letters until Mary was imprisoned in Lochleven and could have no sight of them.

In a fascinating forensic analysis of all the material, John Guy picks apart each of the documents. His conclusion is that almost two thirds of the material is written by Mary, although not always to Bothwell. The lovelorn letters, for instance, were very probably to Darnley, when their marriage was in trouble: 'I will in no wise accuse you, neither of your little remembrance, neither of your little care, and least of all of your broken promises.' Nor was the timeline the lords gave for their composition accurate, as is proven by a number of small errors. The rest of the text, meanwhile, is a series of careful additions, so discreet as to be overlooked if not closely examined by a handwriting expert. On this basis, there is no evidence that Mary was involved in Darnley's death. Many historians agree with Guy, among them Alison Weir, who writes: 'Every single letter poses a problem, whether in sense, style or timing.'

Jenny Wormald takes a different tack. She believed that James's act of 'losing' his mother's letters shows that he thought they were the real thing. Looking at the woman the letters reveal – one utterly in thrall to a domineering man – Wormald concludes that, on balance, they offer strong evidence that Mary was party to the plot to kill Darnley. But she leaves no room for doubt as to where she stands. If they are not genuine, there are still reasons to believe Mary was implicated, even though it cannot be proved. In this assessment, Mary is damned if she did and damned if she did not.

Wormald's convincingly argued verdict is troubling for those who cannot bear to consider Mary capable of such heartlessness. Yet even if the Casket Letters are fraudulent or manipulated, her collusion has to be considered as a possibility. Events in Scotland had shown, as did Mary's flight to England, that she was capable of desperate or illogical decisions. Throughout her marriage with Bothwell she had been as miserable as she was in the months before Darnley's death, when she claimed that if he was not dealt with, she had no wish to live. While at Dunbar, after her abduction by Bothwell, to which she was probably a willing partner, she displayed clear signs of emotional distress. Within a couple of days of their marriage, she was heard calling for a knife to end her life, saying she would drown herself if that could not be provided.

Could her unhappiness have been caused by a painful conscience? In an age when political killings were common, when awkward enemies or liaisons could be disposed of by convenient death, it is not inconceivable that she was persuaded into endorsing such a deed, if only as an act of self-preservation. To those who consider it out of character, it could be countered that many of her wayward actions did not conform to the image we have of her or, more accurately, wish to have of her.

And yet the discrepancies and inconsistencies in the letters, and their belated appearance to aid the rebels' case, all point to tampering intended to frame the queen and secure their position. If I had the unenviable task of adjudicating on the case, I would conclude that Mary played no active part in the murder plot but closed her mind to the very strong possibility that her court would find a way of despatching her husband. She would not have been the first royal to behave in this manner, metaphorically stopping her ears and covering her eyes.

Meanwhile, other arguments have been put forward to explain James VI destroying the letters. Not least of these is that if they were resurrected and shown to be forged, his mother's claim to return to her throne would have been strong.

Ahead of the York conference, as we've seen, the prospect of the letters being cited in evidence made Mary unwell. She might have been reassured had she known that Elizabeth thought they were unreliable and did not intend to take them too seriously. Then again, there was nothing comforting about the way the inquiry unfolded, nor the Queen of England's change of heart while it sat. It was not the Casket Letters that caused Elizabeth's volte-face, since she never believed they were entirely credible. What they did, however, was give her the excuse she needed to keep Mary in England indefinitely. Rarely has such palpably dubious evidence been used to shape the affairs of nations.

From the outset, the York conference was dogged by confusion and double-dealing. Nothing about it was straightforward, nor did it proceed logically as if in a court of law. Instead it was an often fractious, bad-tempered affair. At one point Herries robustly and fearlessly denounced Mary's accusers, who, he said, all stood to benefit from a long minority rather than obey their true sovereign. Patrick Lindsay replied ferociously, accusing Herries of lying 'in your throat', and challenging him to combat, which Herries suavely deflected. But as was evident by now, Elizabeth and her court were keen only to protect English interests, and getting to the truth of the situation between Mary and her subjects was irrelevant to that cause. The outcome they desired was for the danger Mary represented to be nullified; conveniently, the Scottish rebels wanted exactly the same result.

An indication of how compromised the proceedings were to prove was that Norfolk, who was in charge of the inquiry, had by this time been suggested as Mary's possible fourth husband, even though she was still married. Indeed, during the conference, Maitland – who was ahead of his time in wishing for a union between Scotland and England – approached Norfolk to discuss this possibility. No wonder Antonia Fraser believes that of all the players at the inquiry, only Moray was truly single-minded in purpose, his sole aim being to prove Mary's guilt. Maitland was more interested in finding a way of accommodating her restoration to Scotland in a manner that served his political ideals. The same was true of others among Mary's supporters. Norfolk, although not the canniest of men, was nevertheless clear-sighted about what was going on. This inquiry, he told Cecil, was 'the doubtfullest and most dangerous that ever I dealt in', whose participants 'seek wholly to serve their own private turns'.

A week after the proceedings opened, Moray secretly showed copies of the Casket Letters to the English commissioners. Norfolk was appalled at their contents and told Elizabeth that if they were genuine, Mary was undoubtedly involved in the murder. Yet within a few days, after Maitland had spoken privately with him, indicating that the letters were not to be taken at face value, he was showing renewed interest in marrying her. Was the possible prize of the Scottish throne enough to overcome his qualms at being wed to a woman capable of consigning her husband to death? More likely, he had realised how unconvincing the letters were.

Understandably, Moray was reluctant to produce the letters officially before the inquiry, in part because many of Mary's accusers were complicit in Darnley's murder. If the letters were discredited, they might suddenly find themselves accused. If they were forged, or partly fabricated, he also did not want Mary seeing and refuting them. That way lay disaster should she regain her throne. Instead, he needed to determine whether they would provide sufficient evidence to seal the case against Mary before producing them and openly accusing her of murder.

On hearing about the covert appearance of the letters, which suggested the inquiry was getting out of hand, Cecil immediately ordered the conference to relocate to Westminster, where he and Elizabeth could monitor proceedings. But there were other reasons for reconvening it at such a distance from Bolton Castle: in the hard winter months, with snow already heavy in the north, Mary could not make the long journey to London to give her side of the story, even if permitted.

Equally significantly, it is likely that by now Elizabeth had heard of Norfolk's interest in marrying Mary. That he was contemplating this, without consulting her, was bad enough. Worse was that, when she questioned him, he lied, saying he could never marry a woman who might smother him in the night. Even worse was that, by contemplating this marriage, Mary had shown herself willing to conspire behind Elizabeth's back.

Many Scots approved the idea, as did some of Elizabeth's advisors, if only to keep Mary under control. The Earl of Leicester believed 'there could be no better Remedie to provide for so dangerous a Woman . . . considering the present state of the World.' Elizabeth did not know that Mary was only contemplating this union because she felt assured the Queen would approve of it, and hoping that, with her endorsement, the marriage would allow her to be restored to Scotland, with the Protestant Norfolk at her side.

Shortly before the tribunal reconvened at Westminster on 26 November, Elizabeth – urged on by Cecil – assured Moray that if Mary were found guilty, she would acknowledge him as Regent and James VI as King of Scotland. Mary would either be handed over to his party to be put on trial in Scotland or remain imprisoned in England. With his confidence boosted, Moray denounced Mary as soon as the inquiry reconvened. He accused her of being complicit in her husband's murder but also of conspiring with Bothwell 'to cause the innocent Prince, now our Sovereign Lord, [to] shortly follow his father, and so to transfer the crown from the right line to a bloody murderer and godless tyrant'. There was no going back now, which was just as Cecil had hoped.

When Mary's advocates learned that she was not to be given an opportunity to appear in person to answer the charges, let alone be allowed to see the letters she had consistently denied writing, they were shocked. Mary ordered them to leave the conference, and after a delay, during which they were incredulous at not being allowed sight of the incriminating documents, they duly departed. This left the field clear for her enemies. The following day, on 7 December, Moray finally produced the Casket Letters. They were swiftly translated from French into English, and the commissioners pored over them for two days.

At this point, Elizabeth intervened. Although there was no doubt where her best interests lay, she wanted no accusations of being partisan. She increased the number of judges, to Mary's advantage, and relocated the conference to Hampton Court, where she, and the Privy Council, could have oversight of the proceedings. Again Mary demanded the right to see the evidence against her and address the panel in person, and again she was refused.

As a compromise, Elizabeth said she could answer the charges through her commissioners or give her reply to English nobles sent to her at Bolton. She could even put her defence in writing. However, since each course would require her to answer without seeing the evidence on which the accusations was based, Mary rejected all three options, electing only to answer in person before Elizabeth. Not surprisingly, she was outraged at the way she was being treated: 'I am not an equal to my rebels,' she wrote to Elizabeth, 'neither will I submit myself to be weighted in equal balance with them.' She would not be judged by this inquiry on the question of Darnley's murder, she insisted, 'whereof they themselves are authors'.

In response, Elizabeth maintained that by failing to respond she was acting 'as much as she were culpable'. If Mary would not answer before a deputation, she would have to adjourn the inquiry. She also expressed her shock at what had been revealed: 'as we have been very sorry of long time for your mishaps and great troubles, so find we our sorrows now doubled in beholding such things as are produced, to prove yourself cause of all the same. And our grief herein is also increased, in that we did not think at any time to have seen or heard such matter of so great appearance and moment to charge and condemn you.'

Seething, Mary sent a further list of accusations against the rebels, hotly refuting the charge that she had ever plotted her son's death, and citing Rizzio's murder and Moray's illegal regency as evidence of their criminality. As December advanced, she began to realise that the tribunal was a stitch-up. Anticipating how it might end, she anxiously wrote to her son's guardian, the Earl of Mar: 'Look betimes to the safety of the place, and take care that my son be not stolen from you.' Her postscript was plaintive: 'remember that when I delivered to you my son, as my most precious jewel, you promised to protect him, and give him up to no one without my consent'. It must have been a wretched Christmas in the frozen fastness of Yorkshire as she awaited what January would bring.

Chapter 6

'Bound hand and foot'

TUTBURY CASTLE

Whatever torments Mary was enduring in Bolton Castle while she awaited the conclusion of the inquiry, she did not sit idle. Nor did she curtail her ambitions. Early in January 1569, she told the new and combative Spanish ambassador Don Guerau de Spes, 'if his master will help me, I shall be queen of England in three months, and mass shall be said all over the country'. It was fighting talk and, had she been aware of it, would have confirmed Elizabeth's growing suspicion that Mary was neither meek, biddable nor unversed in duplicity. The ambassador's cautious master, Philip II, was not interested, recognising that this was a risky venture. Yet Alison Weir believes this bold approach indicated a new direction: 'It is clear that, from January 1569 onwards, Mary was more interested in claiming the English throne than in regaining the Scottish one.'

In a bid to salvage something from the dying days of the inquiry, Herries and Leslie, without first conferring with Mary, offered three alternatives to the commission. One of these was that Mary would affirm her abdication and live the rest of her life quietly in England. Unsurprisingly, Moray agreed to this, but Mary would not hear of abdicating. She would sooner die, she said: 'the last word which I shall utter in this life shall be that of a Scottish queen'. Her fear now was that, if Elizabeth should die, or her son die before he ascended to the throne, she would be assassinated. Added to which, 'as for my subjects who have an affection for me, if they saw that I deserted them, they would seek protection elsewhere, and I could never hope to regain them'. In conclusion, she wrote, 'I am determined that I shall not lightly throw away what God has given to me, and that I am resolved rather to die a queen, than a private woman.'

The inquiry formally concluded on 11 January, with Elizabeth determining that nothing had been proved on either side: Moray's party was not judged guilty of rebellion, but nor had Mary's guilt been upheld. What happened next ranks as one of the great political betrayals, or sleights of hand, depending on your perspective. Elizabeth allowed Moray and his allies to return to Scotland – she sweetened his journey with a £5,000 loan to aid him 'in his great necessity for the maintenance of peace and resisting the common enemies of both realms', i.e. Mary's supporters. (He had less than a year to repay it.) And, at the end of January, Mary's commissioners were given permission to return home.

But for Mary, home was beyond reach forever. Elizabeth, writing to her cousin on 20 January, made that plain: 'Your case is not so clear but that much remains to be explained.' This, even though, like Moray, Mary had been neither convicted nor exonerated. Elizabeth's promises of restoring her whatever the inquiry's outcome had been hollow. The ambiguous outcome of the conference was dastardly but politically expedient: it helped destroy Mary's reputation and gave Elizabeth a reason to hold her; yet by not directly condemning her, Elizabeth was keeping her options open.

One can only imagine the long, dark hours Mary must have spent in her rooms at Bolton, bitterly regretting her decision to place herself in her cousin's hands. To this gall was added trepidation of what was to follow. Before the commission had concluded, the Privy Council had agreed that this troublesome queen must be moved somewhere more secure than Bolton. Their choice of prison was Tutbury Castle, in Staffordshire. And by now, there was no doubt that it *was* a prison. All pretence of hosting an honoured guest was gone. When informing Mary that her case was 'not so clear', Elizabeth took the opportunity of twisting the knife: 'Hearing from your commissioners you dislike Bolton, I have prepared another place more honourable and agreeable for you, and ordered Knolles and Lord Scrope to escort you there.' It was a calculated and cruel distortion of the truth.

News that she was to be moved again deepened Mary's gloom, and she refused outright. Knollys reported to Cecil that their treatment of Mary made him uneasy: 'We all agree this is a dangerous place for the Queen to tarry in . . . I have told you that she knows we had no authority to bring her from Carlisle; and says plainly she will no more be abused by us, and that we shall bind her hand and foot, and forcibly carry her, before she will go further in the realm.' He also reported that Mary had serious misgivings about leaving Bolton, believing that Cecil 'would cause her to be made away'. The fact that Tutbury was close to the home of Henry Hastings, Earl of Huntingdon, who, as a descendant of Edward IV, had a slender claim to the English throne, deepened her fears of assassination. For the rest of her life she saw him as a mortal threat.

However much she protested, she could not sway her keepers. A Frenchman called M. de la Vergne wrote a secret account of her circumstances to Catherine de' Medici at the end of January. His letter, which was written in cipher and smuggled out in the French ambassador's post bag, suggests the manner in which she was threatened: 'More than wonted rigour has been shewn since the last few days, to the Queen of Scotland: it is to compel her to renounce her crown; and they have threatened her, if she makes any difficulty, that she shall go where it has been ordained to move her (which in truth grieves her very much), that they will lift her up, she and only one other woman with her, in their bed, and carry them by force in a litter close shut up with a lock and key.'

After threats of forcibly removing her if necessary, Mary must have known she had no say in the matter, and was headed for Tutbury, a place she would come to loathe. This castle had been decided upon partly because of its brilliant defensive position, overlooking the plain of the River Dove to the Derbyshire hills. It had the advantage of being as far from London as it was from the border, where Mary might have sought help.

The Bishop of Durham kindly provided her with ten horses and two keepers, and from elsewhere a further six horses with women's side-saddles were found, and sixteen more horses for the guard. With eight carriage horses and six carts for baggage, Mary's over-laden party left Bolton on 26 January, in the middle of a snowstorm. Why they set out in such conditions is unclear, unless it made the risk of rescue slimmer. Mary described that day's ride as 'foule, long, and cumbersome', and over the next ten days, the wind was so strong at times that she had trouble staying on her horse. Given the weather in which they travelled, it is not surprising that the trip was dogged by mishaps. From Ripon, with the journey barely begun, Mary wrote to Elizabeth, complaining about her 'harsh treatment in my forcible removal', and again expressing concern over the safety and care of her son. Referring to the Casket Letters, she added: 'I know nothing about them, and have never written such silly things.'

After spending a night at Pontefract Castle, they reached Rotherham, where Mary's lady-in-waiting Lady Livingston took ill. Too unwell to continue, she had to be left behind. South of Sheffield, at Chesterfield, Mary also fell ill, with the pains in her side that had troubled her so severely in recent years, to which was added a terrible headache. Unable to ride further until she recovered, the entire party, including Knollys, threw themselves on the hospitality of the Foljambe family, local grandees who lived at nearby Walton Hall.

Knollys had been begging to be relieved of his duties since November, but in January he told Cecil that if he was not discharged after taking Mary to Tutbury, he would 'as sure as God is in heaven, repair to court, and suffer any punishment that may be laid upon him, rather than continue in such employment'. His feelings on learning that his wife, Catherine, one of the Queen's ladies-in-waiting, had died at Hampton Court in the middle of January, must have been bitter. Although Elizabeth had been very fond of Catherine, and was often at her side as she lay dying, she refused to allow him to return home for her funeral or to comfort his children.

Whatever warm feelings he had at one time felt for the Scottish queen, these were likely now turned to ash.

Given the timing of Mary's collapse, it seems possible it had been precipitated by stress. For several months, despite being under house arrest, she had been confident of eventually being released. Now, her situation was grim. She was being treated like a convict, in a country where her safety depended on the continuing mercy of her cousin who, as Mary saw it, had proved herself completely untrustworthy. As her entourage made its way towards Tutbury, via Pontefract Castle and Wingfield Manor, she could not know what she was heading into, other than that she would be further still from help. Even without the benefit of hindsight, she must have recognised that this development represented a new and ominous chapter.

Did Mary acknowledge she had played a part in her own troubles? Was she given to self-recrimination? If so, she gave no sign. Heading towards Tutbury, her state of mind was anything but contrite or chastened. Rather, she was shocked and bewildered, feeling herself wronged on every side. That attitude would harden down the years, until she had encased herself in a carapace of martyrdom. It was an outlook that would in time justify all her actions, and reshape her personality.

Eventually, the train of horses bearing Mary reached Staffordshire on 4 February. As she passed through the prosperous market town of Tutbury and rode up the hill towards the castle, she was greeted by the sight of soaring curtain walls and solid towers, the definition of a prison. Like a medieval Italian hill town, encircled by high walls, this sprawling fortress was self-sufficient and braced for attack. In the harshest days of winter, when night fell early and daylight returned late, the compound and its various buildings must have seemed forbidding. Once the portcullis had rattled shut behind them, there was no mistaking the nature of Mary's arrival as a captive.

Tutbury was a market town long before the Domesday Book was compiled. In the Middle Ages it was renowned for its priory and for its Minstrel's Court, where cases were heard and judged annually. This was followed by a Minstrels' Fair, part of which included a bull-running competition. This barbaric and hugely popular event, first recorded in the early fifteenth century, continued until 1778. A bull had its horns removed, was greased with soap and then set loose for minstrels to catch and claim. Once a winner had been declared, the bull was brought back to the village, where it was baited to death for public amusement, and then served as part of a great feast. The crowds this attracted, and the noise they made, would have reached Mary's apartments. As would the aroma of roasting meat.

In the late eighteenth century Tutbury became a thriving mill town. The area is also a rich source of gypsum, which for centuries has been mined to make plaster, alabaster, cement and pale ale. Although today it is best known for its castle, during the Second World War, Tutbury made tragic headlines. At RAF Fauld, a couple of miles away, 3,500 tons of bombs and ammunition were stored underground. On 27 November 1944 the storehouse detonated, killing seventy people, with a further eighteen bodies never found. It was the largest non-nuclear explosion of both world wars, and left a crater 300 feet deep and a quarter of a mile wide.

To the modern visitor, however, Tutbury is charming. My train from Derby passed the famous five cooling towers at Willington power station, denoting the industrial activity of this part of the Midlands, but the scenery grew more rural as Tutbury drew closer. In a field, a dead and bloodied sheep was circled by crows, a glimpse of nature's heartless laws. There is consolation, of a sort, in viewing human brutality through the same lens.

Arriving at the tiny station of Tutbury and Hatton in brilliant sunshine made the journey feel like a holiday. I crossed a busy road bridge over the River Dove and almost immediately saw the ruins of the castle in the distance. The village of Tutbury is a ten-minute walk from the station, past a leafy park where a miniature children's castle and a cricket pitch basked in the early afternoon warmth. Here, only five miles from the built-up brewing town of Burton-on-Trent, the mood was unhurried and calm. Tutbury is a quintessential English village, so festooned with hanging flower baskets and blooming tubs when I was there it was as if royalty was about to visit.

The centre of Tutbury is a mix of Georgian and Victorian buildings, although some look even older. Newbuild houses maintain the illusion of a period village, with tall, narrow redbrick chimneys of a style that would have been familiar to Mary. On the broad curved main street, alongside cafés, a vet's and an interior design shop, there is a half-timbered pub called the Dog & Partridge. Crooked and picturesque, it looks like the backdrop to a Jacobean play, but much of it was renovated in the eighteenth and nineteenth centuries. Formerly a coaching inn, in the fourteenth century it was the town house of the powerful Curzon family, who arrived in England at the time of the Norman conquest.

Just in time for a late lunch, I found a table in a café where the staff were hard-pressed. 'Fancy running out of lettuce on a day like this,' said a harassed waitress, struggling to fulfil orders. Outside the sun beat down. It was six months later in the year than when Mary first set eyes on the town, but whatever the date, the castle would have been sombre. To reach it requires a gradual uphill climb through the village, the road flanked by houses with names such as The Vicarage and The Stables. A strident bird was calling as the pavement grew steeper, and around a corner I found a peacock, sitting on a mossy wall, looking like a model posing on the catwalk.

Ahead lay the castle. In a scruffy field beneath its walls was a small flock of cinnamon-coloured sheep with curved, ribbed horns, sheltering in the shade of a wall. This was a part of the outer bailey of the castle, beneath the windows of the rooms where Mary initially lived. Now scrubland, it is known either as the Queen's Field or the Queen's Garden, which may indicate that it was where Mary strolled when she was allowed out of the gates.

The rutted track continues to a ticket office beside a car park in what, in the fifteenth century, was the upper bailey. Beyond lies the fortified gatehouse, misleadingly known as John of Gaunt's Gate. John of Gaunt, the third son of Edward III, made many improvements to the castle when it was his, including building its distinctive curtain wall. The gatehouse, however, was built at least half a century earlier, by Thomas of Lancaster, in the early fourteenth century.

Lancaster was the richest man in England, after the king, but following defeat by his cousin Edward II at the Battle of Burton Bridge in 1322, he was forced to flee (and was later caught and executed). In 1831, workmen found a huge horde of coins in the River Dove, worth a small fortune in Lancaster's day. This was clearly his long-lost treasury, last seen in three iron-hooped barrels. Thousands of coins disappeared before an official tally could be made, and many are thought to remain in people's possession in the district.

Lancaster's imposing entranceway – to which a barbican was later added – frames a view within of a high grassy knoll, topped by a decorative eighteenth-century mock tower. This mound was the motte of the Norman castle that stood here from the eleventh century, as William the Conqueror stamped his authority across England. With such a commanding position overlooking the shires, it is not surprising the site was previously settled by Stone Age and Iron Age dwellers, Romans and Anglo-Saxons. Not until the Norman invasion, however, did it enter the record books.

Although Mary remains Tutbury's most glamorous, controversial royal connection, the story of the castle was already rich when she reached it, and it would continue to be a focal point of political and military activity for centuries after she departed. Among its most dramatic episodes was its role during the Wars of the Roses, when it was used by Margaret of Anjou from 1457 until 1460. Two centuries later, after it held out for Charles I, an Act of Parliament (1647–48) decreed it should be destroyed, although the job was half-heartedly finished. The ruins as they now stand date largely from then.

What you see today is low-key but intriguing. Stepping inside what remains of the walls, the castle ruins are airy, with a lingering sense of the past. To the background growl of the gardener's sit-on lawnmower, which worked meticulously over the immaculate sward, visitors explored every corner. Atmospheric as it is, though, the castle is nothing like the Tutbury of old. For a start the walls are tumbledown and far lower than in their prime. Even on a sunny day in 1568 its inhabitants would have felt enclosed, possibly claustrophobic, with high walls blotting out much of the sky.

Closely associated with royalty from its inception, Tutbury's heyday was under Henry IV, Henry V and Henry VI – the son, grandson and great-grandson of John of Gaunt – who strengthened its defences and added three towers, two of which survive despite dilapidation. The inner bailey, with its stout defences and elevated position, feels like a self-contained village. On the southern wall lies the South Tower, which is where Mary was taken on her arrival. Its ragged ruins stand open to the sky, floor upon floor of verdigrised stone and gaping windows staring into space. A narrow stone turnpike stair coils between each level with a slack rope handrail. At the top is a precipitous drop and a superb view, worth a moment's vertigo. As well as centuries of inhabitants, almost two hundred years of tourists have climbed these stairs. Tickets for public viewing went on sale in 1847, and the carvings and graffiti on walls and stairs bear testimony to Tutbury's allure: 'T C Greaves 1830', 'HLP 1827', 'Fatty OV Lincs Skin Up' (the last written in white marker pen). The steps have been so often trodden, they are worn to saucers.

Outside the South Tower is a modern replica of the Queen's Garden that Mary once enjoyed: four neat parterres filled with box and roses and lupins. Also on the southern range is the castle's 120-foot deep well, and the kitchen and tea-rooms, which were once part of the early nineteenth-century farm buildings. Alongside is a grand seventeenth-century house, occupying part of the site of the enormous medieval Great Hall and King's Lodgings, where there had been kitchens, butteries and pantries. The hall is furnished in period style, including an intricately carved chair beneath a royal canopy, or cloth of estate, bearing Mary, Queen of Scots's arms at the time she became Queen of France.

This room is now used for wedding ceremonies. Outside, near the gatehouse, is a large permanent marquee, with crystal chandeliers and dance floor for weddings and other celebrations. There are regular historical talks and events too, with titles such as 'Sex and the Tudors Cream Tea', and 'An Evening with Eirik Bloodaxe'. Mary, Queen of Scots events feature frequently, with the castle's curator, a Tudor expert, getting into costume, and character, to tell her story.

The marquee sits close to the site of what is known as the Receiver's Lodging. The Receiver of the Honour of Tutbury was a high-ranking auditor who managed the income of the extensive lordship of Tutbury. This large fourteenth-century, two-storey building, which might still have been standing during Mary's visits, contained several rooms, including a hall, kitchen and buttery. Close by are the foundations of a twelfth- or thirteenth-century chapel. Near to that, and parallel to the north part of the curtain wall, is a row of stones thought to be the footings for the ramshackle two-storey timber building where Mary lived on her last and fateful visit in 1585. Facing the door of the adjacent North Tower is the Healing Herbery, also confined within box hedging, with a profusion of lavender.

From the top of the grassy motte the views towards Derbyshire stretch for miles over the rooftops and factories of Tutbury and Hatton, across swathes of golden fields, to a shimmering stretch of water in the distance. In Mary's day, a marsh lay beyond the walls, its dampness and noxious fumes seeping into the castle. With her love of country pursuits, she might have enjoyed the prospect of Needwood Forest and the far-off hills. Years later, her son would visit on at least three occasions, probably to enjoy hunting in the forest. In this respect at least he was like his mother, never happier than when on horseback with the hounds baying and the huntsman's horn leading the pack on.

But while the views were excellent, Mary chafed miserably at her confinement. It would have become increasingly obvious on the long road from Bolton that she was deep in foreign country and far from an easy escape over the border. Even for a modern visitor from Scotland, Tutbury feels distant from home. A St George's flag flies from the castle battlements, and the proliferation of Union Jacks along Tutbury's streets betokens deeply felt British pride in a way rarely seen in Scotland. Mary, Queen of Scots might give the town a claim to fame, but she is not a heroine in the English story. That would be Elizabeth. Yet as the walls of Tutbury closed around her, Mary would soon be calling upon heroic reserves of fortitude. They would prove essential in the eighteen years that were to come.

Chapter 7

'It is ill with me now I fear worse to come'

THE EARL AND COUNTESS OF SHREWSBURY

Of all Mary's prisons, Tutbury Castle was the place she most detested. 'My imprisonment starts here,' she wrote, and swiftly grew to hate it. Years after that first visit she described the place as 'a walled enclosure, on the top of a hill, exposed to all the winds and the inclemencies of heaven'. In 1561, the castle, which was by then primarily a hunting lodge, had been declared 'decayed in many places'. Repairs were made in 1566, but three years later it was still far from weathertight, profoundly inhospitable for those accustomed to warmth and comfort.

On hearing that Mary was to be brought to Tutbury, its owner, George Talbot, Earl of Shrewsbury, and his indomitable wife Elizabeth – better known as Bess of Hardwick – were thrown into panic. They had visited Tutbury a few weeks earlier, and found it dank, cold and spartan. It was not in any way fit for a queen, even one in invisible shackles. In typically decisive manner, Bess sprang into action: 'I have caused the workmen to make forthwith in readiness all such things . . . most needful to be done before her coming,' she wrote to her friend Robert Dudley, Earl of Leicester, who had informed her husband of the Privy Council's decision to place Mary here. 'And, God willing, I shall cause three or four lodgings to be furnished with hangings and other necessities.'

To that end she had furniture and tapestries removed from Sheffield Castle, Shrewsbury's main home, as well as from her own grand house at Chatsworth. In a rare gesture of largesse, Elizabeth I provided a great number of tapestries and Turkish carpets, beds, mattresses and a variety of items essential to a semblance of sophistication suitable for a sovereign. If Mary ever discovered they had come from the Tower of London, she might well have shivered.

It was at Tutbury that the next phase of her life began. At its centre was the Earl of Shrewsbury, who, along with his wife, would be her keeper for the next fifteen and a half years. On arrival on that wintry February afternoon, Mary was warmly greeted. For a moment, did she almost forget her situation and feel like a guest glad to have reached her destination? It seems unlikely. More probably, since leaving Bolton she had been brooding on the injustices done to her, and planning how to free herself.

Picture the scene: the attractive but travel-weary young queen dismounts from her horse to meet her middle-aged host who, bowing low, treats her with deference. Shrewsbury, who was by nature a worrier, was doubtless honoured at the distinction of becoming Mary's custodian but also aghast at the responsibility. What his wife made of his lovely and vivacious charge can perhaps be guessed.

In appointing Shrewsbury to this arduous and poorly remunerated role, Elizabeth was canny. The earl was one of the richest and most powerful landowners in England, with an eye-watering portfolio of properties. The dissolution of the monasteries under Henry VIII had played a part in engrossing the family's fortunes under his grandfather. As well as Tutbury Castle and Abbey, there was Sheffield Castle and nearby Sheffield Manor Lodge, Wingfield Manor, Buxton Hall, a couple of other abbeys, houses in London and vast swathes of land across the Midlands and Yorkshire. In terms of accommodation, nobody was better placed to house Mary.

The people of Sheffield referred sarcastically to Shrewsbury as 'the great and glorious earl' because of his unbridled spending. Yet there was nothing rash or foolish in his appearance. A portrait shows George Talbot as thin-faced and wary, with hooded eyes, aquiline nose and a wispy waterfall of a beard. His hair is shaved close behind his ears, and on the top of his head is a bushy tuft, neatly parted. If the style is not precisely punk, it bears a similarity. In height he was similar to Mary, at around six foot.

One of Elizabeth's most trusted courtiers, and Lord Lieutenant of the North, the Protestant earl was also recently married to Bess, his second wife. As such he was presumed to be inoculated against Mary's bewitching charms, but in case he might still be susceptible, he was reminded that the Queen of Scotland was said to have murdered her husband and married the man presumed guilty of the deed. When informing Shrewsbury of her decision, Elizabeth sought to flatter him by applauding his sterling qualities. Praising his 'approved loyalty and faithfulness, and the ancient state of blood from which he is descended', she laid out the job description, telling him he was to treat Mary 'with the reverence and honour mete for a person of his state and calling, and for her degree'. It was also essential that the Scottish queen was closely guarded, and never allowed contact with anyone who might help her get away.

Throughout Mary's term of imprisonment under Shrewsbury, the cost of the upkeep of her party was punishing, and a constant torment to the earl, who received a weekly pittance – and sometimes not even that – to provide for a royal household. On the very day of Mary's arrival, he obliged her to reduce her household from sixty to thirty, not including her close attendants. Astonishingly, she accepted this without demur, although shortly afterwards she took to her bed. A few days later she wrote to Elizabeth that 'this place is not habitable, and the cold has given me the rheumatism and severe pain in the head'.

Remarkably quickly, Shrewsbury began chafing under the impositions of his demanding new role: 'the Queen of Scots coming to my charge will soon make me grey-headed,' he complained to Cecil. How prescient he was. There seems little doubt that, over the next decade and a half, these duties exacerbated his declining health and the collapse of his marriage.

With hindsight, knowing the dramatic events that were to unfold during Mary's years of confinement, it is easy to airbrush the reality of her everyday life. What for us is a tempestuous and inspiring tale of hope, despair, courage and fortitude, was for her like anybody's existence: a pointillist portrait made from countless additions of paint, some vivid and uplifting, but many workaday or tediously drab. While her prisons might be stately, unlike most of the country's gaols, and she suffered few of the privations endured by less fortunate inmates of the Tower of London, she enjoyed only the illusion of aristocratic normality. Added to which was the constant presence of her keepers, in this case the often tetchy but considerate earl and his strong-willed but fascinating wife. Although Mary had ladies-in-waiting around her and an entourage including favourites such as young Willie Douglas, the personalities of Shrewsbury and Bess were indelibly to colour the years she was obliged to spend in their company.

In early 1568, when Shrewsbury married the thrice-widowed Bess of Hardwick, who was a year older, he appeared to be in love. She was the wealthy owner of Chatsworth House and Hardwick Hall, and had coal and lead mines on her land, to match his coal and smelting and shipping interests. Yet for him this was not merely the marrying of two fortunes. Calling her 'my own sweetheart', his early letters to her are filled with endearments: 'God send me soon home to possess my greatest joy. If you think it is you, you are not deceived . . .'

Bess did not need to love him to agree to marry and gain the title Countess of Shrewsbury. Although portraits show her as plain rather than beautiful, she was a slim, intelligent-looking woman with ginger hair, who dressed almost as richly as the Queen of England. Most importantly, when she was not being domineering and meddlesome, she appears to have had a winning personality. After three marriages, each ended by sudden death, Bess had accumulated great wealth. Her own efforts in securing her fortune, via the courts, give an idea of her mettle. Born into a well-connected minor family, like other well-bred children she had gone into service with a high-born family at the age of twelve. After the death of her very young husband, she became an attendant of Lady Frances, wife of Henry Grey, Marquess of Dorset. Lady Frances, who considered herself fourth in line to the throne, was mother to the ill-fated Lady Jane Grey and her sisters Katherine and Mary, with whom Bess became close.

By February 1569, when Mary entered her life, Bess was the 41-year-old mother of three sons and three daughters, to one of whom Elizabeth I was godparent. Appointed to the distinguished position of lady of the Queen's privy chamber, she had become a favourite. As Countess of Shrewsbury, she was one of the most eminent ladies at court, and Elizabeth once remarked that 'There is no Lady in this land that I better love and like.' Bess's consuming passion, writes her biographer Mary S. Lovell, was 'the advancement of her children'. Before she and George Talbot married, she partnered off two of her offspring with a son and daughter of his, thereby aiding their progression up the social (and economic) ladder.

Added to her talent as a Tudor tiger mother was her obsession with her house at Chatsworth, which she was to spent thirty years constructing and embellishing. Such was its place in her affections that her third husband, William St Loe, used to address her as 'honest sweet Chatsworth'. Sir William had effectively saved Elizabeth I's life when she was suspected of colluding in the Wyatt rebellion to overthrow Mary Tudor, thereby helping Bess gain the Queen's good favour.

In Mary's early days at Tutbury, she and Bess appeared to get on well. Initially, Elizabeth had instructed Shrewsbury to allow Mary access to Bess only if she was ill. Swiftly, however, that proscription appears to have been ignored. They shared a love of embroidery, and in the coming months, Mary, with her ladies and others of her party, was to spend part of each day in Bess's rooms, sewing and talking. Bess's embroidery work was no mere pastime, since she was making hangings, curtains and bed coverings for her various households. Aristocratic women were expected to be adept with a needle, but while Bess was competent, Mary was more skilled than most. Perhaps hoping to impress on Cecil Mary's meekness, the earl reported a pleasing domestic scene: 'This Queen continueth daily resort unto my wife's chamber where with the Lady Leviston [Livingston] and

Mrs Seaton, she useth to sit working with the needle, in which she much delighteth and in devising of her works. Her talk is altogether of indifferent and trifling matters without ministering any sign of secret dealing and practice.'

Always keen to advance her own interests, Bess in time used Mary's connections to acquire some of the finest silks and threads. During their sessions, Mary produced several works, whose symbolism attests equally to her unhappiness and refusal to be cowed. Among the most famous is the cushion with the title *A Catte*, on which a powerful-looking ginger cat sits, a little grey mouse scampering close to its paws. It was a memorable image of her predicament, as the red-headed Elizabeth sat, as if at a mousehole, ready to pounce. There is no mention of Mary's sentiments towards cats, but her love of small dogs is well known. One, a Skye terrier, was to accompany her onto the scaffold.

Sometimes drawing on Aesop's fables, Mary's work evoked her captivity, sadness, dread and determined resistance in various imaginative motifs. In one a hawk hovers over a caged bird, the caption reading: 'It is ill with me now I fear worse to come'. In another a leopard with a hedgehog in its jaws bears the motto 'It presses on it and it sticks'. Textile artist and historian Clare Hunter describes Mary's needlework as 'her means to reframe, preserve and promote her story'. To analyse Mary's many pieces is to step into her claustrophobic, imperilled world, and come close, sometimes unnervingly so, to understanding her innermost thoughts.

In addition to Mary's individual pieces, she and Bess collaborated on designs for tapestries, as well as jointly making over 100 embroideries, drawing on their own lives, which were to be stitched together in a panel. The scale of such a project would have required Mary's personal embroiderers, other male staff and also children to help, suggesting that at times the castle would have had the atmosphere of a workshop: busy, congenial, productive. Some time after her removal to Tutbury, Mary wrote of her servant Bastian Pages who 'during these troublesome times, comforts me by his designs for needle-work, which is, after my books, the only exercise which is left to me . . .'

Whether they were working on embroidery, making dresses or simply mending, Mary and Bess would talk of fashion and art while they sewed. Bess learned about French style from Mary, and Mary no doubt discovered how to run several properties and hundreds of tenants from Bess, who had a sharp, sometimes ruthless business mind. At this stage of their acquaintance, the pair appear to have been simpatico, each perhaps recognising a remarkable woman surviving – in Bess's case thriving – in an overwhelmingly male world. It was also in their best interests not to provoke each other. Mary's comfort depended on keeping her captors sweet; Bess would have realised that, should the political climate shift, Mary might become Queen of England.

High on its hill, Tutbury was buffeted by winds from every direction, which found their way into Mary's rooms. The stench of the middens into which the privies emptied was offensive, and despite the beds of fragrant herbs and flowers, could be overpowering. Yet within a month of her arrival, Mary was putting on a brave face for visitors. At the end of February 1569 she received a visit from Nicholas White, Cecil's emissary, who was on his way to Ireland on government business. Afterwards he despatched a vivid account. The tenor of Mary's conversation appears to have been largely upbeat, as if she were determined not to whine. She apologised for her poor English, but White understood her easily. Uppermost in her mind, it seems, was the recent death of Knollys's wife, since she kept returning to the subject. In response, White callously told her that Lady Knollys's end was precipitated by 'the long absence of her husband . . . together with the fervency of her fever'. He added that 'although her grace were not culpable of this accident, yet she was the cause without which their being asunder had not happened'.

Hard-hearted though he was, like others he recognised her allure, warning Cecil that 'Fame might move some to relieve her, and glory joined to gain might stir others to adventure much for her sake.' Somewhat surprisingly, he also commented on her coiffure: 'Her hair of itself is black, and yet Mr Knollys told me that she wears hair of sundry colours!' Everything about the enigmatic captive queen, it seems, was considered fascinating.

With the weather too unpleasant for outdoor exercise, White inquired how Mary occupied herself. 'She said that all the day she wrought her needle, and that the diversity of the colours made the work seem less tedious, and continued so long at it till very pain did make her to give it over; and with that laid her hand upon her left side and complained of an old grief newly increased there.' Her household, he reported, comprised fifty members, and she had ten horses. Her advisor, John Leslie, lived not at Tutbury Castle but in Burton-on-Trent, five miles away.

The wording on Mary's cloth of estate, beneath which she would have been seated on a raised platform, puzzled him: '*En ma fin est mon commencement* [In my end is my beginning]', he wrote, 'is a riddle I understand not.' It was accompanied by the image of a phoenix rising from the ashes, the symbol of resurrection that was Mary's mother Marie of Guise's emblem. Others were less bemused, reading it as a statement of intent: Mary was not finished; she still had ambitions.

Chapter 8

'My trembling hand here will write no more'

WINGFIELD MANOR

The ink was barely dry on the inconclusive verdict of the Westminster conference when Moray and Maitland began urging Thomas Howard, Duke of Norfolk, to marry Mary. Could there be any stronger proof that the Casket Letters were forged to tarnish Mary's name? Moray clearly did not regard his half-sister as a murderer, and Norfolk, having had a chance to examine the letters, was plainly of the same view. He was a capable military man, but surely even the most fearless soldier would not willingly have agreed to wed someone who had done away with a previous husband.

A portrait shows Norfolk as a pale young man with a scribble of colour in his cheeks. Dressed in commandingly rich garb, and with a hint of auburn stubble, he stares out of the canvas with dark eyes, his expression anxious or uncertain. For all his rank, however, he was not a glamorous or charismatic individual. Described disparagingly as 'no lover knight', it was also said he was a hopeless dancer, a black mark against one of his high status. As the foremost noble in the country, and at thirty-three not many years older than Mary, he was not a terrible match, even though he had already, like her, been married three times. Indeed, when the Scottish queen had been seeking a husband after her return to Scotland, Elizabeth had proposed Norfolk as a candidate. In that period, she demanded the right of veto over Mary's choice, despite having no authority to control her decision. When Mary, without her permission, married Darnley, who also had a claim to the English throne, her rage was molten.

Under the present circumstances, however, Mary was unlikely to have conspired to marry anyone who would not meet with Elizabeth's favour. Despite the debacle of the Westminster conference, despite her unofficial but undeniable status as a political prisoner and despite her cousin's refusal to meet her, she retained an incomprehensible confidence in Elizabeth eventually restoring her to Scotland. In the following months, as she and Norfolk corresponded in increasingly affectionate terms, she either believed Elizabeth knew and approved of their liaison, or assumed that she would have no objection when she learned of it, or wilfully ignored indications to the contrary.

Meanwhile at Tutbury, Mary's health rapidly declined. Attributing this in part to the parlous conditions at the castle, Shrewsbury asked permission to take her to Wingfield Manor, another of his great houses. He might also have been keen to move on his own behalf, since he suffered badly from gout and arthritis, which the winds and damp and cold at Tutbury did nothing to improve. This was authorised, but shortly before the move, he suffered excruciating pain in his back and legs. What neither he nor Mary could have foreseen was that Wingfield would be even unhealthier for both of them.

The journey to Wingfield, thirty miles from Tutbury, was uneventful. Both Mary and Shrewsbury were so incapacitated they travelled by horse-drawn litter. Hardly anyone noticed the cavalcade arriving in this quiet corner of Derbyshire, where the manor house rises from a hillside close by the village of South Wingfield. This village is recorded in the Domesday Book as having a priest, eight villeins (feudal tenants), two bordars (lower in rank than villeins), three ploughs and four acres of meadow. Small and unspoiled today, it would probably still be recognisable to its eleventh-century serfs.

Mary's thoughts on first sight of Shrewsbury's palatial and well-appointed house must have been favourable. She described it as 'a fair palace', and was allowed more leeway here than at Tutbury. The Victorian journalist and historian J. D. Leader bemoans her behaviour at this critical juncture, believing that 'if Mary had carried herself with discretion at this period, it is quite possible some arrangement in her favour might have been made. But discretion was the one thing the Queen of Scots lacked, and no sooner did she find herself enjoying a somewhat modified restraint, than she plunged into treasonable correspondence with the Duke of Alva, and poured her love letters on the Duke of Norfolk.' Sexism aside, Leader seems overly critical of the Scottish queen, who had every right to try to win her freedom, and overly confident in Elizabeth's good nature.

Even in its present ruinous state, Wingfield Manor has a fairytale appearance. When I arrived around ten on a June morning, the sun was beating down. It was a day like that described by Laurie Lee in *As I Walked Out One Midsummer Morning*, when he left his Gloucestershire village for London: 'White elder blossom and dog roses hung in the hedges, blank as unwritten paper . . . High sulky summer sucked me towards it.'

It sucked at me too, as I made my way alongside fields fringed with pale pink dog roses, heading towards the woods through which the path to Wingfield Manor runs. Ahead and above, the outline of the house peeped through the trees. What I did not realise was that I had already had the best view of it before I arrived. As the road curved towards the village, battlements and chimneys could be seen poking from a lush canopy of trees that fell away steeply, offering an enticing glimpse of medieval splendour standing proud against a cloudless sky.

Uncertain about my route, since I was clearly encroaching on private land, I stopped a young couple walking their golden retriever to ask directions. The man was in shorts, and the woman immaculately dressed in a stylish backless summer dress and flimsy sandals, as if she had confused dog-walking with a fashion show. Pointing me in the right direction, they told me I 'could not miss' the manor. Those words always make my heart sink. The torpid silence of what promised to be a blistering day hung over the hedgerows. Bees were already at work, but most birds had been quietened by the heat.

Reaching the woods, I welcomed the shade, but soon I was over a stile and swiping away nettles from my bare legs as the narrow track rose towards fields. Having carelessly left my straw hat in the car, whenever I broke cover I felt like a sausage under a grill.

Within a few minutes, I reached a wall of forbidding metal barricades. These fringed a buttressed gable-end, some crumbling masonry and farm buildings that, I guessed, were the outlying parts of Wingfield Manor. A sign on a dilapidated iron gate informed me that there was no public access to the manor. Elsewhere, amid the unkempt undergrowth, barbed wire reinforced the message.

Nowhere could I get close enough to see more than the outline of soaring chimneys, battlements and hollowed-out walls. Those who arrive in winter will fare better, when bare trees allow a far better view. At the height of summer, sadly, the place is all but concealed. Although part of a working farm, Wingfield Manor is owned by English Heritage. Currently it is in such poor repair that no sightseers can visit until substantial conservation work has been undertaken. An aerial photo on English Heritage's website offers a flavour of what it describes as 'a monument to late medieval "conspicuous consumption"'. Built in the 1440s by the treasurer of England, Ralph Cromwell, who was also warden of Sherwood Forest, it was bought on his death in 1456 by the Shrewsbury family.

This elegant, decorative house, which is constructed around two courtyards, is described by *The Buildings of England* as 'the most important house of such high status to survive from the mid fifteenth century, with the best-preserved plan and layout of any of the period in the country'. It has a massive Great Hall, beneath which lies an undercroft, and a 72-foot tower, from which the house could be defended. The author says that, such is its elevation, it is 'visible for miles around'. Only when within touching distance does it defy discovery.

Mary's rooms overlooked the manor's orchards and faced onto the main courtyard, making her secure – or so her captors thought

– from escape. What nobody had envisioned was that the sanitary arrangements of this beautiful house would be overwhelmed by the numbers visiting during Mary's time there. Despite her status as a captive, she was allowed a huge number of retainers and guests. Within a few weeks of her arrival her retinue numbered around eighty, and very quickly the stench of the privies became intolerable. Shrewsbury had no doubt that the blame lay with Mary's household: 'Since their coming, there is within these two days, grown in the next chamber by her, very unpleasant and fulsome savour, hurtful to her health, by continual pestering and uncleanly order of her own folks.'

Throughout her term of imprisonment, Mary's life was punctuated by constant transitions from one residence to another. Sometimes this was for reasons of security, but more often it was to allow the 'sweetening and cleansing' of the castle or house where the middens had grown offensively foul. When the party moved out, cleaners and rat catchers moved in, to reduce the stench and vermin. Rodents were to sixteenth-century cats what Whiskas is today. Despite the riches of the aristocracy and wealthy merchants, on this level their existence was primitive by today's standards and, indeed, those of much earlier centuries.

A constant issue was the presence of fleas, which would crawl into the seams of heavy garments. For this problem, a foul-smelling privy could be useful. Such was the whiff of ammonia in these closets that fleas and other bugs were killed off. Hence the term garderobe, indicating the place where dresses and tunics were hung until their uninvited guests were asphyxiated.

What it was like to live with the pervasive smell of middens and privies is not to be dwelt on. Even in summer, windows were often kept shut to hold the farmyard air at bay. No mention is made of cats in the Shrewsburys' households, but wherever Mary lived there must have been an abundance of them, to keep the rodent population in check. Ahead of a feast, servants would be paid to keep watch overnight to make sure no mice, rats or cats touched the next day's cold meats and puddings.

Soon after the Wingfield drains proved troublesome, Mary fell exceedingly unwell. Her ailment was widely assumed to be linked to poor sanitation, which was a common source of illness. Some have suggested that her collapse, which was so serious her priest was called to administer the last rites, might indicate malaria. Prevalent in England in these times, it was known as tertian fever. As on previous occasions when it had been thought she might die, she recovered.

Mary being unwell was not unusual. What was unexpected, however, was the earl's sudden attack of debilitating fever: the result, it was said, of catching a chill. At one point he was in such distress that he expressed the wish to die. To Bess's relief he rallied, helped by a medicinal visit with her to Buxton, a little over twenty miles away, where he owned the healing mineral waters. For both Shrewsbury and his wife to be absent even for a night, let alone several days, is, in hindsight, astonishing. For one as assiduous in carrying out his duties, ever fearful of incurring Elizabeth's displeasure, Shrewsbury made a rare error. When Elizabeth heard of it, she was livid. And had the earl known what was being plotted while he was away, he might have suffered a relapse.

Among the visitors Mary received at Wingfield was Leonard Dacre, from one of the most powerful families in Cumberland. His uncle, Thomas Dacre, Warden-general of the English Marches, had been an ally of Margaret Tudor, and the scourge of the Scots. Leonard Dacre, known as 'Dacre of the crooked back', shared with the Earl of Northumberland the desire to see Catholicism restored and Mary on the English throne. Neither he nor Northumberland approved of her proposed marriage to the Protestant Norfolk.

On Dacre's visit to Wingfield, where he spoke with her privately as she walked on the roof, or leads, of the house, he outlined a plan for her escape. This relied on help promised from among the manor house domestic staff, as well as the Earl of Northumberland and his wife Lady Anne. It also required Mary to reprise her attempt at Lochleven to pass herself off as someone else. In this instance, she was to wear the clothes of Lady Anne, who was to arrive in the guise of a midwife for Bastian Pages's wife. Despite a permanent guard being on duty at the manor, with Shrewsbury away in Buxton, it seemed the plan might just work.

Frustratingly, Mary decided not to act. In the company of such supporters, she would have to give up the idea of marrying Norfolk. He, meanwhile, had vetoed any escape, since it would scupper his chances of marrying her. That Mary put the wishes of a man on the make, whom she had possibly never met, ahead of her own needs, indicates – infuriatingly – how much authority she granted the men in her life. Quite conceivably, she could have fled in the summer of 1569, and perhaps have reached the safety of France. Instead she stayed where she was, allowing the waters, so to speak, to close over her head. Thwarted in his design, Dacre remained bullish about putting her on the throne. A few months later, he would become one of the instigators of the deeply unsettling Northern Rebellion.

From Wingfield, Mary wrote to John Leslie, describing how unwell she had been. Suffering from convulsions and vomiting, she likened her attack to her collapse at Jedburgh, in 1566, when it had been thought she would die. Fortunately, she added, she was beginning to feel a little better. Writing to Norfolk from bed the following day, she kept her note short: 'My trembling hand here will write no more.'

Historians disagree on whether Mary and Norfolk ever met. It is entirely possible that, while Mary was at Bolton Castle, Norfolk's sister Lady Scrope might have introduced them. Some are certain this meeting took place, others think that, since no mention of it was ever made in the couple's effusive letters, it remains unlikely. Mary's terms of endearment might not read the way most of us would address a stranger, but they were typical of that era's courtly manner. When Mary called him 'My Norfolk', saying 'I will live and die with you', this was neither forward nor unusual for the times.

Certainly, there was no doubt that both intended to marry. Norfolk sent Mary a marriage contract while she was at Wingfield, and later a diamond, to seal their bond. Following this, Mary allowed herself to believe she had found a way to freedom. The previous October, when she evidently considered the Norfolk project as hopeful, envoys had been despatched to Denmark to gain Bothwell's agreement to an annulment of their marriage. Now messengers were sent to Rome to further this.

Meanwhile, a few months after Mary's arrival in Tutbury – by which time she had been shuttled between various Shrewsbury residences – an unexpected glimmer of hope appeared. Elizabeth put three options to the Scottish parliament that would enable Mary's restoration. The first proposal was that Mary ratify her abdication and live in England (we already know how she responded to that suggestion earlier in the year); the second was that she and her son rule jointly; and the third was that Mary regain her throne, with assurances regarding religious practice within the realm, and a guarantee of Moray's safety. Given the wretched eighteen years that were to follow, in which suspicion and dread between the two queens would grow cankerous, it should be remembered that when Elizabeth put forward these proposals, each allowing her cousin to regain her liberty, she seemed keen that one of them would be accepted.

How the queen's party in Scotland must have been feeling at Mary's imprisonment is hard to imagine. The past two years had been chaotic, with their monarch accused of collusion in murder, abducted, imprisoned, forcibly made to abdicate, with those who had locked her up in Lochleven Castle taking over the country. Her triumphant escape, which had promised a resurgence of support to her side, had fizzled out in days, ending in a breathtakingly ill-judged flight to England, where she was now – as she herself recognised – the mouse to Elizabeth's cat. In the few months Mary had been in England, her supporters had been persecuted by Moray's party, to the extent of making her tearful and ill. Shortly after the Westminster conference, when hope of the queen's restoration seemed further off than ever, Moray had an act of forfeiture passed on the properties of many on her side. Despite the rumbling civil war between Mary's supporters and those of the young king, Moray's grip on the country was secure, and about to get more so. In April 1569, James Hamilton, Duke of Châtelherault, along with others of the Hamilton family and Lord Herries, who were plotting a rebellion, refused to accept James VI as king and were thrown into prison. Other stalwart Marians felt they had no alternative but to agree to Moray's demands, acknowledging him as Regent and young James as King of Scotland. Like melting snow, Mary's party began to drain away.

The mood was tense. There was still a chance that the rightful queen would win her way back, but the upheaval and unrest this would cause was incalculable. No doubt there was an appetite among those, such as Kirkcaldy of Grange, Captain of Edinburgh Castle, to see right done and Mary restored. But the odds were stacked heavily against him and his fellow Marians. When Elizabeth's three choices were put to the vote at a gathering in Perth in July 1569, they were roundly rejected by forty to nine. Maitland of Lethington and the devoted Huntly were among the nine who stood by Mary, but their loyalty changed nothing. As a result, writes Jenny Wormald, 'Elizabeth was left with Mary on her hands; Moray remained in power.' The gathering also vetoed the annulment of Mary and Bothwell's marriage, which would have allowed her to remarry. Everything was going Moray's way.

That autumn he further strengthened his position by informing Elizabeth of Mary and Norfolk's nuptial plans. As one of those who had urged Norfolk to consider this step, either he had suffered a Damascene conversion, realising the risk to his own position were this marriage to take place, or he had always been double-dealing, knowing that such a venture, when revealed to Elizabeth, would read like a plot. As indeed it did. Mary was promptly removed from Wingfield and returned to Tutbury Castle. There the Puritan Earl of Huntingdon, whom she dreaded, was added to her guard, and many of her privileges were removed. The Norfolk project had not been simply a private matter between Mary and the duke. It had piqued the interest of Philip II of Spain, and of the Pope. At home, it had helped to galvanise England's disgruntled Catholic aristocrats, including the Earls of Westmorland and Northumberland. For each of these individuals, focused as they were on their political and religious mission, this union held out the hope of toppling Elizabeth and returning England to Catholicism.

Chapter 9

'If the vessel was ever so little stirred'

THE NORTHERN RISING

When summoned by Elizabeth to account for his plans to marry Mary, Norfolk wisely disappeared from court. Men armed with 'pistolets' appeared suddenly at Mary's door, demanding to search her belongings for evidence of her complicity in a suspected Catholic rising in the north. In umbrage, Mary complained to Elizabeth at such treatment, during which, she wrote, 'they have forbid me to go out and have rifled my trunks, entering my chamber with pistols and arms, not without putting me in bodily fear, and accusing my people, rifle them and place them under arrest'.

Elizabeth's displeasure at the idea of Norfolk and Mary marrying triggered a national crisis, which ultimately strengthened the position of the Protestant government and diminished the likelihood of another serious Catholic uprising in later years. In the north, there had been long-simmering resentment at the heavy-handed imposition of royal authority since the days of Henry VIII. Elizabeth compounded the insult felt by the northern aristocracy by placing loyal servants in positions of power and, in the case of Thomas Percy, Earl of Northumberland, removing him from his influential and powerful role as Warden of the Middle March.

Word of Norfolk's impending marriage to Mary was welcomed by some, who saw it as an opportunity to restore Catholicism to the country under a Catholic queen. Northumberland, however, did not like that Norfolk was a Protestant. Yet although he was against the marriage, he became one of the leaders of the Northern Rising. To this extent, the fate of Norfolk was only tenuously connected to the rising. There was more than enough anger in the north to fuel rebellion without the marriage, and Mary on her own was a sufficient rallying point, even though she did not approve of the rebellion and sent a message to Northumberland not to proceed with it. This he ignored.

The rising gathered pace, its main aim being to resist 'the new found religion and heresie' imposed by Elizabeth. Underlying this was mounting anxiety about Cecil and his increasingly belligerent foreign policy towards the great Catholic powers in Europe. There can have been few more reluctant rebels than Northumberland. Thomas Radcliffe, Earl of Sussex, who was in charge of security in the north, described Northumberland in a letter to Cecil as timid: 'but that hys wife being the stowter of the too, dothe hasten hym, and yncorage hym to persever'. Keen to oust Cecil and overturn Elizabeth, yet unsure of the legality of doing so unless she were excommunicated by the Pope – which would happen, but not in time to help their cause – Northumberland and Charles Neville, Earl of Westmorland, and their fellow conspirators were debating what action to take when they heard that Norfolk had fled from court. They wrongly interpreted this as the duke returning home to rally his troops for the rebellion, and were on the point of gathering their men when Norfolk astounded them by returning to court to face Elizabeth; shortly thereafter he was imprisoned in the Tower, throwing them into chaos.

Delaying the start of the rebellion, the conspirators were uncertain how to act. What happened next bears out the belief of the loathed Tudor loyalist in the north, George Bowes of Barnard Castle: 'I take this assembly to be more done for fear than there ys any evil pretendyt to be done.' The spark that lit the fuse was Elizabeth's unwise decision to summon both earls to court to be questioned. Rather than await their fate, they took the initiative and embarked on one of the very few and the most potentially serious rebellions of Elizabeth's reign. Close to midnight on 9 November, one of Sussex's men heard the church bells at Northumberland's estate at Topcliffe in Yorkshire being rung backwards. This was the signal for the county to come to arms, and accordingly the north rose to action.

Under shrewder and more strategic command, the Northern Rising might have caused havoc, or worse. An army of around 5,500 to 6,000 men rallied to the earls, which, had it been a well-organised force, would have been formidable. There was also a bone-deep loyalty to Catholicism across the north where, all these years after the Reformation, old religious practices and beliefs prevailed. In the words of Ralph Sadler, writing to Cecil a month later, 'The ancient faith still lay like lees at the bottom of men's hearts and if the vessel was ever so little stirred came to the top.' Yet despite what had initially looked like a propitious time for overturning the new religion, the rebels had no focus, no plan and – most critically of all – too little support. Their crusade came to nothing. The desire to return to Catholicism was neither as passionate nor as widespread as the earls had hoped.

At the outset, however, nobody could foresee that the rising would fizzle out in five weeks. One of the army's first triumphant acts was to storm Durham Cathedral and hold Mass, an event enthusiastically supported by the local populace, which had been smarting under the fundamentalist harshness of the diocese's Protestant leaders. The town of Hartlepool was taken, in the deluded hope that the Spanish might land there and offer support, and Barnard Castle was besieged, leading some of its hungry defenders to leap the walls to join their enemies. A few of them died of their injuries as they fell.

With their eye on rescuing Mary from Tutbury (unaware that she did not wish to be rescued), the army reached as far south as Tadcaster, fifty or so miles away. At this point, however, the rebels turned around and headed back northwards. It had become painfully clear that there was no support for them in Lancashire or Cheshire, which would have been essential in order to carry off the Scottish queen. No help was available from the south, and in Scotland Moray had forbidden anyone to go to their aid. So, despite the depth of grievances felt by its leaders and some of its followers, the rising was more sound than fury.

Shrewsbury, who was greatly alarmed at learning how close the rebels had come to his doors, added 100 armed men to his guard, and sent scouts throughout the neighbourhood. His anxiety mounting, on

25 November he hastily relocated Mary to Coventry. When Elizabeth despatched a large army north, the rebels disbanded. Westmorland and Northumberland took refuge among the lawless clans in Liddesdale on the Scottish border, before heading deeper into the country, where they hoped to raise support from Mary's party. Instead, a moss-trooper – border brigand – called Hector of the Harlowe's Head, sold Northumberland to Moray (for £2,000), who imprisoned him in Lochleven Castle, in the same rooms where Mary had been held. In 1572, after protracted negotiations, he was handed over to the English, who executed him. Westmorland was more fortunate, being taken in by the Kerrs of Ferniehurst, near Jedburgh, before fleeing to the Netherlands, as did Northumberland's wife.

Early in 1570, Leonard Dacre mounted a last-ditch attempt to reignite the rebellion from his family home at Naworth in Cumberland. The result was a crushing defeat at the hands of Elizabeth's army. Thereafter some referred to the Northern Rising as Dacre's Raid. Fleeing over the border, he made for the continent, where he spent the rest of his life. This clash and one other small skirmish were the only truly violent flashpoints in an otherwise remarkably tame challenge to Elizabeth and her councillors.

Yet while the rising resulted in scarcely any killing, Elizabeth was thirsty for blood. The reprisals she ordered were unusually harsh. In the end, around 450 rebels were executed, instead of the 700 she had demanded. In part this was because the atrocious winter weather made rounding them up difficult. But there is also a sense that her military commanders felt enough was enough, and chose to obey her orders in their own fashion. Although a handful of the rebels were hanged, drawn and quartered, the state's most vicious reprisal for treason, many of the wealthier culprits were allowed to live, their estates forfeited to the crown. As a result, by the end of this short-lived, abortive rebellion, Elizabeth had ferociously stamped her authority on the country's Catholic community, and considerably augmented her landholdings.

Equally significantly, in the popular mind Catholics were now synonymous with traitors, an attitude that would further imperil

Mary. In a tub-thumping sermon, the poet Thomas Drant railed against 'Papists', and urged that the Queen's enemies 'feel the punishment of a club, an hatchet, or an halter'. He also upbraided Elizabeth for being too lenient on the rebels. Rightly recognising the danger that Mary posed to the realm, the Privy Council urged Elizabeth to execute Mary, but she prevaricated, and the opportunity passed.

There is a fascinating postscript to these events, which indicates the febrile atmosphere on both sides of the border during and after the Northern Rebellion. A spy called Robert Constable, working for Ralph Sadler to identify the rebels who had escaped into Scotland, was commissioned to entice Westmorland back to England, where he could be captured. When he managed to inveigle his way among the Border reivers at a hostelry at Ferniehurst, what he learned shows how eager Moray was to recapture Mary:

> So I left Farnihurst, and went to mine host's house, where I found many guests, of divers fashions, some outlaws of England, some of Scotland, and some neighbours thereabouts, at cards, some [playing] for ale, some for plack [pennies] and hardheads [tuppences].
>
> So, after I had diligently inquired that here was none of any surname [clan] that had me on deadly feud, nor none that knew me, I sat down and played for hardheads amongst them, where I heard, *vox populi*, that the lord regent [Moray] would not, for his own honour, nor for the honour of his country, deliver the Earls of Northumberland and Westmorland, if he had them both, unless it were to have *their* queen [Mary, Queen of Scots] delivered to him. An' if he would agree to make that change, the borderers would start up in his own country, and *reive* [seize] both the earls and the queen from him; and that he had better cut his own lugs [ears], than come again to Farnihurst; if he did, he should be fought with ere he came over Sowtray Edge [probably Soutra Hill].

Chapter 10

'Smite him to pieces'

COVENTRY

When the rebel army came within two days' ride of Tutbury, Shrewsbury moved Mary to Coventry under a heavily armed escort. She was there for only a couple of months, and was never to return, but for those wishing to get a sense of her times, and the conditions in which she and the well-off lived, it is an illuminating part of her story. By the later sixteenth century, Coventry was a thriving city, its wealth based on the wool trade and cloth-making. During the Wars of the Roses, as the houses of Lancaster and York fought for supremacy, it had briefly served as the capital of England when Henry VI and his wife Margaret of Anjou relocated there in 1456. By 1569, it was one of the most prosperous cities in England. Thinly disguised, the city was immortalised as Middlemarch in George Eliot's masterpiece, portraying all layers of society in an early nineteenth-century Midlands town dependent on the volatile textile industry.

Centuries before Eliot's fictional ribbon-dyers with their scarlet-stained hands refreshed themselves in the Green Dragon, Mary and her entourage arrived late on the evening of 25 November, a time calculated to attract least attention. Initially she was housed in the Bull Inn, on Smithford Street. This was a flourishing, upmarket establishment, with sprawling grounds at the rear. After the Battle of Bosworth, where he trounced Richard III, Henry VII spent the night there as the guest of the mayor of Coventry. Sadly, as with much of Coventry's medieval past, nothing today remains of the inn. Its former site was opposite the present-day Marks & Spencer's in the Upper Precinct, one of Coventry's various malls, although I could not locate the precise spot.

The inn's grounds reached as far as Bull Yard, on Warwick Street, where the town's shopping district begins. Bull Yard, whose name is all that remains of this once grand inn, is a modern square at the entrance to a busy mall and the teeming Coventry Market, where you can find everything from bolts of vivid and sequined dress material and bedroom carpets to fruit, vegetables, fish and meat. A drawing of the Bull Inn, which was also known as the Black Bull, shows a wide-fronted, three-storey whitewashed building with a stone ground floor and timber upper floors. Rows of large windows sit below a roof divided into three pointed hats. Prominent above a central stone arch, through which carriages and carts could drive, was the image of a large black bull, telling those who could not read that they had reached their destination.

Mary's train of carts and horses included around fifty of her servants, so despite Shrewsbury's wish to keep her presence quiet, word must have spread about the city's distinguished guest. Such was the need for security that, during her stay, the townsfolk put on a 24-hour watch at the city gates so no one could enter without being interrogated.

The earl might reasonably have congratulated himself on his speedy response to the Northern Rising, but Elizabeth was unimpressed to learn that Mary was being held in a common inn. She had ordered that she be sent to Coventry Castle, unaware that it was unfurnished. While Shrewsbury protested that it was hard to organise appropriate accommodation at such short notice, after examining various possible venues he found a better location.

St Mary's Guildhall, in the very centre of the city, was where Mary probably spent most of her time, under the joint care of Shrewsbury and the Earl of Huntingdon. First built in the 1340s as the headquarters of Coventry's pre-eminent guild, by the end of the century the hall was being substantially rebuilt as the nerve centre of the city's four most powerful guilds. Acclaimed by a nineteenth-century architectural historian as 'probably the most perfect medieval house remaining in England', it is a sombre red-sandstone building, with stained glass windows that give its exterior a church-like appearance. Located in narrow, twisting Bayley Lane, its nearest neighbour, at the bend in the street, is a crooked white-timbered cottage dating to around 1500; even older are the ruins of the cathedral of St Michael, directly opposite the Guildhall.

During the blitz, the cathedral, which dates to the fourteenth and fifteenth centuries, was all but destroyed by the Luftwaffe. Remarkably, however, its spire was spared. On a warm July afternoon I sat in the open ruins, eating a lunchtime sandwich as visitors roamed its shattered walls. In such tranquil surroundings it was hard to envisage the night of 14 November 1940, when it blazed like an inferno. The stunning but haunting new cathedral, designed by Basil Spence, is only a step away, but continues the mood of tranquillity and remembrance. Side by side, the two monuments to age-old religious belief and the horror of war feel like the heart of the city, fusing the ancient with the modern.

To mark the inauguration of the cavernous, gloomy new cathedral, which was completed in 1962, there was a performance of Benjamin Britten's *War Requiem*, specially commissioned for this occasion. Spence's design is the apotheosis of Coventry's post-war reconstruction, today's city built more of glass, steel and concrete than timber and brick. Nevertheless, there are frequent glimpses of the medieval past, enchanting timbered houses sitting alongside often brutal late twentieth-century architecture. Close by St Mary's Guildhall is probably the most attractive Wetherspoon's in the country, this timbered mansion more a setting for a Shakespeare play, you might think, than for a pub lunch.

Entry to St Mary's Guildhall is through a deep arched gateway with hanging lantern, which leads into a small courtyard. Within, the Guildhall is arranged around a Great Hall. Beneath a high wooden roof, embellished with fourteenth-century carvings, there is a dais at one end, and at the other a minstrel's gallery from the early 1400s, where minstrels would perform during meals. Such was the dedication of Coventry's minstrels, they were also employed as watchmen, roaming the streets playing 'soothing music' to the citizens from midnight until four in the morning.

Many historic figures have passed through this hall, but its greatest claim to fame is that it is home to the most remarkable tapestry in Britain. The Coventry Tapestry, mostly made between 1505 and 1515 in Flanders, is one of the city's finest treasures. Commissioned to hang beneath the north window, it is thought to depict Henry VI, his wife and their court. Henry, who was murdered while a prisoner in the Tower of London, was revered as a saintly figure. His nephew, Henry VII, for whom the tapestry might have been made, petitioned the Pope to canonise him.

This extraordinary work of art complements the stained-glass window above, which shows a succession of English kings, real and mythical, the elephant-and-castle emblem of Coventry (conveying strength) and the coat of arms of Leofric, the Anglo-Saxon earl who ruled Coventry in the eleventh century. His dauntless wife, Lady Godiva, is Coventry's most celebrated figure, far more famous here than Mary, Queen of Scots.

The tapestry is stitched in warm autumnal colours accented with rich shades of blue, appropriate for its central image of the Virgin Mary on her Assumption into Heaven. Incorporating religious and political imagery, such as apostles and angels, as well as creatures such as rats, dogs and dragons, it is breathtaking. This single wall in Coventry conveys the hopes and fears of the late Middle Ages, offering a keyhole into the world its inhabitants occupied or aspired to.

With Mary forbidden to show herself beyond the Guildhall walls, she complained to Cecil that her confinement was making her ill. She also railed against Shrewsbury for removing her palfreniers (grooms) and lackeys 'that did attend upon the keeping of our horses, without whom we could not have travelled this last voyage, nor cannot afterwards be served in case we be forced to remove to any other place'.

Since she was strictly housebound, it is tempting to imagine Mary passing time by poring over the details of the tapestry, which would surely have been of interest to a fellow stitcher. Even though certain elements had been altered after the Reformation, it must still have struck a chord for a devout Catholic. Nor would it have been encased in glass, as it is today, but part of the touchable fabric of this splendid residence in which she found herself immured.

The day I visited, a guide allowed me to take photos as I strolled between the rooms, even though I had forgotten how to turn off the flash. When I reached the Great Hall, however, he consulted a senior guide, who took the camera from me – 'it's a long time since I've seen a camera rather than a phone' – and, to my disappointment, successfully located the off function for the flash. Thereafter, my images of the interior were mistily dark, as if all the fireplaces had been smoking.

Traditionally it was said that Mary's room was in the part of the Guildhall called Caesar's Tower. This tower, reached by a spiral staircase rising from the Great Hall, possibly dates to the earliest hall on this site, or at least to the late 1300s. Now, after bomb damage and renovation, only its lower storey is original. The small, bright chamber on its top floor, known as the Tower Room, has a door so low that anyone over five foot one, says the guidebook, must stoop to enter. The guide told me that during Mary's stay, a portrait of Elizabeth was strategically hung over the door. Rather than appear to be bowing to her cousin, the elegantly tall Mary would enter the room backwards. Perhaps this is just another of the legends that encrust Mary's story, but it catches her refusal to bend before anyone she did not consider her superior.

Given how cramped this room would have been for a queen, it is more probable that she was given what is now called the Draper's Room, on the first floor, overlooking the courtyard. When I made to enter, the senior guide informed me that it was closed to the public that day, since items were being stored there for an upcoming exhibition. I felt awkward, already marked out as a visitor who had not complied with the no flash photography notice, and now determined, having travelled a long way, not to leave without sight of Mary's room.

Eventually, after some persuading, the guide tried the door and, finding it unlocked, allowed me in on the strict understanding I would take no photos. She stood close beside me, and I did not venture further than a few steps. In many ways, apart from the fact that Mary likely occupied it, this is the least interesting room in the Guildhall. The rest of the building is a warren of crooked stairs, sloping floors, low ceilings and highly decorated wood-panelled rooms, where you can imagine conspiratorial conversations. Little of the Draper's Room's original character survives, and its gaslight fittings and stained-glass windows date to the Victorian age. Privacy was rare in the sixteenth century, even for the grandest. Indeed, in part because there was no alternative, in part for protection, most preferred to have others close at hand, even when asleep. Mary was no different. Thus, according to the guide, she and her closest attendants would have slept in this room, while lower servants bedded down in the kitchens, along with other menial staff.

While Huntingdon had Mary under his watch, he proposed that she consider marrying his brother-in-law, Robert Dudley, Earl of Leicester. Years earlier, before Mary married Lord Darnley, Elizabeth had proposed that she marry Leicester, even though her own love for him was widely known. This affection would be retained throughout Elizabeth's life. Whenever Leicester fell short of her expectations – as, for instance, when he supported the secret plan to marry Mary to Norfolk, or when he remarried – he suffered no more than brief banishment from court or from her goodwill. Huntingdon's suggestion, meanwhile, shows the ambivalence of some of the English court towards Mary. They were not unaware that one day she might be their ruler, and that even if that did not come to pass, she could be a useful political pawn.

While in Coventry, from where she wrote so many letters she can have had time for little else, Mary received Norfolk's diamond. In reply she wrote: 'I will remayne yours faithfully as I have promised. And in that condition I took the diamond from my lord Boyd which I shall keep unseene about my neck till I give it again to the owner of it and me both . . . yours faithfully till deth . . .' True to her word, she had it with her at Fotheringhay, seventeen years later.

She in turn sent Norfolk a gold-framed miniature of herself. She also embroidered him a pillow, with a far from benign motif: a hand appearing from the clouds prunes a withered vine, to allow a younger vine to flourish. In the context of her travails with the barren Elizabeth, and her claim to the English throne, the motto, *Virescit vulnere virtus* – Virtue flourishes by wounding – was all too clear. Later, she would also send him a ring.

When visiting the ruins of castles and houses where Mary stayed, it can be difficult to picture the astonishing comfort in which she lived – assuming it was possible to be comfortable with a sword dangling over one's head. St Mary's Guildhall, however, still evokes the opulence with which Mary was surrounded, even in these troubled days. Whether in Bolton Castle, Tutbury, Coventry or the various other gilded prisons she would inhabit during her nineteen years of incarceration, Mary effectively held court. Hers was a toned-down version of the court she had enjoyed as reigning queen in France or Scotland, but it was lavish all the same. Her rooms were hung with rich tapestries, her bedstead draped with embroidered and velvet hangings, and the stools and chairs for herself and her ladies tapestried and padded.

Before and after meals, Mary washed her hands in a silver gilt bowl, and would wipe them on a towel provided by a servant. She ate off silver in a period when many still used bread for a plate or, if they had the means, a wooden board. Pewter was a privilege for the better-off, such as merchants and minor gentry. As a night-owl, Mary's late hours were costly. Often her letters were written by candlelight, the most expensive form of lighting. These were set in gilt 'chaundellours'. Lesser households used rushlights, which took hours to prepare by stripping rushes and repeatedly dipping them in fat. The light of a single reed would last about half an hour, and needed to be constantly wound in as the wick burned. Mutton fat, being the hardest when set, was popular for making rushlights and candles, no doubt making every room smell like a kitchen. Those who could not afford such illumination went to bed when it got dark, or sat by the fireside embers.

Wherever she stayed, at both the main midday meal, and that in the evening, Mary was served a buffet of two courses, each comprising sixteen dishes. Her lower staff enjoyed fewer dishes but were still generously catered for. A financial account of the queen's daily fare at Wingfield and Tutbury for a three-month period in 1584 to 1585 shows how well she ate. Dishes included every imaginable type of meat and poultry, including blackbirds, heron, boar, veal, beef and capons. There was fish in abundance, from eels and sole, herrings and salmon to oysters, pike and carp. Spices used for flavouring included pepper, saffron, cloves, ginger, mace and nutmeg – only the wealthy could afford these rarities – and the table was graced with imported luxuries such as oranges, olives and capers, almonds, dates and figs. Required to provide such variety twice a day, Mary's clerk of the kitchen had a highly pressured role, as did her master cook and his lackeys.

By contrast, ordinary people lived, if they were lucky, mainly on bread, cheese, porridge-like potages flavoured with herbs, and occasional meat or fish. Water being unsafe, they would drink ale or beer but never wine, which was costly. When potatoes reached England from the New World in 1584, only the rich could afford them. The less well-off might have been amused to know that in future centuries they would become the poor man's staple.

The enormous kitchens in St Mary's Guildhall were more than up to the task of catering for a queen. One of the best preserved medieval kitchens in Britain, the airy, vaultingly high-ceilinged room has a louvred wooden vent in the roof to allow steam, smoke and heat to escape without letting in the rain or snow. Two pairs of redbrick fireplaces, set side by side, are typical of the late Middle Ages, and for visitors there is a recording of a roaring fire to evoke their flames and sparks. On these ranges meat would have been roasted on spits or boiled. The combined length of spits used for a feast for Mary's son James VI and I in 1604 was around thirty-three metres, indicating how much food was prepared. Nine spit-turners were employed on that occasion to keep the meat turning. For everyday cooking, however, cauldrons were the most useful vessel, many meals being versions of potages or stews.

Medieval recipes often began with the instruction 'smite him to pieces'. A fourteenth-century recipe for rabbit broth reads: 'Take connynges [rabbits]: smyte hem to pecys: perboile hem and drawe hem with a gode broth, with almaundes, blaunched and brayed [ground]. Do perinne [add] sugar, and powdour ginger, and boyle it and the flesh perwith; flour it with sugur & with powdour ginger & serve forth.' The emphasis on smiting suggests the kitchen would have been a noisy place, as meat was chopped and walloped, pestles pounded and servants were harried by the master cook. Since Mary was at the Guildhall over Christmas, the kitchens must have been at their most hectic, the cook at his most fraught.

The vaulted undercroft beneath the Great Hall is where visitors to the Guildhall begin their tour. Cool and spacious, it was used as a store to augment the butteries, where ale and wine were kept. In addition there was a pantry, larder, jelly house, and a bakehouse with three ovens.

No wonder Shrewsbury fretted about the cost of maintaining Mary's household to the standard she, and Elizabeth, expected. Throughout his tenure as her custodian, he complained constantly, and increasingly sourly, about the paltry allowance the Queen allowed him. He also chafed at the difficulty of finding wood for fuel, and at its price. Such was the demand for wood in Elizabethan times, for building as well as firewood, that by the end of the era there was a national shortage, and coal was becoming increasingly popular for the fireplace.

Shrewsbury did not own Tutbury Castle, which was in the Duchy of Lancaster, but leased it from the Crown. A letter he sent Elizabeth from Coventry in late December, ahead of Mary's return there, shows what was expected of tenants on a royal estate. The earl informed Elizabeth that, because animals and carts had been requisitioned during the Northern Rising, locals' beasts were weak and their carts in poor condition. Part of their obligations whenever the queen was moved was to provide and pay for the transport of goods and for the fuel for her residence. Because of the exceptionally hard winter, he said, roads were 'deep and foul', and sources of fuel at a considerable distance. He warned that, if asked to provide such services for Mary's return journey, tenants would make 'great exclamation'. He requested they be allowed to take wood from the Queen's estate at Castle Hayes Park, a couple of miles from Tutbury, where they could use wood from old trees that were fit only for burning.

A list of the attendants Mary arrived with at Tutbury gives some idea of the luxury she considered essential to her maintenance. There were ten 'chief men', including a surgeon, comptroller, and masters of the household and the horse. There were six varlets of the chamber, among them Bastian Pages and Will Douglas, an usher of the chamber, and a nameless person known simply as The Wardrobe – in charge of robes but also the valuables, such as spices, jewels and important papers, this cupboard held. She had a tailor, an upholsterer and three kitchen staff (two devoted to pastry). Nine men, including a farrier, cared for her ten horses, a ratio today's racehorse trainers can only dream of. Shrewsbury, as she bemoaned, soon reduced her horses to six and her grooms to three, but allowed her farrier to remain.

In a material sense, Mary enjoyed a gilded existence. She expected a change of bed-linen every day and slept on a feather mattress with feather pillows, at a time when much of the country bedded down on the floor and might use a log for a pillow or do without. Ghastly though she found her imprisonment, she survived nineteen years in captivity; in that period, countless Elizabethans died before their time simply because of their woeful living conditions.

While I was taking outdoor photos of Caesar's Tower, which can be reached by a lane behind St Mary's Guildhall, I fell into conversation with a former prison guard who was working for a nearby charity that helps ex-prisoners make a life for themselves. The proliferation of food banks and charities for the homeless in the West Midlands (and across the UK) is a reflection of a country painfully divided, with a growing number on the breadline. Four hundred and fifty years ago, this would also have been a familiar scenario for the residents of Coventry. With an increasingly precarious textile industry, inflation and a rising population, by the middle of the sixteenth century there were too many workers for too few jobs. Poverty in England had reached a level where it was seen as a potential source of social unrest. Few words were more alarming to an Elizabethan than 'vagrant', which conjured up the image of engrained criminality and aggression.

Thomas Harman's popular work, *Caveat or Warning for Common Cursitors Vulgarly Called Vagabonds*, published in 1566, listed a great variety of 'rogues', and helped fuel hostility to the indigent. His exhaustive taxonomy of beggars included dummerers – beggars who pretended to be dumb (they all came from Wales, he said); Abram Men, who claimed to have been in Bedlam and pretended to be insane; and kinchin coves – young male rogues who had no hope of turning straight and might as well be hanged outright. There were doxies as well as horse thieves (priggers or prancers); hookers, who used poles with a hook at the end to filch through windows; and whipjacks, who posed as shipwrecked sailors to beg for money. The length and detail of Harman's inventory suggests a society that believed itself threatened on every side.

For those unfortunate enough to be on the lowest rungs of society, work was unpredictable, and when it dried up, if they had no family to rely on, they might quickly fall into destitution. A run of bad harvests could lead to such scarcity that some died of starvation in the streets. In an effort to ward off insurrection, the government introduced the first of several Poor Laws in 1563. This was the initial step in what was to become a much vaunted, albeit flawed, system of state help for paupers. Like today's welfare system, it was driven by a stern work ethic and a profound mistrust of the 'idle'.

The England in which Mary found herself was, in its essentials, similar to Scotland. It must, however, have felt like a foreign country, and not just because of the language spoken, with which she was slowly accustoming herself: with every passing week, her homeland likely seemed further distant. Still she made no move to seize the chance to escape. While at Coventry, a plausible plot was devised by members of her household. It involved intercepting her cavalcade as she returned to Tutbury and whisking her off to France, with help and accommodation provided en route by her supporters in southern England. Again, this possibility was thwarted by Norfolk's veto on doing anything that would incur Elizabeth's fury. How often in the coming years would Mary reflect on the cost of deferring to his wishes?

Chapter 11

'A waste and howling wilderness'

CHATSWORTH

Elizabeth's harsh injunction that 'the Queen of Scots' head should never rest' was faithfully followed, and on 2 January 1570, Mary was back on the road to Tutbury. The gloom of returning to these miserable lodgings was soon brightened, however, when she learned that, on 11 January, her half-brother Moray had been assassinated. His killer was one of the influential Hamilton family, who were next in line to the throne after the Stuarts.

Even before Moray had imprisoned the Duke of Châtelherault some months earlier, resentment of his treatment of Mary had been simmering. An unsuccessful attempt on his life had been made as he returned from the Westminster conference, but this time his enemies had got their man. As he rode down the high street in Linlithgow, in a scene that carries an echo of the Kennedy assassination, he was shot, becoming one of the first ever to be assassinated by firearm. George Buchanan described the scene: 'The Regent leaped from his horse, saying, he was struck, and walked into his lodgings, as if he had not felt the wound. At first the surgeons pronounced it not mortal, but in a short time, severe pain arising, with great composure of mind, he began to think of death.' By midnight, he was gone.

Unlike JFK, Moray would not be widely mourned or missed except by Elizabeth, who was stricken at the news, recognising she had lost a close ally. His assassin was James Hamilton of Bothwellhaugh, who acted on the orders of his uncle, John Hamilton,

Archbishop of St Andrews. He had taken great trouble to make sure of success, placing a mattress on the floor of the room from which he fired to muffle his footsteps, and draping the walls in black, so his shadow would not give him away. He had even removed part of the arch on the rear gateway of the building to speed his escape on horseback. Mary was exultant. The following year she wrote to her ambassador in Paris, James Beaton, Archbishop of Glasgow: 'What Bothwellhaugh has done was not by my orders.' Nevertheless, she continued, when her widow's allowance, due to her from France, finally arrived, she would compile a list of those to whom she would give a pension. At that point, she wrote, 'I shall not forget that of the said Bothwellhaugh.'

Antonia Fraser describes Scotland's governance by Moray in disparagingly prosaic terms: 'under Moray's brief regency Scotland had not more, but much less stability than in the early years of Mary's rule, and there was nothing in his conduct of affairs to justify his ejection of his sister from the throne on administrative grounds.' A country that was already turbulent now became even more unstable as civil war escalated. After a few months of a power vacuum, during which the English marched into the south of the country, laying waste to towns and villages and the lands of Mary's men, Elizabeth agreed that Moray should be replaced by Darnley's father and James's grandfather, the Earl of Lennox. Although his loyalty was questionable, he was an anglophile with whom Elizabeth could do business. Some historians say she welcomed his appointment, others that she reluctantly conceded to it. Even on a matter such as this, the record is confusing. It was a brave man who would accept this position. Little more than a year later, during a raid on Stirling by Mary's supporters, Lennox too would fall victim to a bullet. No wonder Scotland was internationally viewed as a by-word for treachery and violent death.

Eager for contact with her young son, early in January 1570 Mary sent James a pony, with a touching note: 'Dear Son, I send three bearers to see you and bring me word how ye do, and to remember you that ye have in me a loving mother.' She could not have chosen a gift better designed to please the little boy who, as yet, could still not walk, but would grow into a skilled rider and huntsman. With calculated cruelty, Elizabeth refused to allow this present to reach him.

Mary's three-year-old son was under the care of the Earl of Mar, but being so young was mainly raised by Annabella Murray, Countess of Mar, and his nurse Helen Little. Others at the court at Stirling had a hand in his upbringing; among their duties was ensuring he was not snatched. In time, he would become the pupil of the infamously strict George Buchanan, Mary's most virulent defamer. As he grew into childhood, he was surrounded by those who did not want him ever to create a bond with his – as they saw it – disreputable, heretical and criminal mother. They did everything in their power to make him think she was wicked and that he was better off without her.

In May 1570, Mary was again moved, this time to one of the pleasantest of the many locations she would inhabit. While Tutbury Castle was 'cleansed and sweetened', Shrewsbury took her to Chatsworth in Bess's home county of Derbyshire. Bess of Hardwick's name came from the property owned by her Derbyshire forebears since the fourteenth century. In later life she had a magnificent new mansion built, only a batsman's stroke away from Old Hardwick Hall, where she had been born, and whose ruins still stand. The splendid, glass-filled Hardwick Hall remains one of Derbyshire's finest buildings, yet it was with Chatsworth that she truly came into her own. That building no longer exists, having been rebuilt into the magnificent seventeenth-century palace voted Britain's favourite stately home, but its spirit lives on behind the present house.

Chatsworth became almost as dear to Bess as her children, and ultimately consumed far more of her energy and money. It would take thirty years for the house and grounds to be completed to her satisfaction. She and her second husband, William Cavendish, bought it in 1550 for £600, possibly at her prompting. It included the manor of Cromford as well as Chatsworth, along with seventeen villages, among them Edensor, Bakewell, Chesterfield and Matlock.

Set in the heart of the Peak District, in a steep wooded valley through which the River Derwent runs, Chatsworth's location is as attractive today as during Bess's tenure, and possibly more so. The hillside behind the house was bare in 1550 but is now thickly forested. While building work on their grand design began, Bess and Sir William lived nearby in the original house. When it was completed in 1552, it was a square three-storey house arranged around an inner courtyard with formal gardens and a high-walled hunting park to the rear. By the time Mary arrived, a fourth storey had been added, offering state rooms suitable for the royal guests Bess hoped to entertain.

Chatsworth as Bess knew it disappeared in the late seventeenth and early eighteenth centuries, when the then Earl of Devonshire, later elevated to Duke, radically rebuilt it. There were further alterations early the following century. Fortunately, a copy of a contemporary painting and an intricately embroidered cushion, probably stitched by Bess, give a good idea of how her house had looked. Its aspect was rather severely Tudor. A castle-like structure, with angled towers flanking the entranceway and rear exit, and one at each corner, it had a profusion of small, diamond-paned leaded windows. Although the fashion in Europe by the mid sixteenth century was for more sophisticated and elegant rural architecture, Chatsworth's defensive personality possibly reflects the traumas of the Tudor court and the snake-pit politics that Bess and her husband had to negotiate. In particularly dangerous times – when for instance, Mary Tudor took the throne and those who had supported Lady Jane Grey were in mortal danger – they retreated to Chatsworth and hoped trouble would pass. Bess's biographer Mary S. Lovell writes that she and her husband were neither intellectuals, nor made of the stuff of martyrs: 'The safety of their family and the position Sir William had made for himself were far more important to them than the shade of the Church in which they worshipped.' While their sympathies were Protestant, they astutely courted both sides of the religious divide.

Given the tempestuous times, among Chatsworth's many attractions for the Cavendishes was its remoteness. For those in Westminster, Derbyshire was perceived as the far north. Added to the benefits of its distance from court was its geography. Riders would do well to cover a mile an hour over the fifteen-mile moorland road that brought them to its gates. In the eighteenth century, Daniel Defoe wrote that these moors 'present you with neither hedge, house or tree, but a waste and howling wilderness, over which, when strangers travel, they are obliged to take guides, or it would be next to impossible not to lose their way'.

Despite its inaccessibility, Lovell believes that Chatsworth House had reasonable claims to be 'the first real "country house" built in the north of England'. With thirteen richly furnished bedrooms, their bed hangings decorated with gold, silver and pearls, it was fit for a queen, which was fortunate for Mary. Ironically, although Bess longed for the distinction of receiving royal visitors, she could never have envisaged becoming host-cum-gaoler to the Scottish queen.

Even so, in the many months Mary spent at Chatsworth at various times from 1569 to 1581, the Countess must surely have played the proud chatelaine. When handling Mary, her role was a tightrope act, hovering somewhere between confidante and custodian. Too great an intimacy would bring down Elizabeth's wrath; already she had expressed suspicions that Bess and Mary were growing worryingly close. Too strict supervision, however, could imperil Bess's future, should Mary ever take the throne of England.

The district in which Chatsworth sits is beguiling. Like Umbria and the Abruzzo in Italy, it is heavily wooded, with steep gorges rising from rivers and streams, and outcrops of craggy rocks that lour over the quiet roads snaking alongside sparkling waters below. In the baking heat of a June midday, when I arrived, its parkland, and the pale grandeur of the house itself, appeared like an eighteenth-century artist's idealised landscape. The car park was almost full, all shaded spots taken.

While Chatsworth looks regal from the outside, the opulence of the interior is almost overwhelming. Despite a suite of two rooms that is called the Scots Apartment, in honour of Mary, nothing from her day survives. Where she lived was on the east side of the house, overlooking the river, and directly above what is now the Painted Hall. With the exception of Buckingham Palace, this is one of the grandest domestic entrances in Britain. That Mary's quarters lay above the Great Hall indicates the distinction she was showed.

With the Northern Rebellion quashed, Mary's terms of imprisonment relaxed. It would become a theme of her incarceration that when the state felt threatened, her conditions grew harsher; when things eased, she could have visitors, send and receive letters, and, if she was well enough, go hunting or walking. Cecil told Shrewsbury that while at Chatsworth, Mary could 'take the ayre about your howss on horseback [in] your Lordship's company . . . and not to pass from your howss above one or twoo myles, except it be on ye moors'. Thus, in the summer and autumn of 1570, she enjoyed a taste of the good things in life once more.

Although evidence of Mary's presence is obliterated within the house, relics from her time remain in the gardens and park. Queen Mary's Bower, once part of Bess's extensive complex of fish-ponds, is the more controversial of these. Said to have been built in the 1570s, and described as a 'prospect tower' and a 'fishing station', it is a square, eccentric construction, incorporating a wide flight of steps that once created a bridge over the moat. These lead to a flat, balustraded top. What it looked like in the sixteenth century is unclear, since it was restored in the 1820s. Now overlooking the river, previously it was lapped by the moat, where fish darted temptingly within reach of anglers on the bower.

There is no record of Mary ever fishing – although at Chatsworth she enjoyed practising the longbow and hawking as well as riding – but it is said that in fine weather she and her ladies would sit in the bower for hours, far from eavesdroppers and prying eyes. Historians, however, disagree on whether she actually used it, and there is no conclusive evidence either way. That it was not called Queen Mary's Bower until centuries later might indicate she did not. Yet, since she loved being outdoors, why would she not have taken advantage of such a pleasing retreat? On the other hand, some believe it was not built until after Mary's time. The other building, which Mary might have visited before it was completed, is what was once called the Stand Tower. Located in a clearing in the Stand Wood on the hillside behind the house, and now known as the Hunting Tower, its exterior is almost unchanged since its completion in around 1582.

From the car park, the tower peeps out from the trees above the house, but once I was in the woods, it disappeared from view. These woods are dense, with trails heading off uphill in different directions. Despite signposts, as usual I soon had no idea where I was. Out of the sun, it was pleasant simply to be walking in dappled light past lush banks of rhododendrons, whose lilac petals were strewn on the paths as if it were a bridal walk. Piles of massive boulders encroached on the track, the gaps between them creating caves big enough for bears. As with everything at Chatworth, none of this is accidental or natural. The grounds and gardens of the present-day house were the work of the landscape gardener Capability Brown. At the duke's request, some buildings in the nearby village of Edensor, which were spoiling the view, were demolished. In 1839, a later duke had the entire village rebuilt further afield.

It was a sticky, steep climb, and I was glad to encounter an older man with his daughter and two grandchildren, who stopped to chat. Before they came into sight I had heard him telling them about Chatsworth and its gardens. A retired teacher was my guess. In conversation, he mentioned that in Capability Brown's era, all the villagers were employed by the duke so were in no position to complain, even when Edensor was relocated.

Certainly, the quality of the new village's cottages, houses and villas is exceptional. Now only the spire of the nineteenth-century church steeple intrudes on the outlook from Chatsworth. Among the graves in its churchyard is that of Kit Kennedy, John F. Kennedy's sister, who was married to the Marquess of Hartingdon. On his way to a meeting with the prime minister, the American president visited the church in 1963 by helicopter. When a villager was asked for his response to his arrival, he replied: 'The wind from that machine blew my chickens away, and I haven't seen them since.'

Despite the dense canopy of trees, the heat was growing oppressive. I plodded on, trusting to the loamy path to bring me to the tower. And so, in time, it did. Suddenly, I was out of the woods into a horseshoe-shaped clearing, on one side of which was an open view over Chatsworth's emerald parkland and the wooded Peak District hills beyond. In the centre of the sun-scorched clearing was the Hunting Tower, its appearance dramatic after the gloom of the woods. A lookout where Bess and other ladies would gather to watch the hunt or simply enjoy the view, it has four pepper-pot towers and diamond-paned mullioned windows. Two sturdy mounted cannons, pointing outwards towards the valley, stand guard. Diminutive versions of Mons Meg, they look capable of doing serious damage.

The Hunting Tower's modern front door and lightning conductor are the only obvious nods to the present, though there was also a Mini parked at the rear. I presumed this was not a visitor's lazy way of reaching the top of the 400-metre-high hill, up which the rest of us had sweatily clambered, but rather a guest renting the tower. I had fleetingly considered spending a few nights here, enjoying what must be one of the loveliest prospects in the county. If my Premium Bonds ever come good, one day I still might. The website photos show chintzily appointed rooms reached by a stone spiral staircase. There is an Aga in the kitchen, where a round table mirrors the curve of the walls. The main bedroom is four-postered and filled with light, while the living room is so cosy it might be best to book in January, so there are no pressing reasons to go out.

I could imagine Bess of Hardwick approving of the way the tower has been furnished. The Countess had many sterling qualities: devoted mother and grandmother, dutiful and loving wife (until her relationship with Shrewsbury broke down), astute estate manager, faithful attendant and friend to Elizabeth. To all the above can be added a talent for interior decoration. The attention she lavished on the fittings and furnishings of Chatsworth, and later on Hardwick Hall, was an unabashed act of ostentation, but it was also the work of an artistic sensibility. Despite Bess of Hardwick's depiction by many historians as grasping and ruthless, she was also impressively accomplished. Attributes that would bring men of the period to advancement have too often been denigrated when found in this highly intelligent and independent-minded woman, who had a backbone of steel when it came to maintaining and elevating her position.

During Mary's early months in Chatsworth, there was a thaw in relations with Westminster, with Elizabeth recognising that she had few grounds for continuing to hold her cousin: 'if the Queen of Scots shall not refuse reasonable conditions – we do not see how with honour and reason we can continue her in restraint'. This seemed to bode well for her restoration. However, Mary's pleas for young James to be allowed to visit were not approved by the Scots, a strong hint that trouble lay ahead.

The figure of William Cecil, the Queen's foremost consigliere, hangs over Mary's story like a storm cloud. An immensely able diplomat and advisor, he was former secretary of state to Edward VI, and even before Elizabeth gained the throne, while Mary Tudor was still alive, he had been positioning himself for his future role in her government. Very quickly he became the one to whom Elizabeth turned most frequently for advice, and whose judgement she felt (not always correctly) she could trust.

In October 1570, he was forty years old. Portraits show a man with an expressive, strong face, a silky, well-kept forked beard and deep furrows above his nose. The bags under his eyes suggest that the weightiness of affairs of state did not permit sufficient sleep. This was perhaps not surprising, given how quixotic and unreadable the Queen could be. In his role as secretary of state, and later as lord high treasurer, his time was never his own. He was at Elizabeth's command every hour of the day and never knew what mood he would find her in.

Mary, Queen of Scots had long recognised that Cecil was often the one pulling the strings at the English court. During his visit to Chatsworth, which lasted almost three weeks, she finally had a chance to get the measure of him. Ahead of this encounter, at which

Walter Mildmay, the chancellor of the exchequer, was also present, Cecil sounded anxious. He and Mildmay were to put proposals to the Scottish queen that would allow her restoration but also guarantee England's security. Among the treaty's conditions was that, while she would retain the title Queen of Scots, and have her claim as Elizabeth's successor acknowledged, she would never make a claim to the English throne while Elizabeth or any of her heirs was alive. Her son James was to be raised in England, effectively as a hostage, for several years, along with twelve other leading Scottish nobles, and the government of Scotland was to remain largely in the hands of Mary's enemies. 'God be our guide,' Cecil wrote before setting out for Chatsworth, 'for neither of us like the message.'

Mary burst into tears at their first meeting, complaining at her harsh treatment. Despite her accusatory tone, and despite knowing what a danger she posed, like so many men before him Cecil was charmed by her. She had, he wrote, 'a clement and gentle nature'. The conditions imposed on her restoration were exceptionally stringent, yet Mary wrote to Elizabeth expressing cautious optimism: 'I have some little room to hope, instead of despair, for some good and speedy determination of my affairs.' She might not have sounded so positive if she had known that, before Cecil went to Chatsworth, John Knox had written to advise him that 'if ye strike not at the root, the branches that appeared to be broken will bind again'. Maitland of Lethington's prediction that 'the Queen of England would never free a woman that she had so bitterly wronged' proved prescient.

Thus, several months passed in discussion, and in revisions of the original articles. In Scotland, the king's party, under Morton, expressed its refusal to consider Mary's restoration, while Mary's own commissioners initially strongly resisted the idea of James being handed to the English. Eventually, however, they and Mary appeared to be prepared to consider almost anything, including sending James as a hostage, if it would free her. But when the English increased their demands by asking for six further hostages, including Châtelherault, Argyll and Huntly, it became clear that nothing would come of it. All these negotiations had been pointless, and Mary was if anything more isolated than before, since all hope of her return to Scotland as queen was gone. 'With the end of these negotiations,' writes Steven J. Reid, in his biography of James VI's early life, 'James in effect became sole and uncontested ruler of Scotland, without the spectre of Mary's restoration hanging over Scottish politics.'

Even before the breakdown of negotiations, there was another grave setback to Mary's prospects. In May 1570, a papal bull entitled *Regnans in Excelsis* formally excommunicated Elizabeth, describing her as 'the servant of wickedness'. Mary was not in Pope Pius V's thoughts when he issued this edict – he remained disapproving of her Protestant marriage to Bothwell – but in doing so he made her position considerably more perilous.

In European eyes, England was, in historian Stephen Alford's phrase, 'a rogue state', utterly at odds with the Catholic continent. Elizabeth was a pariah, not merely a heretic but a bastard, because of her father's unlawful marriage to Anne Boleyn. Her overthrow was devoutly to be prayed for. At this distance, it is difficult to appreciate how precarious the new religion of England was. After Henry VIII's break with Rome and the establishment of the Church of England, the country had returned to Catholicism under Mary Tudor. During her reign, Protestants were burned at the stake, and many fled to Europe. Pronounced queen in 1558, Elizabeth reintroduced her father and brother's religious regime, but she was well aware of the Catholic threat to her rule, whether from the empire-building Philip II of Spain, from France, or from within her own borders. With publication of the papal bull, English Catholics had not only been released from loyalty to their queen but actively urged to revolt against her. This made Mary an even more likely catalyst for rebellion.

There was also another imminent problem that gravely undermined Mary's position. In August 1570, Norfolk was released from the Tower, and effectively placed under house arrest. Initially contrite and grovelling, he promised Elizabeth he would forget Mary and behave. Yet within months he was to become embroiled in a convoluted plot concocted by the Florentine banker and papal agent Roberto Ridolfi. A weaselly, self-serving man, Ridolfi had been imprisoned briefly before the Northern Rising for his role in encouraging the duke's marriage to Mary. By associating himself with him, Norfolk was putting his head on the block.

Ridolfi, who worked in London and from whom Mary had recently borrowed money, was the conduit for funds from the Pope to English Catholics. He now devised a scheme which involved an invasion of England, via the Netherlands, under the Duke of Alva, Philip II's governor-general there. In this scenario, England's Catholics were to rise under Norfolk's command and sweep Elizabeth from the throne, to be replaced by Mary, with Norfolk at her side. Ridolfi's plot was riddled with holes and improbabilities, not the least of which was his character. Now a double agent, he trod a fine line between working for the Pope and Norfolk but also for Francis Walsingham, who, as Elizabeth's spymaster, was to become one of the most influential and malign figures in Mary's story. Apart from himself, no one held Ridolfi in high esteem. Alva pronounced him incapable of invading England even with Elizabeth's help.

It is conceivable that, not knowing the flimsiness of his plans or his loyalty, Mary might have been complicit. One of the main instigators of the plot was her ambassador and long-term ally John Leslie, Bishop of Ross, who acted as go-between between her and Ridolfi. She also had long connections with Spain, foremost of which was her friendship with her childhood companion at the French court, Elizabeth of Valois, the wife of Philip II. Her death, soon after Mary's imprisonment in England, grieved Mary deeply. Delusionally, she still hoped to marry her son to one of Elizabeth and Philip II's daughters.

To this day historians disagree in their interpretation of Mary's involvement in the Ridolfi plot, some believing she gave explicit encouragement. According to John Guy, there is no evidence to show she approved of this murderous venture against her cousin: 'The most incriminating letter, intercepted from Mary and written a few months before the Northern Rising, did not say what Cecil needed it to say.' Mary might, of course, have been careful in committing nothing that would implicate her to paper, even in code, to which she was increasingly resorting. It is equally possible that she feared any such plan would simply make her position worse and wanted nothing to do with it.

A few weeks earlier, she had written to Norfolk, assuring him that she remained constant, and insisting that their relationship was in no way 'shameful'. Rather, she wrote, 'I believe the Queen of England and country should like of it.' With rare perspicuity, she continued: 'I will ever be, for your sake, perpetual prisoner, or put my life in peril for your weal and mine.' J. D. Leader was not convinced by her seeming naivety: 'At conspiracy, the Queen of Scots was an adept; at acting, a consummate performer; and she took care during her chequered life never to allow these gifts to rust for want of using.'

When the full details of the so-called Ridolfi plot became known the following autumn, Mary was assumed to be involved, and became a national pariah. The House of Commons was eager to have her executed. In the summer and autumn of 1570, however, as she enjoyed the luxurious delights of Chatsworth, that perilous period was some time away. Whether or not she was complicit, Mary believed her hopes of freedom lay with the great powers of England, France or Spain, not with cloak-and-dagger exploits by enthusiastic supporters. Accordingly, when two escape plans from Chatsworth were hatched by local lords in 1570 and 1571, Mary would not contemplate them unless success was certain. Which, of course, it could not be.

Chapter 12

'Esteemed by you as an enemy instead of a friend'

SHEFFIELD CASTLE

Sheffield Castle was the Earl of Shrewsbury's main and most imposing residence, and it was here, towards the end of November 1570, that Mary was lodged. Less rundown than Tutbury, it was nevertheless dank and dreary, a far cry from the gilded prison of Chatsworth, hammering home Mary's powerlessness. Sheffield Castle was one of the strongest fortresses in the north of England, and in 1648 it was destroyed on the orders of Parliament after Royalists had occupied it during the English Civil War. Such vituperation suggests how powerful a defensive position it held.

Built on the site of a Norman motte-and-bailey castle, on a location that might formerly have been occupied by an Anglo-Saxon longhouse, it was a massive structure surrounded on two sides by the rivers Don and Sheaf, and encircled by a moat. Occupying four acres, it sat amid a forested deer park. An idea of its appearance is found in a report in 1637 by the surveyor John Harrison, who described the castle as 'very spacious, built about an inward court'. On the south side, he wrote, there was 'an outward courtyard or fold built around with diverse houses of officers'. He noted an armoury, barns, stables and 'diverse lodgings'. Maps from the eighteenth century show extensive castle orchards nearby, and some of Sheffield's street names indicate the position of its fish-ponds and deer park. With sheer curtain walls, ramparts and cylindrical watchtowers, it was a textbook medieval castle. As her large party and its baggage train clattered over the drawbridge, and the building's walls closed around her, Mary was enfolded in its grip. Where she was housed is not known, but her rooms overlooked the castle gate and would often reek from the city's main drains, which emptied out near the castle walls.

The razing of the castle was an act of political vandalism, but while it vanished completely, the site, known as Castlegate, remained central to the city's activities. By the nineteenth and early twentieth centuries it was occupied by some of the steel-making factories – the Castle Hill Works, the Phoenix Works and others – from which Sheffield's industrial heyday was built. Alongside the factories were row upon row of slaughterhouses. These are described by archaeologist Professor John Moreland of the University of Sheffield as representing the 'industrial-scale production of meat to feed an industrial-scale production of steel'.

Excavations of the Castlegate at various times in the twentieth century threw up tantalising clues to what lay below, but there was no money for further exploration. In the 1960s, the site was again covered, this time by Castle Market, a focal point of the city centre until its demolition in 2015. Today, Mary's erstwhile residence remains a ghostly presence beneath the ground. At the time of writing, a major archaeological investigation is underway, ahead of redevelopment of the area. The hope is that secrets of the long-hidden castle and its inhabitants will be revealed, reminding us of its once crucial role. Sheffield Castle has been all but forgotten, and with it Mary's long-term residence here and at its sister property, Sheffield Manor Lodge, which lay a mile or so away across the deer park. For fourteen years, between 1570 and 1584, Mary spent the best part of her time in Sheffield, and yet few people are aware of it. Or at least, that's true of those who don't live here. Sheffield citizens who know their history are proud of their city's association with Mary, Queen of Scots.

When I arrived by train on a dreich summer's afternoon, I did not realise I was only a few hundred metres from Mary's old haunts. The landscaped precinct outside the station – a Victorian building, with an elegant Edwardian façade – is attractive, as is much of the newly built city in this area. A short walk away is the bus station, where I went to inquire about reaching Sheffield Manor Lodge, which lies on the edge of town. The official behind the information counter immediately broke off conversation with a colleague to assist. After telling me the number and times of buses to Manor Lodge, he launched into Mary's story without me mentioning her name. Was it my accent that opened the floodgates, or does everyone asking directions to the Manor elicit the same enthusiastic response?

Leading me out the back of the bus station, he pointed towards a quaint timbered building, now a pub called the Old Queens Head. With sagging black beams and fresh white paint, it is dwarfed by high-rise glass offices, offering a glimpse of Mary's era amid modern red brick, glass and steel. An old tunnel once led from here to Sheffield Castle, he informed me. In fact, said his friend, who had joined us, Sheffield is riddled with tunnels – 'Look it up on YouTube.' I did, and discovered that the city has a remarkable underground labyrinth of Victorian storm drains. More pertinently, although not from YouTube, I learned that the Old Queens Head, at Pond Hill, was thought to have been the castle's laundry. A tunnel leading from its cellar was blocked up years ago. In 1925, its landlord said he had been overrun with rats since work laying sewers had begun at Manor Lodge, leading him to assume that this was the tunnel's destination.

The previous year, the workmen laying these sewers discovered a deep tunnel at Manor Lodge, possibly leading to the castle, although by then only about fifty yards of it remained. An intrepid reporter from the *Sheffield Daily Telegraph* ventured down it: 'All sounds from the outside world are cut off, and the thought that people long since dead had trodden the same path was decidedly eerie. The floor, walls and roof are all made of stone, some of the blocks on the floor being of quite considerable size and thickness.'

A 1910 guidebook to Sheffield makes reference to Shrewsbury's father, the fifth earl, whose corpse 'was secretly brought from the said Manor to the Castle', presumably by tunnel. There was thought to be a second passage, perhaps linking Manor Lodge to the Old

Queens Head or, possibly, to Castle Hill. Romantic or unnerving though this network of subterranean routes sounds, it is unlikely that Mary was ever obliged to travel underground. Even so, Shrewsbury might have taken comfort from knowing that, should anyone try to rescue her, she could be moved quickly and undetected from the scene.

Despite the richness of its past, the mood in Sheffield is determinedly modern. Home to thousands of university students, it has a youthful air, especially in the evenings, when the place begins to buzz. My multi-storey hotel was in the centre of town, not far from the Victorian square around Sheffield Town Hall that forms the heart of the district. One evening, on my way to find a restaurant, I watched a handful of teenagers running from a receptionist or manager of a high-class hotel on the square where, I guessed, they had been causing trouble.

The leader of the group was wearing a black mask with eye-holes, and suddenly, while the others ran off, he stopped to dance and wave his arms in his pursuer's face. Onlookers wondered if or when he would produce a knife. Perhaps the same thought went through the hotelier's mind, because suddenly he turned and ran back through the rain to the hotel. The fracas dissolved and the evening crowds continued to stroll, taking their tables in restaurants as if the calm had never been broken.

Early in 1571, William Cecil was elevated to Lord Burghley. At his prompting, Elizabeth allowed her ambassadors to begin negotiations with France for her proposed (but very unlikely) marriage to the Duke of Anjou. Anjou was the brother of the French king Charles IX, and would become Henri III on his death in 1574. During these discussions, the Queen and Anjou played a delicate game of cat and mouse. At the outset she was thirty-seven to his nineteen. A greater impediment than the age gap was his dismay at Elizabeth's reputation for sexual indiscretions, despite his own colourful and well-known proclivities. Even after these negotiations – some might use the word charade – had reached an impasse, both countries agreed to bind themselves to an Anglo-French treaty, which made no provision at all for Mary, Queen of Scots's situation.

When it became clear that marriage with the Duke of Anjou would not take place if Elizabeth had any say in the matter, Burghley suggested Anjou's brother, Francis, Duke of Alençon, as an alternative. When Elizabeth said that he was too young and too small, Burghley claimed that he was the same height as she was. 'Say rather the height of your grandson,' she replied. Nevertheless, some years later, in 1579, the now adult prince, confusingly also called the Duke of Anjou, began to press his suit. For a time their union seemed, if not likely, then not entirely out of the question.

In Scotland, meanwhile, the balance of power was tilting towards the king's party. In April, the Regent Lennox captured Dumbarton Castle, that splendid craggy outpost held by Mary's supporters on the west coast. It was a double blow, both to their authority but also strategically, since the castle rock's location, on a sea firth, made it a safe landing place for their French allies. Showing no mercy when the castle was taken, Lennox had John Hamilton, the Archbishop of St Andrews, hanged.

Although Mary's men were by now in charge of Edinburgh Castle under the command of Kirkcaldy of Grange, who was an experienced and cool-headed soldier, Mary fretted about its capture. Despite constant worrying over how little money she had, she sent much of her income from her French dowry to her supporters, hoping thereby to regain the country in her name. By this time she had no illusions about her cousin's probity, writing to the Archbishop of Glasgow that Elizabeth 'is so full of fraud, that one cannot too sharply check it . . . She uses the fairest words, which she never performs, and promises that she will proceed with the treaty, and replace me in my kingdom; and yet, underhand, she endeavours to get possession of Edinburgh Castle, attempts to bribe the governor, and tries to establish the Earl of Sussex in the government of Scotland.' She told the French ambassador, Bertrand de Salignac de La Mothe-Fénelon, that she depended on Charles IX's support for 'the preservation or the loss of my kingdom'. Entreating Charles to take the castle under his protection, she asked him to provide Kirkcaldy of Grange 'with heavy ammunition and provisions. He only asks five hundred men to defend the place, hold the city at my command, and the country as far as the border and the gates of Stirling.'

The Marians had their revenge for the Archbishop of St Andrews's brutal execution some months later in September when, during a raid on Stirling Castle, Lennox was shot (although some said it was by his own side). Very swiftly, James's guardian, the Earl of Mar, was appointed in his place. It was an eventful month. With details of the Ridolfi plot gradually coming to light, and suspicion again falling on Norfolk, he was arrested and, when it was discovered that he was sending money to support Mary's party in Scotland, charged with high treason. This was as good as a death sentence. As he languished in prison, he must have regretted ever thinking of marrying Mary, recognising that his boundless ambition had led him to calamity.

Also languishing in the Tower of London was Mary's ambassador and official envoy John Leslie, Bishop of Ross, who had been an eager proponent of the Ridolfi plot. Letters and books for Leslie, sent from abroad by Ridolfi, had been found on a go-between, and the presumption of Mary's involvement swiftly followed. Under interrogation, Leslie produced a remarkable statement, throwing Mary to the wolves as a conspirator in the Northern Rising, and condemning her as a husband-killer who had murdered two husbands (Francis II and Darnley), hoped the third (Bothwell) would die in battle at Carberry and would most probably kill her next (Norfolk). Whether he did this while on the rack, or if the mere mention of torture was sufficient to loosen his tongue, it was an unedifying betrayal. Equally remarkable is that several years later, once released from prison, he returned to Mary's service.

Shortly after reaching Sheffield Castle, in late November 1570, Mary once again fell so dangerously ill it was thought she would die. With the assistance of doctors brought from London she recovered, but less than three years into captivity, her health had deteriorated significantly from stress and anxiety, lack of fresh air and exercise, and the damp and draughty conditions of prisons such as Tutbury and Sheffield Castle. For the rest of her life, she was to be plagued by a series of ailments, some more serious than others. She bore these with fortitude, although she also complained constantly to her keepers, and to Elizabeth, about the insanitary and sometimes inhumane conditions in which she was kept.

Even when relatively well, she lived in fear of assassination. In April 1571, she was unnerved by rumours that the Earl of Lennox had ordered her to be poisoned. This might not have been paranoia. Should Mary die in prison, England would breathe more easily, and poison was a common assassin's tool in this period. Bess of Hardwick had once been a target, while her third husband, William St Loe, was very likely poisoned by his grasping brother, who was probably also the culprit for Bess's narrow escape from death. At court and in the nobility's households, antidotes were kept close at hand. There's little doubt that Mary's entourage would have known which herbs acted as an emetic.

Then, as now, poison might be ingested from food and drink or absorbed from contact with surfaces or clothes. A well-known story of medieval Orkney, related in the *Orkneyinga Saga*, tells of the murder of Earl Harald, in around 1128, which was committed by his mother and sister. Jealous of a beautiful robe that they had made for his brother Paul, Harald snatched it and put it on: 'but no sooner was the garment upon his back than his flesh started to quiver and he began to suffer terrible agony. He had to go to bed and not long after that he died.' His parent's and sister's feelings on seeing the wrong man die are not recorded, but his brother, realising he was the intended victim, sensibly banished them from the island.

According to Eleanor Herman, author of *The Royal Art of Poison*, so great was the fear of assassination by this form of poisoning in Henry VIII's reign that pillows and sheets were kissed by his servants before he lay on them, while his son Edward VI's chamber pot was checked before he used it.

Cecil too was alert to the risk to his queen of poisoning, and in 1560 urged vigilance on every front: 'We think it very convenient that your Majesty's apparel and especially all manner of things that touch any part of your Majesty's body be circumspectly looked at.' He warned against any stranger offering perfumed clothes, such as sleeves or gloves, and stressed that 'no foreign meat or dishes being dressed out of Court be brought to your food without knowledge of from whom it cometh'.

Mary dreaded being despatched in this surreptitious manner. In a letter to Archbishop Beaton from Sheffield in 1574, she begged 'for a bit of fine unicorn's horn, as I am in great want of it'. Unicorn horns (narwhal tusks, actually) were thought to protect against poisoning, although only the richest could afford them. Mary was also concerned that the servant whose job it was to oversee her food had not been paid: 'I am not out of danger if my food is not closely watched.' What worried her more than an agonising death was that her captors might claim she had committed suicide, thereby destroying her reputation as a devout Catholic.

There were many vexations for Mary to contend with as she grew accustomed to her unappealing new lodgings in Sheffield Castle. Early that spring, she learned that her great adversary, the internationally renowned scholar and poet George Buchanan, had been appointed her son's tutor. Writing to the French ambassador Mothe-Fénelon, she said she hoped he could persuade Elizabeth to intervene: 'Master George Buchanan, who was engaged to write against me to please the late Earl of Murray and my other rebels, and who perseveres in his obstinacy and evil disposition by all the demonstrations in his power, has been engaged as preceptor for my son: which situation . . . I do not desire that he should be permitted to retain, or that my son should learn anything out of his book.' She added: 'The said Buchanan is aged, and henceforward has more need of a quiet situation than to annoy himself with a child.'

She would soon have reason further to distrust, indeed loathe, Buchanan. In the wake of the discovery of the Ridolfi plot, Burghley had Buchanan's scurrilous *Detection of the Actions of Mary Queen of*

Scots published. This reproduced some of the Casket Letters to bolster his arguments, and more of them were soon divulged in a Scottish edition. It was a bold and brazen attempt to ruin Mary's reputation, but its full English title shows a deeper purpose: *A detection of the actions of Mary Queen of Scots, concerning the murder of her husband, and her conspiracy, adultery and pretended marriage with Earl Bothwel: and a defence of the true lords, maintainers of the king's majesty's action and authority.* This was not just a mud-slinging exercise but a politically astute act of propaganda intended to legitimise the rebels' illegal deposition of their monarch.

Outraged, Mary demanded the printer and author be punished. Even Catherine de' Medici, never Mary's warmest champion, demanded that the book be burned. But by then it was too late. As soon as the Casket Letters became public, Mary's character was torn to shreds by those who believed or wanted to believe they were genuine. It was a form of assassination, if not the sort she had expected.

In these months, security around Mary was tightened, and she was obliged to reduce her staff from forty to sixteen at distressingly short notice. The opening lines of a letter from this time to Elizabeth convey her affront:

> Madam, The extreme severity with which by your orders I am used, so convinces me, to my great regret, of the misfortune which I have, with many others, not only of being in your disfavour, but, which is worse, esteemed by you as an enemy instead of a friend, as a stranger instead of a relative, – even the more detested that it does not permit the exercise of Christian charity between parties so nearly related by blood and propinquity – that for some time past I have felt so perplexed as to hesitate whether I should write to you or not.

She pressed on, requesting to be allowed to contact 'some of [her] people in France', in order to sort her financial affairs, and also to pay her 'old servants, now banished from [her] presence'. Perhaps most importantly, she begged Elizabeth to show 'compassion on a desolate mother, from whose arms has been torn her only child and hope of future joy in this world, to permit [her] to write at least open letters, to enquire into the real state of his welfare, and recall him to his sad mother'.

Unsurprisingly, no leniency was shown. A strict guard was put upon her correspondence, and excursions were vetoed. In a letter to Mothe-Fénelon in November 1571, Mary painted a picture of her unenviable situation, where she was constantly kept ill at ease:

> My people are not permitted to go beyond the gate of this castle, and all Lord Shrewsbury's servants are prohibited from speaking to mine. I am confined to my chamber, of which they wish again to wall up the windows, and make a false door by which they may enter when I am asleep. The Earl of Shrewsbury, as a great favour, said to me the other day that he was willing I should take an airing on the leads of this house, where I was about an hour.

But, she added, he also tried to intimidate her, 'insinuating that I was to be delivered into the hands of my rebels'.

Her postscript touched on a sensitive matter, which she said she would have directed to her mother-in-law, Catherine de' Medici, had she been allowed to contact her, but must instead ask him to convey to her: 'it is to insist . . . that my linen and that of my women, before being washed, shall not be inspected and overhauled by the porters of this wretched prison, who say they have orders from the said queen to do so. That Lord Shrewsbury or his lady may appoint me such laundress as they please, in whom they can confide, and that the men do not put their hands thereto.' She was unaware that this letter was intercepted at Sheffield, and sent not to the ambassador but to Burghley. There is something grubby about the idea of him reading about the humiliation of Mary's garments being closely examined, as if he too had been handling her clothes.

Chapter 13

'It is full of blood'

ST BARTHOLOMEW'S DAY MASSACRE

Sheffield was in the grip of a Yorkshire winter in January 1572, when Shrewsbury was relieved of his command of Mary by the diminutive but dogged Ralph Sadler. Although Elizabeth frequently hinted that she believed Shrewsbury was not strict enough a gaoler, the earl was obliged temporarily to hand over his role not through any failure on his part, but because he had been appointed one of the judges to determine the Duke of Norfolk's fate.

The trial took place in London, and there was never any doubt as to the outcome. After the verdict was pronounced, Sadler wrote to Burghley, on 21 January, that Norfolk's 'offences and treasons were such, and so manifestly proved, that all the noblemen did not only detest the same, but also, without any manner of scruple, by common consent, every one of them did pronounce him guilty'. He immediately told the Countess of Shrewsbury, so that she could inform Mary. But when Bess went to pass on the grim tidings, she found Mary in tears, the news having already reached her. Sadler's letter continues: 'All the last week this queen did not once look out of her chamber, hearing that the Duke of Norfolk stood upon his arraignment and trial.' He added, 'my lady Shrewsbury is seldom from her'.

Unsurprisingly, relations between Mary and Elizabeth had by now grown exceptionally strained, each beginning to believe the worst of the other. In a sharp rebuke the month after Norfolk's trial, Elizabeth chided Mary for a recent letter, which revealed 'an increase of your impatience, tending, also, to many uncomely, passionate, and vindictive speeches'. It was a letter of two halves, she continued, 'the latter being written in a calm, and the former in a storm'. Recommending that in future Mary cultivate the quieter tone, she signed herself 'Your cousin, that wisheth you a better mind'.

With an axe suspended over her would-be husband's neck, Mary began observing a strict Catholic regimen of praying, and of fasting three days a week, in the hope that this would miraculously reverse the decision. Elizabeth, it appears, was hardly less anxious about the duke's welfare. Four times she repealed his death sentence before finally allowing his beheading to proceed. This is not evidence of a queen hell-bent on revenge but rather of one who was almost paralysed by the potential consequences of such an action. Yet while she summoned the resolve to have her foremost noble despatched, she steadfastly stood out against her enraged parliament, who wanted Mary executed also.

In June, the Scottish government sold the Earl of Northumberland, ringleader of the Northern Rebellion, to Elizabeth, bringing him out of imprisonment in Lochleven Castle and handing him over. It was a bloody few months. On June 2 1572, Norfolk went stoically, almost resignedly to the block, leaving Mary distraught. In August, Northumberland was executed without trial. Around this time, it seems that Mary's friendship with Bess grew distinctly cooler. The queen expressed concern in case any of her letters had played a part in Norfolk's downfall, but Bess was dismissive, saying he had been judged fairly and Mary's actions had nothing to do with his sentence. Both were to a degree correct, but Bess's lack of sympathy was unusual and unkind, possibly intentionally. As later events would show, she felt she had reason for treating Mary coldly.

The Scottish queen found a kinder ear in Mothe-Fénelon, to whom she wrote plaintively, shortly after Norfolk's execution: 'My head is so full of rheum, and my eyes so swelled with such continual sickness and fever, that I am obliged to keep entirely in my bed, where I have but little rest, and am in a bad condition, so that I cannot now write with my hand.' Her next sentence put her situation in alarming context: 'Lord Shrewsbury read me a part of the libel which those of the pretended clergy presented against me – it is full of blood.' She was right. Parliament and much of the country wanted her dead, and that animosity was to deepen following one of the most notorious events in French history.

The St Bartholomew's Day Massacre was a shocking and shameful display of religious barbarism, in which tens of thousands of Protestants in Paris and the French provinces were slaughtered. The trigger for the massacre was the marriage of the king's sister to the Prince of Navarre, who was Huguenot, or Protestant. In recent years France had been rocked by religious wars, but a shaky peace had been negotiated. Now, resentment erupted in Paris at a union denounced by the Pope as 'an insult to God'.

On 22 August, shortly after the wedding celebrations, and while Paris was still full of high-born Huguenots, the distinguished Protestant, Gaspard de Coligny, Admiral of France, was shot and wounded. The Duke of Guise was discovered to be behind his attempted murder. The cousin of Mary, Queen of Scots, he was one of the most powerful and ruthless men in the country. Very quickly, under Guise's command and with Charles IX's approval, a hitlist of prominent Protestants was made (including Coligny). Beginning on the Feast of St Bartholomew, on 24 August, and continuing for three days or more, the killing of these targets, and countless others, took place. The Paris mob enthusiastically joined in, throwing Protestants into the Seine, where they drowned if they had not already been shot. Soon, like a fire leaping from roof to roof, the murder spree spread far beyond the city. Estimates of those slain within the capital alone vary from 2,000 to 6,000. The king justified this bloodbath as punishment for an attempted Huguenot coup masterminded by Coligny.

The reverberations made all of Europe quake, and nowhere more so than England. Immediately putting itself on a war footing, the country braced for invasion. Since the chief architect of the massacre was a close relation of Mary's, whose family had raised her as a child at the French court, it is easy to see how panic about the Scottish queen would have intensified among Elizabeth's circle. An anonymous letter from this time, possibly sent to Francis Walsingham in

Paris, where he was ambassador, captures the vengeful and overwrought mood. Claiming that 'our princess's life is in peril, and that her only safety is, with speed, to execute the dangerous traitress and pestilence to Christendom', the writer continues: 'Will Elizabeth leave England, and us all, subject to an adulterous traitoress? . . . Shall we not trust that her majesty, our mother, will not stick to command to kill a toad, a snake, or a mad dog, whom she findeth poisoning or gnawing the throats of her infants and presently threatening the same to her life?'

Elizabeth's main source of information about the massacre was Walsingham, who had the misfortune to be in Paris during this terrifying time. His embassy had served as a haven for terrified English Protestants fleeing the mob, but despite being protected by the king's guard, he must have feared for his own life, and those of his wife and four-year-old daughter, whom he sent back to England as soon as the worst of the danger had passed. Back at Sheffield Castle, responding to the state of national emergency, Shrewsbury increased the number of guards around Mary from forty to seventy, paying for them out of his own pocket, as with so many of Mary's expenses.

Since her accession in 1558, the safety of Elizabeth had been a matter of acute concern for her councillors. Dread of invasion by France or Spain was never far from their minds, but the arrival of Mary, Queen of Scots fanned the embers of suspicion, inflaming an atmosphere at court that at times verged on paranoia. Such was the heightened state of dread that, in Stephen Alford's view, 'the queen's ministers hypnotised themselves with fear'. Lord Burghley was ever vigilant, but equally assiduous in sniffing the air for conspiracies and threats was Francis Walsingham. Ever since Mary had arrived in England, he had been wary and watchful. On that day, he found his vocation.

For the moment, as England's ambassador in France, he was far from court. Yet even while in Paris, his ear was attuned to any whisper regarding Mary and her network – public and covert – of associates and messengers. With many conspirators from the

Northern Rising now exiled in Europe, he was acutely aware of the potential for the seeds of rebellion to be planted on this side of the Channel. If Burghley was Elizabeth's right-hand man, Walsingham was no less useful. A fascinating character, with a quick wit, he combined passionate Puritan convictions with intellectual rigour and worldly cynicism. Although he was deeply devout, in his role as Elizabeth's spymaster he had no qualms about using subterfuge and deception, nor in associating with liars and criminals. In common with covert intelligence gatherers today, his surveillance techniques were often ethically indefensible but highly effective. There is no doubt that he believed the ends more than justified the means.

Were he at work in modern times, his role would be as joint head of MI5 and MI6, in charge of a complex network of informants across Europe and in England, Scotland and Ireland. Indeed, MI5's heraldic arms include a circle of red roses in tribute to Walsingham, whose personal seal was a rose. Certain letters he even signed using the codename 'M', to conceal his identity. Traumatised, one presumes, by what he witnessed during the St Bartholomew's Day Massacre, he understood how lethal religious persecution could become. Believing England vulnerable to the rule of heretics – i.e. Mary and her followers – on his return to England in 1573 he devoted himself to ensuring she never took the throne.

Aged forty at the time of the massacre, Walsingham was the academically able son of a lawyer who had died when his son was a toddler. Like his father, Walsingham trained as a lawyer, at Gray's Inn, after studying at King's College, Cambridge, which was a hotbed of reformist theology. Escaping Mary Tudor's savage reprisals, he spent five years in Europe, where he became proficient in several languages and discovered a love of Italy. Despite his relatively humble origins, he was to rise in the ranks of Elizabeth's circle to become one of the trio she depended upon most heavily, along with Burghley and Dudley, whom she had elevated to Earl of Leicester years earlier, when hoping that Mary would marry him. As the man who pulled the strings of countless puppets, Walsingham was, wrote the contemporary historian William Camden, 'a most subtle searcher of hidden secrets'. He mixed with people who were not of his kind or nature, learning how the world worked, and probing – always probing – to find whatever grubby secrets lay beneath unturned stones.

Walsingham's name is as indelibly entwined with Mary, Queen of Scots as that of Burghley or the Earl of Shrewsbury. His work ethic matched Burghley's, as did his obsession with finding sufficient evidence to convince Elizabeth to execute her cousin. To that end, he worked tirelessly and fanatically to rid the country of a woman he saw as pernicious and ungodly, who would utterly destroy England and its peaceful Protestant population if she got her way. In this respect, as soon as he entered Mary's story he was like a disease that slowly and undetected takes hold, until its victim, unaware of its malign presence, has no chance of surviving. In the following chapters, even when he is not mentioned, he is busy behind the scenes, stealthily weaving a web around Mary from which she could not extricate herself.

The month after the massacre, Elizabeth tried to rid herself of her unwanted captive, offering to hand her over to the Regent Mar to be tried (and doubtless executed) for her role in Darnley's murder. Disobligingly, Mar refused unless paid handsomely – too handsomely. A few weeks later, Mar died after dining with the Earl of Morton, circumstances that some found suspicious, especially since Morton then stepped into Mar's shoes as Regent. The pitiless, self-serving earl, who was foremost among Mary's enemies, was another of Elizabeth's favoured men. Even he, however, was unwilling to continue negotiations for Mary's return, when the blame for killing the queen would be laid upon him.

Thug though Morton was – or maybe because he was so pugnacious and unscrupulous – under his control Scotland would finally grow more peaceful. After becoming Regent, in May 1573, with the assistance of an English army, he took Edinburgh Castle, thereby all but annihilating Mary's party. Kirkcaldy of Grange was hanged, and the ailing Maitland of Lethington died in prison while awaiting trial, possibly after committing suicide by poison. As with the Earl of Huntly many years earlier, he was brought to court in his coffin, a gruesome footnote to a career in which his loyalty to Mary, though it occasionally faltered, had ultimately proved true. One by one the remaining Marians made their peace with Morton, and Mary's hopes of being restored to Scotland evaporated. She acted unconcerned, but as Shrewsbury wrote to Burghley, 'it nips her very near'.

Chapter 14

'Unless she could transform herself into a mouse or a flea it was impossible that she could escape'

SHEFFIELD MANOR LODGE

In April 1573, shortly before the capture of Edinburgh Castle, Mary was moved to Sheffield Manor Lodge for the first of many visits in the coming years. Shrewsbury had intended to take her there the previous autumn, but the news from France about the massacre caused the ever-cautious earl to postpone. In anticipation of her arrival, the lodge had undergone an extensive project of renovation and extension. As a result, although it was only a couple of miles from Sheffield Castle, it was a world apart from that grim fortress, being both tranquil and fashionably appointed.

The road that led from the castle to Manor Lodge was lined with walnut trees, creating an elegant avenue that hinted at the comforts that lay ahead. Situated at the highest point of the vast Sheffield Park, one of the largest deer parks in England, the lodge had spectacular views across Yorkshire, Derbyshire and Nottinghamshire. Such a prospect, for a prisoner, must have made captivity all the more painful. The complex of buildings within the walled enclosure included the recently extended old lodge buildings and, most impressively of all, a Turret House. This squat, dark building, with a single rounded turret, was built in 1574 as part of Shrewsbury's expensive renovations.

Today, despite its proximity to Sheffield city centre, the Manor Lodge compound feels rustic. When the morning rush-hour was reaching its peak, I made my way to the bus station. Waiting for the number 56, I fell into conversation with a retired bus driver wearing a tweed cap with a burnt orange feather that would have looked at home on a Perthshire shoot. He told me which stop to get off at, and the street to follow. His instructions were so clear I was there half an hour ahead of opening.

The Manor Lodge sits to the east of the city, on the edge of a tired housing estate. To get there, the bus made its circuitous way through the centre of Sheffield, navigating a ganglion of roundabouts and fast roads before climbing steeply through a tightly packed residential area. After a few minutes, street names such as Manor Oaks Road indicated the lodge was not far off. As the bus made its slow ascent, I could see traffic on the M1 flashing in the morning sunshine beyond the estate. We passed a shop with a sign above the door advertising 'News and Booze', and soon after came to my stop.

There was nobody on the street, although a white estate car pulsating with music pulled up sharply at the kerb and a young man hurried into a house. Written across the top of his windscreen, in capitals, was the word 'shitbox', which – now I know what it means (a cheap car on its last legs) – seemed a bit harsh. I walked uphill along a wide avenue of houses and turned a corner. At this point on one side houses were replaced by a wall with a pair of attractive wrought-iron gates. One bore a version of the Talbot family crest: the motto *Solo virtus vincit* (Only the virtuous win), with a lion rampant facing a horse on its rear legs. Above them was an armoured helmet. On the other gate was Sheffield's coat of arms: the doughty figures of Thor and Vulcan, bearing a hammer and pincers, and the motto *Deo adjuvante labor proficit* (With God's help our work succeeds). A heavy chain was wrapped around the gates, and beyond them, set in a meadow of bright wildflowers, was the dour Tudor Turret House where Bess of Hardwick had entertained Mary.

Walking on, past high redbrick walls, I was soon on a rough path, lined with flowers and grasses, leading to Manor Lodge. The ticket office and reception, called the Discovery Centre, is a low, hobbitish building, with a turf roof. A number of parents with young children were as early as me, and we ambled around in the weak sunshine, filling time. A trail through trees dripping from a morning downpour led to a plateau at the top of a grassy knoll, beyond which a superb vista of the hills beyond houses and motorway beckoned.

When the doors of the Discovery Centre opened, there was a surge of children. As they charged through the centre and out into the grounds, I doubt any noticed the stylised tableau under glass depicting Mary with her head on the block. Given their tender age, perhaps that was just as well. With something of *The Handmaid's Tale* about it – she wears a scarlet cap and dress – this pared back representation captures the brutality and starkness of her end.

I followed the children into a spacious compound of grass and ruins, at the far end of which is the Turret House. First, however, the tall crumbling chimney and dilapidated walls of the South Range drew my attention. The oldest part of the Manor Lodge complex, which was built around 1516 on the site of an earlier residence – probably a hunting lodge – this range had been the lodge's heart, containing kitchens, cellars and larder.

At a distance from the South Range is a vertiginous wall, which is all that remains of the elegant Long Gallery. In its day, this was a showpiece, the longest such gallery in England until Hampton Court trumped it. Built above stables, the huge, light-filled space was a domestic invention of the sixteenth century, providing a place where people could stroll and exercise in poor weather while enjoying the view, or where they could read, talk and sew. Mary would have spent many hours here, enjoying a stylish setting befitting her status and, no doubt, looking towards the horizon, beyond which lay Scotland.

Today, the Long Gallery overlooks fruit trees and a lavender maze, in which bees were buzzing like drones. In earlier times, the maze was a courtyard. At the end of the gallery wall is a circular ruin, known as Wolsey's Tower or, more evocatively, Wolsey's Toilet. This extension was built in 1530 for the visit of the unfortunate Cardinal Thomas Wolsey, but it is doubtful if he fully appreciated the gesture. The occasion was not a happy one. After failing to obtain an annulment of

Henry VIII's marriage to his first wife, Catherine of Aragon, in order that the king could marry Elizabeth's mother, Anne Boleyn, Wolsey fell from favour. When he arrived at the lodge he was on his way to the Tower of London to face charges of treason. He spent almost three weeks at Manor Lodge, the length of his stay perhaps explained by his becoming extremely unwell, possibly with dysentery, or perhaps as a result of being poisoned. An apothecary gave him medical care, but a few days after departing for London he died in Leicester.

If nothing else, it seems likely he made full use of what was then a state-of-the-art toilet. Visitors to Manor Lodge tend to dwell on this undignified footnote to Wolsey's biography, rather than on his hitherto distinguished career. As manor houses began to replace more primitive defensive buildings, life became more refined. Castle toilets had emptied into a cesspit or moat, but this new design, known as a garderobe, and to which Mary, Queen of Scots, a few decades later, was accustomed, was considered much less basic. To contemporary eyes it is hard to detect much improvement. The tower would have contained two adjacent seats (i.e. holes in a plank of wood), below which was an area filled with straw. This would be regularly (possibly annually) emptied by a farmer, who used its contents to fertilise fields.

Hygiene in the later sixteenth century was an increasingly urgent subject as the population of towns and cities swelled, and cleanliness became more prized (and difficult to achieve). In places, the water supply was so dirty or unreliable that people preferred to jump in a river to cleanse themselves, even in winter. Some did this daily, but most, one suspects, were less fastidious.

An early flushing toilet was invented towards the end of the sixteenth century by Queen Elizabeth's godson, John Harington, and the Queen was quick to adopt it, installing one at Richmond. In rural locations it was far easier to find a supply of running water either to flush toilets or for them to drain into than in towns and cities. There, the cleansing of household cesspits was a Herculean task, conducted at night, and requiring the partial rebuilding of the latrine on each occasion. It was an expensive business, even before, as the author Ian Mortimer writes: 'you factor in the cost of cleaning up the house after sixteen tons of excrement, slopping about in barrels, has been carried through it'. Interestingly, latrine cleaners were amongst the highest paid workers in the Middle Ages, valued in a way that modern cleaners are not.

Today, the sweet-smelling Sheffield Manor Lodge site and park is run by a social enterprise focused on ecological conservation and education, The Green Enterprise Community Interest Company. Swathes of meadow designed to attract pollinators are planted in shades of blue, white, pink and yellow, like Battenberg cakes run riot. And, in a sheltered corner of the South Range, a tidily laid out Apothecary Garden, displaying herbs and plants used for medicines and cooking in Tudor times, provides a haven for butterflies, insects and roving children.

In Elizabethan days, it was the responsibility of the lady of the manor to create a garden that could supply most of the household's medicinal needs. This was the era when gardening as we understand it started to become popular, with books written on the subject to instruct novices. Elaborate knot gardens were a favourite, with low evergreen hedges shaped into intricate patterns and filled, in the warmer months, with herbs and flowers. But the purpose of a garden was as much functional as aesthetic, even though it allowed the lady of the manor an absorbing creative outlet.

Flowers, which were also used as medicines, were often cultivated in raised beds. By the mid sixteenth century, apricots, gooseberries and raspberries were becoming favourites, as were strawberries, although they were half the size of the modern fruit. Flowers as well as fruit were eaten; one delicious-sounding Elizabethan dessert was made with roses and primroses. Why has that disappeared from recipe books?

An Englishman in 1577 said that a wife's quality could be judged by the state of her garden, and in this respect Bess of Hardwick was exemplary. In 1561, as she was getting Chatsworth into shape, she wrote from the court in London to one of her stewards: 'I would have you tell my Aunt Linnacre that I would have the new garden which is by the new house, made a garden this year. I care not whether she bestow any great cost thereof, but to sow it with all kinds of herbs and flowers, and some piece with mallows. I have sent you by this carrier three bundles of garden seeds . . .' Her eagerness to have the garden begun – a project that continued for the rest of her life – shows how important a feature this was becoming for the landed gentry.

By the middle of the century, the Elizabethan diet was expanding as new plants were introduced, among them asparagus, horseradish and artichokes. Seeds were also being imported from abroad, but it was traditional herbs and medicinal plants that mattered most, each with its own special properties. In her account of women's domestic roles down the centuries, Marjoree Filbee gives an outline of how ailments were catered for: 'aniseed, eyebright, lavender, bay, roses, rue, sage, marjoram, and calamint were used to treat complaints of the head; comfrey was advised for lung complaints; the heart could be strengthened by borage, saffron, balm, basil, rosemary, and roses.'

While I browsed the Manor Lodge's Apothecary Garden, the place was alive with children who had dived into that morning's pirate-themed activities. Among these was a treasure hunt that sent them haring after clues through the ruins. One boy was fired up: 'I know where more treasure is!' he shouted, charging around the apothecary garden. A less enthusiastic girl muttered, 'Pirates aren't real.' I didn't like to tell her she was wrong. Not only are they still in business, but they flourished in the days of the Shrewsburys, when the great European powers licensed piracy as a rough form of diplomatic point-scoring. When it came to capturing booty at sea, England had few rivals.

The main attraction for visitors to the Manor Lodge, of course, is the Turret House. Although the earl complained ceaselessly about a shortage of funds, when it came to improving his own estates he did not stint. The Manor Lodge's pamphlet guide tells visitors that the building's original purpose was as a highly fashionable banqueting house and hunting lodge. In this respect it was like the Hunting Tower at Chatsworth, where guests would gather to watch the hunt.

At the same time they might enjoy a lavish picnic, which was eaten standing – perhaps on the tower's flat roof – rather than at table.

Approached by paths mown through the wildflower meadow, the three-storey Turret House can be hired as a wedding venue. Mary's terrible record of husbands and would-be marriages surely stands as a warning to think before committing yourself. Bess's experience of marriage was also eventful and, as her relationship with Shrewsbury broke down, would become even more so. Yet she was an inveterate matchmaker, which perhaps makes the Turret House a fitting place for tying the knot. It's doubtful, however, if anyone today is as relentless in their pursuit of family advancement, through marriage, as was the countess.

Though bijou, the Turret House – well designed, with an expensive, classy interior – retains Bess of Hardwick's personality. The idea of a banqueting house clearly appealed to her, since she had another banqueting room incorporated into the roof at Hardwick Hall. (To give an idea of this mansion's scale, she also had a long gallery built here with three bay windows, each, writes architectural historian Nikolaus Pevsner, 'the size of a twentieth-century council house'.)

Some history books insist that Mary lived in the Turret House when she was in residence, but this is unlikely. A guide, who was sitting outside in the sunshine and warning visitors of the narrowness and trickiness of the spiral staircase, told me that Mary's apartments were most probably in the main part of the Lodge. These would have been close to the eye-catching 60-foot gatehouse towers that Shrewsbury had built from expensive red brick, which could be seen from miles around. There is no doubt, though, that Mary often spent part of her day in Bess's company in the Turret House, to resume her embroidery and conversation.

When she first arrived at Manor Lodge, Mary was under deep suspicion. Following the St Bartholomew's Day Massacre she was allowed few concessions, and she chafed at the strictness of her confinement. If she wished to take exercise, for example, she had to give an hour's notice. In light of the panic around her, such severity was unsurprising. The previous month, Shrewsbury had written to

Elizabeth about rumours of a plot to liberate her. In a long and sombre letter, he made it clear that he was aware Mary would try to escape if possible, and what the consequences would be if she did: 'I have her sure enough, and shall keep her forthcoming at your Majesty's commandment, either quick or dead ... if any forcible attempt be given for her, the greatest peril is sure to be hers.'

To quell alarm at court that she might be rescued, Shrewsbury's son Gilbert Talbot reassured the Privy Council that security at Manor Lodge was exceptionally tight: 'So strictly is she guarded that unless she could transform herself into a mouse or a flea it was impossible that she could escape.' Mary's entourage were under strict orders to leave her rooms at nine at night and could not carry arms of any description. If they left the lodge without permission, they faced execution. Not only was the guard on the queen tight, it was noisy. When a fresh shift came on at five in the morning, drums were beaten. Since Mary would often stay up writing into the small hours, this cannot have amused her.

Outside the Turret House is a long stone coffin. Its now missing lid was inscribed to Thomas de Furnival, who died in 1332, after building Sheffield Castle. By 1708, when the seventh Duke of Norfolk had the manor lodge demolished, the area was already being used as a farm, and the coffin served as a water trough for cattle. You might see this as a metaphor for the transience of power. Inside, the house is cramped, with low ceilings, but its mullioned windows allow light to flood the rooms and, having been occupied until the 1950s, it feels lived in rather than abandoned. With its recessed windows, redbrick fireplaces and tapestries on the walls, it strongly evokes the era when Bess was in charge. There are portraits of her, the Earl of Shrewsbury and his descendants, and of Mary and Elizabeth. On the ground floor, in what is called the Costume Room, there is a rail of dressing-up clothes for those wanting to be transported back almost five hundred years, albeit it in polyester.

In long skirts the spiral staircase would certainly be tricky to climb, as the guide warned. On the second and uppermost floor is one of the house's banqueting rooms, where a table is covered in replica food: boar's head, goose, pheasant, pies and fruit. Blackbird pies, which were popular, would have contained live blackbirds, which had been rendered unconscious after being smoked. As we know from the nursery rhyme, when the pie was cut open, they would gulp in air and fly out singing: the Tudor idea of a spectacle. Presumably the windows were opened to allow them to escape.

Shrewsbury's coat of arms is embossed in plaster above the fireplace: two talbot dogs facing each other. The talbot was a special breed of white hunting hound, with a long lolling tongue, but it is no longer in existence. In this room, the ornate plaster ceiling carries images of flowers associated with Mary: a marigold, her favourite flower; a fleur de lys, which was her mother's emblem; a thistle and a briar rose, referring to Scotland and Catherine de' Medici. Since the Turret House was not finished when Mary first arrived, it seems either that she might have been consulted about its decoration, or that it was devised specifically to please her. If so, it was a gracious and diplomatic gesture by her captor, giving her the illusion, at least, that her comfort and feelings mattered.

Such courtesy, and the sophistication of the Turret House and the Long Gallery, suggest that not everything about Mary's captivity was grim. When the state of national alarm eased, as it did with the regularity of the tide's rise and fall, she was able to socialise with some of the great families of the nearby counties. Such occasions offered the chance to exchange secret letters, which were the lifeblood of Mary's captive existence. Of which more later.

Chapter 15

'The bath has soothed my nerves'

BUXTON

Over the next fourteen years, Mary would be shuttled constantly between residences, sometimes spending a couple of weeks in one location, sometimes several months. The least welcome guest in England, she was treated like an unwanted relative shared between reluctant family members, each of them eager to pass her on. After the disintegration of her party in Scotland, the high drama of her early time in captivity quietened. For three or so years after her arrival in Sheffield, boredom, frustration and, no doubt, despair set in.

There was, however, one place she looked forward to visiting, where her spirits would unfailingly rise. This was the little spa town of Buxton, in the Peak District of Derbyshire. A fourteen-mile ride from Chatsworth through spectacular scenery, Buxton was the highest market town in England, and its bracing air, even in summer, might have done those in search of a cure almost as much good as its warm mineral waters.

These waters had been renowned for their healing powers since Roman times, and possibly long before that too. In the Middle Ages, holy wells drew crowds hoping to find a miraculous cure. There were around 450 such wells across England, where Mass would be said for those seeking help. Supplicants who believed they had been cured would hang up their crutches or shirts or sheets before they departed, testimony to the well's restorative powers. Buxton's well was named after Saint Anne, the mother of the Virgin Mary. As the grandmother of Jesus, she was the patron saint of grandmothers, but also of women hoping to get pregnant, and of miners, which was appropriate for Derbyshire, where there had been mining since the Roman occupation.

In 1536, a mere eighteen years after the well opened, it was closed on the orders of Henry VIII's vicar-general, Thomas Cromwell. It was not just at Buxton that access was denied. All of England's holy wells were to be shut, and any idolatrous remnants of the old religion thrown away. In his history of the spa town, R. Grundy Heape writes that in Tudor times Buxton's spring offered 'a kind of Lourdes where people went to be cured, with greater faith in the healing power of the Saint than in the curative powers of its water'. This was precisely the sort of attitude Cromwell wanted to stamp out. As a result, St Ann's Well was cleared of pilgrims' effects and images of the saint; the baths and chapel were destroyed, sealed and locked up, and its keepers forbidden from taking alms.

This might sound like a footnote to the era's tumultuous history, but the fate of these wells was symptomatic, and even central, to the political and religious unease that threatened to undermine Elizabeth for much of her reign. A fulcrum for the danger posed by those who continued covertly to follow and promote the old religion in the hope one day of seeing England restored to Catholicism, holy wells were deeply vexatious to the Queen and her councillors.

The Oath of Supremacy of 1559 obliged those in public office to affirm Elizabeth as supreme governor of the Church. Catholic diehards who could not in conscience make this oath had sought sanctuary in Europe, and those Catholics still living in England, who wanted to meet associates without fear of apprehension, joined them at the small town of Spa, where the exiles often gathered. Located in the Ardennes region in the Spanish Netherlands, Spa or Spaw as it was sometimes known, became a meeting place for English recusants and European fundamentalists, a pleasant setting in which they could bemoan their persecution, and intrigue against Elizabeth. Those who had fled England in fear of their lives sent 'Spaw rings' to their family and friends back home as tokens to reassure them that they were still alive.

Wily recusants in England, meanwhile, used ill health as an excuse for visiting Spa, although this subterfuge was quickly seen through. Those in genuine search of a cure, and who were faithful to Elizabeth, were given passes allowing them to visit for a period of treatment. One such patient was Shrewsbury's terminally ill daughter Catherine, although her exhausting trip did little to improve her health or her chances of surviving.

Doubtless Elizabeth would have preferred to maintain her father's prohibition on such gathering places, and thereby curtail opportunities for trouble to foment. Yet after the Northern Rising of 1569, when rebels such as the Earl of Westmorland and the Countess of Northumberland fled to the continent and to Spa, a new approach was urgently needed. If those seeking medicinal help could not find healing mineral waters in their own country, European spas would continue to attract rebels, whose company might infect the guileless. What was required was a rethink in the way the old holy wells were viewed, and what they represented. If this could be achieved, a convenient ruse by which recusants could congregate elsewhere would be thwarted.

It was therefore decreed that people would again be allowed to take the waters, but only at sites given government approval. The existence of mineral waters had to be professionally confirmed, and no place where miraculous cures had been reported would be sanctioned. The idea was entirely to disassociate these locations from Catholic superstition. Instead, they were to become a frontier in the burgeoning science of medicine, in which the secular arts of physicians, surgeons and pharmacists were key. From now on, Catholic ritual was to play no part in the medical efficacy of these treatments.

Elizabeth charged her courtiers with the task of promoting this new medical ethos and establishing spa centres across the country. Hence – in part at least – Shrewsbury's eagerness to develop Buxton, which was originally owned by Bess's second husband, William Cavendish, who had bought substantial lands in Derbyshire at her urging. Shrewsbury's son-in-law, the Earl of Pembroke, was the widower of his daughter Catherine. It was he who was responsible for Bath's rising fortunes; in time it would become the pre-eminent spa in England. Elizabeth's long-time favourite Robert Dudley, Earl of Leicester, who considered himself a patron of science, established a new spa at King's Newnham, close to his home of Kenilworth. Unlike at Buxton and Bath, where the water's temperature was akin to a modern jacuzzi, its waters were cold, and it required greater persuasion to attract visitors.

For Shrewsbury, reinventing Buxton was greatly to his personal benefit. In following his sovereign's orders he not only won her approval but was also able to indulge in one of his and Bess's favourite pastimes: making money. Not that he was cynical about the benefits of Buxton's waters. After taking the baths here in 1569 to relieve his gout, he seems to have become a believer. In fact, of all the ailments these warm waters were alleged to help, gout was amongst the most common. They were also good for 'women's problems', and many others besides. (One physician listed eighty-nine conditions that taking the waters at Bath would cure, and even advocated their use for horses.)

When Shrewsbury began turning Buxton into a full-fledged spa town, he had the spring tapped to create three mineral baths. A few yards from them, he built a grand battlemented tower. Known as the New Hall, it connected to the baths by a back door and a covered walkway. All three baths were in the open, with seating around them. Fireplaces provided warmth, which was often essential, even though the waters were over twenty-seven degrees Celsius.

The Welsh physician Dr John Jones was an early advocate of drinking and bathing in mineral waters. In 1572, he wrote a promotional book called *The Benefit of the Ancient Bath of Buckstones*, dedicated to Shrewsbury, in which he described the brand new hotel: 'Joyning to the chief springe, between the river, and the Bathe is a very goodly house, four square, four stories high, so well compact, with houses of office beneath and above, round about, with a great chambre, and other goodly lodgings, to the number of thirty.'

The largest property in Buxton (and today the oldest), it was surrounded by a wall, thereby ensuring its privacy and exclusivity. The imposing New Hall, enhanced by a nearby grove of trees, was designed to accommodate patients for as long as their prescribed period of treatment. Dinner was cooked for patients individually. And it was not only the upper echelons who flooded in. By imposing a levy on visitors to the baths, provision was made for the poor to gain access to the waters. Lodgings for them were also made available in the town. The Buxton Bath Charity, which is thought to have been Bess's idea, allowed general access across the social spectrum. In addition to a registration fee of 4 pence, entrance to the baths was charged on a sliding scale of fees: from 1 shilling for a yeoman and 3 shillings for a gentleman to £1 for an earl and £3 10s for a duke. A duchess paid £2, but a gentlewoman only 2 shillings. There is no note of what a queen was asked to pay. Meanwhile, by charging handsomely for lodgings and meals, Shrewsbury raked in the cash.

Remarkably quickly, a visit to Buxton became part of the social diary for members of the aristocracy, many of whom were at Elizabeth's court. The effect of this influx of the wealthy and powerful on the hitherto quiet and modest hill town of Buxton must have transformed the place. From the outset, the New Hall hosted some of the most prominent members of the Privy Council, which did not please the Queen. Perhaps because of its proximity to the various houses where Mary was being held, she never visited Buxton, although she did go to Bath.

Mary would have been well aware of the Earl and Countess of Shrewsbury's new venture. Suffering as she did from rheumatic and arthritic complaints, it is not surprising that she began to petition Elizabeth and her custodian to allow her to visit. A letter to Elizabeth on the subject in 1571 failed to have any impact, despite being so bluntly worded:

Declare the state of my person, how I have been lately vexed by sickness, with a great vomisement, first of pure blood, and after of congealed blood, flewme and choler, the dolour of my side &ct,

caused by daily augmentation of displeasure. It may bring about my death at length, which before the whole world will be laid upon the Queen and her councillors. Desire them to consider in what reputation it will bring this realm, and how honourable it would be if they caused me to be better treated. Purchase licence for the Earl of Shrewsbury to transport me to Buckstons Well for a few days, as I have written to Burghley by Mr Lowret, physician.

Mary repeatedly pleaded, but to no avail, since Shrewsbury was fearful that she might be intercepted on her journey. He told Burghley that he thought Mary's health was not too bad. Nor could he see what mineral waters would achieve that the herbal baths she already bathed in would not. He did not mention her baths of red wine, which cost him a small fortune. (These, one assumes, were considered therapeutic.) Eventually, however, as so often, he found a way to accommodate Mary's wishes.

Before her first visit to Buxton, in late August 1573, there had been much wrangling between the earl and Elizabeth and her councillors. Given the enduring reputation of spas as hotbeds of Catholic conspiracy, the Queen's anxiety was understandable. Had Elizabeth known that several attempts to help Mary would be made by Catholic or sympathetic visitors to Buxton in the coming years, with some acting as couriers for the Scottish queen's letters to conspirators and others discussing escape, she would never have agreed. Only when she was assured that security would be rigorous did she state the conditions under which the visit must be conducted: no strangers were to be allowed into the town, and the nearby streets were to be sealed off while Mary was in residence. Beggars would also be cleared from the vicinity. Consequently, they deeply resented Mary's visits, since she lost them a considerable amount of income.

When confirming Elizabeth's permission for her cousin to visit, Burghley emphasised to Shrewsbury that as few people as possible should know she was going to the spa, and that strangers must be forbidden from visiting while she was in residence:

> And this I write because her Majesty was very unwilling that she should go thither, imagining that her desire was either to be the more seen of strangers resorting thither or for the achieving of some further enterprise to escape; but on the other part, I told her Majesty that if in very deed her sickness were to be relieved thereby, her Majesty could not in honour deny her to have the natural remedy thereof . . .

Not stipulated was that no members of Elizabeth's court should be in residence at the New Hall at the same time. Over the years 1573 to 1584, during which Mary visited nine times, Buxton became a byword for court gossip and plotting, a place where the likes of Burghley and Leicester would socialise easily with the Scottish queen and, perhaps, fall under her spell. No wonder Burghley tried to prevent Elizabeth knowing he had been in Buxton at the same time as Mary, since this might raise doubts over his loyalty. He, of course, claimed he was there to ensure security was sufficiently strict.

It seems likely that for Mary, being in lively company in a relaxed environment was as good for her health as the waters she bathed in and drank. Even so, she had no doubt as to their recuperative powers, writing: 'It is incredible how the bath has soothed my nerves and dried my body of the phlegmatic humours with which, by reason of feeble health, it was so abundantly full.' Elizabeth's promulgation of England's spas led to a surge of interest in taking the waters and to what Phyllis May Hembry, in her history of the English spa, describes as 'a mania for wellfinding'. Taking a week or two of treatment became quite common, and was, she writes, 'the origin of the secular English holiday . . . The use of prescribed waters for medicinal, as distinct from religious, reasons now acquired an aura of respectability, even of high fashion.'

Buxton's association with Mary and the Earl of Shrewsbury added immeasurably to its political cachet. Indeed, after Mary's execution in 1587 and the earl's death in 1590, it rather fell out of favour with the nobility, although less lofty visitors steadily increased in number. Its fame was such that Ben Jonson mentioned St Ann's Well in one of his plays, and Thomas Hobbes also referred to it in 1678: 'this cures the palsied members of the old, and cherishes the nerves grown stiff and cold'.

Dr John Jones was to spa-going what Monty Don is to gardening: the arbiter of what to do and when. In his 1572 guide to Buxton, he outlined how to get the most out of a visit. On arrival, visitors should take a day or two to recover from their journey before beginning treatment. That should consist of at least a couple of hours' bathing each morning and afternoon, always undertaken before eating but preferably after a little exercise. Patients should then dry themselves and their clothes thoroughly, and at this point might wish to retreat to bed with the Tudor equivalent of hot-water bottles (bladders filled with hot water), which would make them sweat.

Dr Jones allowed patients to eat well, but food was not to be fried or roasted, only boiled. Between sessions in the baths, men should play bowls, practise archery outdoors or amuse themselves 'tossing the wind ball' in the garden. Women, on the other hand, 'may have in the end of a bench eleven holes made, into the which to troule pummetes or bowls of lead, big, little, or mean, or also of tin, copper, wood, either violent or soft, after their own discretion'. This game, he said, was called Troule in Madame. Alternatively, they could stroll the New Hall's galleries. 'Men feeble' could also enjoy playing Troule in Madame, but in another gallery.

A fortnight's regimen was commonly recommended, but some spent as long as forty days. Mary, Queen of Scots's first visit lasted five weeks, although one imagines she wished she could remain indefinitely. Certainly she was eager for a swift return. Writing to the French ambassador, she asked him to pass on her thanks to Elizabeth for allowing her visit and said that if, the following year, when the weather was warmer, 'it should please her . . . to grant me the same permission and to give me rather a longer time, I believe that will quite cure me, if no other accident should happen'.

In winter Buxton was, and still is, frequently buffeted by storms and blanketed in snow. Even in summer time it could be chilly, with breezes that the most vulnerable Tudor spa goers feared might cause a chill. When I visited in the middle of June, however, not a breath of wind disturbed the blanket of heat in which the town was swaddled. I had arrived, with my husband, by way of industrial Yorkshire, driving through the monotone outskirts of Bradford and Huddersfield, with their endless roundabouts and junctions. On reaching Derbyshire and the Peak District National Park, the congested concrete gave way to empty roads winding through woodland and hills, with glimpses of rivers as we passed through villages, at least one with a duck pond. The road to Buxton is steep, since it lies 1,000 feet above sea level. Viewed from the air, this attractive town spreads almost incongruously across the rugged landscape, its elegant crescents and terraces, its magnificent Georgian, Victorian and Edwardian buildings not at all what you'd expect in such a setting. Before Mary's era, however, medieval Buxton would have been all but hidden by trees; since Norman days it lay in the heart of a royal hunting forest.

We reached the town in late afternoon, by which time the heat was more like the Dordogne than Derbyshire. With the sun as bright as memories of childhood summers, our first stop was for a long-overdue pot of tea in a café with glass walls opened to the street. Strangely, it was selling bottles of Harrogate rather than Buxton water, an anomaly we found in several local cafés.

A few hundred yards away lay the heart of Buxton. Its most notable feature is The Crescent, a sweeping Georgian masterpiece by the architect John Carr. Built from pale local limestone, it was designed to accommodate shops and hotels on its arcaded ground floor. Alongside are the Buxton Baths, and close by is the Cavendish Arcade, an emporium of upmarket shops. There is a bijou Opera House, and in the Pavilion Park a domed glass hot-house (the Pavilion) filled with tropical plants. The park itself was a haven on a hot day, with avenues of mature trees, a stream and meandering, shaded paths. At nine o'clock in the evening, families and dog walkers were still idling by the water, enjoying the summer air.

Mary's haunt, the Old Hall Hotel, lies in The Square, directly opposite the gates to the park. Swathed in ivy, which tickles the hotel's name above the door, it looks inviting. Viewed from the front, the tower house that Shrewsbury built is not immediately visible, hidden by seventeenth- and eighteenth-century additions. As in old movies, I parked right outside the hotel's door. Inside, in what felt like gloom after the brilliance of the day, was a long carpeted corridor, its walls hung with memorabilia of Mary. These include a replica of her great seal, her encomium to Buxton Waters, her portrait and a framed article by a historian claiming the Old Hall as possibly the oldest hotel in England.

Further down the hallway, but easily missed, are the remains of the original sixteenth-century entranceway: an arched stone doorway decorated with two gargoyle-like plaster heads. Only from the outside of the building, on the side close to The Crescent, can you clearly see the old tower house, with its dingier walls and small bay windows. Adjoining it, with arched stained-glass windows, is the mid nineteenth-century Natural Mineral Baths, occupying the site where Mary and her peers ventured into the warm waters. Opposite is the elegant Pump Room, its interior a temple to marble. It was built in the late nineteenth century, to relieve pressure on the other baths. By then Buxton's popularity had soared, thanks to the arrival of the railway in the 1860s. Close by is St Ann's Well, which is designed like a shrine.

Inside the hotel and further down the corridor, where the light was even dimmer, I found the bow-fronted glass reception desk. Although sixteenth-century, it looked like something out of a Dickens novel. Several guests were requiring attention, and the staff behind the glass were busy. The hotel's metal-grilled lift had broken down, and people with heavy cases needed assistance. When various queries had been answered and situations resolved, my husband and I were checked into Room 39, on the second floor. By its door is a metal hinge, from which, perhaps, the original door would have hung. The room was old-fashioned but spacious and overlooked the hotel's attic quarters and the town's roofscape. Opening the window as far as it would go, I put on the fan and hoped the temperature would soon drop.

Close below us, on the first floor, was Room 26, known as Mary's Bower, where the queen is said to have stayed. I had called the hotel some weeks earlier, but the room was already booked, and nobody could show it to me while it was occupied. Once we had unpacked, I went downstairs to find it anyway. As with our room, and throughout the old quarters of the hotel, there was a sign above the door telling people to mind their heads. Since Mary was tall by the standards of today, let alone the Stuart era, one assumes she spent much of her time in Buxton, and elsewhere, ducking her head or rubbing bruises.

The Old Hall, as distinct from its relatively modern extensions, has an atmosphere all its own. Hallways lead to narrow back stairs, corridors slant as if the old floorboards are weary, and there are corners of damp on some ceilings. Yet the air of faded gentility feels appropriate for the Old Hall's vintage. One guest remarked on Booking.com, 'it is a bit dated but this is the oldest hotel in the UK so we were happy with it'. Another described it as 'a tad shabby chic', but the staff were widely praised.

At breakfast the following morning, we ate under the gaze of the Earl of Shrewsbury and Bess of Hardwick, as well as Mary herself. The room was large and sunny, and that morning was catering for a large group attending a conference. There were only two waiting staff, one of whom delivered my husband's breakfast to the wrong table. The guest who got it looked slightly bemused to find he'd been given a tomato with his eggs and bacon, but hurried off to make toast. When he got back, the plate was gone and my husband was tucking in, the waiter having assured him, 'It's okay, he hasn't touched it.'

Buxton Crescent Hotel, a sister hotel to the Old Hall, occupies part of the splendidly restored Georgian crescent around the corner. A five-star spa hotel, offering thermal and mineral baths, and with three rooftop swimming pools, this is a deluxe residence fit, one might say, for royalty. Yet to be able to stay in the same house where Mary lived is more memorable, surely, than opulence.

One tangible reminder of her presence sets the Old Hall apart from any other place where she was held captive. On one of the interior windows of the living room, which face onto the corridor, is a replica of the messages and simple drawings Mary, and other guests, left on the hotel's original windows. (In the sixteenth century, glass could be etched with a diamond ring or stylus.) The copy of the original window writing was thought to have been made for Burghley by his secretary Michael Hicks. It is held at Longleat, but the replica at the Old Hall allows visitors to feel they are in direct contact with the Scottish queen.

What is written comes from the heart, so it is no wonder the gimlet-eyed Burghley was keen to preserve not just Mary's words but those of other guests who passed through these rooms. Among them were Mary's secretary Claude Nau, Shrewsbury, Leicester, and Thomas Gerard, who was embroiled in a plot to rescue Mary. Also leaving his mark is the bounty hunter Richard Topcliffe, whose life was spent scouring the country, like a bloodhound, in search of papists. His message, in Latin, is profoundly sinister: *Dulcior vitae finis Aetna mons* – 'Mount Etna is a sweeter end to life' – accompanied by an image of an exploding volcano. He seemed to imply that Mary should burn.

Several of the early messages Mary wrote, in her flowing, confident hand, reflect a preoccupation with what others were saying about her:

> Although people have said so much evil about me,
> Although people have misjudged my faith
> God alone who knows the workings of my heart
> Will one day make my innocence clear
> His virtue attracts me

She hints also at the presence of people she did not trust:

> I hate the one who speaks falsely
> I hate the one who flatters me sweetly
> I hate the one who speaks evil of the person
> Who has never said anything wrong of him

Over the years in her Buxton lodgings, Mary left several cryptic messages about her son, as in this one from the period when she was nursing renewed hopes of joining him on the Scottish throne:

By Mary Queen of Scots about
Her dearest son James Stewart
Message –
Courage calls may you ascend 1582

Another is more opaque. Possibly it suggests that Mary believes James will avenge her deposition and captivity and thereafter be seen as a good king:

Charles James Stewart, King of the Scots.
Message – I shall be called the Just King
Having taken vengeance. This man will be king of you, not through you but for your people

Reading these lines is like dissolving the centuries that lie between her and us. It is a sometimes uncomfortable sensation, since Mary's profound unhappiness is clear in several of her Latin messages. In one, she writes: 'The Lion is cast down and taunted by hares.' In another, from 1576, she vents her rage at Elizabeth's intransigence over acknowledging Mary's claim to the English throne: 'What is difficult becomes bearable through fortitude. It is a wickedness to set anything straight. It is completely against anything I can do to set things straight. You may [word missing?] throughout the family bloodline with a fork. However it continually comes back from the Queen of England.'

In perhaps the starkest indication of distress, she alludes to Acheron and the Styx (mythical rivers over which passengers were ferried to the other side – death), while hinting at suicide as a noble act:

Whoever sees the face of black Acheron
Whoever sees the sad Styx and is not sad

And dares to put an end to her life
She will be equal to kings and gods.

Such an outpouring of despair, while in a place where she could enjoy company and a refreshing change of scene, is unsettling. You wonder how black her thoughts were when immured in the gloom and chill of Tutbury or Sheffield Castle. What is striking about Mary's etched lines is their insistence on her innocence. At all points during her captivity she maintained that she was wronged. Even when found to be lying, or hiding the truth, or conspiring against Elizabeth, she asserted, and seemed truly to believe, that she was faultless. This is not to blame or excuse her, but to see events through her eyes. After being illegally toppled from her throne, and illegally imprisoned by her cousin, she felt she had right on her side. Whatever course she took to reclaim what she had lost, and what she was owed, was legitimate.

Chapter 16

'I immediately burn the draughts of the ciphers'

CODED LETTERS

Despite leaving a voluminous correspondence – few days passed without her taking up her pen – Mary, Queen of Scots remains unfathomable. In part this is what makes her perennially fascinating: her thoughts spill out on the page, describing her emotions, her health, her attendants and her judgements on her political allies and foes, and yet it remains impossible to be sure precisely what sort of woman she was. All that can be said without fear of contradiction is that she is one of history's most prolific, and at times most eloquent, correspondents.

Much of what she wrote, however, was never intended for the public eye. Would she have been appalled to know that her supposedly secret letters were read not only by their intended audience, and by her conniving enemies, but also by readers today? I suspect not. Adamant that she was in every respect justified in her actions, she might even have welcomed the thought that her most private messages, including those that hint at escape, were preserved for posterity. That way, future generations would know how hard she fought to regain her throne and her people.

Were one of these cipher letters to fall into our hands, it would, at first sight, be impenetrable: a grid of markings similar to a mathematician's equations or a shorthand manual. The pages would be filled with letters and symbols drawn from the Greek or Latin alphabets, or from astronomy and alchemy. Or they might be made-up shapes, with no provenance other than the encipherer's imagination.

'I immediately burn the draughts of the ciphers'

This was not how Mary wrote her secret letters, of course. Although capable of putting her words into code, she had secretaries who, after translating her French messages into English, then encoded them for her, using an ever-changing system of ciphers. Pierre Raulet and later Claude Nau were her French secretaries – the same post held, previously, by David Rizzio – and Gilbert Curle dealt with her English correspondence. To make sure that her original letter was conveyed correctly, and contained no unauthorised embellishments, she insisted that this process was done in front of her, and that the missive was then read back to her before being folded and sealed in her presence.

By the time of Mary's captivity, cryptology had become an art form, as had the task of deciphering fiendishly tricky ciphers without a key (cryptanalysis). That challenge required the sort of intelligence that, today, would be found interpreting the Hadron Collider's data. Or cracking the *Times* cryptic crossword in a matter of seconds. Francis Bacon wrote: 'This art of ciphering, hath for relative, an art of deciphering', and rather worryingly believed that 'the greatest matters, are many times carried in the weakest ciphers'.

Folding letters to keep them safe was another art form. In a time before envelopes and a reliable postal service, it was important that the content of letters remained private, even if they contained nothing more than business or personal information. Since the high Middle Ages, techniques of folding a single sheet in such a way that it neither came apart when handled, nor could be opened without the recipient's knowledge, had become increasingly intricate.

If not quite origami, this technique of folding, known as letterlocking, was nevertheless an effective way of ensuring that the letter remained private or, should it fall into the wrong hands, that the recipient would know it had been tampered with. This process involved creasing the paper so that the addressee's name was evident after it had been tightly folded. After this, there were various complicated methods of cutting and tying the letter and sealing it with adhesive, saliva or wax. Mary's final letter, written to her brother-in-law Henri III, King of France, hours before her execution, was carefully folded and locked. To the end, she was determined to avoid prying eyes reading her thoughts.

Far more crucial than letterlocking, however, was finding a way of coding information in a way that others could not fathom, or that would take so long to crack that events might by then have overtaken them. Several systems were employed to outwit decoders. Commonly used letters, such as *e* and *t* in English, or words such as 'and' and 'but', formed obvious patterns of use that could provide a chink in the code, after which its meaning could gradually be grasped.

To avoid this, ciphers were devised to guard against easy reading, and a key to each cipher was sent separately to recipients to allow them to read a letter and to reply in the same code. Each letter of the alphabet would be given a symbol, and the most frequently used letters might be given several symbols, to hide their repeated use. There were decoy symbols that were meaningless, and some that required the reader to delete or duplicate the previous symbol. Some symbols represented commonly used whole words or names. Mary's cipher, as used for her correspondence with young Anthony Babington, which was to lead to her execution, lays out a clear system: as well as each letter of the alphabet having its own sign, several words – such as 'this', 'say', 'my' and 'if', 'but' and 'not' – had their own motif. There were also various symbols for what were termed 'nullers' and one for 'doublets'.

Cryptography is thought to have begun with the Arabs long before it reached the western world. A fourteen-volume Arab encyclopaedia, published in the early fifteenth century and encompassing millennia of expertise, included an introduction to cryptoanalysis, which outlined the basic two methods of creating a cipher: transcription and substitution. In the west, ciphers had been used during the Roman Empire and were in regular use in Europe from at least the tenth century. By the time Machiavelli mentions cryptology in *The Art of War* (1521), his handbook to strategy, duplicity and ruthlessness, they were embedded in political culture, and were to become even more so as the century advanced. David Kahn, a historian of cryptology, writes that 'the growth of cryptology resulted directly from the flowering of modern diplomacy... resident ambassadors sent home regular reports – they have been called 'honorable spies' – and the jealousy, suspicion, and intrigues among the Italian city-states made it often necessary to encipher these.'

Mary's letters contain regular references to the ciphers she sent or received for the laborious process of decoding. In January 1586 she wrote to ambassador Guillaume de l'Aubespine de Châteauneuf: 'fearing that the despatch in cipher, which I lately sent to you by another conveyance, has not been delivered to you, I send you a duplicate, being unwilling to write in it any thing of importance until I am certain that you have received the alphabet here enclosed to serve hereafter between us, for this [i.e. the cipher she was currently using] has passed through too many hands to be relied on.'

Another letter, from 28 August 1571 to the Archbishop of Glasgow, her ambassador in Paris at the time, shows how rigorously the security around her was maintained. She complained that she could not write to him or the French ambassador 'except with much inconvenience and risk'. There was a strict search on the roads around Sheffield: 'I am so watched, and those who are with me, that what I write, or cause to be written, is stolen there; and from fear of surprise, not knowing when I may be visited or my repositories rifled, I immediately burn the draughts of the ciphers...' Later she adds, 'I have received two ciphers, which you sent me, I believe, from the nuncio; but I have not the countercipher for their key. Write to me how this should be done.'

Few nationalities were more sophisticated in ciphering and deciphering than the Italians, but the English were not far behind. The Spanish, by contrast, floundered. Philip II was so astonished that a seemingly unbreakable Spanish cipher had been cracked by the French that he attributed it to the black arts. With underground networks of spies and informants flourishing throughout Europe – as subterranean as tunnelling moles, but a great deal more sinister – spying became as necessary a tool for governance as diplomacy.

From her first weeks in captivity, Mary had been eager to find ways of contacting her allies without her captors' knowledge. There were periods when the guard around her was so tight that nothing could be smuggled out. At other times it was possible to evade detection by various stratagems, some of which she outlined in 1584 to ambassador Michel de Castelnau, Sieur de la Mauvissière:

> by the carriers I find it in nowise safe to write, unless all other means fail: in which event, the best and most secret writing is with alum dissolved in a very little clear water four-and-twenty hours before you wish to write; and, to read it, it is necessary only to dip the paper into a basin of clear water; the secret writing appears white, very easily read until the paper becomes dry again; you can in this way write on white taffeta, or white cloth, especially lawn [linen or cotton]: and, that it may be known between us when there is any thing written, it would be necessary to cut from the piece of taffeta or lawn a small piece out of one of the corners.

Alum was a chemical compound (potassium aluminium sulphate), naturally found in desert regions, such as North Africa, and around the Mediterranean. It was used in the Middle Ages in textile dying, for making glue and preparing paints, although it also had antibacterial and analgesic properties. How Mary managed to get her hands on it is unclear, unless it was allegedly for her apothecary's use. In 1586, after warning Châteauneuf about the risks of trusting in alum, she went on to instruct him how to use it if there was no other alternative. He was, she said, to write between the lines of new books that were sent (presumably for this very purpose) to her secretary Claude Nau. Writing on every fourth page, he must then attach a green ribbon to any book that contained a message.

As mentioned above, she explained that he could write on various different delicate cloths, and her instructions continued with the punctiliousness of a woman who leaves no *i* undotted nor *t* uncrossed:

> As for the packets which you already have, or may afterwards receive in cipher, you can send them to me closed, in place of

cork, in high slippers, this being a species of merchandize which every one has ordinarily to do here. Or rather unfold the letters and spread them out between the wood of the trunks and boxes which you shall send . . . Finally, to show if there is any paper in the slippers, put the marks of the points of the said slippers upon the sole over the heel, and, as for the boxes and trunks, let them have a padlock attached to the fold of the lock.

Nothing better illuminates Mary's vulnerable position in a lethal contest of spider and fly than the reliance she placed upon secret communications. Servants with passes to leave whichever castle or house where she lived (laundresses were particularly helpful in this regard) would be delegated to smuggle out these letters, as would visitors. Their ingenuity in hiding them in places where they could not be found is impressive, since so many reached their recipients undetected – in the early years, at least. That, however, was to change.

In May 1573, Mary's nemesis, Francis Walsingham, returned to England. The horrors he had witnessed during the St Bartholomew's Day Massacre in Paris had seemed to turn an already devout Puritan into an even more fanatical enemy of the Scottish queen and everything she stood for. He could think of no more malign presence in his country than this Catholic figurehead, who – he was certain – was hatching fatal conspiracies that would bring about Elizabeth's end. A clever, ruthless workaholic, Walsingham was consumed by his loathing of Mary, and his determination to destroy her.

Once relieved of his position as ambassador, in December 1573 Walsingham was appointed as Elizabeth's new principal secretary, replacing Burghley, who became lord high treasurer. The Queen now had a loyal coterie around her on whom she could utterly depend. You might see Walsingham, Burghley and her beloved Earl of Leicester as her three musketeers, an intellectual and administrative bodyguard devoted to her safety and, in the secretary's and lord high treasurer's case, working tirelessly on her behalf. Although there was nothing swashbuckling or frivolous about the three, Burghley and Walsingham did have a dry sense of humour that Alexandre Dumas might have appreciated.

In his new post, Walsingham irrevocably changed the face of the English state by establishing a far-reaching web of agents feeding back information from all quarters, both close to home and distant. Some of his sources were upright citizens, others decidedly not. Some were not working under cover but merely passing on knowledge they had gleaned. Others were as shady and double-dealing as George Smiley's slipperiest operatives.

Employing informants, spies and intelligencers was nothing new for governments on either side of the England–Scotland border. There was a centuries-old history of such activity, in which the most seemingly respectable of people could be the most effective informants. (One such was the prioress of Eccles, near the English border, whose information helped thwart a Scottish military campaign against Henry VIII.)

There had been nothing comparable, however, to the reach of Walsingham's reporters and moles, their number running into the hundreds, and their remuneration soon costing the treasury a small fortune. Such a covert and comprehensive system of information-gathering was almost Orwellian. Walsingham was the all-seeing eye, the ever-open ear, picking up word of treacherous talk or news of conspiracies, be it in a London tavern, an English port or a Scottish castle. If evidence were needed for the constant state of anxiety and alarm that characterised much of the Elizabethan era, Walsingham's *modus operandi* is it.

It did not take Mary long to recognise the threat the Queen's secretary posed. In 1574, she described him to the Archbishop of Glasgow as 'my mortal enemy'. Nevertheless, it is doubtful that she ever fully comprehended his efficiency and his nefariousness. Like so many religious fanatics, Walsingham was utterly unscrupulous. He could not afford to be squeamish about some of the spies he dealt with, nor about his own pitiless, shady or illegal tactics. Not when the state of England, the Protestant cause and the Queen's life depended on him.

It is little wonder Mary intrigued and schemed. In the aftermath of the Duke of Norfolk's arrest, the Earl of Shrewsbury's secretary wrote to Burghley informing him that Mary had told Shrewsbury that she would 'use what means she can to help herself to escape if she can, saying she had rather lose her life than lead this life'. Her increasing dependence on covert correspondence is symptomatic of her determination to free herself, at whatever cost. Fleeing her prisons was, of course, only the first step. She would have been well aware that, once she was at liberty, England would be in a perilous situation, at threat either from invading foreign powers or from civil war.

More than five years after entering England, the gulf between the dramatic and daring life Mary had lived in Scotland and her present suffocating confinement was stark. You could see these years, and those that followed, like a stage play: events unfolding beyond the theatre of her current fortress or stately home, while she sat, absorbing everything she could learn from the outside world, and by means of her letters – official and secret – trying to direct her affairs to a better outcome.

The effect of captivity on this once free spirit, who loved nothing more than riding at full tilt across the moors, was in some senses disastrous. Her always precarious health worsened steadily until by the age of thirty she had become a semi-invalid. Yet despite, or more probably because of what she had to endure, both physically and psychologically, Mary gradually matured into a resourceful, resilient woman, very different from her younger self. Religion played a role in this transformation. Though hitherto a stalwart Catholic, she now became devout. Being seen to be a beacon of her faith was a crucial component of her identity and ultimately a defining element of her tragedy. When, fourteen years later, she went to her death, she clung to her image as one persecuted for her beliefs.

The meekness this suggests is misleading. As Mary's own web of informants and secret messengers attest, she was anything but a passive victim. The relish with which she despatched letters and her ability to dissemble suggest she had a talent for outwitting her enemies and enjoyed the excitement of doing so. In some ways she was a born adventurer who only discovered her capacity for scheming and subterfuge when no other path was available. In the words of J. D. Leader, who was no admirer, 'Mary Stuart's was not a life marked by an occasional conspiracy. It was from first to last one long conspiracy of vast intricacy and varying interest.'

As Mary's days in prison lengthened and her prospects of being set at liberty shrank, her life revolved around her coded correspondence, to an unhealthy degree. Living a double life – the docile captive, and the plotter – she spent the most thrilling, hopeful part of her existence in the shadows, writing late into the night, and waiting impatiently for replies to her never-ending stream of missives. There was a feverishness about Mary's conspiratorial efforts that makes it hard to disagree with David Kahn when he writes: 'There seems little doubt that she would have died before her time, the politics of the day being what they were. But there seems equally little doubt that cryptology hastened her unnatural end.'

Chapter 17

'I am very fond of my little dogs'

AMUSEMENTS

In the decade from the early 1570s to 1583, Mary lived between Sheffield Castle, Sheffield Manor Lodge and Chatsworth, with occasional visits to Buxton. Keeping her clandestine existence hidden from all but her closest companions, she ostensibly filled her life with the pursuits of the housebound aristocrat. That she was an avid reader is evident from her letters, although precisely what books she was reading is unclear. An inventory of her belongings taken at Chartley in July 1586 records a Book of Hours, inscribed by her, an '*histoire de la Passion*' and '*grands livres d'histoires*', suggesting her taste for devotional books and history. There is also mention of 'a greate number of bookes', but what these were remains tantalisingly obscure.

Her voluminous correspondence suggests letter-writing must have absorbed at least as much of her time as reading. And, whether in the company of Bess of Hardwick, or with her attendants and servants, she spent long hours embroidering and stitching, to the point where she complained her fingers hurt. Requests for threads and fabrics and dress patterns fill her letters, as in the following note, sent from Sheffield to the French ambassador Mothe-Fénelon: 'all my exercise is to read and work in my chamber; and therefore I beseech you . . . to send me, as soon as you can, four ounces more or less of the same crimson silk which you sent me some time ago . . . The silver is too thick; I beg you will choose it for me as fine as the pattern, and send it to me by the first conveyance, with eight ells of crimson taffeta for lining. If I have it not soon my work must stand still, for which I shall be very vexed, as what I am working is not for myself.'

Mary despatched countless requests and awaited their arrival like an online shopper drumming her fingers for the courier's van. It was, perhaps, a way of reminding herself that she was not entirely immolated or invisible. Despite rarely seeing anyone beyond her immediate companions, it was as important as it had ever been for her to maintain a wardrobe fitting for what has been called her 'mimic court'. Not for a moment was anyone allowed to forget her status as a sovereign. In this respect, her fondness for expensive clothes was not mere vanity but an integral part of the ostentatious display with which Stewart royalty imposed their image. It was also a private passion.

Shortly after Mary arrived in Scotland as a young queen, an inventory of her wardrobe showed how richly she liked to dress once she had abandoned her mourning clothes. Drawing on her household books, the early nineteenth-century antiquarian George Chalmers described her everyday attire. She had 'gownes, vaskenis [petticoats], skirts, sleeves, doublets, veils, fardingales [Spanish farthingales, or hooped skirts], cloikis, . . . wolven hois [woven hose] of gold, silver, and silk, three pair of woven hose of worsted of Guernsey. She had thirty six pair of velvet shoes, passamented [laced] with gold and silver. She had six pair of gloves of worsted of Guernsey.'

Her ordinary gowns were made variously of camlet and damask, and her riding cloaks and skirts were of black serge of Florence, with lace and ribbons adding a flourish. Also listing the embellishments to her household, such as Turkish carpets, tablecloths, chairs and stools covered in velvet and edged with fringes, Chalmers came to the ignorant conclusion that all this, along with her clothes 'might be allowed to have something of the tawdry appearance of a pawnbroker's warehouse'.

As she entered her thirties and forties, there was no sign of Mary's love of clothes diminishing. In July 1574, she wrote to the Archbishop of Glasgow asking him to tell her French dressmaker Jean de

Compiègne, to find 'patterns of dresses, and of cloth of gold and silver, and of silks, the handsomest and the rarest that are worn at court'. At the same time, she requested 'a couple of head-dresses, with a crown of gold and silver, such as were formerly made for me'. From Italy, she summoned 'some new fashions of head-dresses, veils, and ribbons with gold and silver'.

Though she might spend her days only with the countess and her companions, she refused to become slovenly. As her waist thickened and her beauty dimmed, there was evidently consolation in clothes of the finest, softest, most desirable materials. Her diet was equally refined. Dining sumptuously, she also took comfort in liqueurs, which appear frequently in her shopping lists. Eau de canelle, made from cinnamon, one of the world's oldest spices, was a favourite. Today, *l'eau à la cannelle*, when taken as a hot drink, is acclaimed as a *digestif* and a way to control weight, both of which attributes Mary would have appreciated.

Ill health was to cast a shadow over Mary for the rest of her days, and she asked constantly for medicines to alleviate her assorted conditions. Some of these, one suspects, had a psychosomatic root, but there is no question that Mary suffered dreadfully at times, her symptoms suggesting possibly a stomach ulcer as well as rheumatic and other debilitating and agonising disorders. On several occasions, as we have seen, she was believed to be close to death. Her stoicism in the face of such misery was remarkable; despite days when she gave in to self-pity or was engulfed by despair, she was by nature an optimist, determined not to be cast down by her afflictions, and seeking strength from her faith.

A typical medicinal request, made in 1571 to Mothe-Fénelon, reads: 'the ointment which was used rubbing my side and my stomach is exhausted, and both are very much worse. I pray you send me some of it, along with cinnamon water and confected nutmegs. Air and exercise are denied me, and thereby my health declines very far.' Among the more unusual remedies she asked for was a famous antidote to poison (and the plague), much used in the Renaissance era. Writing to Mothe-Fénelon in 1573, she asked him to send 'the

Mithridate of which I wrote to you, the best and most safely as it can be done.' A potion made in Italy and France from dozens of ingredients including acacia juice, cardamom, ginger, frankincense and opium, mithridate was deemed as essential to the royal medicine cabinet as paracetamol is to ours. A pair of ornate, water-tight drug jars, dating to the 1580s and now held in the J. Paul Getty Museum in Los Angeles, are the work of the Milanese sculptor Annibale Fontana. Suitable for display in Fontainebleau or Holyrood, they give an idea of the typical purchaser of this exotic concoction.

From the sometimes imperious tone of Mary's letters, it seems she expected the best of everything. But she was not always granted what she wished. In a revealing aside, she wrote: 'The Countess of Shrewsbury assured me that the right way to cause anything whatever to be denied me, was to signify that it would be particularly agreeable to me, and then I must never expect to have it.' In 1577 she told Archbishop Beaton that she had received the bed he had sent for her 'infirmities', but that it was refused by Shrewsbury's people. 'In the meanwhile,' she continued, 'I am requested to procure half-a-dozen great hall-candlesticks . . . I beg that you will obtain for me the largest, finest, richest and best made that you can, and send them to me, carefully packed, through the medium of M. de Mauvissière, directing them to Nau, as if were some things wanted in the name of some one of his brother-servants, so that they may create no consequence, without being seen at court.' As always, she insisted that she be told what had been spent on her behalf, so that she could reimburse the purchaser. This was a rare trait in royalty, and one in keeping with her sincere concern for the welfare of those who worked on her behalf.

Like many landed gentry, then and today, Mary surrounded herself with dogs, including poodles (known as barbets), greyhounds and hunting dogs. 'I am very fond of my little dogs; but I am afraid they will grow large,' she told the Archbishop of Glasgow. She complained, however, that 'I am a prisoner, and, therefore, cannot form any opinion of the dogs, except of their beauty, for I am not allowed to ride out on horseback, or to the chase.' 'You must buy me two more [dogs],' she instructed him on another occasion, 'for, besides writing and work, I take pleasure only in all the little animals that I can get. You must send them in baskets, that they may be kept very warm.'

In Scotland, she had upwards of thirteen dogs at any time – many of them lapdogs – whose care and upkeep, such as the cost of their bejewelled collars, is recorded in the accounts of the lord high treasurer. While in Sheffield, she urged her ambassadors to send her 'small dogs', and, when they did not promptly arrive, reminded them in her next letter.

But she amassed more than dogs, collecting animals as if they were shoes. Her rooms housed an aviary, the songs and cries of birds filling the too-quiet air. Writing to the ever-obliging Archbishop Beaton in July 1574, she begged him to procure 'some turtle-doves, and some Barbary fowls [a type of partridge]'. She explains:

> I wish to try if I can rear them in this country, as your brother told me that, when he was with you, he had raised some in a cage, as also some red partridges; and send me, by the person who brings them to London, instructions how to manage them. I shall take great pleasure in rearing them in cages, which I do all sorts of little birds I can meet with. This will be amusement for a prisoner . . .

The irony of a captive keeping prisoners of her own cannot, surely, have escaped her. Nor was such an activity always as innocent as it seemed. When Mary asked the Earl of Shrewsbury to allow her to have pigeons, he suspected her intention was to use them as messengers.

The attention and affection Mary showed these creatures could be seen as a symptom of her yearning for her son, although even before his birth she was a devoted animal-lover. Much as she adored them, however, she was even more concerned about the wellbeing of her staff. Pages are consumed by screeds of her complaints about her servants not being paid what they were owed. One particular favourite was young Willie Douglas, from Lochleven Castle, who remained in her service throughout her captive life. He meant so much to her that he was remembered in her final will.

With her son two hundred and fifty miles distant, and her gifts and letters rarely reaching him, Mary fretted about how well he was being treated, and whether he was in good health. Since he had suffered from rickets as a child, which left him with an out-turned foot and weak legs, her anxiety was not misplaced. Had she known the circumstances in which he was being raised – as a staunch Calvinist whose mother was deemed a heretic – she would have been appalled. For many years, Mary lived under the illusion that James loved her as she loved him and would do anything to bring about her release. When that unfounded belief was eventually shattered, so too was Mary. From that point, she had nothing to lose, and was quickly engulfed in tragedy.

For the moment, though, while time was crawling in her various prisons, James was in the care of the Countess and Earl of Mar, in the formidable Stirling Castle. On the earl's death in 1572, James's military guard was put into the hands of Alexander Erskine of Gogar, and between them he and the countess kept a close eye on every detail of the child's upbringing. A portrait of James aged around eight, which is attributed to Arnold van Bronckorst, shows a boy with exceptionally pale skin, pale blue eyes and washed-out red hair, who looks at the viewer with a steady, watchful gaze. One hand rests on his waist, and on the other a falcon perches. There is majesty in this picture, but little joie de vivre. Another portrait, by an unknown artist, which is held in the Scottish National Portrait Gallery, shows a much livelier, more robust-looking child. With closely cropped deep auburn hair and an exquisitely lacy ruff, this boy is smiling, his sparkling eyes filled with life and character. In his delicate complexion and fine features there is a glimpse of his mother.

At Stirling Castle, the young king dressed in rich black velvet, his attendants wearing yellow and red tunics, parading the Stewart colours. In the cheerless schoolroom, James was given a rigorous classical and humanist education by the increasingly irascible George Buchanan, described by the biographer Steven Veerapen as, 'a thoroughly tetchy, sharp-tongued, short-tempered old man, who appears to have sought to batter his student into accepting his ideas under the weight of his rhetoric, his experience, his authority and – when these failed to make an impression – his fists.'

Nightmares of Buchanan would afflict James for the rest of his life, but his education was not entirely miserable. Working alongside Buchanan was Peter Young, a gentle, kindly teacher, who offered light to Buchanan's dark. Among Young's contributions to the king's school years was the recovery of over 220 books from Mary's library. By the late 1570s, James had a library of around 600 books, a priceless treasure for this era. Delivered into Buchanan and Young's scholastic care in 1570, when he was four, James was taught in the company of a handful of other aristocratic boys, including the Countess of Mar's son and Alexander Erskine of Gogar's two boys. He was to retain a lifelong affection for all his schoolfellows, and in later life they would profit handsomely from his patronage.

The education these elite classmates received was rigorous and demanding by today's standards. Thankfully the young king was a quick and eager learner, impressing onlookers with his precocious linguistic skills. Able to speak Latin from an early age, he was soon taught Greek and French, along with history, logic, rhetoric, moral philosophy and theology, a subject in which Buchanan excelled. Some lessons were drawn from Buchanan's own writings, and the diehard Calvinist no doubt relished using scurrilous examples of Mary's behaviour to teach of the dangers of treachery or deceit. He also tried to instil in the boy an appreciation of kingship as a position contingent on moral stature, rather than something divinely bestowed. Some years later, when no longer under his tutelage, James roundly refuted Buchanan's revolutionary – some might say treasonous – views on the monarchy.

His other teachings, however, made an indelible mark. By the time James assumed power, at the age of twelve, he had been not only classically drilled and inculcated with Protestant ideology but also indoctrinated to think the worst of Mary. This was emotional cruelty of a high order, calculated to create an irreparable breach between son and Catholic mother.

The social historian Rosalind Mitchison believes that James 'grew up to be the most intelligent of the Stewarts, the last intellectual to grace the throne of Scotland and, more important, the biggest success of them all'. The intensity of his education allowed his natural precocity to shine, but alongside his academic studies James was tutored in the arts of archery, riding and hunting, pursuits he embraced with equal enthusiasm. At this age he already had his own stables, and staff to look after his horses and hawks; when he was older, these would become one of the most important elements of his household. Also provided for his amusement were the castle musicians, whose playing must have lightened the atmosphere of this imposing fortress. Of this, Mary would have approved. A family from Yorkshire, called the Hudsons, they had been employed by James's father in the fleetingly happy days of his marriage and appear to have become essential to the royal household. As well as playing for the king's pleasure, they taught him how to dance, an essential skill for a monarch.

All this suggests that James was not shackled every hour of the day to schoolwork but could enjoy some of the delights of a noble childhood. And unlike many aristocratic children, after 1571, when the risk of being sent to England as a hostage on his mother's behalf faded, he was never in danger of being placed in another household as an attendant to learn the ropes of his social class. In this, if not in other respects, he was fortunate. Nevertheless, he emerges from the shadows of Stirling Castle as a clever but emotionally needy boy. Those around him treated him with deference (Buchanan excepted) and lavished him with attention and care, but with no mother or father at his side, and no memory of either, he was effectively an orphan, cast on the political tide.

In August 1571, when he was five, James read his first official speech at the opening of Parliament. Written by his grandfather, the Regent, Matthew Stewart, Earl of Lennox, it stated that, being too young to rule, he placed the country in his grandfather's hands. The child fidgeted throughout his time on public view. Discovering a hole in the tablecloth before him, he excitedly announced this to the chamber. Less amusingly, a few days later he was present at his grandfather's

Left. Portrait of Mary, Queen of Scots while on the Scottish throne. Painted by an unknown artist, *c.* 1560–92.
(Historic Images/Alamy Stock Photo)

Below. Workington Hall in Cumbria, where Mary spent her first night in England.
(Author's collection)

Right. Queen Elizabeth I, who resisted Mary's pleas to meet, or be set free.
(iStock.com/Gwengoat)

Below. Cockermouth Castle in Cumbria, where Mary slept in a chair in dread of the Earl of Moray catching up with her.
(Author's collection)

Left. Mary's half-brother, James Stewart, Earl of Moray, who became Regent of Scotland after her enforced abdication. (iStock.com/GeorgiosArt)

Below. The entrance gateway and formidable keep of Carlisle Castle. (iStock/Westhoff)

Above. The site of Queen Mary's Tower in Carlisle Castle, where Mary was kept under close guard. (Author's collection)

Right. Sir William Cecil, later Lord Burghley, Elizabeth I's most trusted advisor. (The Print Collector/Heritage Images/Alamy Stock Photo)

Left. Henry Stuart, Lord Darnley, Mary's ill-fated second husband.
(iStock/RockingStock)

Below. The exquisitely tooled silver casket, made in Paris between 1480 and 1506, in which letters allegedly showing Mary's collusion in Darnley's murder were discovered.
(Image © National Museums Scotland)

Right. Mummified head of James Hepburn, Earl of Bothwell, who was buried near Dragsholm Castle, Denmark. (Author's collection)

Below. The almost impregnable Bolton Castle, Yorkshire. (Author's collection)

Above. Lord Scrope's chamber, on the top floor of Bolton Castle, where Mary is most likely to have slept.
(Author's collection)

Left. James VI, by Arnold Bronckorst, when he was about eight.
(Heritage Image Partnership Ltd / Alamy Stock Photo)

The gateway to Tutbury Castle, in Staffordshire, Mary's most hated residence. (Author's collection)

The relatively comfortable south range of Tutbury Castle, where Mary lived on her early visits. (Author's collection)

Left. George Talbot, Earl of Shrewsbury, who was Mary's custodian for almost 15 years. (The History Collection/Alamy Stock Photo)

Below. The ruins of Wingfield Manor in Derbyshire, described by Mary as 'a fair palace'. (iStock.com/DavidMuscroft)

Right. St Mary's Guildhall in Coventry (behind the timbered building), a superb reminder of the city's medieval heyday. (Author's collection)

Below left. Elizabeth Talbot, Countess of Shrewsbury, known as Bess of Hardwick. (Abbus Archive Images/ Alamy Stock Photo)

Below right. The Hunting Tower at Chatsworth, almost unchanged since its completion in 1582. (Author's collection)

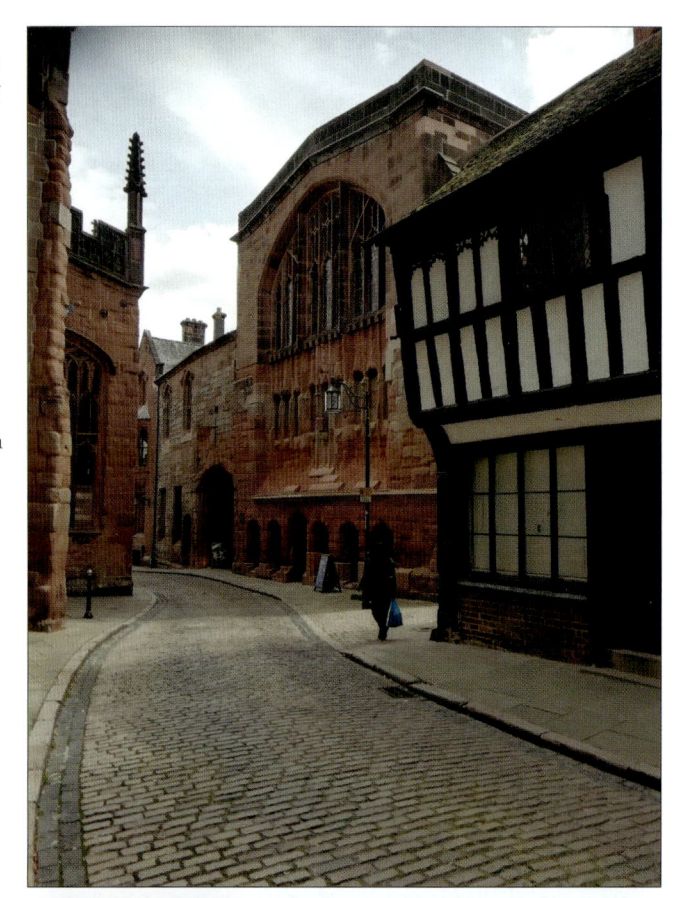

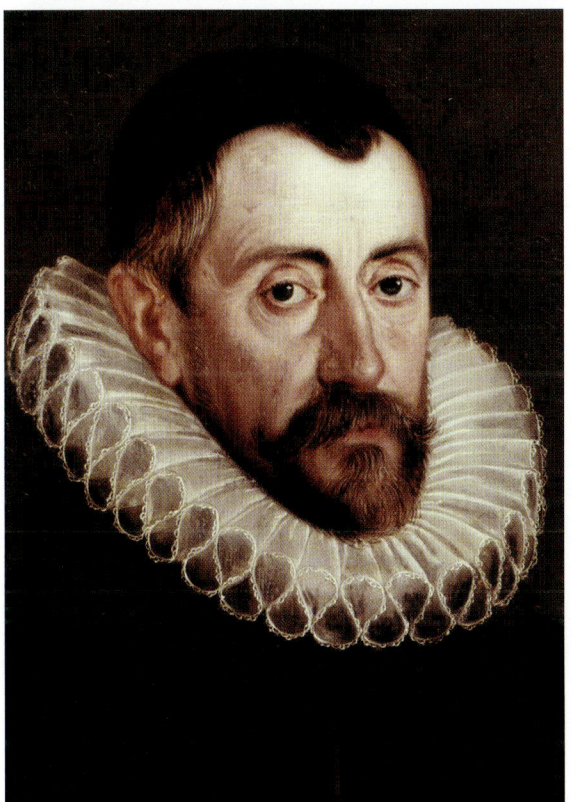

Above. The Old Queens Head pub in Sheffield, thought to have been the laundry for Sheffield Castle, and possibly connected by tunnel to Sheffield Manor Lodge. (Author's collection)

Left. Sir Francis Walsingham, Elizabeth's spymaster. (GRANGER Historical Picture Archive/Alamy Stock Photo)

The Turret House at Sheffield Manor Lodge, where Mary spent many hours embroidering with Bess of Hardwick. (Author's collection)

Old Hall Hotel, Buxton. Mary stayed in the oldest part of the hotel while visiting the spa town. (Author's collection)

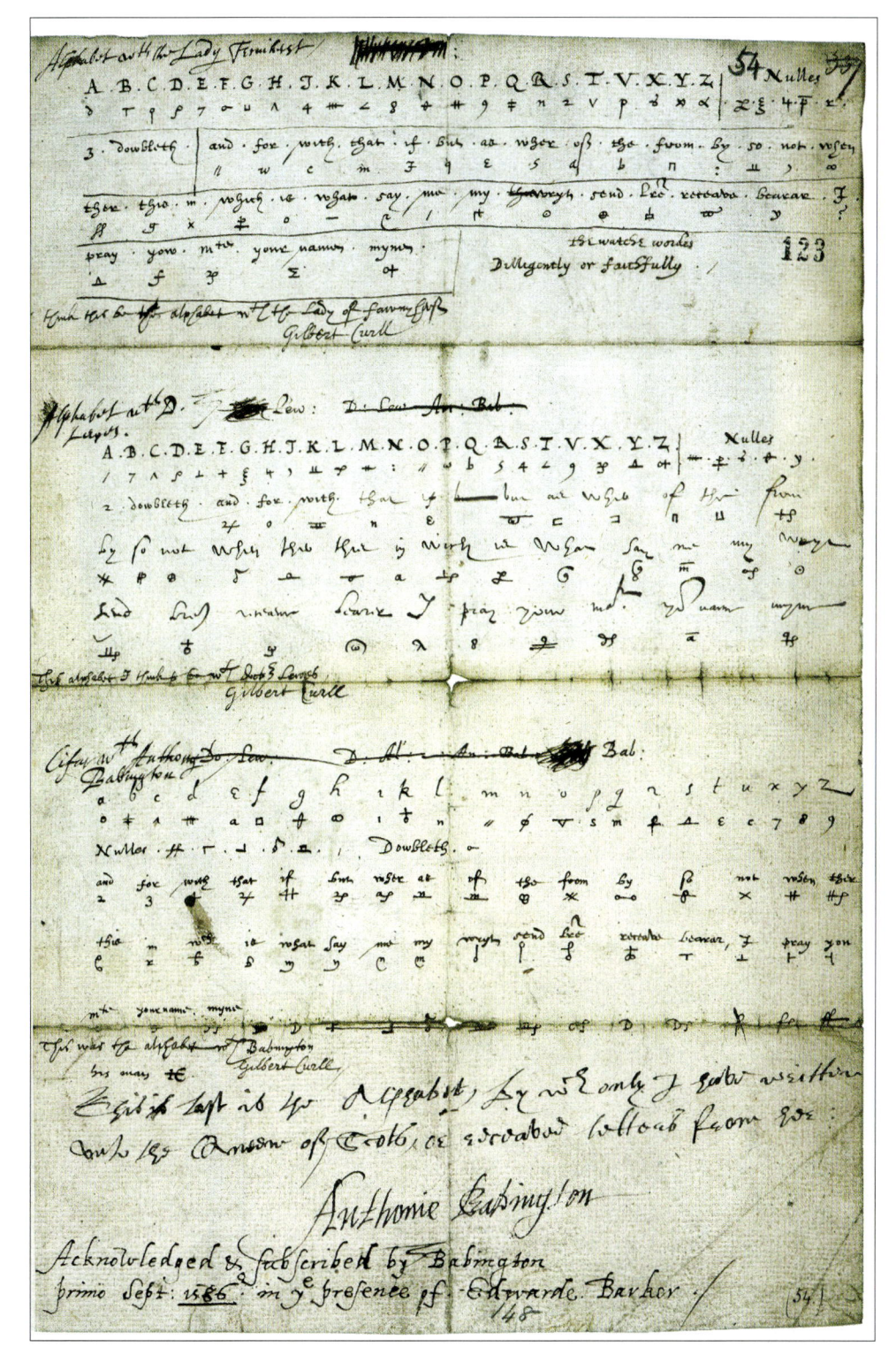

The ciphers used by Anthony Babington and Mary when corresponding. Babington's signed statement reads 'this last is the alphabet by which only I have written unto the Queen of Scots or received letters from her'. (piemags/AN24 / Alamy Stock Photo)

Philip II of Spain, whose territorial ambitions included invading England. (iStock.com/Gwengoat)

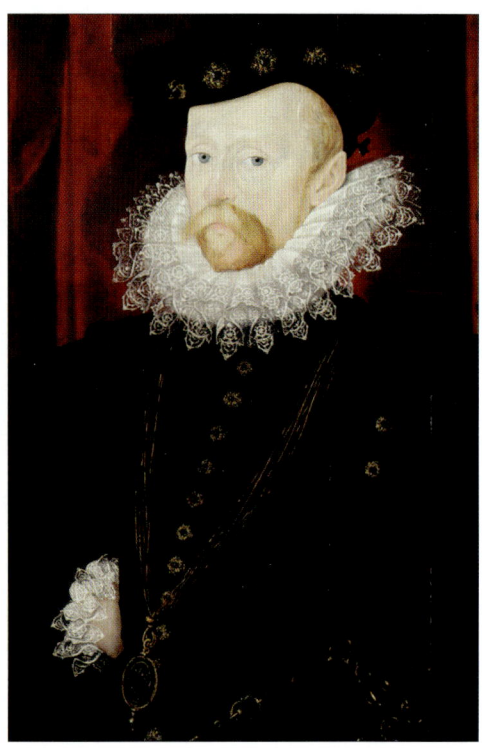

Sir Amias Paulet, Mary's harshest custodian. (The Picture Art Collection/Alamy Stock Photo)

Tixall Gatehouse, all that survives of Tixall Hall. (Author's collection)

Robert Beale's eyewitness drawing of Mary's execution. (Ian Dagnall Computing/Alamy Stock Photo)

Above. What remains of Fotheringhay Castle, with a plaque commemorating Mary's death.
(iStock.com/wzfs1s)

Right. Head of Mary Queen of Scots after Decollation by Amias Cawood. Experts are unable to verify if it was painted at the time of her death or shortly afterwards.
(The Faculty of Advocates Abbotsford Collection Trust)

death. Shot in the back during an attempted raid on Stirling Castle by the Hamilton party, the earl was carried into the castle, where the child witnessed him dying. This bloody episode would have been traumatic, the horror and chaos of the scene something James could never forget. The new Regent, the Earl of Mar, lived only for a year (as mentioned earlier he died, possibly of natural causes, after dining with the Earl of Morton), and Morton, who succeeded him as Regent, was eventually executed. From his youngest days, the heavily guarded James, whose father had been murdered, was uncomfortably aware of the ever-present threat of sudden, violent death.

Mary's feelings for her son were no doubt complicated by the political implications of his role as the now uncontested king of Scotland, occupying the position that was, by right, hers. All such considerations paled, however, beside her concern for his welfare. Her enforced separation from her child, and the machinations of those who worked to alienate James from her, are among the most poignant and reprehensible aspects of her years in exile.

Mary was by nature loving, kind and maternal, showering her attendants and servants with gifts and attention. She must surely have wept at the loss of contact with her son. Doubtless, the arrival of other children in the Shrewsburys' household helped lift her spirits. Bess's first grandchild, Bessie de Pierrepoint, to whom Mary was a godmother, became one of her handmaidens when she was four. Mary was enchanted by her, calling her '*mignonne*', or little one, and made her a special occasion dress in black. Bessie would eat at the queen's table, and even share her bed, as royal companions sometimes did.

Given how much Mary enjoyed the child's company, a letter from 1586, less than a year before her execution, makes sad reading. The queen asks Châteauneuf to make arrangements for Bessie to be returned to her parents, and for her to be well provided for: 'to tell you more frankly, I desire, for many reasons, to be well quit of her, especially on account of her grandmother'. By this time, Mary and Bess loathed each other, a mutual antipathy that began in the mid 1570s, and would make both their lives uncomfortable. Compounding her grandmother's meddling, it was young Bessie's misfortune to have inherited some of the countess's imperious personality, making her presence increasingly irksome to the queen.

Before the rift with the countess, Mary continued to be closely involved with the Shrewsbury family. She stood godmother to another of Bess's grandchildren, George Talbot, heir to the Shrewsbury title, on whose shoulders the family name would, it was assumed, come to rest. But the most significant new addition to the Shrewsbury family, in terms of Bess's dynastic ambitions, was Arbella Stuart. Born at Chatsworth in November 1575, Arbella was the first-born of Bess's daughter Elizabeth Cavendish and her husband Charles Stuart, the younger brother of Lord Darnley. It was natural that, for her first birth, Elizabeth Cavendish chose to be at her mother's residence. Bess's experience at this nerve-racking time would have helped reassure her. Also useful would have been Chatsworth's herb garden, providing medicinal plants such as rue, which helped reduce labour pains, and others, such as thyme and ivy, which could be used for other disorders following birth.

Arbella was safely delivered, in the midst of the political furore surrounding her existence. Her parents' marriage was the result of an unashamed and risky act of matchmaking on the part of Bess and Charles Stuart's mother, Margaret Douglas, Countess of Lennox, who deliberately engineered a meeting between Charles and Elizabeth. Their plans came to fruition when the couple immediately fell for each other. Marriage swiftly followed, but without Queen Elizabeth's permission. Since Charles was a direct descendant of Henry VII, with a claim to the English throne, they had brazenly flouted the convention by which all members of the royal family must gain the monarch's permission before marrying.

The ramifications of this union were potentially serious for Elizabeth I. Almost overnight, the Countess of Shrewsbury's daughter had become sister-in-law to Mary, Queen of Scots, and should she and Charles have a child, he or she would stand next in line to the throne after Mary, James and Margaret, Countess of Lennox. Enraged at their temerity, the Queen had the Countess of Lennox incarcerated in the Tower of London and Bess's daughter and her new husband kept under house arrest in London. After three anxious months in prison, the Countess of Lennox joined them there; their collective confinement eventually came to an end that summer.

Bess, on the other hand, emerged relatively unscathed, and with high hopes. When baby Arbella arrived, Queen Elizabeth was relieved she was not a boy, and Bess was dazzled by the glittering prospects that lay ahead. As Mary S. Lovell writes, 'here was a child with royal Stuart blood, who could be groomed for a great marriage – a possible bride for the boy king James of Scotland, for example.' Were the aged Countess of Lennox and the ever-ailing Mary, Queen of Scots to die, she would be second in line to the throne of England. This was tantalising for a woman like Bess, whose social aspirations were stratospheric. When the Countess of Lennox died in 1578, like an advancing chess piece, Arbella moved one step closer to the crown.

In many respects, the lives of the nobility's children were less enviable than those of the yeomanry or the educated middling sort, and sometimes even of the poor. Rather than be nursed by their mothers, aristocratic infants were often handed to wet nurses, as happened with James VI. The women providing this service were closely vetted, since it was believed that their moral character would be absorbed with their milk. Even so, advice for parents of this era was that infants did best to be nursed by their mothers, and most women did so, as had their own mothers and grandmothers. As well as bonding mother to child, breast-feeding had the advantage of delaying further pregnancies. There was no such reprieve for noble wives, since their paramount role was to provide heirs and 'spares', to ward against the almost inevitable death of some of their brood.

Babies of Arbella's rank were welcomed into the world with real love and affection, but they were also pawns in a competitive, ruthless dynastic system. In lesser households, infants and children were the fulcrum of their parents' lives, much as they are today. Despite evidence of severe treatment, such as Buchanan's thrashing of James and, no doubt, his classmates too, and instances of extreme harshness, such as making a child drink a pint of its own urine after wetting the bed, for the most part parents treated their children with kindness. Even moralists advised merely chastising them for bad behaviour and only resorting to 'the rod' when all else had failed.

As Buchanan's fondness for corporal punishment shows, schoolmasters as a breed seem not to have absorbed this lesson, and grammar schools were rife with savagery disguised as moral instruction. But although there were, of course, cases of appalling domestic abuse and neglect, at every level of society, children were not as badly treated as once assumed. Interestingly, there are accounts suggesting that those from poorer families were less strictly disciplined than their wealthier peers, even though parents often relied on the labours of their youngsters to help keep the household afloat. Tasks suitable to their age – such as spinning, watching flocks or, when older, ploughing – could bring in a vital income.

Children whose better-off families could afford for them to be educated enjoyed a version of childhood that would be recognisable to today's school-goers. Only when they reached fourteen or fifteen were they expected to go into service or bind themselves as apprentices, at which point their independent adult lives commenced. The only generalisation that can be made about children in Elizabethan England is that childhood was short (as, too often, was adulthood).

It has been estimated that in the late sixteenth and seventeenth centuries, around a quarter of all children died before they were ten, with mortality worst during their first twelve months. Yet, contrary to received wisdom amongst many earlier historians, parents were not emotionally detached from their offspring lest they die young. To read diaries, wills or autobiographies from this period – see Samuel Pepys, for example – is to find a depth and range of parental emotion, commitment and pleasure in their response to their children that feels strikingly modern. What you also find are religiously devout parents negotiating with God for their child's welfare, or promising not to love them too much in case this brings calamity upon them.

One father, who believed his prayers had saved his baby son, prayed in his diary 'that we may not sett our affections too much vppon him or any worldly thinge but graunt that we may love the creatures in thee & for thee'. It was a roundabout way of trying to disarm God. As the Reformation expert Alec Ryrie writes, his words 'express a fear that if [they] loved their son in an excessive or disorderly way, it would actually provoke God to take him from them'.

Arbella might have been born into wealth, but her early life was not charmed. Before her first birthday, her father, Charles, died of consumption. After her mother also died, in 1582, she joined the ranks of the countless thousands who lost one or both their parents while they were children. Even so, she was luckier than some, since she was largely raised by the Countess of Shrewsbury. Bess would have been a warm-hearted and careful guardian. She was also determined to protect her granddaughter's prospects. Thus, in her inimitable manner, she fought to have Arbella's right to the Lennox title confirmed. Mary, Queen of Scots seems to have been co-opted into this scheme. In an unsigned will in 1577, she bestowed the earldom on the girl she called her 'niece', although nothing ever came of this.

With youngsters bringing life and cheer to Sheffield Manor Lodge and Sheffield Castle, Mary's thoughts must have turned daily to her own child. In her letters she frequently begged for information about James. Like any mother in this era, she was keenly aware of how vulnerable children were to illness and accidents. Despite this, it was shocking when Bess's first grandchild, the lively and lovable George Talbot, died suddenly in 1577, before the age of three. One day he was mischievous, the next he was gone. The household was stricken, and George's grandparents bereft. Both the earl and the countess could be steely, but they were also devoted to their grandchildren. Bess in particular loved babies and toddlers, and still mourned the loss of two infant daughters of her own.

Where an Elizabethan upbringing differed markedly from our own times is in attitudes to a child's illness and impending death. The Protestant faith offered fewer comforting deathbed rituals than Catholicism. In addition it raised the frightening thought that, if their souls were not saved, the dying might go to Hell. Consequently, parents would not only attempt to comfort a child who was very ill and seemed in danger of imminent death, but would also urge them, if they were old enough to understand, to put their trust in Jesus.

At one of the most dreadful moments of their lives – for the dying and the family they left behind – religious certainties were leaned on for support. The Earl of Shrewsbury echoed the belief of many when he accepted – reluctantly – that George's death was part of God's plan, and that the Almighty had only 'lent' him to his family. Even very young children were taught to believe in the afterlife and the notion that angels would come to carry them away. Some took solace in the knowledge that they would soon be reunited with parents or siblings who had died before them. Others were urged to take heart because they would soon be in the arms of a father even more loving than their own. Those who were told that they were heading for Heaven appear to have found this reassuring. They even, at times, were able to comfort their anguished parents, telling them they were going to a better place.

Because of the high rate of child mortality, the subject of death was openly discussed even with the very young. A minister called James Janeway wrote a book for youthful readers called *A Token for Children* (1671–72). Its opening is startling by modern standards: 'Did you never hear of a little Child that died? . . . How do you know but that you may be the next Child that may die? And where are you then, if you be not God's Child?'

To contemporary readers, death is far too disturbing a subject for young minds. Yet in Mary's age, and in the following century, it needed to be talked about. One of the least comprehensible and disturbing aspects of a sixteenth-century childhood (and far beyond) was the emphasis on children being sinners, no matter their tender age. As a result, emphasising the need to be God-fearing and upright was seen as building a child's armoury against whatever might befall them. Thankfully, despite this unhealthy obsession with sin, there was also a general assumption that when children died, they were bound for heaven, regardless of how they had lived. This seems to have brought a degree of solace to many who were otherwise distraught.

The death of little George Talbot was a miserable time for everyone, and for Mary it followed on from other relatively recent losses. In May 1574, her brother-in-law Charles IX died at the age of twenty-three, to be succeeded by his brother Henri III. The younger brother of her husband Francis, King of France, Charles had grown up with Mary at the French court, a carefree period she would recall with nostalgia. Now another of her childhood companions was gone. It would not be surprising if, on hearing the news, memories of her late husband and his tragically early death filled her thoughts.

Shortly after this loss, Mary realised that her staunchly loyal French secretary, Pierre Raulet, was grievously ill, 'being decidedly consumptive, or I am much mistaken, for he has a continual wheezing, and is quite bent'. She was not mistaken. Despite insisting to the end that he was fit for work, and resenting anyone trying to take over his duties, Raulet died in August. His demise was to create an opening for a new secretary, an opportunity of which Elizabeth and Walsingham appear to have taken advantage. But the blow that struck Mary most closely was the death at the end of 1574 of her uncle, Charles, Cardinal of Lorraine. Despite, or perhaps oblivious to, the underhand financial dealings of her Guise uncles, she was deeply grieved: 'God has bereft me of one of those persons whom I most loved; what shall I say more? He has bereft me, at one blow, of my father and my uncle.'

The late eighteenth-century historian Edmund Lodge took a more detached view: 'he died in 1574, universally detested, as the chief author of those calamities with which the fiery zeal of his family had afflicted France for several years past'. J.D. Leader was no more impressed by the cardinal and Mary's other French relatives, who, knowing she was helpless to do anything about it, had been siphoning off her dowry: 'the authors of the massacre of St Bartholomew were not the people to hesitate to rob a widow'.

Chapter 18

'She cannot do ill while she is with my husband'

MARRIAGE BREAKDOWN

How did Mary feel, being closely bound up in the lives of her captors, yet desperate to escape their hold? To the inevitable resentment and anger can be added suspicion and not a little fear. By 1577, another element was flung into this volatile mix. Since the middle of the decade, the Earl of Shrewsbury had been growing uncharacteristically irascible and unpredictable. Was this because his health was declining, or because he and Bess were spending too much time apart? While she was frequently absent, overseeing work at Chatsworth and enjoying the delights of her sumptuous new home, he was obliged to remain close to Mary. Perhaps, his wife suspected, too close.

A tantalising postscript to a letter from Bess to her husband in May 1577 has been analysed as closely as if it were one of the Dead Sea Scrolls: 'I have sent you some lettuce for that you love them. And every second day some is sent to your charge [Mary] and you; I have nothing else to send. Let me hear how you, your charge and love, do, and commend me I pray.' The words appear to be loaded: accusing him of being in love with Mary, and coldly informing him that she has no affection to spare for him. Such an inference, if correct, was soon confirmed. When asked by Elizabeth how Mary was faring, Bess replied: 'she cannot do ill while she is with my husband, and I begin to grow jealous, they are so great together'. It might have been a throwaway remark, but it seems clear that, whether or not Mary was the root of the problem, the Shrewsburys' marriage was under severe strain.

The precise nature of the earl's relationship with Mary can never be known, but he was sufficiently accommodating of her wishes to cause rumours to fly around the court. This was almost inevitable: any proximity with a woman widely acknowledged to be one of Europe's most alluring royals would have caused tongues to wag. Speculation grew so lurid it was said that Mary had secretly borne the earl one or more children. Such tales were nothing more than malicious gossip, in which all courts excelled. When these allegations reached Elizabeth's ears, she was unlikely to have believed them. In response to Mary's indignation, however, she felt obliged, in 1584, to bring Bess and her sons Charles and William before the Privy Council to answer Mary's charge that they were the source of these stories. All three vehemently denied playing any part in feeding the rumour-mill and were exonerated.

Even so, Elizabeth was perpetually and sometimes justifiably worried that Shrewsbury was over-lenient with his charge. Mary had always been able effortlessly to charm the men in her orbit; even John Knox – more susceptible than his demeanour suggested – had admitted she was beautiful. In her pitiable situation, it would not be surprising if she had used her guiles to win privileges or a loosening of constraints Shrewsbury might otherwise have withheld. On the charge of an actual liaison, however, she must be considered innocent. Notwithstanding public suspicion that she was having an affair with Bothwell while married to Darnley – based solely on speculation and ill-feeling – Mary had always been protective of her reputation. Lovely, lively and engaging, she nevertheless understood the consequences if she was seen to be flighty or promiscuous. Yet if she could sow disharmony within the Shrewsbury marriage, it might rebound to her advantage, the earl being more amenable, at this stage, than his wife. Mary was quite capable of such a heartless stratagem, if it would improve her situation.

By the late 1570s, Bess and Shrewsbury were all but estranged, the earl having fallen out with his children as well as his wife. Irrationally obsessed with money, he began to suspect his wife (not without reason) of ridiculous extravagance, and of setting his family against him. With Mary he seems to have shown his least suspicious and neurotic side, but with Bess his accusations grew increasingly wild.

The marriage that had once been so close and loving appears to have cracked under the pressure of Shrewsbury's custodianship of Mary. There is no doubt that this was an onerous role, especially when his vigilance was constantly in question. An added aggravation was the financial outlay it entailed. For this, Queen Elizabeth was at fault, showing herself reluctant to part with even the inadequate allowance they had agreed, and ignoring his constant complaints about being out of pocket. Not that one need feel sorry for the earl. His financial woes were more a symptom of a general sense of grievance than a cause for real anxiety. Few in England were better placed to afford the cost of keeping Mary's large entourage and the luxuries she demanded, not to mention the heavy guard kept upon them all. While he was petitioning Elizabeth for funds and back pay, he was having a palatial new house built at Worksop.

Mary's biographer Agnes Strickland did not believe it was jealousy of Mary that started the trouble between the Shrewsburys. She points to a letter to Elizabeth, in March 1584, in which Mary blamed her estrangement from Bess on one thing alone: her ambition for her granddaughter. Until the child was born, she wrote, Bess had been as good to her as if she had been God: 'nothing has alienated the Countess of Shrewsbury from me but the vain hope which she has conceived of setting the crown of England on the head of her little girl Arabella [sic] ... But for the notion of raising some of her descendants to the rank of queen, she would never have turned away from me.' It was a revealing glimpse of Mary's arrogance that she had taken Bess's appearance of deference and devotion at face value.

Strickland was persuaded by Mary's assertion that the countess had tried to ruin her 'from the moment of the birth of Lady Arbella Stuart', since it would bring her granddaughter closer to the throne. Are we to assume that Shrewsbury was so repulsed by these machinations that it caused him to fall out of love with his wife? Mary Lovell relates an incident that some regarded as a more likely cause of Shrewsbury's displeasure. When one of Mary's men announced that his mistress should be Queen of England, Bess angrily retorted, in front of the servants, that 'It would be better that the Scottish queen were hanged before this should come to pass.'

It is, of course, possible that it was Bess's determination to marry her daughter to Charles Stuart that rankled Shrewsbury. After all, this put him in an invidious position with Queen Elizabeth. He was quick to inform her that he had known nothing of his wife's plotting, but it must have been galling to be obliged to issue a disclaimer.

Whatever the truth, tension in the Shrewsbury camp was palpable. On one occasion, in 1577, when the earl had some of Bess's craftsmen turned away from Sheffield Manor Lodge, she was so incensed she packed her belongings and left for Chatsworth, even though her husband was due to arrive shortly. The public insult cut Shrewsbury deep, and although both still professed at this point to dearly love each other, that would soon change. One way or another, by the late 1570s the marriage was irreparably damaged, with the earl bemoaning his wife's behaviour to Elizabeth. Some of this can be traced to Mary's presence, but it appears that Shrewsbury's altered temperament, and his violent temper, were as much to blame for the couple's misery, if not more.

A marriage of a very different sort was to occupy Mary's thoughts around this domestically fraught time. Since 1567, her third husband, James Hepburn, Earl of Bothwell, had been imprisoned in Denmark, held by Frederic II, King of Norway and Denmark, as a bargaining tool in his attempt to reclaim Shetland and Orkney. Bothwell was imprisoned first in Copenhagen Castle, then at Malmö Castle and, for the last five years of his life, in the remote fjordside fortress of Dragsholm Castle, where he was said to have been chained to a wall. His wife seems to have airbrushed him from her mind, barely mentioning Bothwell except when, in the hope of marrying the Duke of Norfolk, she urged her envoys to obtain an annulment of their marriage from the Pope. Nothing came of that request.

A curious document came to light in 1576 that offered Mary a fleeting hope of being released and gave her cause to be grateful to her unfortunate husband. Claimed as Bothwell's deathbed confession, it completely exonerated Mary of any part in Darnley's murder, saying that she 'never knew nor consented to the death of the king'. Bothwell shared the blame for that deed, along with various other lords, including Moray, Morton and Maitland of Lethington. He also confessed that he had won Mary over by witchcraft and had drugged her in order to get her into bed – a reference, presumably, to her rape at Dunbar Castle.

Far-fetched as witchcraft sounds today – whereas drugging a victim is familiar – it would have been believable to Bothwell's contemporaries. As a young man, he was rumoured to have learned the arts of sorcery while studying at the University of Paris. His family was notorious for their interest in the black arts, and years later his nephew, Francis Stewart Hepburn, fifth Earl of Bothwell, was said to have been a sorcerer.

Learning of this document, Mary was desperate to know its contents, believing it might persuade Elizabeth of her innocence. Elizabeth had already read it, but remained silent on the subject. On hearing its claims, ten-year-old James excitedly told his court that he now had clear proof of his mother's innocence. You can picture Buchanan raising his hands to the heavens at this infuriating *deus ex machina*, undoing years of assiduous work persuading the boy of his mother's perfidy. The Countess of Lennox also swallowed it whole and, with Mary absolved of aiding in her son's murder, enjoyed a brief rapprochement with her before her sudden death.

Thrilling though this confession sounds, it was far too good to be true. John Guy describes it as a 'blatant forgery', written to exonerate Mary from her part in the murder. Glaring factual errors indicate it was not Bothwell who wrote it but, as Antonia Fraser writes, 'Bothwell would in any case have been unable to write a death-bed confession, since he died insane.'

While in captivity Bothwell did, however, write a memoir of sorts, in which he coloured events to his best advantage. By comparison with his wife's incarceration, his was brutal. Did Mary ever think of him from behind her own bars? Did any spark of affection remain? It is impossible to know. Most probably all love had been snuffed long before they parted at the battle of Carberry Hill, but perhaps even before they married. Had the twins she miscarried while captive at Lochleven Castle survived, she would have had a lifelong reminder of the educated, intelligent but brutish Borderer. As it was, his fate was out of her hands, and she need not bother herself with him any further. Instead, she focused on extricating herself from her prison.

Bothwell was rumoured to be dead when a copy of his confession reached Elizabeth – sent by Frederic II – but he did not die until April 1578, after eleven years of imprisonment without trial. The conditions he endured were vile – it was said he was kept in a room so low he could not stand and latterly was chained to a post. With his mind broken by suffering and drinking, his death might be regarded as a mercy. It was an unjustifiably cruel end for a man who, for all his many faults, had been an unwaveringly loyal supporter of Mary and her mother, and had carried out his duties with brio, and not a little courage.

Bothwell was buried in the church of Faarevejle, twenty miles from Dragsholm, where in 1858 his coffin was opened to reveal his almost mummified body. A photo of his head, with its crooked broken nose, a gruesome relic of a once redoubtable man, can be seen in Mary Queen of Scots House in Jedburgh. It is believed his head was used as a football before at some point being reunited with his body.

The year 1575 saw several significant changes in the members of Mary's inner circle on whom she depended. The first was the arrival of a new French ambassador in London. After seven years in post, Mothe-Fénelon was replaced by Castelnau. In happier days, he had been part of the entourage accompanying Mary on her return to Scotland in 1561, and he rated her highly. He was to serve as ambassador for a decade until 1585, when his successor,

Châteauneuf, arrived from Berry. Like Mothe-Fénelon, both Castelnau and Châteauneuf would be the conduit of many of Mary's letters, both official and secret. This role could no doubt be taxing, since Mary seems to have treated her ambassadors as personal servants whose job it was to respond swiftly to her every request. For Castelnau in particular, it must have been disturbing to observe her grim situation and compare the ailing queen to the young woman who had arrived in Scotland with such optimism only a few years earlier. It was even worse for Châteauneuf, who, in the final weeks of Mary's life, appeared to be working assiduously to save her from execution, until he was placed under house arrest and could do nothing more. At the same time, it seems he had been colluding with Walsingham to increase Elizabeth's fears of yet another plot against her life.

Since the French crown's relationship with the captive queen waxed and waned depending on what was in its best interests, the ambassador had to walk a diplomatic tightrope, satisfying the King of France but also the Scottish queen who might still, one day, ascend to the English throne. Even when such a prospect began to fade, the French embassy would have recognised Mary's legitimate claim, as dowager queen of France, to whatever help it could offer. From the volume of letters Mary despatched to each of her French ambassadors during her imprisonment, it is clear that she imposed a heavy workload (and psychological burden) upon them.

Even without the delicate matter of Mary, theirs was not an enviable position. Resident in the heart of London, they had to deal daily with the English court, which, beneath a veneer of civility, viewed them with understandable suspicion. Relations between England and France in these years fluctuated, as Elizabeth negotiated the minefield of European politics to England's advantage. Throughout the 1570s she attempted to keep both France and Spain onside, hoping that by maintaining a good relationship with France she might guard against the menace posed by the all-powerful Spain. In both endeavours, Mary complicated matters. Her captivity displeased the French and, increasingly, she represented a useful focal point for Philip II's ambitions to invade England and replace Elizabeth with the Catholic queen. Meanwhile, the French ambassadors were umbilically attached to the woman who represented a mortal threat to the country and did everything they could to support her without causing a diplomatic firestorm. In this they were a great deal more successful than their Spanish counterparts.

On the home front, Mary had to adjust to the new French secretary appointed to handle her correspondence. The death of Raulet had robbed her of a devoted servant who, despite being curmudgeonly and querulous, had been a stalwart aide. He worked alongside the more amiable Curle – described by one onlooker as 'good but stupid' – who dealt with matters written in English. Raulet had been adept at enciphering her covert messages. Curle, for his part, also served the queen faithfully, and in due course married her attendant, Barbara Mowbray. They soon had a child, whom Mary baptised herself. One of Mary's closest gentlewomen was her secretary Gilbert Curle's sister Elizabeth Curle, who, along with Jane Kennedy, was with her on the scaffold, giving her courage in the minutes before her death.

Raulet's absence was keenly felt. By this point, the coterie around Mary was akin to a family, tight-knit, supportive and presumably occasionally fractious. Filling the tetchy secretary's shoes would have been daunting for most, but his replacement, Claude Nau, had a high opinion of himself. It was Nau who took down Mary's memoir, which she dictated to him, and she appears to have trusted him implicitly. In later years, he caused some friction in the household when he was consumed by unrequited passion for Bessie Pierrepoint, the Countess of Shrewsbury's haughty granddaughter. Mary's froideur at learning of his unauthorised use of her top-secret 'pipeline' for covert correspondence to contact Bessie would have unnerved a lesser man.

Despite this faux pas, Nau was to remain in Mary's service until a few months before her execution when, under interrogation by Walsingham, he turned Judas. Wherever he went, Walsingham carried about him the whiff of the rack and the thumbscrews, and his appearance often spelled the end of a suspect's stoical silence or denials. That, however, is a story for a later chapter, in which the upright Curle also helped incriminate Mary. Both might be excused, given the false evidence they were presented with, and the prospect of torture that hung over them. Indeed, Antonia Fraser goes to some lengths to exonerate Nau of treachery, likening his betrayal to that of Mary's envoy John Leslie, Bishop of Ross, who, when interrogated about Mary's part in the Duke of Norfolk's regicidal plans, denounced his queen as the murderer of not one but two of her husbands: a temporary lapse of judgement caused by mortal fear.

Yet a letter from Elizabeth to the Earl of Shrewsbury suggests Nau might not have been such a hapless innocent. In March 1575, when discussing replacing Raulet, she referred to the dead secretary's 'evil offices' while in post, indicating his cast-iron fidelity to Mary. She informs the earl that a Frenchman called Nau has been recommended to her by the King of France, and that Nau himself had promised not to 'practise any hurtful or offensive thing . . . with offer that, if at any time he shall be found faulty, he submitteth himself to any punishment'.

This passage, writes Agnes Strickland, suggests that Nau 'was recommended and even forced into the service of Mary, Queen of Scots by Elizabeth herself'. There is further incriminating evidence, in the form of a payment by Elizabeth in 1584 'to Monsieur Nau, the Scottish Queen's servant, 73l 10s 2d'. Strickland believed Nau was 'the paid agent of Queen Elizabeth. The Queen of Scots always paid his wages and expenses, and had even appointed payment of his arrears of salary in her will, if he was found to have deserved it.' For her this fee, along with Elizabeth's letter, 'proves a lamp to lighten the dark places of history and to discover iniquity'.

So was Nau one of Walsingham's plants, sent to undermine Mary's household from within? It is certainly possible, especially given Walsingham's reliance on undercover operatives. Yet until his arrest in 1586, when he ratted on the Scottish queen, Nau's behaviour gave no sign of duplicity. On the contrary. It was he who warned her not to reply to Anthony Babington's reckless letter outlining his plans for overturning Elizabeth. Mary ignored his advice and, by replying, gave Walsingham's agent the opportunity to forge an incriminating postscript that led directly to her death.

All the same, it is suspicious that after Nau's testimony against Mary, he lodged in Walsingham's house and was allowed to return to France, whilst Curle languished in prison for a year. Who are we to believe, then: Strickland or Fraser? This is a dilemma for which the verdict of not proven is perfectly suited. In such treacherous times, it is not hard to imagine Walsingham finding a malleable man who could infiltrate Mary's entourage and act as a sleeper until called upon to prove his worth. Why, though, would he urge his mistress not to write anything that her enemies could use against her, when the point of the exercise was to bring her down?

If – and it remains in doubt – Nau was working against Mary, John Leslie, Bishop of Ross, was merely a man caught in the riptide of Tudor paranoia and unable to withstand its pull, which is to say the terror of torture. After spending almost four years in the Tower of London, he was released, and – astonishingly – taken back into Mary's service. She was so delighted at his return that she wrote a poem to mark the occasion. Once back in harness, among Leslie's first commissions was to attempt again to get Pope Gregory XIII formally to annul Mary's marriage to Bothwell. This request was refused, on the grounds that it would make Mary's position unsafe. Nevertheless, it was widely assumed, including by the Pope, that Mary was now free to remarry, even though her husband was still alive, albeit in no mental state fully to comprehend the world beyond his walls.

Chapter 19

'Being in constant dread lest my son should fall into the hands of the Earl of Morton'

EL ESCORIAL

During her lifetime, Mary wrote several wills, a melancholy task at the best of times. Like many wealthy women, she had composed a detailed last testament before giving birth, a time fraught with the possibility of dying. And as a captive she anticipated death at any moment, either from ill health or by assassination. Leaving a list of bequests and instructions for the care of servants was usually a way of securing the future for loved ones left behind. Sometimes, however, it could be an act of aggression or revenge. This appears to have been the case with a will she drafted in February 1577, which was composed more in rage than in immediate fear of mortality. Among its various provisions, Mary bestowed the earldom of Lennox on Bess's granddaughter Arbella Stuart, in the (futile) hope that her son James would grant Arbella that title. She also expressed the wish that James would marry one of Philip II of Spain's daughters and convert to Catholicism.

Although such a desire showed her reluctance to accept the fact that James was now a devout Protestant, what makes this document particularly illuminating is her instruction that, should James not embrace the Catholic faith, she would bequeath her rightful claim to the throne of England to Philip II. It was an extraordinary statement of pique, insecurity and frustration. The following year, James would officially become ruler of Scotland and, in theory, be capable of making decisions on his own. Yet already Mary understood that he had been turned into an enemy of the Catholic cause and thus to herself. To declare her intention to hand over her claim to the English throne to the most powerful Catholic monarch on the globe suggests a flash of something akin to vindictiveness, and also despair.

If nothing else, it shows Mary's embattled state of mind, even if in the end she never carried through on this threat, and the will remained unsigned. What she needed at this time was Philip II's support. In that light, this document was perhaps nothing more than a way of signalling to him that she was willing to switch allegiance from France to Spain. It was not a one-off. In 1586, by which time she had lost all faith in her son, who had publicly abandoned her in favour of Elizabeth, Mary repeated her intention to make this bequest, explicitly including with it her claim to the Scottish throne as well as the English. But again, it seems, she was merely sabre-rattling. After her death, Philip II had the archives scoured to find what is now known as the 'phantom will'. Picture the scene when searcher after searcher reported back to him empty-handed.

It says much about the way in which Philip viewed Mary that he believed her capable of enriching him in this way. From her earliest days of imprisonment by Elizabeth, she had turned to Philip II as well as to France for help, willing to jettison her French connections if he would extricate her from her predicament. Although she was almost as French as Scottish, she had dearly hoped to marry James to one of her childhood friend Elizabeth of Valois's children by Philip. As with many of her aspirations for her son, this was doomed to failure.

For his part Philip wavered over whether to help her. As Mary Tudor's husband, he had for a brief period (1554–58) included England in his ever-expanding empire. Even though he devoutly desired England to return to Catholicism and, naturally, to include it in his conquests, initially he could not countenance the idea of a queen on England's throne who was closely bound to the French crown. He was also impressed by Elizabeth, Mary Tudor's half-sister and his sister-in-law, and was keen to remain on good terms with her. It is intriguing that, for a decade and more, the rulers of these two great European powers had no wish to go to war with each other, despite their often bellicose members of court, and despite their own devious attempts to undermine each other's kingdoms.

In the months after Mary's imprisonment, Philip's attitude changed, putting Elizabeth at a disadvantage and Mary into a position of greater potential power. By the time of the poorly conceived Ridolfi plot of 1571, which he had supported, Philip even considered it possible that, should the plot succeed, Mary might marry his illegitimate half-brother, Don Juan of Austria, thereby setting the pair on the English throne. He planned to send 10,000 crack troops from the Netherlands, under his brutal general, the Duke of Alva, to assist an English Catholic uprising if the plot came good. Fortunately for Elizabeth, the conspirators were arrested before any rebellion could be mustered. An attempt in 1580 to aid the invasion of Ireland by English Catholics also fizzled out. Undeterred, during the remainder of Mary's captivity, Philip repeatedly considered schemes for supporting a Catholic uprising and putting Mary in Elizabeth's place.

Relations between England and Spain were combustible. Most pressing of the tensions between them was the Protestant rebellion in the Spanish-occupied Netherlands, which began in 1568. Although Elizabeth had an innate mistrust of rebels, she recognised the need to help defend them against a European superpower that posed a serious danger to her own rule. Consequently, for many years English funds were sent to William I, Prince of Orange, to bolster resistance against Catholic oppression.

It was not until William's assassination in 1584, however, that the situation dangerously escalated. The following year, Elizabeth signed a treaty committing English troops under the command of the Earl of Leicester to come to the aid of the rebel Protestant provinces in the Netherlands. Seeing this as tantamount to a declaration of war, Philip, buoyed up by unimaginable power and wealth from his world-dominating empire, decided to move against England. It was arguably the worst decision in an otherwise impressive if fanatical career.

This, then, was the man with whom Mary was willing – indeed

eager – to ally herself. Philip, nicknamed 'the Prudent', was a monarch whose empire, by the early 1580s, encompassed territories throughout Europe, including the states of Milan, Sicily and Sardinia and the Netherlands; across the Atlantic he added Mexico and the south and central Americas to his portfolio; and, across the Pacific, the Philippines, which took their name from him. An idea of Spain's naval prowess in this era can be found in the Museo Naval in Madrid, situated in the headquarters of the Armada, or navy, and run by the Spanish Ministry of Defence. Showing Spain's exploratory and military triumphs, from the fifteenth century to the present day, with arrays of model ships, weaponry and scientific instruments used in global navigation, it gives an idea of the scale of the maritime power wielded by Philip II and others on the Spanish throne. Among its treasures is the first map made of the American continent, in 1500, by Juan de la Cosa, who visited three times in the company of Christopher Columbus. This remarkable document is a reminder of the enormity and hazards of such voyages, and of Spain's pre-eminence in this sphere.

The defeat of the Spanish Armada off England in 1588 is one of the most famous events in English history. (In a gesture designed to antagonise England, Scots rescued many Spanish sailors shipwrecked off the Scottish coast as they sailed the long way home after this ill-fated venture.) Philip made further attempts to invade later in the century, but although he was thwarted on each occasion, his biographer Geoffrey Parker believes he came closer to taking England by force than either Napoleon or Hitler.

Had Spain succeeded in invading England during Mary's lifetime and rousing English Catholics – assuming there were sufficient numbers interested or brave enough to rally to the call – Mary would have become the puppet of a ruthless religious fanatic. Pity not her but England in that terrifying enterprise. For a man of God, Philip was anything but gentle or forgiving. A portrait of him by Alonso Sánchez Coello in 1587, the year of Mary's death, shows an unnervingly piercing stare. With pallid skin and wispy moustache, his fleshy Habsburg face is framed by a penitentially high-necked ruff. His severe black tunic and hose, alleviated only by the white of his collar and cuffs, indicate the asceticism of a zealot. In his bedroom he kept his father's blood-stained scourge. His use of the Spanish Inquisition against heretics, notably in the occupied Netherlands, where tens of thousands were persecuted, makes sickening reading.

There is no doubt that Philip was driven by genuine religious fervour. Earlier in his reign, in 1566, he had told the Pope: 'rather than suffer the least damage to religion and the service of God, I would lose all my states and a hundred lives if I had them; for I do not propose or desire to be the ruler of heretics'. Geoffrey Parker argues that Philip's religious convictions, and his missionary drive, were central in shaping his policies, at home and abroad.

El Escorial, his imposing – indeed sinister – residence, an hour by train from Madrid, is testimony to the centrality of his Catholic faith to everything he did. Built between 1563 and 1584, the austere El Escorial overlooks tussocky countryside grazed by cattle and goats. Sitting at the top of the small town of San Lorenzo de El Escorial, it is enormous, sheer-faced and uninviting. With row upon row of small windows and a tower at each of its four corners, it has the demeanour of a prison. The only softening feature is a formal parterred garden which lies beneath its walls, beyond which is a grove of olives.

The afternoon I visited, local schoolchildren were kicking footballs against the palace walls, a pleasing note of normality for a place that is anything but ordinary. In Philip's day, the townsfolk must have viewed it like the ogre's castle. Superstitious as well as devout, Philip was fascinated by the occult and magic, and the palace housed a laboratory where medicines and drugs were concocted for the royal apothecary. There was also a medicinal garden, filled with herbs for potions.

The layout of El Escorial is unsettling. It was designed on a floor plan modelled on a gridiron as a reminder of the implement on which the third-century Saint Lawrence was martyred by roasting. It is recorded, although it sounds apocryphal, that during his ordeal

Lawrence said to his torturers: 'I am cooked on that side; turn me over, and eat.' Philip intended El Escorial to serve a triple purpose: as a monastery and a royal palace but also as a fitting burial place for his beloved father, the Holy Roman Emperor Charles V. So great was his regard for Charles that he could not contemplate returning to England to be with his dying wife Mary Tudor, since he was fully occupied making preparations for his father's funeral. Nor did he find the time to attend her funeral.

Philip's palace is a monument to hubris and carnage. Recognised as a masterpiece of the Spanish Renaissance, it is filled with sombre religious works of art by the likes of El Greco and Titian. Its rooms and echoing stone corridors are patrolled by unsmiling, inflexible staff. When I made to leave a room by the wrong door, I was barked at as if I'd whipped out a can of spray paint. Evidence of Philip's intellectual breadth and global ambitions can be found in his magnificent library. In this barrel-vaulted, light-filled room, with a painted ceiling Michelangelo would not have been ashamed of, thousands of books are arranged with their spines to the back of the bookcases. This shelving system, disapproved of by the librarian who visited with me, was designed to allow the page edges to be painted gold, thereby catching the sunlight and reminding onlookers of the king's magnificence.

Philip's remains are preserved in the castle's bowels in a Royal Pantheon that could have come from the imagination of Bram Stoker. Reached by a steep and narrow staircase down a windowless wooden-panelled passage lit by hanging lamps, the mausoleum is a claustrophobic circular room with a richly decorated domed ceiling. Only after a period of twenty to thirty years in El Pudridero ('rotting room'), where the corpses were covered in lime until they had been reduced to bones, did the dead eventually go to their final resting place.

Stacked four-high to the ceiling around the walls are twenty-six black marble coffins on gold clawed feet and embellished with gold name plates. It is here that Philip is entombed, on a shelf beneath his father Charles V and above his successors Philips III and IV. Almost every Spanish monarch since Charles V is here. Elsewhere in the palace, in a further region of the basement, is an interconnecting series of rooms, filled with the white marble sarcophagi of Philip's wives (with the exception of Mary Tudor), family, relatives and descendants. Truly a place of death.

Every room in El Escorial is stamped with the king's personality, but it is in his bedchamber that one gets closest to the inner man. An austere room, containing a narrow four-poster bed draped in gold and maroon, beside which is a chair, this is where Philip retreated, in 1598, for the final fifty-three days of his life. These were spent in an agony of foul-smelling sores and the shame of incontinence, which the fastidious king, who had a modern sensibility when it came to hygiene, would have found repulsive and humiliating. Was he tormented in his dying days by remorse for the horrors he had inflicted on heretics? More likely he saw them as his fast-track to heaven. At the side of the bed is a small window, looking down into the chapel from which, in better times, he could watch as Mass was celebrated. Apparently as the end approached, Philip clutched the crucifix his parents had held as they died, and passed quietly from this life.

The month after making her sensational will, Mary wrote to the Archbishop of Glasgow, expressing her fears that, should the Spanish invade England, she would be in danger, since she was unfairly suspected of being in league with Philip's brother, Don Juan of Austria. In the same letter she begged for news from Scotland – 'for I have heard that there is a new design to bring up my son here, for fear, it is said, that in the event of the death of Morton, who has been extremely ill, he should fall into some better hands'. A few weeks later she urged the archbishop to send her several thousand crowns, so that she could continue to send messages.

James's vulnerability to those around him was a running theme of her letters while he was a boy. In March 1578, a group of nobles who resented Morton's aggressive, greedy and partisan regency effected a coup. Led by the Earls of Argyll and Atholl, this group persuaded

James to become the figurehead of this change of governance. Roundly trounced, Morton was forced to resign and retired to his estate at Lochleven, where he planned to occupy himself by levelling the paths in his garden.

Mary saw this coup as the first step in her restoration and was keen that James be taken immediately to France. None of the leaders behind the rebellion, however, would even consider this. At various points in her captivity, Mary tried ineffectually to have James removed, either to France or Spain, where she hoped he would marry and convert to Catholicism. Still only a child of twelve, James seemed comfortable with the new regime, but a counter-coup in April 1578, led by his former classmate John Erskine, now Earl of Mar, shocked him with its violence. During the assault on Stirling Castle, when young Mar pressed his claim as custodian of the castle and of the king, one of James's oldest and most trusted companions, Alexander Erskine of Gogar, was badly injured, and his son trampled to death.

A new government was convened, whose members included some of the instigators of the initial coup. Morton was restored as First Lord of the Privy Council, with Atholl next in importance. It had been a traumatic few weeks for young James, but this difficult and bloody episode saw what Steven Reid describes as the 'transformation of the royal nursery into a fully functioning royal court'. James was not yet acting as a wholly independent king, but with the passing of an act announcing the start of his adult rule a few months earlier, he now played a small role in the Privy Council, and was beginning to make his presence felt. He was no longer to be treated as a child but as a fledgling king. He was also growing aware of the deadly nature of Scottish politics. The death of Atholl shortly after a reconciliatory feast held by Morton shocked the court. Morton denied any wrongdoing, but a post-mortem convinced all but one of the presiding doctors that Atholl had been poisoned. The dissenting doctor licked the lining of Atholl's stomach to prove his point, and thereafter fell so ill that he never fully recovered.

It was essential to replace Atholl, to whom James had been close, with another on whom he could depend. In search of a suitable candidate, he and his advisors summoned his cousin Esmé Stuart d'Aubigny from France. In September 1579 Esmé arrived. Handsome, quick-witted and respectful to the young king, he quickly became his favourite. An English onlooker described James as 'in such love with him as in the oppen sight of the people, often-times he will claspe him about the neck with his armes and kisse him'. But if James's life was soon to be transformed, so too was that of the Scottish court.

Locked away in Sheffield Castle and the Manor Lodge, Mary learned of these developments belatedly and third-hand. When it became clear how much influence Esmé Stuart was wielding at court, she grew anxious, and her letters reflected her dislike, and perhaps even fear, of what she and others considered a cuckoo in the nest.

Known as Monsieur d'Aubigny, or simply as Monsieur, Esmé Stuart was born in the same month as Mary, Queen of Scots. When he was invited to Scotland, he was a married man with five children. Arriving with a large entourage, he immediately dazzled the court, especially James, who very quickly bestowed on him first the earldom and later the dukedom of Lennox. In so doing, he deliberately deprived his mother's protégé, Arbella Stuart, who was a rival for the English throne, of what the Lennoxes considered her rightful inheritance.

Tall, auburn haired and red-bearded, Esmé Stuart was the son of John Stuart, brother of James's grandfather Matthew Stuart, Earl of Lennox. For centuries he has been viewed as an essentially malign, self-serving figure who enchanted the young James and tried to shape the court in his own interests. James's biographer Caroline Bingham writes that the court invited him 'without stopping to compare themselves with rash dabblers in the unknown who, Faustus-like, having summoned a spirit to serve them, most often fail to control it for their purposes'.

The nature of the king's relationship with his much older distant cousin has been the source of fascination: was he a father-figure, a close friend or possibly even a lover, as some contemporaries claimed? The facts give no conclusive answer, but Reid suggests that the more lurid interpretations of the Frenchman's position might be wide of the mark. Esmé Stuart, he writes, was the first courtier to treat James as an adult ruler. He showed him affection, calling him his *petit maistre*, but also the deference he was due.

Far from the Scottish king being duped into showering him with privileges, both sides benefitted from his presence. The glamorous Frenchman earned himself a dukedom, while James and his coterie had introduced a powerful new player at court. Steven Reid describes this move as 'a means by which to re-energise the power of the Lennox earldom as a counterweight against the Morton-Mar faction'. But Esmé Stuart's role went further than this. Appointed lord chamberlain, he reshaped the court in the French model, moderating access to the king. In effect, he headed up the new regime, with James delegating authority to him. Unsurprisingly, this made him unpopular. He grew even more disliked when it was rumoured that he was an agent of the Guise family, sent to prepare the way for the return of Catholicism. This possibility greatly alarmed Elizabeth who, writes Bingham, 'feared that his coming was the first move in a game that the Catholic powers were certain to open sooner or later'.

If a Catholic mission was part of Esmé Stuart's original remit, evidence suggests he made no moves in this direction until towards the end of his stay in Scotland. His was a brief moment in the sun, an episode that was to last a mere three, albeit eventful, years. From afar, Mary watched the turmoil in Scotland with consternation. In May 1578, shortly after the coup against Morton, she wrote to the Archbishop of Glasgow, outlining her anxiety over James's safety: 'being in constant dread lest my son should fall into the hands of the Earl of Morton, or of those of his faction, who would secure him to England in any way that they could'.

Every few years there is a flurry of excitement at the unearthing of a letter or object relating to Mary, Queen of Scots that adds colour to the story. In 2022 the discovery of a treasure trove of fifty-seven secret letters made international headlines. The letters, written between May 1578 and October 1584, were found in the digital archive of the Bibliothèque Nationale de France, where they had lain misfiled. A team from the DECRYPT Project, an international, cross-disciplinary group that scours international archives for interesting enciphered material, did not at first appreciate the significance of what they had stumbled upon. Only when they began deciphering did they realise that the letters were in French, their author was a woman who had a son, and that she was in captivity. Mention of the name Walsingham confirmed that they had been written by Mary, Queen of Scots.

Most of the letters are to the queen's French ambassador, Castelnau, and mention further letters enclosed for him to pass to others, most often the Archbishop of Glasgow. Sadly those enclosures are long-gone, but they give an indication of the reach of Mary's underground correspondence. Hailed as the most significant addition to Mary's archive in a century, this cache helps illuminate her state of mind and preoccupations in the years 1578 to 1584, when she was being held by Shrewsbury in Sheffield. The team who found and decoded Mary's prison letters are a latterday version of the men Walsingham, and all European courts, employed to crack codes and gather intelligence. Although they come from different intellectual backgrounds, they are all skilled in taking complicated patterns of symbols, which were designed to be impenetrable, and converting them into words.

The team comprises the French computer scientist George Lasry, whose achievements include deciphering papal messages from the sixteenth, seventeenth and eighteenth centuries, and messages from the First and Second World Wars. His colleagues are the German musician Norbert Biermann, a pianist and music professor at Berlin University of the Arts, for whom historical cryptography is a hobby, and the Japanese patent expert, Satoshi Tomokiyu, who studied astrophysics at the University of Tokyo. He too works on historical cryptography in his spare time, and maintains the website Cryptiana. When the three had finished the fiendish work of deciphering (for details visit the Cryptiana website), it was for experts in Middle French to translate. This was no easy task, since the messages are in places arcane, misspelled and confusing. That work is proceeding at the time of writing, but synopses of all the letters allow a glimpse of their contents.

A few of the ciphered letters recovered from the Bibliothèque Nationale are already familiar, having been intercepted by Walsingham, decoded, and added to the official record of Mary's correspondence. Many, however, are entirely new. What they reveal is that the queen was preoccupied with many of the same subjects she addressed more cautiously and in less detail in her open correspondence. In the first of these letters, for instance, Mary told Castelnau that she would agree to remain in captivity so long as her and her son's rights to the English succession were upheld.

Over the period these letters cover, Mary wrote frequently about the channels by which her secret communications were delivered and received. Fear of double agents, spies and interception is constant, with Mary often showing great acuity in discerning danger. 'Beware of Archibald Douglas,' she told Castelnau in October 1584, 'for he has not been as sincere as he would like you to believe.' In an irritable letter from October 1582, she expressed concern about the laxness of security after an official box of letters, which concealed a coded letter from the Archbishop of Glasgow, was inspected by Shrewsbury. Fortunately, Beaton's letter was not found, but Mary would have fretted that, on another occasion, they might not be so lucky.

Referring to her official letters to Castelnau, to which the Privy Council had access, she said dismissively that she would never write anything in them she didn't want her worst enemies to read. In that same letter, she warned Castelnau that Walsingham falsely presented himself as a friend, and said she was afraid that the Earl and Countess of Shrewsbury might join the Earl of Leicester and the Earl of Huntingdon against her.

An indication of the state of alarm throughout the country comes from a letter written a day earlier, on 6 January 1580, in which she claimed that the Puritans were allying with the Scottish rebels, openly objecting to the rule of women. It was feared that they might capture both Elizabeth and Mary. In the same letter she added that representatives from England had been sent to a Protestant synod in France, under Walsingham's instruction, with the ultimate purpose of converting all Frenchmen to Huguenots. If what she wrote was true, then of all the secretary's ventures, this was surely the most unlikely and far-fetched.

Anxiety over her personal safety features persistently, and Mary frequently expressed dread at the prospect of being put into the hands of captors who wished her dead. Not everyone was a foe, however. She wrote often about Robert Beale, Walsingham's brother-in-law, who was sent on several occasions to discuss conditions for her release, as in this letter from June 1582: 'Should you find Beale, please let him know that I have a good opinion of his sincere way of proceeding with everything he has been charged with for me, and that I feel very grateful to him, despite the little effect that has ensued, which I attribute only to the passions of those whom he is obliged to obey.' Clearly this was a man she respected. The same cannot be said of Robert Dudley, Earl of Leicester; her barbed comments about him reveal great mistrust, dislike and on occasion fear.

Other recurrent subjects include the welfare of her son James, of whom she received far too little news. Not long before the Ruthven Raid, in which he was held prisoner for several months, she warned that Walsingham and Elizabeth were stirring trouble in Scotland, and that if there was a rebellion there, she wanted Castelnau to persuade the King of France to intervene.

When James was taken captive during the Ruthven Raid, his mother's extreme distress was evident. Desperate for further information, she asked Castelnau to request from the King of France that her Guise relatives 'secure' James and his servants. In October 1582, while her son was under house arrest, she thanked her ambassador for sending her a portrait of him. However, because it was not like other portraits, she wished to know who painted it, and when. You can imagine her disquiet at receiving an image of her son that did not correspond with her idea of him, knowing there would be no opportunity to see him for herself any time soon, if indeed ever. Yet while James occupied much of her thoughts, her letters indicate she did not understand what sort of a young man he had grown into, nor that her hold over him was nothing compared to that of Elizabeth.

Among the main themes of the letters from 1579 to 1582 is the painfully protracted and ultimately futile negotiation of Elizabeth's marriage to Francis, Duke of Anjou, Henri III's younger brother. As an aside to her detailed discussion of this – for her – hopeful union, Mary was concerned that because of these negotiations, France was neglecting Scottish affairs. As a result, she worried that James might be driven toward a course different from hers and that of her predecessors – into the arms of England, in other words, rather than France.

Of paramount importance was the matter of Mary's restoration to her throne, to rule jointly with her son. This dominated her thoughts between 1582 and 1583. Indeed, in June 1583, when she was eager to speed up the process, she mischievously told Castelnau to spread alarm about Spain and France among Beale and his associates, hoping this would rattle them and help her cause.

Not everything in these letters is politically significant, but they often offer a vivid glimpse of the times. Complaining to her ambassador that the doctors recently sent to her were not what they seemed, she wrote: 'they are my great enemies, and depend heavily on Walsingham. Smyth is an ardent follower of Paracelsus and demonstrated it quite clearly in the argument that took place on the day of his departure regarding the liquid gold and other remedies from the alchemist, about which you had written to me.'

In several letters from 1583, she referred to a disturbing situation, in which the late Kirkcaldy of Grange's mistress refused to support their illegitimate daughter. With uncharacteristic venom, Mary wrote that she did not want to offer the girl's mother help, and accused her of being a man-chaser who simply wanted to live in another country (presumably France). Rather than come to her aid, she said, she would have her whipped while tied to the back of a carriage if she had the authority to do so. Eventually, however, she relented towards the unwanted child: 'I have written to Monsieur de Glasgow to take hold of this girl of the Laird of Grange and appoint her to one of my relatives in France . . .'

What becomes apparent from her covert confidences is that Mary remained fully abreast of the politics of her own country, and those of England and the continent. She also assiduously, and almost obsessively, sent instructions and passed on information in the hope of influencing events. In the first of these letters, for instance, she wrote that she believed Walsingham and the Puritans were working against Elizabeth by supporting the Earl of Huntingdon's claim to the throne. She also admitted that she wished to bring England back to Catholicism, but not by force. Trapped she might be, but as this hidden correspondence shows, she did not behave like a woman in despair, nor one who recognised that her active role in political life was negligible, her fate in the hands of those she could not control.

Chapter 20

'Tribulation has been to them as a furnace to fine gold'

ELIZABETH'S LAST CHANCE TO MARRY

Esmé Stuart's prominence at the Scottish court spelled the end for the Earl of Morton. As his implacable enemy, Stuart engineered his denunciation, in December 1579, for his part in Darnley's murder. Accused on the evidence of Captain James Stewart, one of the more thuggish of James's adherents, Morton was dramatically confronted in the presence of James, who did nothing to protect him. When Elizabeth heard of his behaviour, she was outraged: 'That false urchin! . . . what can be expected of the double dealing of such an urchin as this!' It was, at the same time, no less than she expected from the Scottish crown. Morton was thrown into prison and executed eighteen months later, in 1581. As the guillotine fell, the country was rid of a Machiavellian presence which had nevertheless managed to control its troublesome factions and bring a measure of stability. Told of the death of the man who had worked remorselessly against her interests, Mary professed herself 'very glad'.

There were other reasons to be cheered in these months. Among them was the peculiar courtship and romance of Queen Elizabeth, who, at the age of forty-five – in an era when the average life expectancy was thirty-seven – appears to have fallen in love and contemplated marriage and children. Since 1570, when Charles IX, King of France, had suggested the 37-year-old Elizabeth might marry his 19-year-old brother Henri, Duke of Anjou, there hovered the (unlikely) possibility of the Queen of England taking a French husband. It made diplomatic sense; if nothing else, this proposed union would act as a warning to Spain that England was not entirely friendless. It might also allow Elizabeth to help the beleaguered Huguenots in France. For the French, the alliance offered support against the Spanish occupation of the Netherlands on their doorstep. For both countries it raised the possibility of bringing about peace there.

The marriage negotiations were protracted and irritable. Throughout this process, Elizabeth expressed her unwillingness to marry such a devout Catholic (he was also licentiously bisexual and in later life flamboyantly transvestite). Nor was Henri enthusiastic. When this doomed project eventually foundered, his younger brother, Catherine de' Medici's youngest son Francis, Duke of Alençon, was tentatively put forward in his place. The young man was described to Elizabeth as 'not so obstinate, papistical, and restive like a mule as his brother is'. Again Elizabeth bridled, since at sixteen the duke was little more than a boy. He was also very short. When she complained to Burghley, he replied that Henri was the same height as himself. 'Say rather the height of your grandson,' she snapped, referring to the five-year-old.

But seven years had wrought a considerable improvement. Francis, Duke of Alençon, had taken the title Duke of Anjou when his brother became King Henri III in 1574. By the spring of 1579, as plans for this improbable marriage started to gain momentum, Francis was still a mere twenty-three. He was conducting a military campaign in the Netherlands, where he hoped to become the protector of the Huguenots, despite being a Catholic. In his absence, the silver-tongued courtier, Jean de Simier, descended with a flourish on the English court to pave the way for his arrival. He proved so persuasive an emissary that it was rumoured that Elizabeth had fallen for him. When Anjou made his appearance in August, however, she seems genuinely to have been charmed. She adopted pet names to show her affection, such as 'little fingers' and 'our frog', and was untroubled by the pockmarks that disfigured his face, the result of a bad case of smallpox.

After the duke's departure, the pair corresponded warmly: 'I confess there is no prince in the world to whom I would more willingly yield to be his, than to yourself, nor to whom I think myself more obliged, nor with whom I would pass the years of my life, both for your rare virtues and sweet nature,' wrote Elizabeth. Anjou was no less effusive: 'If Your Majesty will consent to marry me, you will restore a languishing life, which has existed only for the service of the most perfect goddess of the heavens.'

For all his flattery, the duke's feelings were almost certainly mercenary. Catherine de' Medici remarked that, once back in France, he was embarrassed when 'he called to mind the advanced age and repulsive physical nature of the Queen'. 'The lust to reign will contend with the lust of the flesh,' she suggested, 'and we shall see which of these two passions possesses the greater force.'

For several months it seemed as if, after a lifetime of hesitation and resistance, Elizabeth was about to take a remarkable step. Although the Earl of Leicester, her lifelong love, had recently married the Countess of Essex in secret – the Queen was furious and upset on hearing this news and temporarily banished him from court – marrying him had only briefly been a possibility. The sudden death of the earl's first wife, Amy Robsart, whose lifeless body was found at the bottom of a flight of stairs, fuelled rumours that he had had her murdered, which dogged him for the rest of his days and ended any hope of marriage to Elizabeth.

In one of the more gossipy of Mary's newly discovered letters, the Scottish queen told Castelnau in January 1580 that for more than a year the Countess of Essex had been signing her secret letters as 'L. Leycester', and that he should use the information of the covert marriage against the earl. She also referred to an instance, clearly burned on her memory, when Leicester told her that she owed him her life, since Elizabeth had once wanted her dead.

Elizabeth's previous offers of marriage had left her cold, but some believed the young Anjou had captured her heart. Or so, at least, she made it seem. Historians differ on this point, some certain she was genuinely smitten, others convinced it was all a show for political ends. That seems the more likely interpretation, and yet when a Puritan pamphlet by John Stubbs appeared, lambasting the proposed marriage, Elizabeth was so incensed she threatened to execute Stubbs, along with his printer and publisher. Eventually she merely ordered that Stubbs's and the publisher's right hands be chopped off.

None of this indicates Elizabeth's real feelings. The biographer Jane Dunn writes that 'For a while she believed she could be as other women, pursue her love, share sexual pleasure, even give birth to the heir which would secure her beloved father's dynasty.' If that was the case, it seems most likely that the Queen allowed herself to indulge the dream of possible happiness and fulfilment, all the while knowing, if not acknowledging, that it could not be. Always attentive to public opinion, what most worried Elizabeth during this protracted courtship was not that she was too old to marry or bear children, but that her subjects disapproved. She knew that they believed her too old. Worse still, after the St Bartholomew's Day Massacre, they could not trust a Catholic Frenchman.

While the country held its breath, Mary anticipated the union with excitement. Should a French ally share the throne, it might lead to her liberty. In a state of hopeful anticipation, she asked the Archbishop of Glasgow to find out Anjou's attitude towards her. Towards the end of 1579 she requested that Castelnau update her on the marriage negotiations, and in a later letter she offered invaluable advice to be passed to Anjou, to improve his prospects of winning Elizabeth:

> you must advise the said Duke, when he is here, not to persist in the request that he is said to have made for the rehabilitation of the Earl of Leicester, whom he does not need in order to fortify himself, and he needs even less to fear [Leicester's] strength and power if he takes care of it in good time. I know that some Catholics have already been greatly offended by this, fearing to see themselves again under the persecutions of the past. Such fear will make them constantly affectionate toward the Duke of Anjou, all the more so if they see him animated against their common enemies.

Mary's letters concerning Anjou and Elizabeth reveal the febrile atmosphere at court, with many secretly against the proposed union. In January 1582, she wrote that she had learned that Leicester and Burghley were acting with Spain against Anjou and the Low Countries. Members of the Privy Council had professed their affection to France and the Duke of Anjou, but in fact, she wrote, they were acting against the proposed marriage, spreading rumours that the duke planned to usurp the English throne, and that, if the marriage took place, they were ready to take arms. She added that Bess of Hardwick was trying to bring her husband into the faction against the marriage.

Meanwhile, Catholics in England hoped that Anjou would act in their favour, as several Jesuits had been recently executed. The Earl of Huntingdon, however, was trying to convince some Catholics that the duke was not really interested in religious matters, and that those supporting the marriage would be punished anyway. Mary said Castelnau should warn the Queen against those actions, but that he should not reveal that the information came from her. In her next letter, Mary reported that Bess had been won over by the faction against the Elizabeth–Anjou marriage, having been promised that her granddaughter Arbella Stuart would be married to one of the Countess of Essex's sons, either by her first husband, or by the Earl of Leicester. In the end, Leicester and Bess's machinations came to nothing, since Leicester's son died in 1584, aged three, leaving his father grief-stricken. While little Robert was alive, however, Mary's newly discovered letters show her fretting that Leicester would attempt to take both the Scottish and English thrones, and kill James.

Gradually, however, as the weeks rolled by, England relaxed and Mary's optimism over the likelihood of an impending wedding faltered. The Earl of Shrewsbury's son George Talbot told him as early as May 1579 that odds of three to one had been laid against the negotiations coming to anything. By late 1580, the Spanish ambassador was offering a bet of 100 to 1 against, a gamble no one was willing to accept. They were wise, since in 1582, at the end of Anjou's second wooing visit, Elizabeth gave him a hefty sum for his campaign against the Spanish in the Netherlands, where he had been made sovereign of the United Provinces. Shortly thereafter, he finally left the court, and Elizabeth reportedly danced for joy. On his departure, her final chance of married bliss evaporated, if it had not already done so years earlier. Meanwhile, wrote Mary in one of the recently decrypted letters, Leicester, who had accompanied Anjou to the Low Countries, was bragging that he had convinced him he was his best friend in England, and had encouraged him to stay in Flanders, thus committing to protect the 'drunk' people of Flanders. She said she was ashamed the duke was being mocked.

While Anjou was in the frame, Elizabeth attempted to pander to French interests by making a rare concession to Mary. In conciliatory mood, she allowed her to send her secretary Claude Nau to the Scottish court with gifts for her son. For months Mary had been secretly writing about her hope for this. Sadly, it turned into a humiliating debacle, since Mary's letter for James failed to address him as King but as 'Prince of Scotland'. Nau was refused access and turned away, meaning neither messenger nor presents reached the boy. It was consistent with the way the mother and son's relationship was controlled. As well as presents being withheld, their letters to each other were often confiscated, thereby deepening the silence and suspicion between them.

Little wonder that in 1580 Mary produced an *Essay on Adversity*, into which she poured her personal frustrations. Drawing on the lives of troubled rulers as far back as biblical and Roman times, she wrote: 'Tribulation has been to them as a furnace to fine gold – a means of proving their virtue, of opening their so-long blinded eyes, and of teaching them to know themselves and their own failings.' This philosophical treatise was in essence a meditation on how to put life's reverses to good purpose.

Few had faced greater adversity than the benighted Mary. Not knowing what would happen to her next, and with the dread of murder never far from her thoughts, she turned to her religious devotions in a way she never had as a young queen. By the time of her execution, she had shaped her image into that of a Catholic martyr; this was a clever, calculated political statement, but it genuinely reflected how she had come to see herself. As is evident from her letters, her sense of dignity and position never wavered, her ego too large for the rooms in which she was held. Her conviction that she was suffering for her faith rather than for anything she had done can be seen as a redirecting of her previous insouciant confidence in her God-given position as sovereign. Thwarted in this expression of herself, it seems that the role of martyr gave her solace, strength and, ultimately, a remarkable degree of power.

By now a captive of more than twelve years, Mary was very different from the woman who stepped ashore at Workington. Under duress, her character had been tempered, from a headstrong and entitled sovereign to a more contemplative – though still occasionally reckless – personality. Mary's youthful beauty had long since faded, and, with exercise severely restricted and many periods when she was bedbound, she had gained a considerable amount of weight. Yet she never lost her winning personality and wit, her generosity to those around her and her indomitable sense of what was owed her as lawful Queen of Scotland. In the long, slow years leading to her terrible end, she leaned on her faith as her only steadfast support. What had once been a conventional Catholic obedience was by now bone-deep, as much a part of her nature as her former vivacity and carefree spirit. To meet the middle-aged Mary was to encounter a woman steeped in the scriptures and prayer, who believed that not just she but also the religion she represented were under mortal threat.

James was to be at the forefront of Mary's thoughts in the coming few years. His was not an enviable position, as he grew into his kingship and attempted to navigate between the competing demands of his mother and Elizabeth while maintaining his independence and dignity. By the time of Morton's arrest, he had shown himself skilled in the art of political manoeuvring. He was also aware that Elizabeth was a more powerful and fruitful ally than his mother, the person whose support would better advance his ambitions. One of the ironies of James and Mary's relationship is that Mary's claim to the English succession was inherited by her son. His determination to succeed Elizabeth on her death was thus the wedge that came between him and his mother.

In March 1580, however, James was still a child, as far as Mary was concerned, and she was distressed at hearing he had been unwell. 'I myself had the same indigestion about the same age,' she wrote to the Archbishop of Glasgow. 'I remember especially that they made me wear ivory on the stomach, and that I used confected nuts and nutmegs before refection.' Despite having been reassured that the king was not in danger, she asked the archbishop to make arrangements to 'send his weight in virgin wax' to the church of Notre-Dame de Cléry, near Orléans, where she had been with her husband Francis II as he died. She asked that a novena be said there and Mass be sung daily, for a full year. On each day thirteen pennies were to be handed out to thirteen 'poor persons'.

Recognising that Elizabeth's marriage to Anjou was a lost cause, like a sunflower turning towards the sun, Mary looked to Spain. She urged the Archbishop to contact the Spanish ambassador and propose 'the removal of my son to Flanders or Spain, according as shall be agreeable to the king his master'. Spain was now her preferred ally, her relatives in France, including the king, having failed to come to her aid as she had expected. In several of the newly decoded letters she bemoaned France's abandonment of her and of James, leaving her no alternative, she suggested, but to seek Spain as an ally.

Among France's many inadequacies was the continuing mismanagement – and appropriation – of her dowry, which, as her letters official and secret show, was a perpetual source of bitterness. In one covert message, for instance, from April 1583, she thanked Castelnau for sending her money, since what she was receiving from her dowry was half of what she was owed. As a consequence of this disgraceful treatment, Mary struggled with lack of funds throughout her captivity. Her greatest concern always was to pay her servants what they were due, although, as well as their wages, the many luxuries which made her life bearable doubtless placed a considerable strain on her income.

In 1580 Mary wrote at length to Elizabeth, reminding her of her rightful claim to the English succession, and pleading to be set free. Since her health was wretched, she also requested a visit to Buxton: 'I have not found here any remedy more efficacious for the complaint in my side, with which I am excessively tormented.' The spa visit was granted, her liberty not. But despite their beneficial effects, Buxton's waters could only offer temporary relief. A letter to the French ambassador from Mary's physician, Dominique Bourgoing, points to the root of her ailments: 'I see nothing that can give hopes of her health but freedom and deliverance from the evils to which she has been so long exposed.'

By now the damp, cold and draughty conditions in which she had been confined, without any recourse to outdoor exercise, had led to irreversible illness, including rheumatic complaints that often made it difficult for her to walk unaided. Since her time at Carlisle Castle, Mary had been the subject of various escape plans, few of which she had entertained. Perhaps because of her worsening health, or because she had endured so many years of misery, it seems she was beginning to lose faith in effecting her release by diplomatic channels. In a letter to the Archbishop of Glasgow, she intimated that if Elizabeth continued to deny her demand to be set free, she would consider gaining her release another way, whatever the risk: 'I shall omit no possible means, nor refuse any just condition, to arrive thereat.' It was a marked change of position, and the first indication of the dramas the new decade would bring.

Perhaps the saddest aspect of Mary's story is the misplaced faith she put in her son, who she believed loved and honoured her as she deserved. The misunderstandings, deceptions and treacheries that underlay their relationship are a tragedy in themselves, their political, religious but, above all, personal ramifications worthy of Shakespeare. With Morton's arrest and the stellar rise of Esmé Stuart – now Duke of Lennox – Mary wrongly assumed that Scotland was under the control of a regime close to the House of Guise and sympathetic to her cause. Galvanised by fresh hope, she proposed a scheme that would bring about her restoration. All it required was her son's and Esmé Stuart's approval, and the meeting of a series of imperious and misjudged demands. With Morton's malign interference at an end, Mary had no doubts that James would rally to her: 'with time he will submit himself entirely to my devotion . . . and by this means I think that my liberty could soon follow'.

With high expectations of what lay ahead, she asked her cousin Henri, Duke of Guise, to act as her agent for what she called an 'Association' between her and James, which would allow them jointly to share the Scottish throne. This agreement would acknowledge James's right to the throne – which Mary and all of Catholic Europe currently refuted – while also upholding hers. Wishing for a speedy resolution, she set up a commission, led by James Beaton, Archbishop of Glasgow, to handle negotiations.

Perhaps the best thing to come of Morton's downfall was the sudden relaxation on mother and son directly contacting each other. For the first time since Mary left Scotland, they could correspond without interference. In three letters from 1581, James was courteous and cautiously enthusiastic. In his first, written in January in French, he was eager to show that he recognised 'the honour and duty which I owe to you, having hope that with time, God will give me grace to offer you my good and loving services, knowing well enough, that all the honour I have in this world I hold from you'.

Mary had already sent him a ring, and he returned the compliment with a ring of his own. 'You have made it appear very plainly, by your last letter, how good a mother you are,' he wrote, signing himself 'Your obedient son for ever, Jacques R.'

James made positive noises about the Association, despite saying it would need Elizabeth's approval, but in reality he, and Esmé

Stuart, whom James delegated to communicate with Mary over its details, were cool on the idea. It was in their best interests to keep negotiations open, and to use the situation to their advantage, but even James's lukewarm response was misleading. As Steven Veerapen writes, he was keeping his options open, 'hoping – quixotically – for a solution to the insoluble problem of how to keep Mary Queen of Scots alive, out of trouble, out of Scottish affairs, and all in a way which would keep his active conscience quiet'.

With an English army menacing Scotland at the border in protest at Morton's treatment, Esmé Stuart asked for and was sent money and gunpowder from the Duke of Guise. Rather than a demonstration of commitment to Mary's proposal, though, this was sheer opportunism.

As early as February, Mary was requesting greater freedom, telling Castelnau, 'I should feel obliged if the Queen of England . . . would pay a little attention to the things necessary for the complete recovery and preservation of my health, such as exercise on horseback round about here, when I shall get well.'

With no concessions granted, in October Mary wrote to Elizabeth in a frankly threatening manner, stating that if the strictness of her guard was not eased to allow her to exercise, she would make over her title to the crown of Scotland to James, along with everything else in her possession. Should her enemies continue to try to persecute her, she added, they would find themselves faced only with 'a sickly, dying body'.

Alarmed in part by the thought of Mary dying because of ill treatment, but more by the Association she was planning with James, Elizabeth sent Robert Beale, Walsingham's useful brother-in-law, to Sheffield Castle in November. Her ostensible reason was to find out more regarding Mary's list of complaints about her captivity and the effect this was having on her health. What she really wanted to know was where things stood between Mary and James.

The queen was so unwell when Beale visited that she could not get out of bed. He reported to Walsingham that she told him that 'the want of fresh air had brought her into such a weakness and impotency of her limbs, as that she could not go six steps, nor sit up and therefore was forced to keep her bed and if the like restraint continued still, she said she could not long endure'. By now, she said, she had no thought of ever marrying again, 'and besides her body was in such case as that she was not fit for any such matter now'. She told him that she was old, 'if not in years, yet in health of body; all her hair was grey, and when she had made over her interest to her son, who would care for her when she could bring nothing?'

Beale's visit lasted several weeks, and on one occasion Mary seems to have staged a tableau to convince him of how close to death she was. When he entered her room there was so little light he could scarcely see her. A feeble voice emerged from the gloom saying she did not know how long she had left to live and begging for physicians to be sent to her from London. Beale was aghast, but Shrewsbury and Bess were unmoved, thinking it merely a ruse to allow her to smuggle out messages. It is a miserable portrait of Mary, even if she was exaggerating. Beale returned to London unsettled by what he had witnessed.

In Scotland, meantime, when the list of Mary's terms and conditions for the Association arrived, all consideration of a joint venture ended. Among countless provisions, Mary insisted that she officially clear her son of acting as king in her absence. Her preferred option was that there be a 'new coronation'. (Since her abdication had been revoked for being illegally procured by force, it could be argued that James and his nobles had technically been committing treason.) After this situation was publicly rectified, Mary would proclaim his right to rule alongside her. Among other unthinkable demands was a policy of toleration for Catholics in Scotland, allowing priests to preach and debate with Kirk ministers. Showing she had no conception of how Scotland stood, she added her wish that James might yet convert.

Steven Reid writes that Mary's wildly inappropriate demands showed a 'wholly unrealistic sense of her enduring significance both in Scotland and in James's affections'. The only measure that did appeal to James was his mother's promise to write to the Catholic heads of Europe instructing them henceforth to refer to him as King of Scotland. So far, they shared his mother's view that he was merely Prince of Scotland. But on receipt of Mary's conditions, James went quiet. It was the strongest indication yet that the son she imagined would help and protect her had other priorities.

Chapter 21

'I look this day for no kingdom but that of my God'

THE RUTHVEN RAID

The ciphered letters Mary smuggled out of Sheffield Castle, and her other prisons, were often dangerously open about her willingness to bring about Elizabeth's downfall. During this period, Mary was troubled by the loss of two dependable undercover go-betweens, and by the tightness of security at the Scottish border, which made getting letters in and out of the country even more difficult. Confiding to the Archbishop of Glasgow her hope for the Spanish to land in Scotland to help bring about her restoration, she was equally upfront about her support for England's arch-enemy, Philip II. Sinisterly, she described gaining her freedom as synonymous with her taking the English throne. Since the letter in which she discusses all this, which had been encrypted and sent secretly, is in the official archive, it was presumably intercepted by Walsingham and either confiscated or sent on to the Archbishop once its contents had been copied.

To Walsingham, Mary's double-dealing would not have come as a surprise; he expected nothing less. More surprising is that the correspondence was not used to build a damning case against her and put an end to further plotting. Such restraint might suggest that these letters were a useful way to monitor where danger lay, and that the greater risk was to be taken unawares. Seemingly tireless, despite her woeful health, the captive queen fired off messages as if they were emails, bombarding her contacts for information, issuing directives and voicing opinions with the confidence of one who still had a seat at the high table of international affairs.

There is something manic about this activity. Something sad, too, in how out of touch she had grown with the outside world, and her relevance to it. Interestingly, the volume of her letters and her increasingly emphatic tone correspond directly with the decline in her influence. Despite being astute, intelligent and worldly-wise, she was by now suffering from delusion, seeing herself as far better informed and a great deal more important than was the case.

During the negotiations for Elizabeth's marriage to the Duke of Anjou, for instance, as found in one of the recently discovered secret letters, she asked her ambassador to convince Elizabeth that 'she has no one in her realm to better rely upon' than herself. Mary was also confident that Anjou's intentions towards her were entirely positive. When it was subsequently rumoured that Mary had been briefing against Anjou, she was outraged and demanded Castelnau find the source of this slander.

The Anjou marriage consumed much of her attention, but another preoccupation was the urgent matter of returning England and Scotland to the Catholic faith. Such determination befitted her position as a religious figurehead, and in July 1581 she asked Pope Gregory XIII for his help to make it happen. Six years earlier, in 1575, he had issued an order to reconvert England, calling his mission the 'Enterprise of England'. Progress was slow, and it was not until 1580, when he reissued the papal bull excommunicating Elizabeth, that the project began to gather momentum. To encourage action, the Pope affirmed that assassinating Elizabeth would not imperil the murderer's soul: 'there is no doubt that whoever sends her out of the world with the pious intention of doing God service, not only does not sin but gains merit. And so, if these English nobles decide to undertake so glorious a work, they do not commit any sin.'

Following this call to arms, in the summer of 1580 missionary Jesuits began to arrive secretly in England and Scotland from the Continent. Around the same time Philip II also planned to attack, and Mary asked her French ambassador for information on that front: 'Do not fail to write to me particularly what you shall have been able to learn of the king of Spain's army, and of that of the Pope; for which they are in great alarm here, and fear that there is to be an invasion of Ireland, according to the confession of a Spanish soldier who had been taken prisoner, to whom they have applied the rack.' Five hundred Spanish and papal troops did indeed land in Ireland, but when the support they requested from European leaders did not materialise, they were brutally defeated by an English army.

In England, the appearance of Jesuits, risking their lives to bring about the overturn of Elizabeth's rule, created panic at the prospect of insurrection or invasion. New laws were introduced, making such subversive activity punishable by death, and torture was condoned. It became a treasonable crime to be reconciled to Catholicism, and in 1585 it was a treasonable act for Jesuits to return to England.

In Scotland, the Kirk was put on high alert for any sign of Catholic spies. The prime players of this wave of Jesuit incursion were Robert Persons and his fearless side-kick Edmund Campion, who had a gift for rhetoric and writing. His intention in returning to England, Campion wrote, was 'to cry alarm spiritual against foul vice and proud ignorance, wherewith my poor countrymen are abused'. He declared that priests carrying out this mission must never give up hope 'while we have a man left to enjoy your Tyburn, or to be racked with your torments, or to be consumed with your prisons'.

These words come from an open letter Campion composed to be circulated in the event of his capture. Published as a pamphlet, it was used, together with clandestine prayer meetings and masses, to nurture the thirsty spirits of England's Catholic community. As with illegal Conventicles in Scotland in the following century, devotional gatherings were conducted with the utmost secrecy. But for the hardiest souls, dread of reprisals proved no deterrent.

Despite the state's vigilance and fury, over the next twenty years, writes Alison Weir, 'no more than 250 Catholics would be executed or die in prison. There is, however, evidence that about ninety of these persons were tortured.' Of 471 priests working in England over a period of forty years, writes Stephen Alford, '116 were executed; at least 294 were sent to prison; 17 died in jail; and 91 were eventually banished from England'. When Campion met his inevitable grisly end, relics were made from his 'holy rib'. But in 1581, some months before his martyrdom, he and Persons looked to Scotland, where Esmé Stuart, Duke of Lennox, was proposing the restoration of Catholicism – as also in England and Ireland – with the help of the troops sent by the Duke of Guise and Philip II.

Early in 1582 a Jesuit priest, Father Holt, who brought with him written confirmation of Philip's support from the Spanish ambassador Mendoza, was despatched north to talk to Esmé Stuart and help bring about the Association between Mary and James. He was joined by Father Crichton, another Jesuit then at large in Scotland, and between them they secretly agreed that a 'papal army' of 20,000, drawn from Spain, Italy and Scotland, under the leadership of Esmé Stuart, James and the Duke of Guise, could achieve their purpose. By toppling Elizabeth, they would free Mary – although James would retain the title of King of Scotland – and the old faith would sweep the board. Confident of success, Esmé Stuart informed Mary of their invasion plan, raising her hopes yet again.

While it sounded good in theory, Philip baulked. He remained ambivalent about ousting Elizabeth and was unwilling to risk so much money and so many men for Mary. Thus a promising venture came to nothing. In fact, it was worth less than that for James and Esmé Stuart, because by now Stuart's Catholic sympathies – despite his public assertion of having converted to Protestantism – were causing consternation at the Scottish court. He had only a few months left before his spectacular fall from grace and expulsion.

In the months following Morton's arrest, the anti-Morton faction began to fracture. Esmé Stuart fell out spectacularly with Captain James Stewart, who was by now Earl of Arran (the unfortunate incumbent earl was clinically insane, and had his title effectively stolen from him). This rift resulted in the ridiculous situation in which there were two privy councils, one sitting at Holyrood under the Earl of Arran, and the other at Dalkeith, under Esmé Stuart.

Though aged only sixteen, James had already experienced his share of drama. Few personal events in his life, however, would match what was to come for shock and alarm. While on a hunting trip in August 1582, he was persuaded to spend the night at Ruthven Castle (now Huntingtower Castle), the seat of William Ruthven, Earl of Gowrie. When he made to leave the next morning, his way was barred. Frightened and angry, he realised he had fallen into a trap. He was now the victim, or pawn, of a faction at court that could no longer tolerate the Esmé Stuart–Arran regime, with its rapacious demands on nobles and restriction of access to the king.

Esmé Stuart's policies threatened ruin for the country and the man himself seemed to hold his *'petit maistre'* in thrall. The tub-thumping but undoubtedly courageous Andrew Melville, John Knox's successor as leader of the Kirk, described their relationship more colourfully, denouncing the Duke of Lennox for keeping James 'in a mistie night of captivity and blak darknes of schameful servitude'.

Now James truly was captive, like his mother. He was held under heavy guard first at Ruthven Castle, then at Stirling and finally, for most of the rest of his ten-month imprisonment, at Holyrood. His kidnappers, who called themselves the Lords Enterprisers, had several demands, but their first priority was that James banish the malign Esmé Stuart and promote the country's own nobility rather than strangers and foreigners. In a way unimaginable today should there be a similar coup d'état, they had the backing of the Kirk, which had been appalled at James's plan to bridle its power by imposing a form of episcopal governance upon it. The Kirk also reviled the regime's immoral behaviour, and its collusion with Mary, Queen of Scots and the Catholic cause, rumours of which hung over the court like a toxic cloud.

Led by William Ruthven, who had been told (mistakenly or maliciously) that Esmé Stuart planned to murder him, the Ruthven Raid was carried out by a powerful cabal, the main players of which included Mar, Glencairn, Angus and Lindsay. A daring protest against the country's misgovernance, the conspirators' intention was to ensure that James would in future follow a Protestant, pro-English policy, and acknowledge the Kirk's right to independence. They were equally eager to institute reforms that would reduce the royal household's outrageously heavy expenses.

On hearing the news of James's kidnapping, Mary became so ill it was thought she would die. When able to gather herself, she frantically urged the Archbishop of Glasgow to arrange for French troops to come to Esmé Stuart's aid and liberate James. As she confided in a recently decoded letter, she felt helpless, knowing James was in the hands of their worst enemies. But no help from France arrived. Esmé Stuart made one wild attempt to rescue the king, which was foiled, after which he fled for Paris via London. There he appears to have charmed Elizabeth, but not Walsingham.

He died the following spring, refusing Catholic rites and passing out of this world as a Protestant in the hope that it would benefit his children's fortunes. His embalmed heart was sent to James, along with a letter begging him to protect his children. One of his brood would soon arrive in Scotland and become a close friend of the young king. This child, the nine-year-old Ludovic, who was raised to the earldom of Lennox, was brought to Scotland by Patrick Gray, Master of Gray, one of Mary's people in Paris. Gray was supposedly working on her behalf, but on reaching the Scottish court soon turned against her.

That James's capture had the support of the Kirk was an added humiliation to an already miserable situation. Alone, with his beloved Esmé Stuart gone and Arran imprisoned and then forbidden access to the king, he had to rely largely on his own wits for his escape. But he was not entirely friendless. The French ambassador, Mothe-Fénelon, and the Marquis de Mainville, sent by Henri III to control the situation, made noble efforts to set the conspirators against each other. They also managed to unite a party of Esmé Stuart's supporters in opposition to the kidnapping party, including Huntly, Bothwell, Angus, Argyll, Montrose and Seton. And, in a wholly unexpected stroke of good fortune, the Earl of Gowrie, on learning that Esmé Stuart had never intended to kill him, repented of snatching the king, and began to waver in his commitment to the cause.

The Ruthven Raiders' regime was awash with rival foreign ambassadors, since two English ambassadors, Robert Bowes and George Carey, joined the court alongside the French, and proved almost as powerful. One of the Raiders' first moves had been to restore the relationship with England, which had faltered with Morton's arrest and execution. As well as shoring up this new accord, the English ambassadors' remit was to curb the amity growing between James and the French. To this end, Elizabeth appeared willing to entertain ideas for Mary's liberation. The French, for their part, were there to renew the Auld Alliance and press upon the king Mary's willingness for an Association.

Eventually, while on the pretence of a hunting trip around the country, in June 1583 James made his escape on horseback from Falkland Palace to St Andrews. There he was met by supporters he had summoned, and, after the threat of recapture had been averted, he was restored to power. Although he reinstated the loathed Arran to high position, James was now more in command – and more politically skilled – than ever before. His new Privy Council alarmed the English by being dominated by Catholics.

During James's captivity, Mary had been on tenterhooks. In November 1582, in a particularly plangent letter to Elizabeth, she reproved her for mistrusting her, for her refusal to allow her access to her son and for the lack of information she received about James during this anxious time. It was a resounding *j'accuse*, and it would have taken a hard heart not to be moved by its depiction of a decade of cruel and unjust confinement. Added to this, in a now familiar refrain, Mary stated that her time on this earth would not last long: 'For I protest to you upon my honour, that I look this day for no kingdom but that of my God, whom I see preparing me for the better conclusion of all my afflictions and adversities.'

Some weeks later, Elizabeth despatched Robert Beale to Sheffield, with a list of responses to Mary's complaints. In this duel of words, Mary had the moral upper hand, her treatment from the start indefensible. But while her words must have stung the Queen, they had no tangible impact. And while in the coming months Elizabeth made a show of finding out the terms on which Mary might come to an accommodation that would allow her to be liberated, these were little more than window-dressing. Beale, recognising how unwell Mary was, seems to have behaved kindly towards her. Trying to dampen her expectations, he indicated that he believed James had no intention of agreeing to an Association, since it was not 'desired by the King or the nobility'. To this warning, Mary appears to have been deaf.

Chapter 22

'I know my duty to you, as much as any son in the world towards his mother'

RENEWED HOPE OF RESTORATION

The Earl of Shrewsbury was, by 1582, in poor health, suffering severely from arthritis, gout and, in the coming months, from what he described as 'colic and the stone' – renal colic and kidney stones. His worst episodes were worrying enough for Mary to mention in her letters, including a reference in one of the newly discovered secret cache, from 1580. In this she wrote to Castelnau that although the earl was not as close to death as was rumoured, she nevertheless expected him to die in the near future. In light of this, she asked the ambassador to ensure her safety by secretly trying to influence the choice of her new guardian. Clearly her concern for her captor was prompted as much by fear that she would be placed under a less sympathetic guardian as by concern for his welfare. But perhaps that is unfair. For all her faults, Mary did have a tender heart, and if there was any subject on which she could fully commiserate, it was the ordeal of being unwell.

Shrewsbury had many other problems to contend with beyond his ailments. Financial worries over the cost of his royal prisoner were a constant aggravation but so, increasingly, was his wife's behaviour. The year 1582 had been a sad one at Sheffield Manor Lodge, with Arbella Stuart's mother Elizabeth dying there in January, leaving her child an orphan. Nine months later, Shrewsbury's eldest son and heir Francis Talbot died of the plague. After this blow, it appears that the earl's paranoia over his place in Bess's affections deepened.

Francis's death meant that Bess's youngest daughter, Mary, who was married to Shrewsbury's younger son Gilbert, would in time become Countess of Shrewsbury. The earl feared that, with Mary's social elevation all but assured, he was no longer necessary to his wife's plans. The bickering between them sharpened into spite.

There was, however, one bright spot in Shrewsbury's life. His palatial new manor house, at Worksop, in Sherwood Forest in Nottinghamshire, was nearing completion. Adapted from his father's hunting lodge, it was designed by Robert Smythson, who had worked on Longleat and would later design Hardwick Hall. Magnificent in scale, and filled with modern glass that banished any vestige of medieval gloom, Worksop was as bold a statement of wealth and influence as can be imagined. Possibly intended to cast Chatsworth into the shade – which it undoubtedly did – it was a last hurrah from the melancholy and beleaguered earl, who hoped to show himself fit to entertain (and harbour) royalty. Burghley was so impressed by the size of the gallery he called it 'the fairest' in England.

Never one to miss an opportunity, Bess hired Smythson in 1582, while construction on Worksop was going slowly, to design the hunting tower at Chatsworth. The following year, even as building at Worksop continued, Shrewsbury relocated Mary there on two occasions, in June and September. For the first time in over a decade, she enjoyed an entirely new change of scene. Given the splendour and comforts of this 500-room palace, set amid abundant woodlands, it must have been a welcome interlude. Today, sadly, almost nothing is left of Shrewsbury's manor house, which was destroyed by fire in 1761. The rebuilt Worksop Manor is part of a stud farm, with no public access.

The earl was not the only one afflicted by periods of serious illness. For the past couple of years, Mary's closest companion Mary Seton, who had been at her side since she was a child, had been increasingly frail. Some might consider her life as well as her health to have been blighted by her mistress's incarceration, but the intensely religious and, in Antonia Fraser's word, 'spinsterish' noblewoman had, in fact, twice had the opportunity to marry during Mary's years in prison. Unfortunately, her first suitor was executed for treason and the second died of smallpox.

Eventually Seton became so sickly that, in 1583, Mary permitted her to retire to France. She would live in the convent of Saint-Pierre at Rheims for the rest of her days, which, now she was liberated from her own quasi-imprisonment, outnumbered Mary's by thirty years. One can only imagine how the queen mourned the loss of such a trusted, devoted and sympathetic friend, when she felt herself surrounded by enemies and was growing weaker politically and physically with every year.

James, meantime, was coming into his own in Scotland. An attempt by Arran's enemies to topple him had led to their exile and the crumbling of the pro-English party. Now Arran and his cousin Colonel William Stewart, captain of James's guard and a favoured privy councillor, headed a loyal, partisan (and intensely disliked) group around the king, upholding the position of the Stewarts, and thereby unnerving England.

In a letter in November 1583, James wrote to Mary indicating that he was keen to negotiate with the Duke of Guise over an Association: 'Be assured, that in all the adversities which I have sustained for love of you, I have never failed of, or been turned from my duty and affection towards you but, on the contrary, it greatly increases and augments with every trouble that I have: at any rate I would make appear to you that I know my duty to you, as much as any son in the world towards his mother.' Had they reached her, his warm words would have brought some comfort – cold comfort as it would transpire – but the letter was intercepted and confiscated, and she knew nothing of it.

Elizabeth, angered by James's seeming eagerness to make an ally of France, sent a very reluctant Walsingham to the Scottish court, to remind the young king what he stood to lose if he bound himself to France rather than England. The secretary was far from well, suffering from such severe pain he could not ride. (On his death, in 1590, he was found to have a growth in his testicles.) His snail's-pace journey from London by litter was extremely uncomfortable. 'I shall have more ease in another world,' he hoped, 'than I do in this.' With diplomatic hold-ups at the border causing further delays, odds were placed in Scotland against him ever making it as far as Stirling.

But it was always a mistake to underestimate Walsingham, as those who lost their bets would attest. Although he would have been relieved to reach his journey's end, his reception when he arrived at the Scottish court was cold. James left him to stew for two days, and when they had the first of two meetings, it was on the inauspicious date of 9 September, the anniversary of the Battle of Flodden. There is no record that Walsingham, who was accompanied by the English ambassador Robert Bowes, mentioned the Scots' dreadful defeat at England's hands, although both would surely have been aware of it. Nevertheless, he spoke sternly, refusing either to fawn or to cajole James into returning to Elizabeth's fold. Instead, he made it clear that England would prosper with or without Scotland's support.

With no prevarication, Walsingham laid out England's request that James cease persecuting the Ruthven lords, and rebuked him for altering the members of his government without informing Elizabeth or asking her permission. Morton's execution was also a sore point. Reverting to Puritan mode, he sermonised about the role of an honourable king compared to that of a tyrant. There is an irony in a man, professedly bound by the ethics demanded by the gospels, using any means, fair or foul, to ruin James's mother and those who would harm England. Evidently – conveniently – he drew a line between his private morality and that demanded in his governmental role.

Duly chastised, James appeared to fall back into line, professing himself prepared to do Elizabeth's bidding. Walsingham, however, was unconvinced, deeming the young man slippery and untrustworthy. His time in Stirling was made even more uncomfortable by the scold, known as Kate the Witch, whom Arran had hired to hurl abuse at Walsingham and his party at the palace gates. In addition, a diamond ring that James gave to the secretary on his departure had been replaced by Arran with a crystal ring. Irked on every front, the secretary returned to London empty-handed and tormented by pain.

James's disrespectful treatment of Walsingham, and by inference Elizabeth, and his friendliness towards France were not adolescent whims but calculated to strengthen his own position. As Steven Reid writes, 'James used the threat of a possible rapprochement with France to underline his autonomy from Elizabeth and the English government.' At this very early point in his adult reign, he wanted to be treated as an equal to Elizabeth, not a child to be patronised and manipulated. Reluctantly, Elizabeth and her court had to revise their attitude towards him and give him the respect he was due.

Until he had wreaked revenge on the Ruthven lords and those ministers of the Kirk who had applauded his kidnapping, James refused to be constrained by England's representations on their behalf. His reprisals were harsh, and included the execution of Gowrie. Yet ultimately he knew that his future lay with England. During these difficult months, which lasted until late in 1584, although he tugged against Elizabeth's hold over him, he frayed rather than severed the cord between them. Young he might be, but his sights had long been fixed upon the English succession. As a result, his seeming rebellion against Elizabeth could only go so far.

Shortly after Walsingham's unsatisfying visit, the ambassador Castelnau wrote to Henri III, painting a discouraging picture in which he noted that some pessimists feared Elizabeth would be so angered by James's behaviour she would move against Scotland. He was quick to reassure Henri that she 'has resolved not to declare war against the King of Scotland upon any slight pretext or trifling occasion, but allow him to proceed his own way and sow his wild oats; but she should be on her guard against him . . .'

Even so, the mood of country and court was uncertain, with the ambassador worrying that James was in peril: 'the ill-will which the nation bears him, and which is further excited by the English faction, may reduce him to great extremity, like his predecessors, most of whom have been killed or come to a tragical end'. In that unhappy band he included Mary.

For her part, Mary was stating her terms with Elizabeth's envoys for the stringent conditions on which she would accept her liberty, which included ruling jointly with James, not dealing with foreign powers, and recognising Elizabeth as Queen during her lifetime but not relinquishing her and her son's claim to the English throne. Elizabeth, keen to undermine James's association with France, made a show of being prepared to consider Mary's release, albeit with strict conditions attached.

Mischievously, in a comment surely designed to embarrass Walsingham if the letter were intercepted, Mary confided to Castelnau that she believed she could create a rapport with him: 'If I were but sure that the said Valsingham was dealing uprightly, I should be very glad to make friendship with him, looking upon him to be a plain, downright man, and whose disposition would easily agree with mine, if he were acquainted with it otherwise than from the reports of my enemies.'

Among Walsingham's various coups – and there were many still to bear fruit – was turning one of the French ambassador's secretaries into a spy. A clerk in a position to copy Mary, Queen of Scots's correspondence to and from Castelnau, his role effectively was that of a photocopier. Consequently, Walsingham read everything that passed between them, which revealed not only that the ambassador was aware of a simmering plot but also that Mary was enthusiastic about it.

In May 1582, the authorities in the north of England had apprehended a man in an old grey cloak, claiming to be a dentist, who was arrested. His belongings were confiscated, but he was allowed to go on his way after giving his captors a large bribe. It was only later, when John Forster, Warden of the Middle March, was examining the man's possessions, that he made a remarkable discovery. Secreted away in the dentist's looking-glass was a piece of paper. This was an encrypted message from the Spanish ambassador Bernardino de Mendoza to the Jesuit priest William Crichton, containing information on the Pope's 'Enterprise for England'. Alerted to the dangers of an imminent invasion, Walsingham worked deviously and doggedly to prove a link between Mary, Queen of Scots and those intent on destroying Elizabeth and Protestant England.

It took only a single, decidedly odd assassination plot against Elizabeth to justify a national state of alarm. That autumn, a Catholic gentleman from Warwickshire called John Somerville set out to shoot the Queen. Unwisely, he told several people of his plan 'to see her head on a pole, for she was a serpent and a viper', thereby leading to his arrest and imprisonment. Clearly he was not of sound mind. Charged with treason, he was condemned to death but hanged himself in his Newgate cell the night before his execution. Others who had known of his intentions were also arrested, among them his father-in-law and a missionary priest called Hall, who were both executed. There seemed to be no direct link to Mary in this strange episode, beyond the Pope's urging of good Catholics to kill the heathen Elizabeth. But there was a far more disturbing plan brewing, to which the insane Somerville's personal mission pointed. His peculiar venture put the government on even higher alert.

For some time, Secretary Walsingham had been well aware that secret messages were being smuggled in and out of Mary's prisons. He discovered that these were being conveyed by Francis Throckmorton, a Catholic gentleman and nephew of Nicholas Throckmorton, the English ambassador who had offered Mary sound advice when she was a captive at Lochleven. On his first appearance in Mary's newly discovered letters, in April 1582, she referred to him as '*la Tour*'. Aged twenty-nine, Francis Throckmorton had come under the influence of Catholic missionaries while he was at Oxford University, and later, after his law degree, when he was travelling on the continent, where his brother Thomas was consorting with Catholic rebels. By the time of his return to London, he was acting as a secret agent for the Duke of Guise's plan for invasion. He became a friend of Castelnau, whose house near the Fleet was under constant watch by Walsingham's men, and his frequent visits to the Spanish embassy to see Bernardino de Mendoza raised further mistrust. Until Somerville's apprehension, however, the secretary had been in no hurry to arrest Throckmorton, awaiting more tangible evidence of treason. Now, unnerved by Somerville's outspoken desire to kill the Queen and fearing immediate danger to her life, he could no longer leave Throckmorton at large.

When the constables knocked on his door, Throckmorton was in the process of writing in cipher to Mary. A search of his houses in London and Kent threw up several incriminating documents, including a list of prominent English Catholics and of potential ports where an army could land, along with a polemic by John Leslie, Bishop of Ross, proclaiming Mary's right to the English crown. Although Throckmorton denied the lists had been written by him, under interrogation in the Tower of London, and the persuasive threat of a second session on the rack, he revealed all.

What Walsingham learned was profoundly alarming. This was not some amateur attempt to liberate Mary but an international plan for invasion, involving the Duke of Guise, Philip II, the French and Spanish embassies in London and some of the highest placed nobility in England. Two armies, of French, Spanish and Italian soldiers were to land in the south-west and the north-east of England, aided by the Earls of Northumberland and Arundel. Also involved was Lord Henry Howard. An open supporter of Mary, whom his unfortunate brother, the Duke of Norfolk, had hoped to marry, Howard was already on Walsingham's radar. Thanks to the secretary's mole within the embassy, Howard was known to be a furtive night-time visitor to Castelnau. All these men were in on it, said Throckmorton. As was Mary herself, and a man called Charles Paget. Indeed, as the recently deciphered letters show, Mary was not merely aware of the plot but also offered to give up to £2,000 to her Guise cousins to aid their efforts.

Paget had previously roused Walsingham's suspicions. As an émigré in Paris, he was a close associate of James Beaton, Archbishop of Glasgow, who ran Mary's embassy there. Paget worked alongside

Mary's agent, Thomas Morgan, dealing with her French affairs. A few years earlier, he had offered himself as a spy, intending to play the double agent, but Walsingham had realised what he was up to. Henceforth, he had been kept under watch.

Paget and his older brother Thomas were from a venerable English Catholic family. Thomas was involved in the invasion plan, but maintained a low profile. Charles, however, was a key player, acting for Mary's cousin, the Duke of Guise, in helping strategically to organise the French landing. Ahead of the invasion, he was commissioned by Guise secretly to visit England and identify likely landing places for thousands of French troops in Sussex. He was also to ascertain vital practical information, such as how many weapons and supplies would be needed for English Catholics to play their part in this invasion-cum-uprising. He was to liaise with Mendoza, the Spanish ambassador in London, and with Henry Percy, Earl of Northumberland, whose brother had been executed after the Northern Rising. Despite being a Protestant, Northumberland was now behind the push to put Mary on the throne.

For his role in enabling the plotters, the Spanish ambassador was thrown out of the country, hurling threats as he departed. There would not be a Spanish embassy again in Elizabeth's lifetime, and few doubted it would be long before England and Spain were at war. Throckmorton was hanged, drawn and quartered at Tyburn, going to his death in an agony of remorse for betraying Mary: 'I have disclosed the secrets of her who was the dearest thing to me in the world.'

On his revelation of such a wealth of dismaying information, Walsingham recognised the immediate risk to Elizabeth and England. In early 1584, another assassination plot by Dr William Parry was foiled. An eccentric Member of Parliament, he was one of Walsingham's agents who had, you might say, gone rogue by converting to Catholicism and attempting to double-cross the English government. Mary expressed her horror at Parry's schemes, as well she might, because he had been close to her agent Thomas Morgan in Paris, who had encouraged him to kill the Queen of England.

Morgan was thrown into the Bastille and was fortunate to survive, given Elizabeth's eagerness to have him returned to England where he could be properly dealt with. More worrying for Mary was that, even if only by association, she was personally implicated. Evidence and suspicion of her perfidy was mounting.

Chapter 23

'I seek the quiet with all my heart'

THE BOND OF ASSOCIATION

If this story were a symphony, the tempo would be quickening, sawing strings and rolling drums indicating that the final movement had begun. In no time the whole orchestra will be discordantly, electrifyingly at work, before crashing cymbals bring the piece to a resounding finale, and a shattering silence descends.

Events began to escalate when in July 1584, Prince William of Orange, leader of the Protestant rebellion in the Netherlands, was assassinated. The shockwaves rattled Europe, and England braced itself for what was to come. A few months later, the Jesuit, Father William Crichton, who was in league with the Duke of Guise, was captured at sea with a colleague, on their way to Scotland. He carried with him details of an earlier plan for a French-Spanish invasion, in which Mary was implicated. Mary's involvement in attempts to liberate her by force had already been suspected, but, writes the author Stephen Budiansky, what was news was 'the involvement of her followers in a plot directly against Elizabeth's life'.

As the threat-level intensified, Elizabeth was moved to Windsor Castle for safety. Castelnau, who does not seem to have had much of an imagination, could not believe there was a traitor in his ranks. Revealed as an accessory to plans for invasion, with Mary's letters to him explicit in her support for Throckmorton's cause, he became putty in Walsingham's hands. From now on, all letters between him and Mary would – without her knowledge – be passed through the secretary. It did not matter that Walsingham considered Castelnau a good friend; he would still twist the screw to help build a case against the Scottish queen. For his part in this, the ambassador's reputation was ruined.

Complicit from this point in Mary's undoing, the chastened Castelnau was never the same man again. Although his name was kept out of Throckmorton's trial to protect the identity of the embassy mole, he was mistrusted equally by Mary's supporters, by the English court and, when his posting ended the following year, by the French court too.

At the start of 1584, as we saw earlier, Mary had been advising him on how best to communicate secretly by writing in the chemical compound alum. Soon after, however, she would realise this was far too easily detected, and tell him to find other ways of communicating covertly. Already by February of that year, she was expressing doubts about the security of their correspondence: 'I am informed that your house is surrounded day and night with spies, and that all the agents of my correspondence with you have been discovered. Some suspect that your servants are bribed, and that is my own supposition.'

Wilfully blind to the existence of a spy, Castelnau reassured her that all was well, and they continued to exchange letters, despite the queen's nervousness. Now, of course, Walsingham was privy to the Scottish queen's machinations. He might have been looking over her shoulder as she wrote. And there was no end to these conspiratorial letters. As John Guy writes, in these years 'her sense of reality was ebbing away and intrigue became a substitute for activity'. Certainly, few in England could match the reams of correspondence she produced. Even though gaining her release by military intervention remained a possibility, Mary hoped for a better, more peaceable conclusion. In March 1584 she wrote to Burghley about the proposed Association with James and Elizabeth: 'This treaty is the only thing in this world which can ease me either in body or mind; for I feel so depressed by my seventeen years' captivity, I can bear it no longer.'

She seemed not to recognise that her enthusiasm for the Throckmorton plot signalled the end of any chance of returning to

Scotland to rule with her son. Elizabeth had been incandescent to learn of her duplicity. She could no longer pretend that Mary was not capable of endorsing the murder of her cousin who, on several occasions, had thwarted her Privy Council's desire to send Mary to the scaffold. Not that Mary was involved directly in the Throckmorton or Parry plots. After so many years in captivity she was oddly peripheral to Catholic Europe's hopes of restoring England and Scotland to the true faith. Naturally, in their plans she would be placed on the throne of England, but her role was perceived as passive: a figurehead – perhaps even a puppet – rather than a crusader. Now aged and ailing, her value was increasingly symbolic.

While international events pitched England, Scotland and Europe into ferment, Mary had more pressing worries at home. This year marked a turning point in her fortunes, its series of endings foreshadowing the future. The events of 1584 did not represent the shutting of one door and the opening of another, but rather the closing of her remaining hopeful avenues, leaving her in an unlit corridor with only one exit.

On the domestic front, Mary was about to be uprooted. By now, Shrewsbury was fighting several fires, some set – he believed – by his wife. There was open rancour between the pair, and he was estranged from his son Gilbert, who sided with Bess, as did Bess's own children. Feeling financially pinched, Shrewsbury petulantly withheld Bess's allowance while still profiting from the rents on her estates. Unwisely, he wrote disparagingly of her to the Queen, justifying his sense of grievance. Elizabeth was not well placed to offer matrimonial advice, but the couple were urged to mend their differences.

Bess for her part laid the blame for their failing marriage squarely on Mary. By now, the couple were effectively estranged. Outrageous rumours of Shrewsbury's prisoner bearing him one or more children electrified the court, although such tittle-tattle had been circulating for years. On hearing what was being said, Mary immediately suspected Bess and her sons of malicious gossip, and insisted that Elizabeth investigate: 'I shall never have any pleasure until their wickedness is known.' If the Queen did not clear the matter up, she told Castelnau, 'I shall be obliged openly to attack [prosecute] the Countess of Shrewsbury herself.'

Bess, as described in an earlier chapter, appeared with her sons before the Privy Council in late 1584, to answer the accusations of slander. Unsurprisingly, all three emerged blameless. Instead, improbable scapegoats for the source of the scandal were found in two men from Islington, one an innkeeper, the other a vicar, who were charged with spreading malicious rumours.

As Shrewsbury's erratic and aggressive behaviour escalated, there was no hope that he and Bess would be reconciled. Already burdened by personal worries, the earl was rocked at news of the Throckmorton plot and fretted that local Jesuits might cause trouble. Oddly, however, he seemed not to see the risk in allowing his brother-in-law, Edward Manners, Earl of Rutland, to visit him at Worksop. Rutland had been named by the Duke of Guise as among the English lords sympathetic to the Catholic rebels, and to have him in the vicinity of Mary was an extraordinary lapse of judgement. Elizabeth, when informed, was deeply perturbed. Her patience had been sorely tried by the Shrewsbury marital saga; perhaps she also recognised that Shrewsbury was not the man he had been, his mental health giving serious cause for concern.

So it was that, in August 1584, Elizabeth relieved him of his duty as Mary's custodian. What did he feel on relinquishing his charge of fifteen-odd years? On the one hand, he had complained from the start about the heavy responsibility of the role and its exorbitant strain on his purse. On the other, he had spent much time in Mary's company and must have felt some sympathy for her, and possibly even affection. When he was dismissed, relief was probably tempered by regret, and perhaps anxiety over his place in Elizabeth's esteem.

Shrewsbury's replacement was the wealthy but elderly Ralph Sadler, one of Henry VIII's loyal servants, who had reported to him from Linlithgow Palace shortly after Mary's birth. Well-versed in Scottish affairs, he had been one of Elizabeth's commissioners at the York and Westminster conferences in 1568, where the Casket Letters had created a sensation. In his late seventies and suffering from gout, the old soldier diplomat arrived at Sheffield Manor Lodge with fifty heavily armed men and spent several days recovering from the journey. Ordered to take Mary from Sheffield Castle to Wingfield, he questioned the wisdom of moving from such a well-defended position, but dutifully carried out his orders. Thus, early in September 1584, Mary's long years at Sheffield came to an end, as did her restorative trips to Buxton and Chatsworth.

Wingfield Manor in Derbyshire was elegant, with an attractive prospect, but on her previous visit Mary had complained bitterly about the appalling stench of drains. This time she travelled in the company of Sadler's son-in-law, John Somers, who wrote an extensive account of their conversation for Lord Burghley. During the journey, he recalled, Mary emphasised her love for her son, telling him that 'nothing can ever sever me from him, for I live for him and not for myself'. She then proceeded to deny having anything to do with the recently revealed plot to invade England: 'as to the enterprise you spoke of, by my troth, I know not, nor heard anything of it; nor, so God have my soul, will ever consent to anything that should trouble this state, whereof I seek the quiet with all my heart'.

If she were released, she told him, she would go to Scotland 'but only to see my son and give him good counsel'. She would never stay long in Scotland or govern 'where I have received so many evil treatments'. 'For her heart,' Somers went on, 'could not abide to look upon those folk that had done her that evil, being her subjects, whereof there are many yet remaining.' What she now desired, she said, if Elizabeth did not allow her a maintenance to remain in England, was to go to France – 'and live thenceforth among my friends . . . and never trouble myself with government again'.

Her sublime conviction of innocence is admirable, allowing her to call on God as her witness. Believing as she did in his omnipotence, she must have assumed he knew exactly what she had been plotting. When it came to survival, Mary could lie without hesitation and defend herself with every deceit in her armoury. Added to which, she had the assurance that God was on her side, rather than that of the heretical Protestants. Since, as a foreign sovereign, she had never recognised Elizabeth's or her councillors' right either to imprison or judge her, she believed whatever actions she took to free herself or be restored to her rightful place were entirely justified. Given her situation, it is hard to disagree.

With international turmoil simmering, and assassination plots being discovered with alarming frequency, the hazard that Mary posed to Elizabeth's life could not have been starker. In response, in October 1584 Burghley drafted a truly remarkable document, called the Bond of Association. This directive decreed that anyone found involved in a plot that endangered Elizabeth's life would be executed. So far, so run-of-the-mill. What made this bond extraordinary is that, in addition to punishing the conspirators, it decreed that anyone – i.e. Mary – who stood to benefit from their actions, even if they had no knowledge of them, could not succeed Elizabeth and would also be put to death, since they would be deemed guilty by association. It was, writes John Guy, 'a licence to kill'. With so many conspiracies already thwarted, it could be no more than a matter of months before another was attempted, at which point Mary could finally be dealt with and despatched.

Eager to show their loyalty to Elizabeth, and their determination to defend her and their realm, thousands of citizens queued to sign this document, pledging to protect their queen and uphold the Protestant cause. Stacks of paper covered in signatures landed on Burghley's desk, evidence that the country was behind him. To show her good faith, even Mary put her name to it, declaring that she deplored the idea of 'an act so wicked as an attempt against [Elizabeth's] person or her kingdom'. In light of recent events, she must surely have recognised that, whether she signed or not, this document represented her winding sheet.

The Bond of Association was passed into law in March 1585 as the Act for the Queen's Safety, which was subtly different from the Bond. Its measures stated that anyone with a claim to the throne found to be plotting against the Queen would be tried by a commission and, if found guilty, barred from the succession and executed. In the event of an assassination attempt on Elizabeth, the same conditions were applied to the culprits and whomever would benefit from this plot. The Act's provisions sound almost identical to the Bond, but the difference lies in the Act's insistence on a public trial of the defendants – stipulated at Elizabeth's instigation – whereas the more primitive Bond allowed for instant reprisals by anyone who had pledged their allegiance.

Keen to avoid stirring up trouble with Scotland, Elizabeth specifically excluded James VI as a beneficiary of any plot, unless he was proved to have been directly involved. The last thing she needed, as tensions with Spain intensified, was a disaffected neighbour in the north where Philip's army could find a toehold. By dangling the tantalising possibility of the English succession in front of James, she ensured he would not turn against Elizabeth and would side with her over his mother. How well Elizabeth understood James. His mother meant little to him compared to his ambition to inherit the English throne. The Bond of Association marks the turning point in his relationship with Mary, since he believed it made it impossible to maintain contact with her without fear of being considered complicit in any of her conspiracies. Thus the Bond was one reason why, after protracted negotiation, the proposed Association in which mother and son would rule jointly was finally, and with shocking abruptness, dropped.

For some months before this, Mary had been employing the devious young Scot Patrick Gray, Master of Gray, who was one of the Archbishop of Glasgow's many agents in Paris. He had a long connection with Mary, and his remit was to petition hard on her behalf at the Scottish and English courts for the Association. This he did not do. Arriving in Scotland in the autumn of 1584 and being warmly welcomed by James (in a very short time, Gray would supplant the increasingly unpopular Arran), Gray overnight became James's rather than Mary's man. Sent as ambassador to the English court, he showed his worth by gaining Elizabeth's agreement to an Anglo-Scottish league. While doing so, he made it clear to Elizabeth that Mary was no longer a necessary part of any conversation regarding James. In that breath, Mary's last chance of being granted her liberty disappeared. Hitherto, as Antonia Fraser writes, she had considered her only hope of liberty depended on James making her release 'one of his conditions of treating with Elizabeth'. But neither James nor Gray had any intention of pressing Mary's case, and, like a climber whose rope is severed by those who have reached the summit, she was ruthlessly cut loose.

Patrick Gray has gone down in history as Mary's Judas, although her son is more deserving of that title. All the same, Gray's double-dealing with Mary is painful to observe, as is her obvious distress as she began to realise she was being conned. Her letters to him grew more and more panicky until, in desperation, she offered to relinquish her claim to the English succession as one of the conditions of her release. It is unlikely that Gray ever passed on this message.

Early in 1585, James raised the idea of the Association before his Privy Council. As he would have expected, they gave it short shrift, considering it 'detrimental for both king and the country' and saying it should be 'annulled forever'. When Mary heard this, on 5 January 1585 – the day she signed Burghley's Bond of Association – she was stunned. Betrayed by her son, whose protestations of love and honour had been empty, and indeed duplicitous, she was devastated. Writing to Castelnau, she expressed her heartbreak: 'I am grieved to the heart by the crosses which I have to endure, but especially by the estrangement of my son from me, and his being set against me; praying to God to let me die rather than learn for certain that such a thing can be.'

To Elizabeth she wrote, 'it may please you at once to bring to a conclusion the treaty for my liberty, and permit me to retire, with your good grace, out of this isle into some solitary place'. She added to this a thundering denunciation of James. If he tried to make a treaty with Elizabeth, she said, 'I will disavow him for my son, lay on him my malediction, and disinherit him, not only from what he holds now, but from all that, through me, he can pretend to elsewhere, abandoning him to his subjects to do to him as he has been instigated to do to me . . . And I will take from him – and with good right – the protection of God . . .' Vituperative and vengeful, she was also threatening, not only to James but to Elizabeth: 'in all of Christendom I shall find enough of heirs, who will have talons strong enough to grasp what I may put into their hand'.

This molten response to James's mistreatment of her showed how much she had invested in him on a personal as well as a political level, and how cruelly betrayed she felt. Yet no matter what she said or threatened, it made no difference to James. He had too many reasons for allying himself with Elizabeth to return to his mother's side. Watching with dispassion, the childless Elizabeth must have marvelled at James's coldness and calculation. Perhaps now she recognised that having a son and heir was a mixed blessing, or, as in this case, no blessing at all.

As if she were not suffering enough, Mary's woes were to deepen. Keen for her to be under better guard, Elizabeth ordered that she be relocated to her most hated prison, Tutbury Castle, under Sadler's watch. The symbolism was clear. A self-contained fortress on a hill overlooking the Staffordshire plain, it was sealed off from the world. Even though the village of Tutbury lay only a short step away, Mary was all but immolated, unable to receive or send letters and left to brood on how wronged she had been. Preferring comfort to self-pity, she quickly itemised her requirements if she was to survive incarceration in so inhospitable a place: two chamber ladies, two gentlemen and two valets de chambre, from France or Scotland. Above all, she wrote to Castelnau, she required 'a small stud of twelve horses, besides my coach, it being impossible for me to take the air without them, since I am unable to walk fifty paces together.'

On her previous visits to Tutbury, between 1569 and 1571, Mary had been lodged in the South Tower of the castle, which, though not luxurious, had been reasonably appointed. In the intervening years, while Bess of Hardwick and the Earl of Shrewsbury were lavishing attention and money on their pet building projects, Tutbury had been allowed to fall into disrepair. By the time of Mary's return in the middle of January 1585, the wind whistled through its walls and under its doors like a banshee.

Already in a state of high aggravation, Mary wrote a vivid description of the castle, giving vent to its many discomforts. On this visit, her accommodation was in a long, two-storey hunting lodge, whose probable foundations have been found within the gardens near the North Tower. It was a gloomy location, with light blocked by the high curtain wall. An artist's impression of what the lodge would have looked like shows a simple but attractive Tudor wooden-framed structure. As Mary's letters reveal, however, it was little better than a stable in terms of its provisions, and a great deal worse-smelling, thanks to the nearby drains.

At the end of the summer, Mary wrote a dignified but forceful letter to her ambassadors Castelnau and his replacement, Châteauneuf, who took up the post that month. In a vigorous account of her requirements, which runs to many pages, she demanded that they get an answer from Elizabeth about allowing her to receive information from France about her dowry, and be given permission for an increase in her staff, which was necessary for her health. Most pointedly, she wanted them to convey to the Queen the abject conditions in which she was being detained. It is worth quoting at length, since it shows that, despite ill health and devastating setbacks, she remained self-assured and regal. There is nothing in this of a spirit cowed. After everything she had endured, that is nothing short of remarkable.

> I am in a walled enclosure, on the top of a hill, exposed to all the winds and the inclemencies of heaven; within the said enclosure ... there is a very old hunting-lodge, built of timber and plaster, cracked in all parts, the plaster adhering nowhere to the wood-work, and broken in numberless places; the said lodge distant three fathoms or thereabouts from the wall, and situated so low, that the rampart of earth which is behind the wall is on a level with the highest point of the building, so that the sun can never shine upon it on that side, nor any fresh air come to it; for

which reason it is so damp, that you cannot put any piece of furniture in that part without its being in a few days completely covered with mould. I leave you to think how this must act upon the human body; and, in short, the greater part of it is rather a dungeon for base and abject criminals than a habitation fit for a person of my quality, or even of a much lower . . .

The only apartments that I have for my own person consist . . . of two little miserable rooms, so excessively cold, especially at night, that but for the ramparts and entrenchments of curtains and tapestry which I have had made, it would not be possible for me to stay in them in the day-time . . . Sir Amyas [Paulet, her gaoler] can bear witness that he has seen three of my women ill at once from this cause alone; and my physician himself, who has had his share of it, has several times declared 'that he will not take charge of my health during the next winter if I am to remain in this house'.

Of the garden that had been created to allow her to take the fresh air, she wrote that it was 'fitter to keep pigs in than to bear the name of garden: there is not a sheep-pen amidst the fields but makes a better appearance'. Even worse was the smell: 'this house, having no drains to the privies, is subject to a continual stench and every Saturday they are obliged to empty them and the one beneath my windows, from which I receive a perfume not the most agreeable'. As if this were not dismal enough, she added a further layer of paint by describing a priest who, after being persecuted for his beliefs, hanged himself from the wall opposite her windows. Four or five days later, she wrote, another man died after falling into the castle well. Mary concluded her miserable inventory with a patrician command: 'Learn, then, if you please, gentlemen, if the queen my good sister intends to treat me in future like a condemned criminal.'

To his credit, before leaving post, the disgraced Castelnau managed to secure the promise that Mary would be relocated to a more healthy and spacious location. This promise came good on

Christmas Eve, when she was taken to Chartley Manor in Staffordshire. For this achievement alone, and for many years of faithful service, he deserved her gratitude. That for the past eighteen months he had been privately showing their correspondence to Walsingham, thereby conniving in her misfortune, does not entirely negate the good work he had done on her behalf all those years.

Mary knew nothing of his duplicity, although by now she had learned how few of her associates and closest aides she could trust. If she heard of it, his betrayal might not have greatly surprised her. But far worse was still to come from within the ranks of her supporters. This time, it would prove disastrous.

Chapter 24

'One of the most whimsical and austere persons whom I have ever known'

TUTBURY AND CHARTLEY

Amias Paulet, who was to be Mary's final keeper, arrived at Tutbury in April 1586, and a very grateful, relieved Sadler was allowed to return home. Although Sadler was one of the few courtiers Elizabeth could fully trust with Mary's care, he was too aged to hold the position for long. For the few months she was in his care, however, he had been kind. Having seen her as a baby in her mother's lap, full of life and happy prospects, he must have found being her captor a melancholy duty. Perhaps for the sake of the young princess he had known, or maybe because he was a humane man, he allowed her to go hawking outside the castle walls, affording her a rare moment of pleasure in these careworn months.

Paulet was another man entirely. Although he was considerably younger than Sadler, being in his mid fifties, his appointment startled many. A portrait of him, attributed to Nicolas Hilliard, shows a granite face above a flamboyant, lace-tipped ruff. Wearing a black velvet bejewelled cap, he has elfin ears, such finely arched eyebrows they could be plucked, a long nose and a russet moustache that droops over his mouth like a fur stole. It is his expression, however, that is arresting. His clear blue eyes are flint hard and, despite the colour in his cheeks, they hold no warmth. Implacable is the word. Châteauneuf described him as 'a man of honour . . . but otherwise a great Huguenot, and partisan of those who are esteemed enemies of the Queen of Scotland'. He was, he added, 'a man very rigorous', as Mary would soon learn.

The Governor of Jersey, Paulet had been Elizabeth's ambassador in Paris from 1576 to 1579. There, he had earned his spurs as a zealous Puritan, dedicated to the Protestant cause and equally committed to the downfall of Mary, Queen of Scots. Questions flew around court as to why a man who was neither wealthy nor of particularly high rank, and far from well, should be given this onerous distinction. John Somers recommended more suitable candidates, but Walsingham and Elizabeth would not budge. Amias Paulet it was to be. (His name was probably pronounced Amice, and his surname is variously given as Poulet or Paulet.) Mary, awaiting his arrival at Tutbury, had no illusions about what to expect.

As she had no doubt anticipated, he had been selected specifically for his animosity towards her. John Morris, a Victorian Jesuit, was editor of Paulet's voluminous series of *Letter-books* covering his time as Mary's custodian. In his introduction, Morris cites correspondence from earlier in Paulet's career in which he is shown to be terrier-like in his desire to snare Mary. (At one point he rather recklessly urged Elizabeth to spend more money on gaining intelligence, for which Walsingham rapped his knuckles.)

Among his appealing credentials was that he was not squeamish in how he achieved his ends, being willing to consort with all manner of disreputable individuals if they could help bring about this objective. In Morris's view, 'Poulet was all eagerness and self-importance. Clearly Heaven had destined him as the man whose wisdom should unravel every clew and winding of conspiracy, and above and beyond all else, provide the swift "occasion" for applying Cecil's "remedy".' In other words, despatching Mary. His greatest strength as her captor was that he would 'approve and abet the worst intrigues against Mary Stuart'. Unsurprisingly, the relationship between gaoler and captive was tense from the start. And yet, while Mary expressed anxiety for her safety under his charge, the irony is that she and her followers would in fact have cause to be grateful to him (not that she would ever know this). For, in one sense at least, he saved her life.

The month after Paulet assumed his post, Mary wrote 'now I am very differently warded and watched'. Yet she admitted that she and her servants were well treated. A little later, she described him as 'one of the most whimsical and austere persons whom I have ever known; and, in a word, fitter for a jail of criminals'. If Elizabeth were to die, she added, 'I should think my life very insecure in his hands.' Elizabeth responded swiftly, keen to reassure her prisoner that she had been put into the hands of a reputable man: 'You need not doubt that a man that reverenceth God, loveth his Prince, and is no less by calling honourable than by birth noble, will ever do anything unworthy of himself.' To her chagrin, she was soon to learn how accurate this assessment was.

From Paulet's letters, written mainly to the Queen, Walsingham and Burghley, a vivid picture emerges of Tutbury under his control. From the outset he was harsh, remorselessly carrying out Elizabeth's command to tighten the guard around Mary and cut her off completely from the outside world. He was so assiduous that soon he had to defend himself against accusations of undue strictness by insisting his measures were necessary. There was no doubting how pitilessly he would carry out his orders. Should there be any attempt to rescue the queen, he said, 'she shall die before me'. For her part, Mary was unsettled that whenever her party took a walk they were accompanied 'with so many horsemen, all furnished with snaphaunces or cases of pistols, and a good number of harquebuziers on foot with their matches lighted'. (Snaphaunces were firearms that worked by a struck flint lighting the powder, and harquebuziers were cavalrymen, armed with long guns.)

Restrictions on Mary's servants and coachman prevented them, among other things, from walking on the walls, riding beyond the castle, as before, or strolling into Tutbury. What seemed most to upset Mary was that she was no longer allowed to give alms, something she had been doing all her life. This act of generosity was an instinctive gesture from a woman who felt pity for the poor, but it was also a spiritual directive, something her religion demanded of her. To be thwarted in this expression of her faith was intolerable, and she told Paulet this intervention was 'barbarous': 'You fear lest by giving alms I should win the favour of the people', she said, 'but you ought rather to fear lest the restraining of my alms may animate the people against you.'

Applying to Walsingham for his and Elizabeth's orders on the matter, Paulet listed the Maundy Thursday alms Mary had had distributed the previous Easter: to forty-two 'maidens' she had given a half yard of woollen cloth, two yards of linen cloth, and 13 pence. The same was given to eighteen 'little boys', in respect of her son, and on Good Friday £6 was shared among 'the elder sort of poor of Tutbury town', who were selected by her priest.

Mary's living quarters were a constant source of complaint for her and her retinue. 'This Queen's servants are always craving,' complained Paulet, 'and have no pity at all of English purses'. The Scottish queen's retinue at Tutbury, as itemised by Sadler before he left, consisted of forty-eight. This included the queen, five gentlemen, fourteen servitors, three cooks, four boys, three gentlemen's men, six gentlewomen, two wives and ten wenches and children. The queen had two chambers for herself, and there were fifteen allocated for the entire party, several of which were for the use of her two secretaries, her physician Bourgoing and Melville, master of the household. At dinner, Mary was served sixteen dishes for both courses; for her attendants and other servants, the number of dishes was reduced according to their status. 'This Queen before my coming, and some time after,' wrote Paulet in astonishment, 'had upon the fish days twenty-four dishes at every meal for her whole family, which I reduced to twenty.'

It was hardly the stuff of gulag prisoners. Nevertheless, it is impossible not to feel intense sympathy for her, after so many years of unjust imprisonment, to which was added great emotional distress and increasingly grave ill health. Her life might have been luxurious compared to many, but only those lacking the basic necessities of life could possibly have envied her.

Even under these conditions, Mary retained her mordant humour and her talent for a well-turned phrase. Informing Paulet that she had cut all ties with foreign supporters, so that she depended solely on Elizabeth, she told him that 'she had proferred her heart and body to her Majesty: her body is taken and great care taken for the safe keeping of it, but her heart is refused'. She added piteously that 'if she had desired great liberty, her Majesty might instantly have been jealous of her, but she desired only reasonable liberty for her health'.

Complaints from her household seem designed to fray Paulet's nerves. They grumbled about the state of the linen, and the lack of sea fish. When Mary asked for Turkish carpets to improve her chambers, Paulet reported, 'She hath the best of the old long ends [of carpet] to walk on in her chamber, which is matted, but yet too hard for her sore foot. The dining-chamber floor is plaster, very cold, though strewed with rushes.' Mary could not tolerate the least draught in her rooms, he wrote, and had been given double hangings for her chamber. Any cold, he told Walsingham, made her unwell, and 'caused a distillation into her legs, and now bereaved her of the use of them'.

Throughout these months, her poor mobility is frequently mentioned, as is her declining health. At one point, she was more ill, he wrote, than her attendants could ever remember. Often, she could not leave her bed, and her legs appear to have been swollen and painful for much of the time. Paulet believed they were in such a state that she would never recover the use of them. It is a wretched portrait of invalidism, some of it – but arguably most – directly attributable to the conditions in which she had been held.

Repeatedly she asked for her lodgings to be repaired, and to be relocated somewhere healthier. Although Mary was eventually moved to Chartley Manor, Paulet regarded her immobility as a bonus: 'The indisposition of this Queen's body, and the great infirmity of her legs . . . is no small advantage to her keeper, who shall not need to stand in great fear of her running way, if he can foresee that she be not taken from him by force.'

For the duration of their time at Tutbury, Paulet was on edge about the dangers of the neighbourhood, which he believed to be filled with 'Papists'. He also posted guards throughout the area, mounting a 24-hour watch on towns and parishes within ten miles of Tutbury. The slipperiness of Mary's servants and attendants also troubled him. He bore a particular animus against laundresses, whom he suspected – probably correctly – of smuggling messages for the queen. He also had doubts about Mary's embroiderer, Audrey, and especially his wife, who 'may prove a dangerous messenger in this dangerous [time]'. He wrote that coachmen, laundresses and 'suchlike' had previously been used to convey letters. Currently there were three laundresses, working and living in a small house in the park just outside the castle walls. From now on they were to be searched on their way to and from the castle, during which he ordered that they be 'stripped unto their smocks'.

Left to make his own decisions, Paulet would likely not have moved Mary, even though she was obviously unwell. Thanks to pressure from the French, however, Elizabeth agreed that she should be relocated. Paulet was ordered to scout out suitable nearby locations. When he visited Chartley Manor in Staffordshire, his gout was so severe he had to travel by coach. After some deliberation, Chartley was chosen as the best option. Among its several advantages was the proximity of Protestant loyalists, such as Walter Aston of Tixall Hall and Richard Bagot of Blithfield, who could be swiftly summoned, with their men, in an emergency.

The decision made, on Christmas Eve 1585 Mary and her household were duly relocated to Chartley Manor. The property of one of Elizabeth's most unruly favourites, Robert Devereaux, Earl of Essex, it was a double-moated, timbered Elizabethan house, sitting in a thousand acres of parkland. A print of Chartley, made in 1685, shows a two-storey, attractive building with two wings attached to either side of the central house, and an elaborate fountain in the courtyard.

Essex was most unwilling for this elegant residence to become Mary's new prison, fearing, as Paulet reported, that 'in respect of her mislike both of his father and of himself, those of her train should abuse, or rather spoil it'. He pressed the suitability of another nearby house (owned by the father of one of Walsingham's agents, Gilbert Gifford), but in the same breath begged that, should Chartley be chosen, his woodlands were not felled to provide fuel. His bourgeois worries at a time of national emergency carry a foretaste of the requisition of Britain's country houses during the First and Second World Wars.

Unfortunately, Chartley Manor was destroyed by fire in 1781, and only traces of it remain, inside and outside the nineteenth-century Elizabethan-style manor house that stands in its place. There is no public access to the grounds, where earthworks that were once part of the ornamental water garden and parterres Mary knew can still be seen. From the main road that passes present-day Chartley Hall, the two pale drum-towers of the medieval Chartley Castle are prominent on the hilltop, like the backdrop for a play. In Mary's day this motte-and-bailey castle, protected by a deep and wide dry ditch, was already a picturesque ruin. As she grew accustomed to her new quarters, it must have afforded a pleasing outlook beyond the gardens and parkland.

As Mary's doctor had predicted, the move exacerbated her condition, and for more than two months she was too ill to leave her bed. As a rare concession, Paulet granted her wish for a better bed, the one she had being stained and uncomfortable. It was a worrying time for her entourage, but in due course she recovered so well that she could be helped outdoors to enjoy watching duck hunts by the manor-house ponds.

Despite this gratifying improvement, her health continued to fluctuate that summer, and in July she was writing to Châteauneuf about the need to have a fixed residence, 'being but as one passing from inn to inn'. She said she was 'very ill attended to' and had lost her appetite. 'There are no means left for preserving my life by strengthening my nerves, from the weakness of which, by want of exercise, all my maladies proceed, but' – as her physicians had told her – 'by some natural very warm baths of Italy.'

Today, the countryside around Chartley Castle is lush and pleasant, with fields of dairy cattle and roadside hedges that look as if they have been trimmed with the help of a plumb line. Once Mary was in her new abode, Paulet kept her and her retinue under such tight guard that, he boasted, 'I cannot imagine how it may be possible for them to convey a piece of paper as big as my finger.' He described the queen's quarters in glowing terms, reporting that she could enjoy the facilities of 'a very fair great chamber, which may serve her to walk instead of a gallery'. There was also plenty of space for all her gentlewomen, 'all within her own chamber door, which is good for her, and no less good for me'.

Life within her party continued as always, with Paulet noting that Bastian Pages's wife was about to have a baby and commenting sourly that 'It is likely that Curle's wife will be sick of the same disease very shortly, and some say she complaineth already. As likewise it is to be expected that there will be no end of marrying in this great household, when they may marry without controlment, according to their own religion.' The presence of midwives, gossips and nurses was always a security hazard, given the opportunities they presented for the smuggling of messages. Previously, Mary had assured Paulet that she had asked her people not to marry, in order to keep a limit on the numbers in her household. This seems to have had little impact, if indeed she ever did issue such a command.

Other irregularities in Mary's party also irked her gaoler. He strongly suspected that a Frenchman, Camille du Préau, who was called her 'reader' and had been heard to speak in Latin, was in fact a priest. His presence was as galling to Paulet as a tick burrowing behind his knee, and he told Walsingham that 'no known Popish Priest ought to dwell within these gates . . . these open doings reach not only to the actors, but to all such others as shall wink at them'. Rather than adopt the drab dress suitable to his alleged status, Du Préau's appearance made him hard to miss. Paulet scoffed that he went about 'apparelled in court-like suit, a brooch in his hat, silver buttons, his garments of all colours'.

Du Préau was indeed a priest, having taken the place of Mary's previous secret chaplain, John Morton, who had died years earlier. It says much for the rigour of Shrewsbury's oversight that these men had hitherto escaped undetected or, more likely, been allowed to practise under his nose.

Chapter 25

'Eated in the face with small pocks'

THE BABINGTON PLOT

Mary's new French ambassador, Guillaume de l'Aubespine de Châteauneuf, was a cooler, more calculating character than Castelnau. He took up his post in September 1585, and within a few months Mary was warning him about the danger of spies within his own house. Even so, he seemed entirely unaware that his secretary, Cherelles, was in Walsingham's pocket, alerting him to everything relating to Mary that crossed his desk.

Once she had been placed under Paulet's guard, Mary instructed Châteauneuf on the various stratagems, mentioned earlier, for passing on messages undetected, including writing between the lines of books marked with green ribbons and putting packets into the heels of shoes. The world beyond her doors must have felt exceedingly hostile, but while in some respects Mary was no longer entirely in tune with reality, having been cut off from news for almost two years, her fear of treachery was justified. In this, her instincts remained keen. As she feared, Châteauneuf was indeed being spied upon, although neither could have imagined he was at the centre of one of the most devious and clever acts of espionage of the sixteenth century. So too was Mary, for whom an entire edifice of betrayal, deceit and counter-deception was constructed, in the hope of trapping her in its web.

In his bid to destroy the Scottish queen and catch her in the act of conspiring against Elizabeth, Walsingham was to excel himself in the use of his network of agents. If her treachery could be proved, then she would have fallen foul of the Act for the Queen's Safety, and Elizabeth would be justified in executing her. But, given Elizabeth's unease at publicly executing a fellow monarch and the repercussions that would follow, the burden of proof would need to be overwhelming.

There were many moving parts in Walsingham's Machiavellian machine, each of them essential to the unfolding of his plot. Historians tell the story with varying degrees of complexity and digression, often contradicting each other. One of the clearest and most revealing accounts is offered by Stephen Alford in *The Watchers*, which illuminates an intensely complicated episode. What follows draws, broadly, on his narrative.

Central to Walsingham's scheme was Thomas Morgan, Mary's agent in Paris whose influence, writes Alford, 'lay behind many of the plots against Queen Elizabeth of the 1580s'. Despite being incarcerated in the Bastille, Morgan continued to work on Mary's behalf, including managing, or mismanaging, her French dowry. Since the discovery of the Throckmorton plot and the heightened guard around the Scottish queen, it had been impossible to get messages secretly to Mary. What Morgan badly needed was someone who could act as a courier and find a way to take letters from Paris and the French embassy in London to Mary, and the same in reverse.

At the same time as Morgan was searching for a go-between, Walsingham recognised that blocking Mary's secret pipeline was counterproductive. It would be far more useful to know what was passing between her and her supporters than remain in the dark. Even better, it would allow him to manipulate them into revealing themselves.

Enter Gilbert Gifford and Thomas Phelippes, two of the most skilful and effective of Walsingham's countless operatives. Indeed Phelippes, who was one of the finest cryptographers in history, was Walsingham's equal in imagination, dedication and ruthlessness. Born in 1556, the son of a cloth merchant, and thought to have been educated at Cambridge University, Phelippes had a facility for languages, speaking French, Italian, German, Latin and Spanish. He had known Paulet when in Paris, so the pair needed no introduction. Although very different in temperament, both had their eyes trained on the same prize, towards which they devoted all their energies.

At Christmas 1585, Phelippes visited Paulet at Chartley Manor, where Mary was now in residence, to set things in place for their sting operation. On one of his return trips, Mary described him in a letter to Morgan, providing the only record of his appearance: 'of low stature, slender every way, dark yellow haired on the head and clear yellow bearded, eated in the face with small pocks, of short sight, thirty years of age by appearance, and, as is said, Secretary Walsingham's man'. It is a colourful portrait of a man whose unscrupulous part in helping to send Mary to the scaffold has earned him equal plaudits and condemnation.

Gilbert Gifford, who was to become Phelippes' right-hand man in this nerve-racking project, was one of many young Catholic English gentlemen who had offered his services to Morgan in Paris to aid Mary's and the Pope's cause. Born in 1560, which made him similar in age to Phelippes, he was the son of a well-known recusant who had been imprisoned for his refusal to conform. He was also related to Francis Throckmorton, who had so recently been executed for conspiring to free Mary. Educated for several years by the Jesuits in Europe, and ordained as a deacon, Gifford had been expelled from the English seminary at Rome, after which he entered the seminary of Douai, which at this time was relocated to Rheims. While there, he had a peppery relationship with its founder, Dr William Allen, who was a figurehead for supporters of a Catholic invasion of England.

With these credentials, Gifford seemed to be the courier Morgan had been looking for. Not only was he capable of acting as a conduit, but his father owned Chillington Hall in Staffordshire, near Mary's prison, which offered an excuse for his visits. (It was one of the houses Paulet inspected as a possible prison for Mary.) Gifford was later to assure Châteauneuf, the suspicious French ambassador in London, that when acting as a courier for Mary, nobody would know him as an Englishman since he had been out of the country since he was a boy of ten or twelve. Even his own family would not recognise him now, he said. Writing Mary a warm endorsement of Gifford's reliability and trustworthiness, with which the Archbishop of Glasgow and Charles Paget agreed, Morgan anticipated soon having Mary's correspondence in his hands. That Gifford was so easily taken into Morgan's trust suggests what sort of a man he was: intellectually able with a winning personality and an apparent openness of character that was beguiling.

Nicolas Berden, one of Walsingham's best agents, who was working in Paris, noted that Gifford had left Paris and might be conspiring on behalf of the Catholic rebels. Thus, when Gifford was set ashore at Rye, Walsingham's men were waiting. Soon he was in London, under interrogation, and shortly thereafter he was in Walsingham's pay, having been almost effortlessly turned into a double agent.

At the same time as he enters the picture, so does another of Morgan's eager operatives, who was also working for Walsingham while appearing to be in the service of Mary. This was Robert Poley, a nominal Catholic recently released from Marshalsea prison, where he had been incarcerated for a year by Walsingham in order to gain information. Once released, Poley threw open his London home to the Catholic conspirators and acted as a gregarious, generous friend, thereby gaining confidences he then passed on to Walsingham.

While behind bars Poley had, like a true undercover operator, won the trust of the persecuted Catholics with whom he had been kept, one of whom enthusiastically vouched for him. As a result, Morgan had placed him in the household of Walsingham's daughter and her husband, the poet Philip Sidney. It seemed like a terrific coup to have deployed Poley so close to the heart of power when, in reality, his situation allowed him to pass information to Walsingham without raising suspicions.

These men, some motivated by conviction, some by money and the thrill of adventure, were to bring about Mary's destruction. Yet it was Thomas Morgan who, by employing them so unquestioningly, had brought the wolves within the gates. With Morgan putting them into Mary's orbit, he was doing Walsingham's job for him. Was his lack of judgement a sign of desperation, or was he just fatally unsuited to the task?

Now firmly in position, Gifford was able to pass letters between the three sides of the triangle – Châteauneuf, Morgan and, at its apex, Mary. As soon as she was safely lodged at Chartley Manor, Walsingham devised a convoluted system that would satisfy everyone's need for subterfuge. It would also allow him – and Paulet – sight of every scrap of intelligence that came from or was put into Mary's hands. Walsingham told no one about the trap he had set for Mary apart from Elizabeth and the Earl of Leicester. At this stage not even Burghley was aware of it. Even informing Elizabeth made the secretary queasy, as he confided to Leicester: 'My only fear is that her Majesty will not use the matter with the secrecy that appertaineth.'

Muriel Spark said of the teacher on whom she based Miss Jean Brodie that she was 'a character in search of an author'. The same could be said of the man who was pivotal to the functioning of Walsingham's plot. Known as the Burton brewer, he was the tradesman who provided Chartley Manor with its beer every week, removing the empty casks as he did so. There is no record of his appearance, but you might imagine him shaped like his barrels, wearing a long apron and a greedy expression. Gifford approached him with a bribe to place and retrieve messages in the barrels by means of a waterproof receptacle (Châteauneuf described it as a 'small box of hollow wood'), which he could insert through the bunghole of a beer barrel. This would then be retrieved by Mary's butler and passed to Nau when the beer keg reached Chartley. The process worked in reverse when Mary's letters were smuggled back out for the brewer, and then Gifford, to collect.

The Burton brewer was led, naturally, to believe that Gifford was one of Mary's agents. Not that he cared what side anyone was on, so long as they paid up. No doubt to his surprise as well as his delight, he was richly rewarded for each delivery, since Paulet also bribed him secretly to show him the barrel letters before passing them to Gifford. A stickler for security, Paulet needed to know exactly what was passing through the brewer channel since, like Phelippes – and indeed the French ambassador – he was not entirely certain of Gifford. Mary, who for her part was grateful to the brewer and tipped him handsomely, trusted Gifford without a second thought.

An interesting detail in this labyrinthine plot is that the brewer was housed by Walsingham in the forfeited home of Charles Paget's brother, Lord Paget, who had escaped to the continent after the discovery of the Throckmorton plot. With Gifford delivering the letters to this house in Burton, it became the place where Mary's fate was decided. Had Lord Paget known of this he would, no doubt, have been sickened. His brother Charles, who had also evaded capture, continued to work in Paris in the interests of Mary and a Catholic invasion of England. He too had been fooled into trusting Gifford.

Burton-on-Trent, from where the brewer operated, was twenty miles from Chartley Manor. The town's first brewers had been the monks at Burton Abbey in the early Middle Ages. By the nineteenth century, Burton was considered the world capital of beer and is renowned to this day for its beer and pale ales.

Recognising how essential he was to everyone in this process, and despite being paid triply for his clandestine services, the brewer soon hiked up the price of the beer he supplied to Chartley. In their cagey correspondence, Gifford, Phelippes and Walsingham sarcastically refer to him as 'the honest man', knowing the type they were dealing with. Regardless of the cost, it was worth it.

In May 1586, Mary wrote to Mendoza, who, after his expulsion from England for his connivance in the Throckmorton plot, was now Spain's ambassador in Paris. As well as promising to bequeath her right to the English succession to Philip II, should her son not convert before her death (which she considered unlikely), she also begged the king to take her 'under his special protection, and likewise the state and affairs of this country'. The contents of this letter were probably evidence enough to charge her with a fatal conspiracy against Elizabeth, but Walsingham hoped for better: something so explicit she could not evade justice.

To that end, he now had all the players in place for his boldest and riskiest venture. Gifford had sufficiently gained the trust of Mary's French ambassador to be allowed to convey messages between the London embassy and Mary. Not that Châteauneuf was entirely gullible. He had for some weeks suspected a plot was afoot, and that the supposedly secret channel of letters was not so secret after all. As he wrote to the King of France, his suspicions grew during an audience with Elizabeth. 'You have great and secret communication with the Queen of Scotland,' she said, 'but believe me that I know everything which is done in my kingdom; and as I was a prisoner in the time of the queen my sister, I know what devices prisoners employ to gain over servants and have secret communications.' Nevertheless, the work of Walsingham's team continued undiscovered, as did that of Châteauneuf's nefarious secretary Cherelles.

Before handing letters to the brewer – or when gathering Mary's replies from him – Gilbert passed these directly to Phelippes, who began his painstaking deciphering work. Phelippes then despatched the decoded letters to Walsingham while allowing Gifford to ferry the originals to their intended destination. Since Mary had recently sent a new cipher to Châteauneuf by beer keg, not trusting the old one she had used with Castelnau, Phelippes' work was made considerably easier. To ensure that the seals did not appear to have been tampered with, a government agent called Arthur Gregory, who was expert in breaking and resealing them without leaving a trace, was employed.

Now that the system had been proved effective, the conspiracy to entrap Mary moved up a gear. It was to Walsingham's great advantage that, rather than manufacture conspirators against Elizabeth, he could draw on what appeared to be a never-ending supply of religiously motivated gallants, eager to liberate Mary. Foremost among these were two ill-fated individuals. The first was an English priest, John Ballard, who, thanks to Walsingham's spies (of which he had once been one before repenting), was known to have consorted in Paris with Charles Paget and Mendoza.

In May 1586, Ballard, who was something of a bar fly, met the elegant young gentleman Anthony Babington, who was also a frequenter of pubs. They rendezvoused in the Plough Inn in London, the haunt of many of the conspirators in this plot. The unfortunate Babington's name is among the best known in Tudor and Stuart history. From his first appearance in the records as a page for the Earl of Shrewsbury while he was Mary's captor, his terrible end hangs over his head. As Shrewsbury's servant, he developed an intense admiration for the captive queen, a devotion that never dimmed. In those far-off days he was, in Châteauneuf's words, 'very simple', but now, in his mid twenties, he was a more dangerous political animal, albeit one sometimes described by historians as 'dreamy'.

Babington was a complicated figure. A portrait believed to be of him shows a man of slight build, with a heart-shaped face and deep brown eyes, who was fashionably and expensively dressed. From a wealthy Derbyshire family, he was married with a daughter, but seems to have been innately restless. Although he was intelligent, and had begun to train as a lawyer at Lincoln's Inn, he had been easily lured away by the pleasures of life at court and soon abandoned his studies. Charismatic, lively and thoughtful, Babington was surrounded by like-minded young gentlemen who were willing to follow his lead. Raised clandestinely as a Catholic, as a teenager he had formed part of a group that protected missionary Jesuits in England, among them such notable individuals as Edmund Campion and Robert Persons. He had also conveyed messages from France to Mary. But despite his sunny disposition, he had a conspiratorial nature. In his biography of Elizabeth I, Paul Johnson writes that 'the previous autumn he had drawn up a plan to murder the entire Privy Council'.

In light of the danger Babington and his fellow plotters represented, it is no surprise that they attracted the attention of Walsingham's spies, who were on the hunt for Catholic traitors. When he met Ballard, Babington was unsettled by the growing anti-Catholic mood of the government and dreaded a bloody invasion.

To avoid both, he was contemplating leaving England for a protracted period of travel in Europe. In pursuit of a passport, that summer he twice met Walsingham, who seems to have hooked him like a salmon. Walsingham urged him to reveal whatever he knew, as if this was for his own good, and expressed interest in Babington reporting on affairs in Europe, on behalf of Elizabeth, while he was abroad.

It is unsettling to think that, at this stage, Babington did not see himself as a danger to the state but as one who might prove useful to Walsingham, whereas in the secretary's mind, whatever happened next, the young man was already on his way to the scaffold. Now that he was firmly on Walsingham's radar, Babington was befriended by Poley, who from this point clung to him like a leech.

As they drained their tankards in the Plough Inn, Babington was unconvinced by Ballard's optimistic expectations that Spain would soon launch an attack on England. He was right to be sceptical, and wrong to allow himself to be persuaded that if Elizabeth were assassinated, help from Europe would swiftly follow. But persuaded he was, as were his friends. During the summer of 1586, they would meet at the Plough Inn, and elsewhere, to work out the details of yet another conspiracy to free Mary, kill Elizabeth and return England to the Catholic faith. The man selected for the unsavoury task of doing away with Elizabeth was called John Savage. He had lived up to his name when, at the seminary of Douai in Rheims, he had sworn to murder the Queen of England. Gifford, who had heard him make this vow, was determined to hold him to it.

Without any difficulty, Gifford had wormed his way into Babington's inner circle of ardent Mary sympathisers and, whenever he sensed hesitation in their mission, would egg them on. Meanwhile Poley reported diligently to Walsingham on what he had learned of their doings. His bulletins included the conspirators' palpable unease about the legality, and morality, of murdering the Queen of England. As Châteauneuf would later write in his account of the plot to the King of France, the main hurdle for Gifford was to persuade Babington and his associates 'that they could execute this enterprise against Queen Elizabeth without doing violence to their conscience.'

In the end, while Babington swithered, it was Mary who lit the fuse that led directly to his door. When Morgan suggested that she should give the young man some encouragement, she wrote a vaguely worded letter that hinted at her interest in whatever proposed venture was on hand. In his unguarded reply, on 7 July, Babington laid bare the plot that was being hatched. This comprised an invasion from Europe, a Catholic uprising in England, Mary's rescue by a posse of ten gentlemen and one hundred soldiers, the 'despatch of the usurping competitor' and the placing of Mary in her stead on the throne. He hoped to receive her endorsement before he and his friends proceeded, and, perhaps to underline their serious intent, said that Elizabeth's 'tragical execution' would be accomplished by 'six noble gentlemen'. Once this letter was put into Mary's hands, Walsingham, Phelippes and Gifford held their breaths, waiting to see if she would respond.

Several days passed before she composed a reply, during which she must surely have lost sleep over how to proceed. By this stage, following her son's refusal to press for her liberation and his veto on sharing the throne of Scotland with her, Mary was running out of options. Her son's support was gone (if she had ever had it), as was her health. But there was more. The day before Babington sat down to write his fatal letter outlining the plot, a treaty had been signed at Berwick between Scotland and England. News of that dreaded alliance, formally aligning James with Elizabeth, must have ended whatever hopes Mary retained of being restored or, as she now preferred, allowed peacefully to retire to France.

The timing of that life-changing treaty, and of Mary's equally life-changing reply, cannot be coincidence. On 17 July, against the advice of her secretary Nau, who recommended she leave Babington's message unanswered, she wrote the most fateful letter of her life. As when she ignored the counsel of her companions not to sail for France in 1568 – to this point the worst decision she ever made – so, before taking the most unwise step of her career, she swept aside the better judgement of her secretary and followed her own path.

Nau translated Mary's dictated French response into English, and Curle put it into cipher, for its conveyance by beer barrel and thence to the house at Lichfield where Babington had told Mary he would be waiting. Knowing the risks she ran, she destroyed the notes from which she had dictated her letter, and urged Babington to burn her reply. The letter itself, which was long and thoughtful, was that of a pragmatist, focusing on the minutiae of the plan:

> Now, to ground this enterprise substantially and bring it to good success, you must examine deeply:
> 1. What forces on foot and horse may be raised amongst you all, and what captains you will appoint for them in every shire in case a general in chief cannot be had.
> 2. Of what towns, ports, and havens you may assure yourselves in the north, west, and south, to receive succour from the Low Countries, Spain and France.
> 3. What place you esteem fittest and of great advantage to assemble the principal company of your forces, and the same being assembled, whether or which way you are to march.
> 4. What foreign forces on horse and afoot you require from the three said foreign Princes – which would be compassed according to the proportion of yours – for how long paid, what munition and forts fittest for their landing in this realm.
> 5. What provision of armour and money, in case you want it, you would ask.
> 6. By what means do the six gentlemen deliberate to proceed.
> 7. Also the manner of my getting from this hold.

She urged Babington to make sure she was rescued before Elizabeth became aware of the plot, since otherwise, if she were caught, the consequences would be dire. '[The Queen would] enclose me for ever in some hole from which I should never escape, if she used me no worse, and to pursue with all extremity all who had assisted me, which would grieve me more than all the unhappiness that might fall upon myself.'

Showing how much consideration she had given the matter, Mary presented three scenarios in which she believed the rescue could be carried off successfully:

> First, that at a certain day appointed in my "walking" abroad on horseback on the moors between this and Stafford, where ordinarily you know very few people pass, fifty or three score men well horsed and armed, come to take me there, as they easily may, my keeper having with him ordinarily but eighteen or twenty horsemen with daggers only.
>
> The second means is to come at midnight or soon after to set fire to the barns and stables which you know are near to the house, and whilst my guardian's servants shall run to the fire, your company – having a mark whereby they may know one another at night – might surprise the house . . .
>
> And the third. Some that bring carts hither ordinarily, coming early in the morning, their carts might be so prepared with such cart-leaders that being just in the middle of the great gate the carts might fall down or overwhelm, and thereupon you might come suddenly with your followers to make yourself master of the house and carry me away. So you might do easily before any number of soldiers, who lodge in sundry places forth from this place, some a half and some a whole mile off, might come to the relief.

Hoping to raise further support, she added, 'I will essay . . . to make the Catholics of Scotland rise and put my son in their hands to the effect that from thence our enemies here may not prevail by any succour. I would also that some stirring in Ireland were laboured for.'

As all this shows, there was nothing tentative about her response to Babington's plan. But one paragraph, in its implicit acceptance of Elizabeth's assassination, was particularly incriminating:

> The affairs being thus prepared and forces in readiness both within and without the realm, then shall it be time to set the six gentlemen to work, taking order, upon the accomplishing of their

design, I may be suddenly transported out of this place, and that all your forces at the same time be in the field to meet me in tarrying for the arrival of the foreign aid which then must be hastened with all diligence.

When Phelippes deciphered what he dubbed 'the bloody letter', he drew a gallows on it and passed it to Walsingham. He believed its contents would almost certainly spell Mary's end, but hoped that at the very least Nau and Curle would hang for it. But, as was ever the case, Walsingham wanted more. Here, his cunning moved into the territory of outright criminality. At his behest, Phelippes forged a postscript to the letter, asking who had been appointed to assassinate Elizabeth ('I would be glad to know the names and qualities of the six gentlemen which are to accomplish the designment'). This would not only make Mary's complicity beyond doubt but, if Babington responded, allow Walsingham to mop up the leaders of the plot.

Babington replied only to acknowledge the letter, but by now he was rattled. As Stephen Alford writes, 'was Babington a conspirator or merely a young man caught up in a plot?' He told Poley of his intention to reveal to Walsingham the danger Elizabeth faced, in the hope that in return he would be given permission to leave the country. Poley urged him to reveal all to the secretary, but Walsingham had other plans. He had no intention of allowing Babington to escape, let alone act as an informant on the government's behalf. On the contrary, he was on the brink of arresting him and all his associates and wringing from them every drop of information they possessed.

Babington's acknowledgement of Mary's reply was written on 3 August. The following day Ballard was arrested. At this, some historians claim Babington urged Savage to kill Elizabeth the same day, but that for lack of clothes fit for the assassin to wear at court, time was lost. Babington then wrote a fond but suspicious letter of farewell to Poley, whom he had never fully trusted, and, along with his fellow conspirators, fled to the safety of St John's Wood, a few miles from the centre of London. There he tried to disguise himself by rubbing walnut juice into his face and hands. After several days as a fugitive he and several of his companions were captured and, in a bedraggled state and doubtless terrified, brought to the Tower of London. The rest of the group were hunted down and imprisoned, fourteen of them in total. Gifford, meanwhile, fearful that he would be caught up in the wave of retribution, and not trusting Walsingham to play fair by him, wisely fled to France.

Under threat of torture, Babington confessed all, blaming everything on Ballard. For his part, Ballard, who was put on the rack, confirmed that there had indeed been a conspiracy. Believing he might be pardoned if he told them everything he knew, Babington regurgitated the contents of Mary's letters from memory, with a little help from his inquisitors, who of course already knew their contents. Alford damningly concludes, 'It was evidence offered by Babington that finally caught Mary in Walsingham's trap.'

Historians disagree over Elizabeth's reaction to the Babington Plot, some claiming she was in terror for her own life, others that since she knew of Walsingham's hand behind it, she was not shocked. Nor, the same theory goes, did it make her suddenly eager to see Mary executed. Others, however, believe she now became implacable over Mary's fate, wanting her gone, even if not on the scaffold. Whatever the truth, Elizabeth had recently retreated to Windsor Castle for safety. And although she was in on Walsingham and Phelippes' shady dealings, it was felt she need never know of their forgery. In their minds, this useful postscript to the original letter could be filed in the cabinet labelled 'end justifying means'.

The next few weeks for Babington, Ballard and their cronies were dreadful. After a trial in which they pleaded guilty to plotting to free Mary and turn England back to Catholicism, but not to planning regicide, they were nevertheless found guilty of treason. On 20 September, Babington and six of his inner circle, including Ballard, were treated to a ritual medieval punishment. Dragged on horse-drawn sledges from the Tower, they were taken to St Giles' Fields in Holborn where, before an enraged throng, they were hanged on a scaffold. Cut down while still breathing, they had their genitals cut off, were then disembowelled and quartered, all while conscious. Their entrails and 'privities' were then burnt in front of them. At such savagery, the onlookers' mood turned from righteous fury to something like sympathy. Recognising that she had gone too far, Elizabeth ordered that the next day's seven victims were to be hanged until dead before being disembowelled.

Chapter 26

'Her Majesty might have her body, but her heart she should never have'

TIXALL HALL

In better health than for many months, Mary was surprised but gratified when, on 11 August, Paulet invited her to take part in a stag hunt at nearby Tixall Hall, the home of Walter Aston. A more suspicious person would have wondered at her captor's sudden lenience, but Mary accepted the offer at face value. Accompanied by servants and companions, she anticipated an enjoyable outing.

It was on this inauspicious day that her French physician, Dominique Bourgoing, began a journal he was to keep until her execution. In 1895, the Hon. Mrs Maxwell Scott of Abbotsford, Walter Scott's great-granddaughter, used this to reconstruct the last months of Mary's life, from which most of his memories here are selected.

With a journalistic eye for detail, Bourgoing noted that, as the party prepared to set out, 'Her Majesty arrayed herself suitably, hoping to meet some pleasant company, and was attended by M. Nau, who had not forgotten to adorn himself.' Others around her included Bastian Pages, acting as 'mantle bearer', and a servant who carried her crossbows and arrows. All looked forward to a relaxed day, taking advantage of the fine summer weather. As they made their way towards Tixall, Mary noticed a line of horsemen approaching fast across the moors. For a fraction of a second she possibly believed that these were Babington's rescuers, coming to her aid. If so, it was to be her last-ever moment of hope.

Thomas Gorges, the leader of the men, dismounted and approached Mary as she sat on her horse. Bourgoing mentions, with contempt, that the Queen of England's messenger was wearing green serge, which was 'embroidered more than necessary for such a dress'. Gorges baldly informed Mary that Elizabeth knew she had been conspiring 'against her and her state'. Her secretaries were to be arrested, and she was now under his guard.

What had started as a bright, pleasant morning had turned into a nightmare. Mary stridently denied involvement in any treachery and ordered her party to draw their swords. They were quickly disarmed, and as Nau and Curle tried to approach her, they were roughly dragged away. Soon they would be in a London prison where interrogators initially could not get them to implicate their mistress in any wrongdoing. Eventually, however, they mistakenly confirmed the authenticity of the gallows letter, having not been shown the forged postscript, which would have caused them to discredit it. As a result, each acted as Mary's unwitting nemesis. Along with them, Andrew Melville, the head of the queen's household, was also taken, while her companion Bessie Pierrepoint was obliged to return to Chartley.

As the soldiers and Paulet led the queen's party away, Mary realised they were not returning to Chartley. Feeling suddenly very unwell, she dismounted and sat on the ground. It seems she thought she was being taken immediately to her death. Informed by Paulet that her destination was Tixall Hall, she refused to budge from where she was seated, saying she preferred to die there. In response, Paulet threatened to call for her coach and forcibly remove her to Tixall. Only her physician's encouragement led her to mount her horse and continue on her way, but not before she had knelt to pray aloud, piteously beseeching God for his mercy in a manner that suggested she believed she had only hours to live.

The stone and timber-framed Tixall Hall, which was less than eight miles from Chartley, no longer exists. Nor does its Georgian replacement, which was demolished in 1927. All that remains is the Tudor gatehouse, which sits stranded amid pastureland and trees.

Without the grand hall behind it, the gatehouse serves no purpose except as an unusual period residence or – as now – an upmarket holiday let.

The original Tixall Hall, built in 1555 on the site of a previous building, was a sombre but elegant mullioned Elizabethan affair, exuding wealth and influence. Walter Aston was obviously proud of his estate, telling Paulet that it supported about 100 people and that 'he is sufficiently provided of corn, hay, grass about his house, and of all other things necessary for so great a family. He hath threescore milch kyne [dairy cows], three ploughs of oxen, and one of horses.' In 1580 Sir Walter added the gatehouse as a statement of grandeur. One commentator, in 1598, wrote that in so doing he had 'beautified, or defaced (I know not which to say)' the house his father built. Yet this architectural critic seems to have approved, calling it 'one of the fairest pieces of work made of late time in all these counties'. To Mary, as she was led under the gatehouse arch and into the manor house's enclosed compound, it must have felt menacing.

Even today and in sunshine, the gatehouse has a forbidding, faintly minatory air. There is an aura of venerability about it, and of watchfulness. A rather graceless, square, three-storey edifice, it has pepperpot towers at each corner and a balustrade around its flat rooftop. When I visited, the weathervanes flashed in the sunlight; I later learned they had been regilded with gold leaf paint a decade or so earlier.

Parking the car off the road, I climbed the five-bar wooden gate into the field in which the gatehouse sits and gingerly made my way along a path trodden in the grass, trying – not entirely successfully – to avoid a minefield of recent cowpats. Too recent, in fact, since after I had been admiring the building for a few minutes, a herd of dairy cattle suddenly came into view, trotting my way in single file. I was back at the wooden gate, heedless of muck, by the time they reached the gatehouse.

Tixall Gatehouse's location is idyllic. Five miles from Stafford, it lies on the edge of the hamlet of Tixall, with a canal running nearby. On a hot summer's day, the atmosphere was bucolic and somnolent, despite a municipal-sized green recycling bin by the gatehouse walls, an incongruous element in an otherwise Tudor scene. The gatehouse is owned by the Landmark Trust, which buys and restores historic properties and turns them into holiday homes. When it acquired the gatehouse in 1968, it had no roof, floors or windows, and was used only as a shelter for cattle. A few years ago a Tudor historian stayed here while working, the setting perhaps helping the chapters to write themselves. With its roof terrace, turret bedrooms, wood-panelled living rooms, and top-floor table-tennis room beneath the beams, it is appealingly comfortable, at odds with the severity of its exterior.

Mary, of course, was never in the gatehouse. She was to spend only two weeks at Tixall, every day of them miserable. While here, her rooms at Chartley were turned upside down as her captors sought evidence of her involvement in the Babington Plot. Elizabeth urged Paulet to search 'all the secret corners' of her lodgings and Bourgoing, who was allowed to stay only one night with Mary at Tixall, watched three coffers of papers and other material being carried off. Among them were around sixty ciphers and alphabets used in her secret correspondence.

An inventory of some of the items taken from the queen's rooms suggests magpies as well as intelligencers were at work: 'a little chest garnished with diamonds, rubies, and pearls, a little pincase of gold, a chain to wear for a girdle for a woman, enamelled in white and red . . . two carcanets [chains or collars of jewels], other blackset with pearls'.

A mere handful of servants was allowed to attend Mary while she was at Tixall. On her return to Chartley, she was met at the gatehouse by a group of what Paulet called 'poor people', hoping for charity. 'I have nothing for you,' she told them, 'I am a beggar as well as you, all is taken from me.'

Paulet might have raised his eyebrows at such hyperbole, but he would have been pleased to see no money going the beggars' way. His lack of feeling for the poor, and his refusal to countenance Mary's almsgiving, were evidence of his inflexibility towards his prisoner, but also of this period in Elizabeth's reign. People had grown steadily less tolerant of paupers as fear of social unrest mounted. Now, the middling sort and gentry condemned rather than pitied them.

For a wealthy Catholic such as Mary, giving alms was an expression of her religion. Not only was it a kind deed, but since alms givers expected beggars to pray for them in return for their charity, it was also a way of saving their souls. The social historian Steve Hindle, who calls this the 'supernatural economy', contrasts the pre-Reformation attitude to that of the Calvinist Protestant age, in which such acts were not necessary for a believer's salvation. Instead, he writes, the motto 'heaven helps those who help themselves' 'perfectly captured the moral economy of Protestantism'. The biblical authority for such an uncompassionate response was found in 2 Thessalonians 3:10 – 'if any would not work, neither should he eat'. As the wretched procession left Tixall Hall, and the poor departed penniless, Paulet's and Mary's attitudes typified both sides of this spiritual coin.

Back in her rooms at Chartley, Mary was horrified at the scene of devastation left by the ransackers. In anger, she turned to Paulet's men, telling them that there were two things that could never be taken from her: her royal blood and her religion, 'which both she would keep until her death'. Only her money had been left untouched, and that was soon taken also. One day, when Mary was lying ill in bed, Paulet ordered all her women and servants out of the room. Armed men filled the antechamber, causing consternation. Accompanied by Richard Bagot, a Staffordshire magistrate who lived only a few miles away and formed part of the Protestant loyalist group that made Chartley a fitting prison for the queen, Paulet informed Mary that he had been ordered to seize her money. She responded by assuring him, 'Her Majesty might have her body, but her heart she should never have.'

She refused to hand over the key to the cabinet where her money was kept, but when Paulet instructed his servants to fetch bars to break the door open, Mary reluctantly told her companion Elizabeth Curle to open the cabinet. Inside were 5,000 French crowns and two leather bags filled with gold and silver coins, representing a small fortune. As Paulet and Bagot began to gather them up, Mary dragged herself from her bed and, without putting on slippers or shoes, as Bourgoing writes, told them that this was money 'she had long put aside as a last resource for the time when she would die, both for her funeral expenses and to enable her attendants to return each to his own country after her death'. But her protestations made no difference. Shortly after, Paulet and Bagot found more money and valuable items in Nau's chamber, which were likewise taken.

Paulet was pitiless in removing all trace of money, carrying out Elizabeth's commands to the letter. The Queen had also ordered that Mary be separated from her servants. John Guy writes that, rather than face the prospect of putting Mary on trial and having her executed, she hoped that 'by seizing her money and keeping her as far as possible in solitary confinement, she would become so seriously demoralised, her existing illnesses and afflictions would worsen fatally'. It was execution by stealth, but Mary was more robust and resilient than they expected.

Unsure what was coming, but knowing it would not be good, Mary spent her last days at Chartley in a state of suspense. Paulet questioned her about what she knew of Babington's plot and told her to expect more of the same. There was, however, one uplifting episode. While Mary had been at Tixall, Gilbert Curle's wife had given birth to a daughter. Since the secret chaplain had been dismissed some time earlier, Mary asked Paulet if he would allow his minister to baptise the infant. Paulet reported that when he refused, Mary 'came shortly after into Curle's wife's chamber, where laying the child on her knees, she took water out of a basin, and casting it upon the face of the child she said, "I baptise thee in the name of the Father, the Son, and the Holy Ghost", calling the child by her own name Mary.' He could not let this pass without comment: 'This may not be found strange in her who maketh no conscience to break all laws of God and man.'

Not long after, Paulet informed Mary that she was to be moved again, to a place not far from London. Bourgoing writes that she was not told exactly where she was headed, and was kept in the dark until she reached her destination. One or two locations had been discussed, including the Tower of London, but the place chosen for her final prison was Fotheringhay Castle in Northamptonshire, one of the Queen's properties. On the day of her departure, 21 September 1586, Gorges and Nicholas Stallenge, who was Usher of Parliament, entered her chamber, carrying pistols. Despite their alarming appearance, they treated her with unexpected civility. Paulet, meanwhile, conducted himself with typical caution, having her servants locked up so they could not communicate with her as she left.

So immobile that she had to be carried to her coach, Mary spent four days on the road, accompanied by Paulet, Gorges and a heavy guard of soldiers. On 25 September 1586, she and her escort finally passed through the intimidating gates of Fotheringhay Castle. She was never again to see the world beyond its walls, and knew as much.

Chapter 27

'Look to your consciences'

FOTHERINGHAY CASTLE

Fotheringhay Castle was a spectacular twelfth-century motte-and-bailey construction, thirteen miles from Peterborough and eighty-five miles north of London. Originally a wooden castle, built in Norman times by Simon de Senlis, it passed for a time into the Scottish royal family when Senlis's widow married David I. The birthplace of Richard III, it was a state prison with such a grim reputation that Henry VIII's first wife, Catherine of Aragon, said she could only be imprisoned there if 'bound with cart ropes and dragged thither'. This, despite the fact her husband had granted the castle to her on their marriage, as he would do for all his wives.

In its heyday, Fotheringhay – also spelled Fotheringay – must have dominated the gentle Northamptonshire landscape, a perpetual reminder of the power of the state over its people. Protected by a double moat and a massive keep, it had an imposing gateway set between two towers and was guarded by a drawbridge and thick defensive walls on which soldiers could patrol. A chapel stood alongside the castle, which was built around a large courtyard. Inside, the various spacious state rooms included a Great Hall, which would one day become infamous as the scene of Mary's execution. The whole complex was considered such a feat of architectural strength that people came from across Europe to admire it.

Today, to the great disappointment of all those following in Mary's footsteps, almost nothing remains of it. It was said that when James VI became James I of England, he had it razed out of rage, but that is not the case. After Mary's execution, the place began to fall into disrepair and dilapidation, much of it being appropriated by local builders. Officially demolished in 1628, the castle's stone was used to construct the Talbot Inn in the nearby village of Oundle. (The inn's stately staircase is also said to come from Fotheringhay.)

Visitors will find only a knuckle of old wall, fenced off by railings bearing plaques to Richard III and Mary, Queen of Scots. The River Nene, with its houseboats and moorhens, runs past the enclosure, which stands on the edge of a tussocky field. Overlooking it is the grassy hill that was formerly the castle's motte. From its summit there is an excellent view of the much-altered fifteenth-century church of St Mary and All Saints, with its octagonal lantern tower. The church dominates the bijou village of Fotheringhay, with its tidily thatched cottages, neat stone houses and farm steadings. A quintessentially English settlement, with finger signposts and the occasional passing horse rider in high-vis jacket, the village is set in low, fertile agricultural land that floods when the river is high. It is not difficult to imagine the place in the depths of winter in Mary's day, when mist would swirl around the river and creep up the castle walls, the silhouettes of leafless trees offering little in the way of cheer.

On her arrival, Mary complained about the inadequate size of her rooms. Several of the castle's fine state apartments were unused, she remarked, before realising they were intended for another purpose, one whose meaning she immediately grasped. They were being kept for the day she was put on trial. As he reported in his journal, Bourgoing was impressed by the queen's demeanour during this profoundly unsettling interlude. With few illusions about what lay ahead, Mary nevertheless displayed astonishing strength of mind: 'she was not in the least moved,' he wrote; 'on the contrary, her courage rose, and she was more cheerful and in better health than before'.

On 1 October, Paulet, with a show of courteousness that instantly put Mary on her guard, informed her of the forthcoming trial, at which she was to be interrogated about aiding a plot to harm Elizabeth. He urged her immediately to confess all, at which

Elizabeth would be merciful; she parried this by saying he was treating her like a child, to be bribed into admitting wrongdoing. In the first of many assured and shrewd responses over the coming days, Mary reasserted her view of her position. Foremost among these was that she had nothing to confess. Down the years her words ring with timeless clarity: 'As a sinner I am truly conscious of having often offended my Creator, and I beg Him to forgive me, but as Queen and Sovereign I am aware of no fault or offence for which I have to render account to any one here below.' Paulet duly relayed her sentiments to Elizabeth.

In these darkening days, there was some good news in the return of the steadfast Andrew Melville, her steward, and of her devoted servant Bastian Pages. More sinisterly, her coachman was dismissed without her permission, a clear indication that Mary would not be going anywhere. Not that she needed to interpret the runes. Even before reaching Fotheringhay, she knew the end was close. This may have come as a relief. Nineteen years of unjust imprisonment, of promises of clemency that came to nothing, of Machiavellian plotting at both the English and Scottish courts had wearied her. Remarkably, however, while her body had been worn down by her tribulations, her mind and spirit appear only to have grown stronger.

Accepting that she would be found guilty and executed no matter what she did or said, Mary turned her thoughts to a good death, as defined on her own terms. The first sight she had of Fotheringhay must have sent a jolt through her, but its brutal appearance and reputation made it a fitting stage for what she later described to the Spanish ambassador Mendoza as 'the last scene of the Tragedy'.

Since arriving in England and discovering she was a prisoner rather than a guest, Mary had been assiduously shaping her identity into that of an innocent Catholic persecuted for her religion. All these years later, and in such poor health she believed that even if freed, she would have only two or three years of life left, she had transformed herself from a brave but headstrong young queen into a stoical exemplar of religious devotion and endurance. As she entered her final months, she went almost willingly to her end, embracing – indeed relishing – the role of martyr. Perhaps eager for the conclusion of her life, she had her cousin's measure and had no expectation of reprieve. So when Paulet hinted that Elizabeth might show mercy, she correctly interpreted this as meaningless.

Meanwhile in London, Elizabeth and her councillors had read Babington's and Mary's correspondence, along with his confession and those of Mary's secretaries Nau and Curle. There was no doubt in anyone's mind that the Scottish queen must be put on trial. Elizabeth therefore summoned forty-eight commissioners to make their way to Fotheringhay, where Mary would face the charge of conspiring against her life. When he received the order to attend, the Earl of Shrewsbury tried to wriggle out of this most unwelcome duty by claiming poor health. With menacing directness, Burghley warned him that his non-attendance would damage his standing, and heighten suspicions that he had been a lax guardian during Mary's captivity. In the end he grudgingly made his way to Fotheringhay. But, to Elizabeth's surprise and anger, several others did not. As a result, Mary was to appear before a gathering of fewer than forty nobles.

On Saturday 11 October, Elizabeth's faithful courtiers began to arrive in Northamptonshire. Some stayed in the castle, others were put up in the nearby village of Fotheringhay or in local farmhouses and lodgings. Among them were Walsingham and his brother-in-law, Robert Beale, Elizabeth's tireless clerk of the Privy Council, for whom Mary had a high regard. There were also Robert Dudley, Earl of Leicester, Christopher Hatton, one of Elizabeth's long-time favourites and second only to Leicester in her affections, and Mary's former gaoler, Ralph Sadler. Burghley did not reach the castle until Sunday. On that day, the assembled nobility attended chapel, where doubtless they silently prayed for a swift guilty verdict to be delivered, and an equally swift end to the woman who had caused two decades of ceaseless trouble. Later that day, a delegation comprising Burghley, Walter Mildmay, Paulet, Stallenge and Elizabeth's notary Barker handed Mary a letter from the Queen, addressed simply to 'The Scotish'. Its contents were curt and its ameliorative last sentence, appearing to hold out the prospect of mercy, reads as if tacked on for form's sake. Elizabeth's tone was imperious and accusatory:

> You have in various ways and manners attempted to take my life and bring my kingdom to destruction by bloodshed. I have never proceeded harshly against you, but have, on the contrary, protected and maintained you like myself. These treasons will be proved to you and all made manifest. Yet it is my will, that you answer the nobles and peers of the kingdom as if I myself were present. I therefore require, charge, and command you make answer for all I have been well informed of your arrogance. Act plainly without reserve, and you will sooner be able to obtain favour of me.

Mary treated the idea that she would submit herself to a jury of her inferiors with disdain. Only Elizabeth, as a fellow sovereign, was her peer and in a position to judge her. Equally importantly, she was not a citizen of England, and did not consider herself bound by its laws.

In the course of two days of arguing with Burghley and his delegates, in which Mary seems rather to have enjoyed pitting her wits against theirs, she lucidly explained her situation, and outlined a well-rehearsed list of grievances. These stretched back to her arrival in England in the hope of gaining Elizabeth's support, but included the illegality and unjustness of expecting her to defend herself in the proposed trial. She had nobody to act as counsel, and there were no witnesses for the defence. Above all, she would rather die than 'answer as a criminal person' since 'By such an avowal, I should betray the dignity and majesty of kings, and it would be tantamount to a confession that I am bound to submit to the laws of England, even in matters touching religion.'

She declared herself willing to answer all questions before a free Parliament but 'not before these Commissioners, who doubtless have been carefully selected, and who have probably already condemned me unheard'. In shaping the climax and conclusion of her life, Mary showed a touch of theatrical genius. Her ringing last words to Burghley and his party sound like a pay-off line before the curtain drops on the penultimate act: 'Look to your consciences, and remember that the theatre of the world is wider than the realm of England.'

And yet, in the end, she capitulated: not because she was weak or defeated, but because she recognised the truth when Christopher Hatton remarked that, if she was absent at the trial, it would be read as an admission of guilt; whereas by attending, she had an opportunity to prove her innocence by answering the accusations against her.

Mary was not so naive as to suppose that she would be found innocent, but she saw that by putting her testimony on record, along with her refusal to recognise the trial's authority over her, she would be leaving a historical record of her persecution and resistance. This was her way of marking what might be seen as one of the stations of the cross on the way to her wrongful execution. But there was another, even grislier inducement to go along with this so-called trial and whatever punishment resulted from it.

If the trial's legality were later questioned, as it might be without her attendance, other means might be found for quietly disposing of her. Mary dreaded murder far more than death itself, since lies could be told about the manner in which she died. This was a constant and well-founded concern, and a few months earlier, she had confided to the Duke of Guise, 'I expect poison or some other secret death.' If it were a public event, however, she could act her part, and uphold her protestations of faith and innocence to the end.

So it was that, on the understanding that she was to answer only to the charge of plotting Elizabeth's assassination, and that her protest against the trial's legitimacy would be duly noted in the trial proceedings, Mary agreed to face her interrogators. This momentous decision left her feeling faint, and she required a glass of wine to revive her.

Among Burghley's many administrative attributes was his talent for meticulous organisation. A careful and often cautious man, he liked to be in control of every situation. Ahead of the trial, he drew a picture of the large state room in which it was to take place, recording its precise measurements and instructing where tables, benches and chairs were to be placed. A contemporary drawing, found in the papers of Robert Beale, and similar in style to Beale's eyewitness drawing of Mary's execution, captures the scene as the trial took place, although the placement of its players differs a little from Burghley's instructions.

A rail, with a gate, divided onlookers from the court, which occupied the larger part of the chamber. At the head of the room on a dais stood a chair of state, beneath a canopy embellished with the English arms. This empty seat represented Elizabeth, whose absence was in body only. Metaphorically she was in the room, staring down at Mary. Below the eerily vacant dais, to one side, was positioned one of Mary's own red velvet high-backed chairs, with a red velvet footstool. Around three sides of the court-room sat the commissioners, while in the centre of them at a long table, as if awaiting a feast, were Elizabeth's notary, lawyers and other representatives of the crown, with their documents piled before them.

At nine o'clock on the morning of Wednesday 15 October, Mary entered the room, accompanied by an escort of armed soldiers. Supported on either arm by Melville and Bourgoing, she was attended by three of her ladies-in-waiting and her surgeon and apothecary. Scanning the room as she was led to the front, Mary was startled to see Elizabeth's canopied chair set higher than her own. This was an unmistakable slight. Composing herself, she took in the commissioners, who had removed their hats at her entrance. 'Ah, here are many counsellors, but not one for me,' she remarked to Melville.

Dressed in a black velvet gown and cloak, with a cambric cap and a flowing white veil, she was helped into her seat, her maid arranging her train behind her. This would have been the first time most of the commissioners had seen her. Her dress was reminiscent of that she wore when she arrived in Scotland as a beautiful young widow, but the queen who was demonised by almost all of

England as 'the monstrous and huge dragon', was no longer lovely. Rather than a public threat, she would have looked pitiable, being overweight, almost unable to walk, and appearing much older than her forty-three years. Was there any compassion for her condition as she shuffled towards her chair? Surveying their faces in the following hours, Mary convinced herself that she had spotted signs of sympathy. Yet by the trial's conclusion, only one did not judge her guilty. Tellingly, that one was not Shrewsbury, who knew her best of them all.

The first day of the two-day trial was to be especially gruelling. The Lord Chancellor started proceedings by stating Elizabeth's demand that Mary be questioned about her part in attempting to kill her. Mary opened her side of business by putting it on record that 'in consenting to appear before this Commission I do so, not as a subject to Queen Elizabeth, but only from my desire to clear myself'.

Much of the morning passed discussing Mary's correspondence with Babington, of which she denied any knowledge. Her secretaries' corroboration of the letters she had exchanged with him was awkward, but she was not daunted, insisting on seeing the original letters, with her signature.

She must have been shaken to discover that Walsingham had had sight of them, despite the fact he could not produce the originals Nau and Curle had taken down at her dictation. Yet she would not be bowed. It would have been easy, she said, for her enemies to tamper with her ciphers (how right she was). But while casting the blame for these incriminating letters on Nau and Curle she did willingly, indeed enthusiastically, concede two important points:

> I have written to my friends, I confess; I appealed to them to assist me to escape from these miserable prisons in which I have languished for nearly nineteen years. I have also, I confess, often pleaded the cause of the Catholics with the Kings of Europe, and for their deliverance from the oppression under which they lie, I would willingly have shed my blood. But I declare formally that I

never wrote the letters that are produced against me. Can I be responsible for the criminal projects of a few desperate men, which they planned without my knowledge or participation?

Learning that she had been betrayed by Nau and Curle, she said that Curle would only have done so if forced into it by Nau, who in turn must have acted under fear of torture. 'If they were in my presence now,' she said, 'they would clear me on the spot of all blame.' Evidence against her was produced in haphazard order, leaving Mary bewildered. A break for lunch did nothing to improve matters, since the blizzard of accusations continued afterwards over Babington's and the secretaries' confessions, and her letters to Babington, which she repeatedly denied having written. Saying that, unless her word as a sovereign was believed she demanded another trial, Mary emphasised how unfairly she was being, and had been, treated. Taking a ring from her finger, she announced: 'Look here, my lords, see this pledge of love and protection which I received from your mistress – regard it well. Trusting to this pledge, I came amongst you. You all know how it has been kept.'

Ignoring this, Burghley charged Mary with having always coveted the throne of England. She in turn accused Walsingham of tampering with her letters. Perhaps because she struck so close to the truth, Walsingham defended himself angrily: 'I protest that my soul is free from all malice. God is my witness that, as a private person, I have done nothing unworthy of an honest man, and as Secretary of State, nothing unbefitting my duty.' By such legalistic distinctions he managed to pacify his conscience and sleep at night. The afternoon turned even more unpleasant as the infuriated commissioners began to hurl accusations at Mary, and the session descended into chaos. When Mary was led back to her rooms at the end of the day she was reeling, likening her experience to that of Christ when the crowd bayed for his crucifixion.

The following morning, after a disturbed night and early morning prayers, she resumed her place in the courtroom. Very pale but determined, she began by condemning the clamour and confusion of the previous day, during which the commissioners had tried, she said, 'to vanquish by force of words a solitary and defenceless woman. There is not one, I think, among you, let him be the cleverest man you will, who would be capable of resisting or defending himself, were he in my place.' Perhaps to her surprise, Burghley now adopted a less aggressive stance, and the trial recommenced in a more mannerly fashion. Nevertheless, everything produced before the court was designed to affirm her guilt.

The record of the proceedings, and Mary's self-defence, is long and fascinating. It might be seen as her finest hour to this point in her captivity, showing her as courageous, spirited, intellectually fleet-footed and unintimidated. In one exchange, Burghley accused her of acting in concert with her agent Thomas Morgan, who had sent Parry to murder Elizabeth. Suddenly Mary seemed to see Burghley in his true colours: 'You are indeed my enemy,' she said, as if only now recognising his malign hand behind her downfall. His answer was that of a professional, admitting to no personal animus: 'Yes,' he said, 'I am the enemy of the enemies of Queen Elizabeth.'

As the hours dragged on, Mary was questioned about her communications with foreign powers, especially Philip II of Spain. She was asked what she would have done if there had been an invasion of England. Again denying any involvement in a plan to murder Elizabeth, she asserted that 'I have no other desire than the overthrow of Protestantism and the deliverance of myself and the afflicted Catholics, for whom (as I have often said) I am ready to shed my blood. I shall esteem myself very happy if God gives me the grace to suffer and to endure death for His holy name and in the defence of His quarrel.' She repeated her desire to appear before Parliament, and for a meeting with Elizabeth. Then, rising from her chair, she signalled that her part in this charade was over.

Regally surveying the room, she pardoned them all for what they had done, saying she wished no ill to any of them. Before departing she had a brief word with Walsingham. What he said is not known, although he did not appear happy at their conversation. Turning from him, Mary announced: 'I place my cause in the hands of God,' as if she had just had confirmation that she could not hope for justice here on earth. Sweeping past the table of lawyers, she said, with a smile, 'May God keep me from having to do with you all again.'

The queen's composure during this ordeal was exceptional. She had maintained to the last her innocence, her refusal to accept the commissioners' right to sit in judgement on her, and all with a dignity, chutzpah and charm undimmed by years of confinement, dread and illness.

With the queen gone, the commissioners were eager to pronounce Mary guilty. Burghley, who had received instructions from Elizabeth not to impose a sentence yet, had to tell them this was not the time. Instead, the commission was to be prorogued for ten days, after which it would reconvene at Star Chamber in Westminster. Thwarted, the commissioners began to make their way homewards. Mary, exhausted by her performance and stricken by the visible loathing of some of her adversaries, returned to her chambers to await what would next happen.

Chapter 28

'I pray God grant you as much happiness in this world as I expect in leaving it'

LIMBO

An atmosphere of melancholy hangs over Mary's story as the hour ticks towards her execution, and yet she was neither gloomy nor fearful. Rather, she seems to have been energised by her impending doom and to have regained some of the lightness of spirit of her youth. By now, she was brimful with Catholic fervour and mission. She might have worked hard to refashion her image into that of a martyr, but her conviction was genuine. Her physician writes that in these weeks, 'I have not seen her so joyous, nor so constantly at her ease for the last seven years.' Paulet reported that Mary knew nothing of the commission's prorogation, and was 'utterly void of all fear of harm', seeming to misread her serenity as a sign of ignorance, rather than assurance that she would soon be with God.

Always a keen reader, Mary at this point pursued her particular interest in history. An inventory of her belongings, taken at Chartley, includes books on history, along with illuminated prayer books. Paulet recorded a conversation in which she remarked on the bloodiness of England's history: 'I answered that if she would peruse the chronicles of Scotland, France, Spain and Italy, she should find that this realm was far behind any other Christian nation in shedding of blood.' Ever the preacher, he added, 'although the same was often very necessary where dangerous offences did arise'.

On 25 October, the commission reconvened at Star Chamber in Westminster Palace. This light-filled courtroom, its ceiling painted with gold stars on a blue background, was the domain of the Privy Council and judges of the common law. Originally a court of appeal dealing with people of such high status that lower courts might be too intimidated to convict them, by Elizabeth's time it dealt with a variety of offences, often involving property or public disorder. As England had grown more unruly, its provisions had become harsher. Its powers included ordering torture and imposing fines and prison sentences, but not the death penalty.

It was in this deceptively pleasant chamber that an almost unanimous verdict of guilty was delivered upon Mary. Nau and Curle had been ordered to attend, and although they did not address the assembly, they confirmed that their testimony had been voluntarily obtained, without pressure. Their presence clinched Mary's fate, since almost all the commissioners were convinced that their evidence left no room for doubt as to Mary's actions and intentions. The only peer who stood out from the crowd was Edward la Zouche, who was not persuaded of Mary's participation in an assassination plot. Sadly, a solitary naysayer could not stem the vengeful tide. (Aged around thirty, Zouche was an interesting character. A friend of Ben Jonson, as a young man he quickly ran through his inheritance, largely because of his passion for gardening.)

The commission's entirely expected outcome left Elizabeth in a quandary. The Privy Council demanded Mary's execution, both for the Queen's and England's security. She, however, did not want to be rushed into taking this fateful decision. Despite growing pressure, she still hoped to find a way of ending this long-running saga in a manner that left no stain on her reputation and did not stir her enemies in Europe into action. For weeks she was paralysed, in such emotional turmoil that some believe she was suffering a form of breakdown.

With the guilty verdict now official, nobody was in any doubt that the last chapter of Mary's captivity had begun. Security around Fotheringhay was heightened, the numbers of soldiers considerably increased and Paulet allowed more powder and shot.

Following the Star Chamber verdict, on 29 October Parliament upheld its findings and added its own embellishments. In what John Guy describes as 'a frenzy of invective couched in the language of biblical fundamentalism', Mary was denounced not just for attempting to promote the killing of Elizabeth but also for adultery with Bothwell and her part in Darnley's murder. Under the guiding hand of Burghley and Walsingham, Parliament immediately and strenuously petitioned for Mary's execution. Still Elizabeth swithered. She wanted Mary condemned under the provisions of the Bond of Association – essentially a private citizens' bill – whereas Burghley wanted the Queen to sign Mary's death warrant, thereby legitimising her execution as state regicide. This last course was not to Elizabeth's taste.

After making it clear she hoped to find a way of ensuring her own safety without publicly executing Mary, Elizabeth let time pass. In the meantime, she ordered Paulet to urge Mary to repent and beg forgiveness. This, of course, Mary would never do. Instead, she verbally jousted with Paulet, to the point that he could scarcely bear being in her presence. In truth, he was thoroughly tired of his charge and wished to have as little to do with her as possible. Bored by her ceaseless religious talk, he did not bother to convey everything she said in this vein when writing to Walsingham or Burghley. Instead, he referred disparagingly to such conversations as 'superfluous and idle'.

As the days passed without any sign of Elizabeth agreeing to the execution, the strain on Burghley's nerves began to tell. He told Walsingham's secretary William Davison that 'the sentence is already more than a full month and four days old. It was full time it should also speak'. On November 19, not long after Drue Drury replaced Stallenge as Paulet's deputy, Robert Beale arrived at Fotheringhay. He was in the company of William Sackville, Lord Buckhurst, a decent man, who would later succeed Burghley as lord high treasurer. Not unsympathetic to Mary's plight, Buckhurst began by informing her that the death sentence had been passed on her by Parliament. Elizabeth had not signed the warrant for her execution, but because 'The person of the Queen, the state and religion are no longer safe,' he explained, 'it is impossible for you both to live, and therefore one must die. For this end then, in order that you should not be taken by surprise, Mr Beale and I have been sent to warn you to prepare for death.'

'I expected nothing else,' Mary replied, adding: 'I do not fear death, and shall suffer it with a good heart.' Refusing as ever to repent, she riled them by maintaining she was dying for her beliefs. Countering this, they insisted she was to be executed for plotting against her cousin.

After Buckhurst's departure, Mary believed her execution was imminent. Gathering her companions and servants, she instructed them on her final wishes regarding her death and what they were to do afterwards. She also emphasised that she died a true Catholic and was innocent of the crimes alleged against her. One can only imagine the atmosphere among her entourage at hearing her long-rehearsed instructions, knowing that she was soon to be gone.

At this delicate time, Paulet made matters worse. Entering Mary's rooms, he told her that Elizabeth had ordered that her cloth of state be removed. Mary's servants flatly refused to take this down, and it fell to his men to do so. Paulet informed her that this was being done because she was 'now only a dead woman, without the dignity or honours of a queen'. He also had a billiard table taken away; Mary remarked that it was just as well she had never had time to use it.

From this time, Paulet appeared in her presence 'with his head covered', a gesture intended to insult. Yet, aware that he had been excessive in removing her canopy without the Queen of England's specific command, he relented a little by offering to ask for Elizabeth's approval to restore it. Treating his back-pedalling with contempt, Mary simply pointed to the crucifix that she had hung on the wall in the canopy's place. The message was clear: worldly status mattered little to her now, her eyes being fixed on a higher realm.

Expecting to die within a matter of days, perhaps hours, on 24 November Mary sat down to compose final letters to the Archbishop of Glasgow, the Pope, Bernardino de Mendoza and her cousin, the

Duke of Guise. The pain and difficulty of writing meant that this task occupied her for two days. In her message to Mendoza, the Spanish ambassador in Paris, she said she could hear the sound of hammering: 'They are working in my hall; I think they are making a scaffold to make me play the last scene of the Tragedy. I die in a good quarrel, and happy at having given up my rights to the King your Master.' She said of Philip that if James did not convert to the Catholic faith, 'I confess I know no prince more worthy, or more suitable for the protection of this island.' She also told him to expect to receive a token from her. Unlike today, a token did not denote something trivial but rather referred to a ring. Her gift was the diamond the Duke of Norfolk had given her when, she wrote, he 'pledged me his faith, and which I have nearly always worn'.

To the Duke of Guise, she wrote, 'You will receive tokens from me to remind you to have prayers said for the soul of your poor cousin, destitute of all aid and counsel but that of God, who gives me strength and courage to withstand alone so many wolves howling after me.' That last phrase captures how threatening she found the atmosphere, and how feral her foes must have appeared.

These vivid, moving, elegantly composed letters reveal Mary as ready to die, and calm at the prospect. For those of us who find the thought of her final weeks harrowing, it is comforting to see how composed and even content she was. All the evidence suggests she was far less unhappy or distressed during these weeks than she had often been in the previous nineteen years.

Meanwhile, the impasse over Elizabeth signing the death warrant continued, during which the Queen appears to have been in torment. Never one to make swift decisions, she had to balance her desire not to be seen as bloodily vengeful, like her father, with retaining her authority. She did not want to lose allies such as Scotland and France when tensions between England and Spain were escalating, yet by not acting on her counsellors' advice she risked alienating her own parliament.

Aware that she was trying their patience, she begged both Commons and Lords to suggest an alternative to beheading the

Queen of Scots. None was forthcoming. In a piteous speech before Parliament, which demonstrated her acute anxiety and indecision, she thanked its members for its good advice — namely to execute Mary — and asked them to 'excuse my doubtfulness, and take in good part my answer, answerless'. She then adjourned Parliament until the middle of February the following year, by which time it was hoped she would have summoned the resolve to sign Mary's death warrant, or have found some other way out of this deadlock.

Despite her indecisiveness, Elizabeth allowed the death sentence to be publicly proclaimed on 4 December. Trumpets sounded across the country as the news was relayed, and in London the populace was ordered to light bonfires in front of their doors, which took place to the background accompaniment of day-long bell-ringing.

The previous month, a Scottish delegation had arrived in London to plead for a delay in Mary's execution until members of the Privy Council could reach London and try to persuade Elizabeth to find a better course. The French ambassador Châteauneuf noted that when James had initially heard that his mother was to be put on trial, his response was chilling: 'his mother might drink the ale and beere which her selfe had brewed,' he said.

But when she was judged guilty of treason, and the death sentence loomed, James's tone altered. Increasingly desperate representations were made to Elizabeth. However, to the great discredit of the Scottish court, James's delegates, among them Archibald Douglas (widely believed to be Darnley's murderer), who had been one of Walsingham's spies, and the treacherous Patrick Gray, made it known privately that James's bluster was for show. He had no intention of risking the Anglo-Scottish agreement made at Berwick, and with it his hopes of the English succession.

A letter from Gray to Douglas some months earlier, when representations began, shows the double game they played. The task of mediating on behalf of James for Mary, wrote Gray, 'shall be a staff [to break] our own heads'. He said that James had earnestly commanded him to negotiate on Mary's behalf, but that for his part, so long as relations between Elizabeth and James remained good, he did not care if Mary 'were out of the way'. Agnes Strickland shares the view of other historians that Gray 'advised the execution of the Queen of Scots at the very time he was sent by her son to prevent it'.

The Scottish king's final delegation to Elizabeth, in which Gray played a leading role, arrived at the palace during the Christmas festivities. A genuine attempt on James's part to save Mary's life, it was coolly received by the Queen. Whereas the earlier ambassadors had made the bizarre proposal of a marriage between James and Elizabeth (tactfully ignored), this embassy pressed for a sensible compromise: for Mary to be taken out of England and put under stricter guard by members of her family in another country. But, if this was not to Elizabeth's liking, then James was prepared to accept any alternative, so long as his mother lived.

Such fervour was not so much a sign of filial affection as a ploy to protect James from the growing clamour in Scotland against England's outrageous treatment of their former queen. As he wrote to Elizabeth, the mood in Scotland was such that he hardly dared set foot outside 'for crying out of the whole people'. Throughout the increasingly tense last weeks of Mary's life, James hoped in vain to coax or shame Elizabeth into showing mercy. Yet while threatening to sever their recent alliance might have had an effect, he did not do so. In his political and personal calculations, staying on the right side of England and its queen was more important than Mary's fate. Antonia Fraser succinctly sums up the situation: 'his fulminations and his embassy were both intended to save his face in Scotland; they were not intended to save his mother's life in England.'

The French also petitioned Elizabeth to have mercy, Henri III sending an envoy called Pomponne de Bellièvre, to no avail. Nor was Châteauneuf any more successful. He was put under house arrest in January 1587, although he appears to have colluded with Walsingham in raising the spectre of another plot against Mary's life. By this time, despite public displays of outrage, Henri III had effectively washed his hands of Mary, considering her a liability.

The year drew to a close, and as December advanced, Mary was given permission to write to Elizabeth. This, the penultimate letter she would ever compose to her (Paulet withheld the final letter), was a cleverly calibrated personal and political statement. In it Mary claimed not to comprehend the loathing of the Puritans against her, saying she wished ill to no one and forgave everyone. She gave instructions on how she hoped to be buried close to her mother in France. Still the dread of murder was at the front of her mind, although she believed it was Elizabeth's people who would carry out such an act, never imagining that her cousin would, very soon, be the one to order it: 'I beg you not to permit me to be executed without your knowledge – not from fear of the pain, which I am ready to suffer, but on account of the rumours which would be spread concerning my death if it were not seen by reliable witnesses.' For this reason, she asked that her attendants be present at the end, 'and that afterwards they shall all together withdraw quickly, taking my body with them as secretly as you wish, and so that the furniture and other things which I may be able to leave them in dying, be not taken from them, which will be, indeed, a very small reward for their good services'.

Her parting shot was designed to prick Elizabeth's conscience: 'on the eve of leaving this world, and preparing myself for a better, I remind you that one day you will have to answer for your charge . . . I desire to think of the time when, from the earliest dawn of reason, we were taught to place our soul's welfare before all temporal matters, which should cede to those of eternity.' She signed herself 'Your sister and cousin wrongfully imprisoned'. The final letter she wrote to Elizabeth, a few days before her execution, and which Paulet did not send, ended with a barb that, despite its gravity, reads almost as an aphorism: 'I pray God grant you as much happiness in this world as I expect in leaving it.'

Paulet was a man of many faults, foremost among which was his hardness of heart. But in one respect he cannot be criticised. As a custodian he was eagle-eyed and imaginative, anticipating danger around every corner. During the seemingly endless weeks between Mary's death sentence and her execution, he fretted for the deed to be done. Every additional day spelled possible peril. A week before the queen went to the scaffold, when the risk of her escape was high, he reiterated his commitment to carrying out his mission, come what may: 'by the grace of God I will not lose this lady, my charge, without the loss of my life, neither shall it be possible for any force to take her out of my hands alive.'

Even as simple a matter as Mary's letter to the Queen was cause for concern. Bluntly, he told her that it would have to be tested in case it contained anything to harm Elizabeth. Nobly, Drury offered to be a guinea pig and test it for 'subtle poison', but Paulet insisted he would handle and read the letter himself. This proved unnecessary, since when it was written, reports Bourgoing, 'Her Majesty showed him her open letter, and tested it by striking it against her face, then closed it with white silk and sealed it with Spanish wax.' Paulet's version of events is even more colourful, describing how Mary, 'holding the leaves open, did wipe her face with every part of both the leaves'.

Though the letter was safe to despatch, Paulet held onto it for as long as possible, for fear that it might contain something to soften Elizabeth's heart and prevent her signing the death warrant. John Morris, editor of Paulet's letter-books, writes that 'It may have been the knowledge of this cruelty and injustice . . . that encouraged Walsingham to think him capable of a still more grievous crime.' When finally the letter did reach Elizabeth, Leicester reported that although it made her cry, nothing more damaging came of it.

The striking scene in which Mary proved her letter was untainted carries echoes of our own age, when Novichok and polonium are political poisoners' substances of choice, whether deployed in teapots or on door handles. Paulet's caution might seem extreme, but although he had misjudged Mary entirely in believing her personally capable of cold-blooded murder, he was not being paranoid. Had he not been suspicious, he would have been considered lazy or negligent.

No doubt his vigilance was heightened by the anxiety reverberating throughout the country. While Elizabeth could be heard murmuring '*Aut fer, aut feri; ne feriare, feri*' – 'Either suffer or strike; not to be struck, strike' – Burghley and Walsingham were stoking national panic. They helped spread stories of another plot against Elizabeth's life, likely invasion by France and Spain, a rebellion in the north, a Scottish army already over the border, London set alight by Papists and, perhaps most terrifying of all, that Mary had escaped.

Paulet's response to all this is telling, his imagery Bosch-like. Writing to Walsingham's secretary Davison in late January 1587, he complained about the 'dangerous and most pitiful delay' in bringing Mary to justice, 'especially in these declining days, wherein Satan with his complices goeth roaring up and down with open throat, seeking by most horrible and execrable complots, as well domestical as foreign, how to devour our most gracious queen'.

Such was the state of alarm that notices of hue and cry were sent out around the country. One of these instructed the Mayor of Exeter, upon pain of death, 'to make diligent search, and hue and cry for the Queen of Scots, who is fled, and to lay all highways, and stay all barks and shipping in your harbours'. Another, also to Exeter, demanded the parish 'make your armour and artillery in readiness, and that with all speed . . . for London is set on fire'.

The contemporary Tudor historian William Camden wrote that these rumours were intended to terrify Elizabeth and induce her to sign the warrant, and they seem to have produced the result Burghley had so long desired. After weeks of excruciating uncertainty, and shortly following Burghley's instruction to the Queen to double her personal guard, she acted. When Davison, under orders from Lord Howard, Lord High Admiral, presented her with a sheaf of papers to sign, she breezily did so, making it seem she had not noticed that among them was the warrant for Mary's execution. This, despite Davison informing her that the bundle included a document Howard had specifically asked him to give to her. Then, as if suddenly ashamed of this pretence, she asked Davison if he was troubled by seeing her sign Mary's warrant. He replied that he preferred to see a guilty person die than an innocent one. Poor Davison. He was soon to be the scapegoat for Elizabeth's guilty conscience, thrown into the

Tower of London for two years following Mary's execution, put on trial in Star Chamber and fined the exorbitant sum of £10,000. There was an element of farce about his treatment: he continued to receive his salary during his ordeal, and was never called on to pay the fine. By 1588 he was a free man, if battered.

Chapter 29

'Laughing with the angels'

THE LAST ACT

Elizabeth might have put her signature to the death warrant, but she still hoped for a better solution. In previous weeks she had shocked her councillors by berating them for not acting on the provisions of the Bond of Association; she was, in short, disappointed that they had not taken the initiative and killed Mary for her. Most unusually, at this critical moment Walsingham, who was ill in bed, was absent from court. As a result, much responsibility fell on his sidekick Secretary Davison's shoulders. The same day that Davison placed the warrant in the hands of the Lord Chancellor, who would attach the great seal of state upon it, Elizabeth had him write to Paulet. This letter, which must have made Mary's gaoler break out in a cold sweat, is testimony to the lengths to which Elizabeth was prepared to go to spare herself public and political opprobrium; the verdict of posterity, however, can only be damning.

This extraordinary letter, signed by both Davison and Walsingham, informed Paulet that Elizabeth was upset that 'you have not in all this time . . . found out some way to shorten the life of that Queen'. She was, the letter continued, most unhappy that he had not done so, 'knowing as you do her indisposition to shed blood, especially of one of that sex and quality, and so near to her in blood as the said Queen is'.

Paulet was appalled. A punctilious servant of the Queen, he nevertheless lived by an ethical code that would permit nothing criminal. His reply, which was signed also by Drury, is electric with shock: 'I am so unhappy to have liven to see this unhappy day, in the which I am required by direction from my most gracious sovereign to do an act which God and the law forbiddeth . . . God forbid that I should make so foul a shipwreck of my conscience, or leave so great a blot to my poor posterity, to shed blood without law or warrant.' Aware of the danger of crossing Elizabeth, Paulet ignored Davison's instruction to burn the letter once read. Instead he made copies of it, which he kept with his family, as evidence of how he had answered this clear directive to murder Elizabeth's prisoner.

Angry at his squeamishness, Elizabeth dismissed Paulet as 'dainty and precise'. But she did not despair. She now hoped Mary could be despatched secretly by Robert Wingfield, a Northamptonshire gentleman, and Burghley's nephew, known to history for the vivid eyewitness account of Mary's execution he wrote for his uncle. 'I have Wingfield,' Elizabeth said, 'who will not draw back.' Before she could follow up this plan, the Privy Council acted. Burghley bound the council to absolute secrecy, not wishing Elizabeth to know anything about the execution until it had been done, nor for any last-minute rescue to be mounted to save the Queen of Scotland. Beale swiftly made his way to Fotheringhay with the warrant for Mary's execution, travelling with Shrewsbury and the Earl of Kent, who were to be in charge of proceedings. While he was thus occupied, Walsingham found an executioner, by the name of Bull, whom one of his own servants hired for a fee of £10.

To avoid raising suspicions, Shrewsbury and Kent took rooms in Orton, a few miles from Fotheringhay (and near where Robert Wingfield lived). Another of Walsingham's servants, called Digby, asked Walter Mildmay if he would put up the axeman in his own house, which was only a couple of miles from the castle. 'Misliking thereof', Mildmay refused and instead Bull took a room at the inn in the village of Fotheringhay. On Friday 3 February, Walsingham informed Paulet of these preparations: 'I send down the executioner by a trusty servant of mine, who will be at Fotheringhay upon Sunday at night. His instrument is put in a trunk, and he passeth as a servingman. There is great care taken to have the matter pass in secrecy.'

That instrument was his axe. If the innkeeper noticed his guest's unusual luggage, what he made of a serving man carrying a trunk is left to our imaginations. Snug in the darkness of its leather case, the lethal blade takes on the significance of a character in these events. Gleaming, sharpened, it lay ready for service. Despite all this, the possibility of assassinating Mary was discussed by Beale when he reached Fotheringhay. Eventually, after raising the spectre of the murders of Edward II and Richard II, which had gone down in history as heinous crimes, 'it was not thought convenient or safe to proceed covertly: but openly, according to statute'.

Unaware that events were finally moving at speed, Mary's household was troubled by a couple of unsettling domestic problems. Knowing the execution was fast approaching, Paulet had ordered that Mary's steward, Melville, and priest, Du Préau, were no longer allowed access to her. This was a serious blow, since Mary relied heavily upon both, as much as friends as for their professional advice. It also heightened her fear of being poisoned, since Melville's role included 'carrying the rod' ahead of the servants bearing the dishes for dinner. When she delegated this task to her butler, this too was forbidden. That Paulet would interfere with this minor ritual roused Mary's suspicion, and she told Bourgoing to inform Paulet of her unease.

Her gaoler responded angrily, amazed that the queen would believe that Elizabeth, or the Privy Council, or he himself 'wished to undertake anything so unworthy or so insulting as to kill, to poignard, or murder her secretly, or of a sudden, whether by night or day; that he felt heart-broken to think he was supposed capable of committing such butchery, or of permitting such.' Mary could not know how wounding her suggestion was, in light of his recent refusal to murder her. At the back of her mind – as of Beale's – was what had happened to King Richard II, who, as a captive in Pontefract Castle, had been badly treated, and then murdered. She feared, said Bourgoing, the same would happen to her.

Under such strain, Mary's health worsened, and on Saturday 4 February, Bourgoing pleaded with Paulet to allow him to collect herbs from the gardens of gentlemen in the village to make a remedy. Very reluctantly Paulet granted permission, less from concern for Mary's well-being, some have said, than to prevent Mary's party from suspecting the warrant for her execution was on its way. But shortly after Bourgoing and the apothecary picked the herbs, on Sunday 5 February Mary learned that Beale had arrived at the castle. Immediately understanding what this portended, she announced that there was no longer any need for remedies.

Her household now held its breath, and when more nobles arrived at the castle, it became clear that the day they had long dreaded was upon them. Bourgoing writes that, seeing Shrewsbury and Kent, they were 'in great fear, having for three days imagined all kinds of things as to her Majesty's end, fearing the blow was certain.'

The final hours of Mary's life had arrived. This last chapter has been endlessly reprised yet never fails to disturb with its brutality and horror. Although it is not all dark. At the centre of a barbarous punishment is a woman who refused to consider herself a victim, and who outwitted her foes by the grace and courage with which she faced death. After dinner on the evening of Tuesday 7 February, a delegation led by Beale, comprising Shrewsbury, Kent, Paulet, Drury and the Sheriff of Northamptonshire, asked for an audience with Mary. She had begun undressing for bed but, after taking a few minutes to prepare herself, received them sitting in a chair at the end of her bed, in the company of her household.

Conspicuously, none among the delegation removed his hat. It fell to Shrewsbury to tell her that, having been accused, found guilty and condemned to die, she must listen to her sentence. Beale, holding a sheet of parchment stamped with the dangling yellow wax of the Great Seal of England, duly read out the warrant for her execution. When he had finished, Mary, who had listened with utmost composure, thanked the delegation 'for news so welcome . . . she was very glad that it had pleased God, by their means, to take her away from so many troubles'.

Holding a copy of the New Testament, she swore her innocence of the crimes alleged against her. She was offered the Dean of

Peterborough 'for her consolation', but asked instead for her own priest, Du Préau. This request was refused in the language of zealots: 'It is our duty, to prevent such abominations which offend God.' Even at this late hour, her captors hoped she would finally 'recognise the true religion'. This, she refused to do.

When she asked if Elizabeth would permit her to be buried in France, either beside her husband at St Denis, or her mother at Rheims, she was informed that this could not be sanctioned. As if eager to tie up the loose threads of the story, she then inquired what had become of Nau. Drury told her, 'he still drags his fetters'. At this, Mary remarked that 'she would die for the life of him who accused her and caused her death to save himself'. There was, however, an unexpected moment of vindication when Kent burst out with the real reason she was to be killed: 'Your life would be the death of our religion, your death will be its life.' This left no doubt that she was to be viewed as dying for her faith. Unwittingly, her fundamentalist enemies had given her the best parting gift she could have hoped for.

Still her questions continued. Had there been representations from foreign powers to save her? Yes, they said, but none had offered a good reason why she should not be executed. When she complained about the way James had treated her, they urged her to show charity, because he had 'done all that was in his power'. No further proof was needed that he was in Elizabeth's pocket.

Inquiring what time she was to die, she was told at around eight the following morning. This was very short notice, she said, but it was her servants who begged for a delay, since this did not allow their mistress enough time to arrange her affairs, and they feared they might be left destitute as a result. Beale appeared open to a brief deferment, but Shrewsbury was inflexible, saying 'he had no power to grant the smallest delay'.

One can imagine the mood in the room when the earl and his associates departed. Mary's household would have been in a state of horror and distress; she, by contrast, was perfectly calm. After praying with her ladies, she divided up her money into packets, with the name of each servant on them, to be handed to them in the morning. She ordered supper to be served early, and after eating scantily, writes Bourgoing, sent for her servants, whom she urged to be charitable to each other when she was gone. This would be easier, she said, without Nau stirring trouble between them. She also begged them to pray for her.

Then, from her bedside chair, with an inventory in her hand, she busied herself dividing up her possessions among them, bestowing on them her clothes, jewels and whatever other objects, writes her physician, had survived the pillaging at Chartley. She also gave them items to be given, once they were at liberty, to her son and other relatives and friends. Benevolent to the end, she announced that, if Nau could clear his name, he was to be awarded his pension. After revising her will, which Bourgoing witnessed for her, it was well into the evening when she sat down to write to Du Préau. Begging him to pray for her, she also asked what prayers he recommended she say in the hours before her death.

Her final obligation was to inform her brother-in-law, Henri III of France, what was happening. This is the last letter she would ever write. In the keeping of the National Library of Scotland, its firm handwriting shows no sign of her infirmity nor suggests she was in a state of terror. It was a generous farewell, and far more than Henri deserved. Telling him that she had only hours to live, she wrote: 'The Catholic faith and the assertion of my God-given right to the English crown are the two issues on which I am condemned, and yet I am not allowed to say that it is for the Catholic religion that I die, but for fear of interference with theirs.'

Explaining that her chaplain had been taken from her, and she could not therefore receive the Last Sacrament, she referred briefly and coldly to James: 'As for my son, I commend him to you in so far as he deserves, for I cannot answer for him.' She told him that she was sending him 'two precious stones, talismans against illness, trusting that you will enjoy good health and a long and happy life. Accept them from your loving sister-in-law, who, as she dies, bears witness of her warm feeling for you. Again I commend my servants to you.'

Mary finished this letter shortly after two o'clock on the morning of Wednesday 8 February. It had been dark for many hours by the time she asked that her feet be washed, in imitation of Christ, before lying on her bed, fully dressed. In the ensuing hours she was kept company by her ladies, who were already in mourning clothes. Lit only by candlelight, with Mary's women in black, the room must have presented a dismal picture. As she did every night, Mary requested Jane Kennedy to read to her from the lives of the saints, choosing the story of the good thief, who was crucified on Calvary alongside Jesus Christ. 'In truth,' she said, 'he was a great sinner, but not so great as I have been. I wish to take him for my patron for the time that remains to me.' When the reading ended, the rest of the short night passed in silence, save for the sound of hammering from the Great Hall, where the scaffold was being built. Deep in prayer, Mary lay almost motionless, but could be observed at times smiling faintly. It was, said Kennedy, as if she were 'laughing with the angels'.

Before daylight, the queen rose and dressed. Fastidious as ever about her appearance, she told her companions it was necessary that, in going to death, she was 'creditably dressed'. She wore a black satin skirt and bodice over a dark reddish-brown petticoat, bodice and sleeves, their rich colour symbolising Catholic martyrdom. Over these she placed a black satin cloak, trimmed with fur, with a long train and long wide sleeves. Around her neck was a chain with a cross, and a rosary was tied around her waist. Placing a white cap on her head, from which fell a long white veil, she was almost ready to face the day.

As on so many other mornings, this one began with prayer. She spent so long on her knees that Bourgoing grew anxious, and, seeing her pallor, encouraged her to eat some bread and take a glass of wine. These she gratefully took from him before returning to her devotions. This man, who the previous evening had served her supper with tears running down his face, had been a faithful, devoted servant. Distraught at what was now happening he had to confess that, like her other attendants, he could not assist Mary to the scaffold, since he could not bear to be the one to lead her to her death.

When, at eight o'clock, the sheriff knocked on the locked door, saying it was time, Mary requested a little longer to finish what she was doing. Paulet's men returned with the sheriff at nine, expecting to have to kick in the door and forcibly drag her to the scaffold, but to their surprise she went willingly, carrying a small ivory crucifix and her illuminated book of prayers. Since she was not allowed to have her servants in attendance, she needed assistance from Paulet's guards, who helped her down the long staircase that led from her rooms to the Great Hall.

At the first landing were Shrewsbury and Kent, and at the foot of the stairs she found her steward, Melville. Seeing her, he fell to his knees, in tears: 'it will be the sorrowfullest message that I ever carried, when I shall report that my Queen and dearest mistress is dead.' Mary, also in tears, replied, 'You ought rather to rejoice than weep, for the end of Mary Stuart's troubles is now come. For know, good servant, all the world is but vanity, and subject still to more sorrow than a whole Ocean of tears can bewail.' Asking him to commend her to her son, 'and tell him that I have not done any thing that may prejudice his kingdom of Scotland', she said farewell, kissed him, and asked him to pray for her.

In an antechamber to the Great Hall various other lords were assembled, including Paulet. Mary made him promise that her servants would receive the gifts promised them in her will and be allowed safely home once she was dead, and to all this he agreed. Her final request was more irksome. She required the company of her ladies at her death, she insisted, in order 'that they may report when they come into their countries that I died a true woman unto my religion'.

The Earl of Kent baulked at this, saying her women might make speeches that would disturb her, or cry loudly and dip their handkerchiefs in her blood. Mary refuted this and became tearful. Only minutes earlier, in her chamber, she had begged her ladies 'not to forsake me, and be, if you please, near me at the hour of my death'. It was the only sign she ever gave of fear. Their presence at the end was something on which she had depended, and with a flash of hauteur, she reminded her captors of her royal lineage and credentials. Reluctantly, the lords granted her wish. Mary quickly named six of her party, including Melville and Bourgoing and her ladies, Jane Kennedy and Elizabeth Curle.

The Queen of Scots entered the Great Hall with her most trusted attendants around her, Melville carrying her train. Some months earlier Paulet had noted of Mary that 'When she was at her lowest, her heart was greatest.' There is no doubt that during this dreadful ordeal, she exceeded herself in maintaining her courage and dignity. The enormous hall into which she was ushered held a crowd of three hundred. They had been there all night, keeping warm by the roaring log fire; outside the castle walls a throng had gathered, awaiting the grisly outcome of a nineteen-year saga, and kept in check by a troop of armed horsemen.

At the sight of the scaffold Mary appeared undaunted, raising the small ivory crucifix over her head. In fact, her untroubled and even joyous demeanour greatly impressed onlookers. One witness wrote, 'Those who were there present, marvelled to behold the great beauty and courage of this poor princess.' The scaffold, which was raised a couple of feet from the floor and balustraded on three sides, was surrounded by a guard of halberdiers, all Huntingdon's men. The person Mary had dreaded might do away with her when she was in captivity had been charged with making sure there was no last-minute escape.

The tableau that greeted her must have been unnerving, since the entire hall was draped in black, as was the scaffold. On it stood the executioner Bull and his assistant, wearing long black gowns and white aprons. Their faces were covered by black masks, and in Bull's hand was his axe, described by one witness as being 'of the same shape of those which they cleave wood withal'. Before they mounted the scaffold, Paulet offered Mary his arm, for which she thanked him: 'this will be the last trouble I shall give you, and the most agreeable service you have ever rendered me.'

Leading the way was Shrewsbury, carrying the white wand with which, as Earl Marshall, he would signify when the axe was to fall.

Chairs were placed near the block for Shrewsbury and Kent who, as she took her place on a black-draped stool, stood to one side of Mary. Once seated, she asked for her chaplain, which was curtly refused. Beale then read aloud the warrant for her execution, to which Mary listened with imperturbable calm. It was almost, said Wingfield, as if she did not understand English. Nor was she disconcerted when, once Beale had finished, the assembly roared 'God Save the Queen!'

For Shrewsbury, this day must surely have ranked among the worst of his life. 'Madame, you hear what we are commanded to do,' he said, as if to suggest he was only obeying an order. 'Do your duty,' Mary replied. Then, addressing the hall, she made a long, clear speech, in which she stated her innocence of the crimes imputed to her, forgave everyone, and prayed for friends and foes alike.

When the Dean of Peterborough, Dr Fletcher, as instructed by Elizabeth, attempted to prepare her for her death, she asked him to be quiet. He would not be silenced, however, but pressed on, asking her to repent. As he continued to harangue her, she began to pray aloud in Latin. Even Shrewsbury found the dean's persistence excessive, and roughly told him to cease and say a prayer. Fletcher's prayer was long, but Mary's was even longer, during which she often kissed her crucifix and made the sign of the cross. Eventually, when she had finished, she hugged her servants, and then took her seat.

By now her ladies were in a state of anguish. As they helped her to disrobe, she commented wryly that she had never had to do so before so many. Bourgoing describes how Jane Kennedy and Elizabeth Curle removed 'her veil, her mantle with train and her stomacher'. The executioner removed a gold Agnus Dei from around her neck, which she took back from him to give to Jane. One account says that Mary handed it to her and promised Bull he would be given money in its place. Another says that, despite this assurance, he grabbed it from the queen, saying it was his right, and put it in his shoe.

For the final time, Mary embraced her attendants, making the sign of the cross on their foreheads, and begging them not to cry, since she had promised they would not. Once Jane had tied a white handkerchief over her eyes, she asked them to leave the scaffold. The executioners knelt before her, making the ritual plea to be forgiven. 'I forgive you with all my heart,' she replied, 'for now, I hope, you shall make an end of all my troubles.' After this, she sat on her stool, stretching her neck as she prayed in Latin, '*In te Domine confide...*', repeating this prayer again and again until the blade should swing. One witness recounted that, in adopting this pose, it would seem she was 'expecting her head to be taken off with a stroke of the sword, as they do in France'. This, after all, was the manner in which Anne Boleyn had been beheaded, by a French executioner skilled in making the act as swift and painless as possible.

Mary's death was not to be as quick. The executioner, seeing her misunderstanding, helped her place her neck on the low block. To make it easier to breathe, she placed her hands under her chin, but it was only as Bull raised his axe that his assistant noticed this error and quickly removed her hands, so that they were not cut off also. Then, at Shrewsbury's signal, Bull swung his axe, misjudging it so that he sliced into Mary's skull rather than her neck. It took two further strokes to sever her head. Robert Wingfield writes that during all this 'she making very small noise or none at all, and not stirring any part of her from where she lay', which suggests the first blow had rendered her unconscious. As was customary, Bull then lifted her head, proclaiming 'The head of Mary Stuart!', at which her linen head-covering fell off and she was seen to have closely cut grey hair, concealed all these years by the cleverness of her hairdresser, Mary Seton, and by headpieces and wigs. Wingfield notes that 'her lips stirred up and down for a quarter of an hour after her head was cut off.'

The hush that had fallen was broken by the Dean of Peterborough crying, 'So perish all the Queen's enemies!' Not to be outdone, Kent stood over Mary's headless body, declaiming: 'such an end of all the Queen's and the Gospel enemies'. It was noted that many onlookers had tears in their eyes, among them Shrewsbury. Perhaps the most poignant detail of this indelible scene is the one children remember best: Mary's Skye terrier, which had accompanied her unnoticed onto the scaffold, was found cowering under her skirts, refusing to come out. When it did emerge, it took up its position between her body and her head. Covered in blood, it had to be carried out of the hall, to be washed. 'As all things else were that had any blood,' writes Wingfield, 'was either burned or clean washed.'

Aftermath

'Now I am sole king'

When the execution was over, onlookers were quickly dispersed. They had witnessed one of the greatest moments of historical theatre, and its reverberations would remain with them for the rest of their lives. Everything that Mary had worn or touched during her execution was burned or destroyed, to prevent objects becoming relics. Paulet had insisted that it was he who removed all her belongings from her body. It feels like the last insult and dishonouring, the behaviour of a carrion crow.

Some accounts say that before Mary's corpse was taken away, the executioner placed her head on a dish and showed it at the window to the crowds in the courtyard. One of Mary's entourage, Amias Cawood, allegedly – and improbably – made a painting of the queen's severed head, which is now on display at Abbotsford House, Sir Walter Scott's home in the Scottish Borders. Mary's body was then taken to one of the castle's state rooms. Through a keyhole her servants saw that her remains had been ignominiously covered in the baize cloth from her billiard table. They were not meant to see this, having been banished to a room of their own, and it would have done nothing to console them. Under instruction from a physician, two surgeons embalmed Mary, and her heart and other organs were buried in Fotheringhay's grounds, concealed for fear of becoming a shrine. With her head returned to her body, she was wrapped in a wax winding sheet. She was left to lie for so long, one witness said, that the corpse began to smell and had to be salted to prevent further corruption before it could be encased in a heavy lead coffin.

To prevent the news travelling abroad, all of England's ports were closed. Shrewsbury's son Lord Talbot was sent post-haste to London to inform Burghley. The news of Mary's death would have been welcomed by him and all the Privy Council, but when Elizabeth learned of it she was convulsed by grief, rage and, quite possibly, remorse. Anne Boleyn's tragic execution cannot have been far from her thoughts; that she had condemned another to the same fate as her mother must have caused profound emotional turmoil. In a state of extreme distress, she had Davison locked in the Tower, spoke of having him hanged, and refused to see Burghley or Walsingham. London, however, enjoyed a second Christmas, with bells ringing all night and bonfires blazing to celebrate the death of a woman viewed as England's mortal enemy.

At Fotheringhay, none of Mary's party was allowed to leave. Inside, while their mistress had escaped this life, they remained captive. On the day after the execution Du Préau was allowed to conduct Mass for Mary's soul, after which the altar was dismantled. Paulet brought the rest of Mary's staff from Chartley to hold them at Fotheringhay and, despite his assurances that her entourage would be allowed to depart for their homes after her death, they were kept there for another eight months until October.

During this period, while the rest of the world went about its business, Fotheringhay Castle was wreathed, fog-like, in sorrow. Walsingham had ordered that the coffin be placed on an upper shelf in the village church at Fotheringhay, but this did not happen. As a result, Mary's traumatised household was kept company by the dead queen, lying in her leaden casket. Not permitted passports, her servants were unable to proceed with their own lives. This unnerving limbo was a gratuitously cruel finale to the haunting drama of which they had been part.

On 14 February, by which time Elizabeth had composed herself, she wrote a weaselly letter to James. Intending to exculpate herself of all blame, her description of Mary's execution is embarrassingly gauche: 'My dear brother, I would you knew (although not felt) the extreme dolour that overwhelms my mind for that *miserable accident*, which, far contrary to my meaning, hath befallen . . . I beseech you that as God and many more know, how innocent I am in this case.' This would not for a moment have fooled James, and nor would her seemingly benign sign off: 'think not you have in the world a more loving kinswoman, nor a more dear friend than myself'.

Elizabeth told Châteauneuf that 'it was never her intention to put her to death, unless she had seen a foreign army invade England, or a great insurrection of her subjects in favour of the aforesaid Queen of Scotland; then she confessed that perhaps she might have put her to death, otherwise she would never have given her consent'. She added that in executing Mary her council had played her a trick, 'which she could never forgive; and she swore, by God, that but for their long services, and also because, what they had done had been out of consideration for the welfare and safety of her person and of the state, they should have lost their heads'.

Eager to mend bridges, Elizabeth despatched her courtier Robert Carey north to explain to James how Mary had been executed against her wishes, but James would not countenance meeting him. Briefly, he suspended all dealings with England. Accounts differ as to how he reacted to the news of his mother's beheading, some claiming he was secretly relieved – 'Now I am sole king' – others that he retreated to his bedchamber without eating. He must have been profoundly shaken, even though his feelings for his mother were little more than platitudinous. How could they be otherwise, after a lifetime's absence, and an upbringing in which she had been vilified? Nevertheless, her brutal execution would have been deeply distressing.

James, if not callous, was hard-headed and ambitious, and had no intention of severing his ties with England. His people, however, felt differently. Scotland was in uproar about Elizabeth's treatment of their former queen, and there was talk of taking up arms against England. Walsingham's informants told him that the streets of Edinburgh were plastered with posters denouncing Mary's killing. To underline the point, an example of their savage mood was sent to him: a hemp rope, tied in the shape of a noose, with a verse attached:

To Jezabel, that English whore;
Receive this Scottish chain
As presages of her great malheur
For murdering our queen.

The Scots were far more exercised by Mary's death than her son, with public demonstrations and considerable unrest in the Borders. When finally James was prepared to listen to Robert Carey's message, he told him not to cross the border, for fear of the consequences. 'Given the fury [the people] were in,' Carey relates, 'no power of his could warrant my life at that time.' Instead he was to deliver his message at Berwick. Not for a second did James believe that Elizabeth had no hand in Mary's death, but it was politic to make a show of accepting her version of events. In her telling, she had never intended Davison to use the warrant she had signed, and it had been put into effect without her permission.

With Davison imprisoned in the Tower, and Elizabeth continuing to treat Burghley as a pariah – for him this was emotional torture – the Queen had to be warned not to make too great a show of her disapproval, since this would give Mary's supporters cause to believe her execution had not been legal. When it became clear that even Mary's son would not challenge Elizabeth's conduct, however, the furore in Scotland eventually died down. In France, there was a splendid show of grief for its former Queen. During a long, tearful Requiem Mass in Notre Dame, the priest recalled happier days, contrasting Mary's wedding at the cathedral with the present dark occasion. Henri III paraded his fury, even though he had done nothing to help his cousin in the preceding nineteen years, and had no intention of making an enemy of England.

A memorandum Beale wrote some time later explaining the reasons for Mary's execution recorded that he was told by an English diplomat, in August 1588, that the Count of Arenberg, a prestigious figure in the Habsburg Netherlands, believed 'that it had bin better don to have poisond her or choked her with a pillowe, but not to have putt her to so open a death'. The English diplomat sent to

France to explain the execution confirmed that Henri III, and others, held the same view.

But although there were crocodile tears as well as genuine sorrow among France's nobility and royalty, as in Scotland, public anger spilled out onto the streets, where there were demonstrations. There was also a growing sense of Mary as a martyr to the Catholic cause. In Spain, meanwhile, Philip was urged by his priest to go to war with England in part to avenge Mary's killing. It is a measure of her posthumous significance that the arrival in July 1588 of the Spanish Armada in the English Channel was a direct consequence of her death. Historians have been quick to note the irony that Philip was willing to send his fleet on Mary's behalf once she was gone, but not while she was alive.

The cloud that hung over Fotheringhay finally lifted in July. Following an emotional debate over where Mary was to be buried, she was allowed a state funeral and burial in Peterborough Cathedral, one of the finest Norman cathedrals in Europe. As a sop to James, Elizabeth bore the cost. Mary's double coffin – the lead one encased in a wooden coffin – left Fotheringhay as she had arrived: with a heavy escort, and as inconspicuously as possible. The cortege accompanied a royal funeral carriage draped in black velvet, with four horses, also draped in black velvet, that must have strained under the tremendous weight of the burden they had to pull. The bier was surrounded by a consignment of soldiers, members of Elizabeth's household and heralds. Some of Mary's entourage also accompanied the procession, among them Bourgoing, Melville, Du Préau, Elizabeth Curle and Jane Kennedy.

Leaving the castle at around ten at night, the torchlit party reached Peterborough in the small hours of Sunday 30 July. It was met by the Bishop of Lincoln and the Dean of Peterborough, the man who had badgered Mary on the scaffold. So it was that, before the hot summer's day dawned, and with minimal ceremony – 'without bells or chanting' – Mary's coffin was placed in a vault in the south aisle of the cathedral. She was to lie opposite the tomb of Catherine of Aragon, Henry VIII's first wife, whose grave had been prepared by the same gravedigger, by the name of Scarlet, who prepared Mary's tomb.

Before the vault was bricked up, save for a small opening, heralds broke their staves and placed them in the grave, as was customary. In the funeral of any royal this is a poignant moment, but even more so for Mary, conducted as it was in the hours of darkness, in what can only have felt like a shabby, secretive operation. With the breaking of the staves, her time on earth visibly ended.

The funeral proper, such as it was, took place on Tuesday 1 August, after a lavish dinner, the previous night, at the bishop's palace. At the head of the funeral procession were two yeomen of the guard, followed by a lord carrying the ceremonial helmet and heralds bearing the royal sword and tabard. Behind them came a recumbent wax effigy of Mary, beneath a black canopy carried by four knights, which proceeded into the cathedral, surrounded by flag-bearers, their colourful banners representing Mary's ancestry, marriages and coats of arms. The cathedral interior was swathed in black cloth, and every second pillar was adorned with bright escutcheons bearing the arms of Mary, Francis or Darnley.

One hundred poor women, dressed in black at the Queen's cost, entered the cathedral in pairs. Their presence was appropriate, given Mary's bequest of alms for the poor in her will. Pride of place was given to the chief mourner, the Countess of Bedford, who was representing Elizabeth, assisted by the Earls of Lincoln and Rutland. Numbering around 350, the gathering of invited guests, most of them high-born, filed into the cathedral. Elizabeth had paid for their mourning clothes, as she had for the paupers, but some of Mary's party refused this gesture and preferred to wear their own mourning clothes. Apart from Andrew Melville and Barbara Mowbray, who were Protestants, Mary's Catholic entourage walked out of the Protestant service as soon as the choristers began to sing in English, and kicked their heels in the cloisters until the service was over. Great offence was taken by Protestant mourners at the large gold cross Mary's priest Du Préau held in his hand.

Aftermath

The Bishop of Lincoln conducted a strange, undistinguished ceremony. Beginning his sermon by talking about the 'happy death of the high and mighty Princess Mary', he distanced himself from her tragic end by saying, 'I have not much to say of her life or death, knowing little of the one, and not having assisted at the other.' Those who attended were witness to the whitewashed official narrative, which was that Mary had died while in England, rather than that she had been executed by the state. No mention was made of her marriage to Bothwell, nor of the events in Scotland that had led to her fleeing her homeland, nor of the years she had spent imprisoned. The bishop also managed to hint nonsensically that, at the very end, Mary might just possibly have converted to Protestantism.

After the ceremony there was a wake, presumably almost as grand as the previous night's dinner, since the cost of both feasts accounted for a third of Elizabeth's outlay on the whole affair. Those responsible for preparing the banquet arrived in Peterborough a week before the funeral, which is not surprising given the quantities involved: 192 rabbits, 52 capons, 12 gulls, 39 ducklings, 18 heron, 18 bitterns, 90 mallards, 163 teals, four oxen (providing 512 servings), 40 mutton (1,600 servings), 1 ton of Gascony claret (1,680 pints), 10 tons 1 hogshead of beer (17,220 pints), 3 tons 1 pipe of ale (5,880 pints). And finally, around two tons of wheat, which was turned into about 2,000 loaves of bread.

Needless to say, Mary's servants did not celebrate, being still wrapped in grief. Refusing to join the other mourners, they ate in a separate room, where they could express their sadness without watching what they said. Nor did the funeral bring about their release. Perhaps because they had not joined the wake, or because they had not taken part in the service, it was a further three months before eventually, after James protested, they were freed. Only on their release could Mary's final letters at last reach their recipients.

Once back in Scotland, Andrew Melville and Jane Kennedy married. It seemed they had a chance to put their sorrows behind them, but tragically, at Leith, on her way to escort James's bride

Anne of Denmark to Scotland in 1589, Jane drowned. Like Elizabeth Curle, she had remained perpetually dressed in black, in honour of her dead mistress. This choice also portended her own untimely demise.

Paulet, who had returned to London after Mary's execution, died eighteen months later, on 26 September 1588. He was initially buried in St Martin-in-the-Fields in London, but his imposing tomb was relocated in 1728 to the parish church of Hinton St George in Somerset. Various tributes in Latin, French and English embellish his tomb. One acknowledges his role as Mary's captor:

Never shall cease to spread wise Poulet's fame;
These speak, and men shall blush for shame:
Without offence to speak I do know,
Great is the debt England to him doth owe.

Shrewsbury – who had been Mary's gaoler for almost fifteen taxing years, to the detriment of his health, his wealth and his marriage – would keenly have felt the snub if he ever read this encomium.

Mary lay in Peterborough for twenty-five years until in 1612 her son, by now King James I of England, had her removed to Westminster Abbey. Here he commissioned a stupendous white marble tomb, its grandeur surpassing even that he had erected for Elizabeth I. Some believe that Mary would have been pleased to take her place among England's royalty, seeing it as belated recognition of her right to the succession to the throne. I am not convinced. In the will she wrote at Sheffield Manor Lodge in 1577, she requested that if she died in prison, her body was to be buried alongside her first husband, Francis II, in St Denis. In a much later letter to her cousin the Duke of Guise, she asked that her heart be buried by her husband, and her body beside her mother at Rheims. Towards the end, she again expressed her wish to be buried in France, the country she had come to think of as home. Among her last words to Elizabeth were clear instructions: 'I require you to ordain that when my enemies have slaked their cruel thirst for my innocent blood, you will permit my poor disconsolate servants altogether to carry away my corpse, to bury it in holy ground, with the other queens of France my predecessors, especially near the late queen my mother.' She then specifically asked *not* to be buried 'near the kings your predecessors, who are mine as well as yours; for according to our religion, we think much of being interred in holy ground'.

With her execution only weeks away, Mary was primarily concerned with the state of her soul, although also needing the comfort of knowing her final resting place would be beside those she had best loved. She had wished for reunion in death with either her husband or, as she most keenly desired, with her mother at Rheims. Unhappily, as with so many of Mary's hopes and ambitions, it was not to be. In death, as in the last nineteen years of her life, she was to remain an exile.

Further Reading

Few historical figures have been written about as extensively as Mary, Queen of Scots. For *Exile*, as with *Homecoming*, I turned frequently to the biographies that cover her in closest detail, in particular Antonia Fraser's brilliant *Mary Queen of Scots* and John Guy's meticulous *My Heart is My Own*. Of the many other biographies, Jenny Wormald's blistering *Mary Queen of Scots: A Study in Failure* is distinguished by its incisive – some might say pitiless – analysis; Alison Weir's *Mary, Queen of Scots and the Murder of Lord Darnley* is painstakingly detailed, and Jane Dunn's *Elizabeth & Mary: Cousins, Rivals, Queens* covers the queens' strained relationship with subtlety and insight. However, the source I drew upon most heavily was Mary's own letters, and for these I turned mainly to the volumes gathered and edited by Agnes Strickland and Prince Alexander Labanoff. Also compelling, and worthy of a book to themselves, were the letters written by her gaoler Amias Paulet. Both offer an extraordinarily vivid insight into the two queens' personalities, the one fighting for her life, the other determined that she be brought to account. What follows is a partial list of books, articles and records I have used, many of which, I hope, will be of interest to readers keen to follow Mary's story for themselves.

Peter Ackroyd, *The History of England*, vol. II, *Tudors* (London: Macmillan, 2012)
Stephen Alford, *The Watchers: A Secret History of the Reign of Elizabeth I* (London: Penguin Books, 2013)

Jill Armitage, *Bess of Hardwick* (Sheffield: Bradwell Books, 2018)

Katie Barclay, Kimberley Reynolds and Ciara Rawnsley, eds, *Death, Emotion and Childhood in Premodern Europe* (London: Palgrave Macmillan, 2016)

Caroline Bingham, *The Making of a King: The Early Years of James VI & I* (London: Collins, 1968)

Stephen I. Boardman and Julian Goodare, eds, *Kings, Lords and Men in Scotland and Britain, 1300–1625* (Edinburgh: Edinburgh University Press, 2014)

John Bossy, *Under the Molehill: An Elizabethan Spy Story* (New Haven and London: Yale Nota Bene Press, 2002)

Fernand Braudel, *Civilisation and Capitalism, 15th–18th century*, 3 vols, trans. Siân Reynolds (London: Collins, 1981–84)

David J. Breeze and Gordon Donaldson, *A Queen's Progress* (Edinburgh: HMSO, 1987)

Keith M. Brown, *Noble Society in Scotland: Wealth, Family and Culture, from Reformation to Revolution* (Edinburgh: Edinburgh University Press, 2000)

Keith M. Brown, Alastair J. Mann and Roland J. Tanner, eds, *Records of the Parliaments of Scotland to 1707* (University of St Andrews) http://rps.ac.uk

George Buchanan, *The Tyrannous Reign of Mary Stewart*, trans. and ed. W. A. Gatherer (Edinburgh: Edinburgh University Press, 1958)

Stephen Budiansky, *Her Majesty's Spymaster: Elizabeth I, Sir Francis Walsingham and the Birth of Modern Espionage* (New York: Plume, 2006)

Joseph Bain, ed., *The Border Papers. Calendar of Letters and Papers Relating to the Affairs of the Borders of England and Scotland* (Edinburgh: 1894–96)

Joseph Bain et al., eds, *Calendar of State Papers relating to Scotland and Mary Queen of Scots 1547–1603* (Edinburgh: 1898–1969)

William Camden, *The History of the Most Renowned and Victorious Princess Elizabeth*, trans. R. Norton (London: 1635)

Annie Cameron, *The Correspondence of Mary of Lorraine* (Edinburgh: Scottish History Society, 1927)

Jamie Cameron, *James V: The Personal Rule, 1528–1542* (Edinburgh: John Donald, 2011)

George Chalmers, *The Life of Mary, Queen of Scots*, 2 vols (London: 1818 and 1822)

Patrick Chapman, *Things Written in the Glasse Windowes at Buxstons* (Buxton: Merit Publications, 2012)

J. Keith Cheetham, *On the Trail of Mary Queen of Scots* (Edinburgh: Luath Press, 2000)

Samuel Cowan, *The Last Days of Mary Stuart: And the Journal of Her Physician Bourgoyne* (London: Eveleigh Nash, 1907)

Robert Crawford, *Scotland's Books: The Penguin History of Scottish Literature* (London: Penguin, 2007)

T. M. Devine and Jenny Wormald, eds, *The Oxford Handbook of Modern Scottish History* (Oxford: Oxford University Press, 2012)

Gordon Donaldson, *All the Queen's Men: Power and Politics in Mary Stewart's Scotland* (London: Batsford, 1983)

Gordon Donaldson, *Mary, Queen of Scots* (London: English Universities Press, 1974)

Susan Doran and Norman L. Jones, eds, *The Elizabethan World* (London: Routledge, 2011)

Jane Dunn, *Elizabeth & Mary: Cousins, Rivals, Queens* (London: HarperCollins, 2003)

Francis Edwards, *The Dangerous Queen* (London: Geoffrey Chapman, 1964)

Francis Edwards, *The Marvellous Chance: Thomas Howard, Fourth Duke of Norfolk, and the Ridolphi Plot 1570–1572* (London: Hart-Davis, 1968)

Elizabeth Ewan, '"Hamperit in ane hony came": Sights, Sounds and Smells in the Medieval Town', in Edward J. Cowan and Lizanne Henderson, eds, *A History of Everyday Life in Medieval Scotland 1000–1600* (Edinburgh: Edinburgh University Press, 2011)

Marjory Filbee, *A Woman's Place: An Illustrated History of Women at Home from the Roman Villa to the Victorian Townhouse* (London: Book Club Associates, 1980)

Anthony Fletcher and Diarmaid MacCulloch, *Tudor Rebellions*, 5th edn (Harlow: Pearson Longman, 2008)

Antonia Fraser, *Mary Queen of Scots* (London: Folio Society, 2004)

George MacDonald Fraser, *The Steel Bonnets: The Story of the Anglo-Scottish Border Reivers* (London: HarperCollins, 1995)

Frances and Joseph Gies, *Scenes of Medieval Life: Life in a Medieval Castle, Life in a Medieval City, Life in a Medieval Village*, 3 vols (London: Folio Society, 2002)

John M. Gilbert, *Hunting and Hunting Reserves in Medieval Scotland* (Edinburgh: John Donald, 1979)

Julian Goodare, *Queen Mary's Catholic Interlude* (Edinburgh: Edinburgh University Press, Innes Review, 1987)

Rosemary Goring, *Homecoming: The Scottish Years of Mary, Queen of Scots* (Edinburgh: Birlinn, 2022)

Robert Grundy Heape, *Buxton under the Dukes of Devonshire* (London: 1948)

John Guy, *Elizabeth: The Forgotten Years* (New York: Viking, 2016)

John Guy, *My Heart is My Own: The Life of Mary Queen of Scots* (London: Fourth Estate, 2004)

Clare Hartwell, *Derbyshire* (Buildings of England series) (New Haven: Yale University Press, 2016)

Phyllis Hembry, *The English Spa 1560–1815: A Social History* (London: Athlone Press, 1989)

R. A. Houston and W. W. J. Knox, eds, *The History of Scotland from the Earliest Times to the Present Day*, vol. I (London: Folio Society, 2006)

Clare Hunter, *Embroidering Her Truth: Mary, Queen of Scots and the Language of Power* (London: Sceptre, 2022)

Clare Hunter, *Threads of Life: A History of the World Through the Eye of a Needle* (London: Sceptre, 2019)

Paul Johnson, *Elizabeth I: A Study in Power and Intellect* (London: Futura Publications, 1976)

David Kahn, *The Codebreakers* (London: Sphere, 1978)

Sir Arthur Keith, 'The Skull of Lord Darnley', *British Medical Journal*, 2, 8 September 1928

Krista J. Kesselring, *The Northern Rebellion of 1569* (London: Palgrave Macmillan, 2007)

John Knox, *The History of the Reformation in Scotland*, trans. and ed. W. Croft Dickinson (Edinburgh, 1949)

Prince Alexander Labanoff (A. I. Lobanov-Rostovsky), *Lettres et mémoires de Marie, Reine d'Écosse*, 7 vols (London, 1844)

Prince Alexander Labanoff, *Letters of Mary Stuart, Queen of Scotland: Selected from the 'Recueil Des Lettres de Marie Stuart'*, trans. William Barclay Turnbull (London: Charles Dolman, 1845)

George Lasry, Norbert Bierman and Satoshi Tomokiyo, 'Deciphering Mary Stuart's Lost Letters from 1578–1584', *Cryptologia*, 47(2), 2023

J. D. Leader, *Mary Queen of Scots in Captivity: A Narrative of Events* (Sheffield: 1880)

Maurice du Pont Lee, *James Stewart, Earl of Moray: A Political Study of the Reformation in Scotland* (New York: Columbia University Press, 1953)

Mary S. Lovell, *Bess of Hardwick, First Lady of Chatsworth, 1527–1608* (London: Little, Brown, 2005)

Michael Lynch, *The Oxford Companion to Scottish History* (Oxford: Oxford University Press, 2001)

Michael Lynch, *Scotland: A New History* (London: Pimlico, 1992)

Norman MacCaig, *Collected Poems: A New Edition* (London: Chatto & Windus, 1990)

Norman MacDougall, *James IV* (East Linton: John Tuckwell, 2001)

Rosalind K. Marshall, *Mary, Queen of Scots: 'In the end is my beginning'* (Edinburgh: National Museums of Scotland, 2013)

Rosalind K. Marshall, *Queen of Scots* (Edinburgh: Mercat Press, 1986)

Rosalind K. Marshall, *Virgins and Viragos: A History of Women in Scotland from 1080 to 1980* (London: Collins, 1983)

David McKinnon-Bell, *Philip II* (London: Hodder & Stoughton, 2001)

Clare McManus, 'Marriage and the Performance of the Romance Quest' in L. A. J. R. Houwen et al., eds, *A Palace in the Wild: Essays on Vernacular Culture and Humanism in Late-medieval and Renaissance Scotland* (Leuven: Peeters, 2000)

Hon. Mrs Maxwell-Scott, *The Tragedy of Fotheringhay, Founded on the Journal of Bourgoing and Unpublished MS Documents* (London, 1905)

James Melville of Halhill, *Memoirs of his Own Life* (Edinburgh, 1827)

Haydn Middleton, *Tudor Children* (Oxford: Heinemann Library, 2003)

Rosalind Mitchison, *A History of Scotland*, 3rd edn (London: Routledge, 2002)

Ian Mortimer, *The Time Traveller's Guide to Tudor England* (London: The Bodley Head, 2012)

Claude Nau, *Memorials of the Reign of Mary Stewart*, ed. J. Stevenson (Edinburgh, 1883)

Geoffrey Parker, *The Grand Strategy of Philip II* (New Haven, London: Yale University Press, 1998)

David Parkinson, ' "A Lamentable Storie": Mary Queen of Scots and the Inescapable Querelle des Femmes', in L. A. J. R. Houwen, A. A. MacDonald and S. L. Mapstone, eds, *A Palace in the Wild* (Leuven: Peeters, 2000)

Maria Perry, *Elizabeth I: The Word of a Prince. A Life from Contemporary Documents* (London: Folio Society, 1990)

Nikolaus Pevsner, *Cumberland and Westmorland* (Buildings of England series) (London: Penguin, 1967)

Nikolaus Pevsner, revised by Elizabeth Williamson, *Derbyshire* (Buildings of England series) (London: Penguin, 1979)

Sir Amias Poulet, *The Letter-books of Sir Amias Poulet. Keeper of Mary Queen of Scots* (London: 1874)

Maud Stepney Rawson, *Bess of Hardwick and Her Circle* (London: Hutchinson & Co, 1910)

Steven J. Reid, *The Early Life of James VI: A Long Apprenticeship, 1566–1585* (Edinburgh: John Donald, 2023)

Graham Robb, *The Debatable Land: The Lost World Between Scotland and England* (London: Picador, 2018)

Joseph Robertson, *Inventaires de la Royne d'Ecosse, Douairiere de France, 1556–1569: Catalogues of the Jewels, Dresses, Furniture, Books and Paintings of Mary Queen of Scots, 1556–1569* (Edinburgh: Bannatyne Club, 49, 1863)

William Robertson, *The History of Scotland during the Reigns of Queen Mary and King James VI till his Succession to the Crown of England* (London: 1759)

Alec Rylie, 'Facing Childhood Death in English Protestant Spirituality', in Katie Barclay, Kimberley Reynolds and Ciara Rawnsley, eds, *Death, Emotion and Childhood in pre-Modern Europe* (London: Palgrave Macmillan, 2016)

Margaret Sanderson, *Mary Stewart's People* (Edinburgh: Mercat Press, 1987)

Jade Scott, *Captive Queen: The Decrypted History of Mary, Queen of Scots* (London: Michael O'Mara Books, 2024)

Walter Scott, *The Abbot* (Edinburgh: Edinburgh University Press, 2000)

Robert Stedall, *The Challenge to the Crown: The Struggle for Influence in the Reign of Mary Queen of Scots 1542–1567* (Leicester: Book Guild Ltd, 2012)

Agnes Strickland, *Letters of Mary Queen of Scots and Documents Connected with her Personal History*, 3 vols (London: 1842–43)

Alice Taylor, *The Shape of the State in Medieval Scotland, 1124–1290* (Oxford: Oxford University Press, 2016)

David Templeman, *Mary, Queen of Scots: The Captive Queen in England 1568–87* (Exeter: Short Run Press, 2017)

A. Teulet and Prince Labanoff, *Lettres inédites de Marie Stuart* (Paris: 1859)

G. B. Thornton, *The Rising in the North* (Hexham: Ergo, 2010)

William Barclay Turnbull, *Letters of Mary Stuart, Queen of Scotland* (1845)

Steven Veerapen, *The Wisest Fool: The Lavish Life of James VI and I* (Edinburgh: Birlinn, 2023)

Retha M. Warnicke, *Mary Queen of Scots* (London: Routledge, 2006)

Alison Weir, *Elizabeth, the Queen* (London: Pimlico, 1998)

Alison Weir, *Mary, Queen of Scots and the Murder of Lord Darnley* (London: Jonathan Cape, 2003)

Kate Williams, *Rival Queens: The Betrayal of Mary, Queen of Scots* (London: Hutchinson, 2018)

A. N. Wilson, *The Elizabethans* (London: Random House, 2011)
Jenny Wormald, *Mary Queen of Scots* (Edinburgh: Birlinn, 2018)
Jenny Wormald, *Lords and Men in Scotland: Bonds of Manrent* (Edinburgh: John Donald, 1985)
Thomas Wright, *Queen Elizabeth and Her Times* (London: 1838)
Keith Wrightson, *English Society 1580–1680* (London: Hutchinson, 1982)
Stefan Zweig, *The Queen of Scots* (London: Cassell, 1987)

Index

Alençon, Francis, Duke of 116, 202
Alford, Stephen 109, 125, 217, 254, 266
Alva, Fernando Álvarez de Toledo,
    Duke of 74, 110, 188
Angus, Archibald Douglas, Earl of
    45, 218–19, 291–2
Anjou, Duke of (later Henri II of
    France) 115–16, 201–06, 208, 215
Anne of Denmark (bride of James VI)
    315–16
Aragon, Catherine of xx, 132, 275,
    314
Argyll, Archibald Campbell, Earl of
    108, 192–3, 219
Arran, Captain James Stewart, Earl of
    201, 217, 218, 224, 225–6
Articles, Book of (Buchanan, G.) 29
Aston, Sir Walter of Tixall Hall 249,
    268, 270
Atholl, John Stewart, Earl of 192–3

Babington, Anthony 154, 184–5,
    260–7, 268, 278, 282, 283
Babington Plot 266, 271, 273
Bacon, Francis 30, 153
Bagot, Richard of Blithfield 249,
    272–3

Ballard, Father John 259–60, 265–7
Barker (notary) 278–9, 279–80
Barnard Castle 83, 84
Beale, Robert 199, 281, 300;
    assassination of Mary and 299;
    delivery of execution warrant 298;
    explanations for Mary's execution
    312–13; illness of Mary, visit on
    concerns about 211–12; respect of
    Mary 198, 278; responses to
    Mary's complaints and 220–1;
    warning of death sentence to Mary
    from 288–9
Beaton, James, Archbishop of
    Glasgow 100, 116, 155, 256;
    agents in Paris 238; Anjou's
    attitude, request for news about
    204; association between Mary
    and son, negotiations about 210;
    coded letter to Mary from, lucky
    escape for 197; diminishing
    wardrobe, Mary's request
    concerning 162–3; dogs, Mary's
    concerns about 164–5; final letter
    from Mary to, pain in 289–90;
    freedom for Mary, letter on
    continued denial to 209; health of

James, Mary's concerns about 208; liberation of James, call for French troops in 219; Mary's description of Walsingham to 158; Paget and, close association between 229–30; protection against poisoning, Mary's plea for 119; safety of James, message of anxiety about 195; Spanish arrival in Scotland, Mary's hopes for 214; Spanish invasion of England, Mary's concerns about 192

Beaton, John, Master of the Household 9, 22

Berden, Nicolas (Walsingham agent) 256

Bess of Hardwick, Countess of Shrewsbury 64, 66, 77, 118, 122, 148; Arbella Stuart, raising of orphan 173; blaming Mary for failing marriage 234–5; breakdown of marriage 176–9, 222–3, 234–5; building projects, lavishing money on 240; Buxton Bath Charity and 142; Charles and William, sons of 177; Chatsworth, love for 101–04, 107; cooling of relationship with Mary 123, 169–70; family machinations, failure of 205; favour of Elizabeth for 67–70; gardening skills of 133–4; intelligent and independent-minded 107; marriage, eventful experience of 135; Mary's captivity with, tightrope act of 103; Mary's relationship with 68–70, 135–6, 161–2, 164, 169–70, 212; money-making, favourite pastime for 141; shrewd and opportunistic xvii;

Stuart-Cavendish marriage, ramifications for 171

Bingham, Caroline 194, 195

Boleyn, Anne xx, 5, 109, 132, 307

Bolton Castle xvi, 33–9, 43–4, 49, 51, 53–6, 65, 78, 93

Book of Hours 161

Bothwell, James Hepburn, Earl of 3, 14, 15–16, 29, 79, 80, 109, 117, 219, 315; alleged adultery with, Mary's denouncement for 288; Casket Letters and 45–6; deathbed confession 180–1; imprisonment in Denmark 179; Mary's abduction by 47; murder of Darnley, accusations of conspiracy in 4, 50; public suspicion of affair with 177; refusal of Pope to annul Mary's marriage to 185

Bourgoing, Dominique (Mary's physician) 209, 268–9, 271–4, 276, 281, 294, 299–300, 302–03, 313

Bowes, Robert 220, 225

Buchanan, George 29, 99, 101, 119–20, 166–8, 171–2

Buckhurst, William Sackville, Lord 288–9

Bull Inn, Coventry 87, 88

Burghley, William Cecil, 1st Baron 115, 116, 149, 202, 205, 223, 246, 257, 310; Bond of Association, involvement in proposal for 233, 236, 237, 239; Buxton visits, involvement in 143–4; dedication to Elizabeth and enmity towards Mary 125–8; Mary's execution, demand for secrecy from Privy Council on 298; Mary's

reputation, scurrilous attempt at ruination of 119–21; Mary's schemes for escape, vigilance on 159; national panic, stoking of 295; Norfolk's guilt, letter from Sadler about 122; pariah status post-execution for 310, 312; part of Elizabeth's faithful bodyguard 157–8; petition for Mary's execution 288; trial of Mary at Fotheringhay, involvement in 278–9, 279–81, 283–5
Buxton 77, 78, 138–47, 161, 209, 236

Camden, William 127, 295
Campion, Edmund 216, 217, 260
Carberry Hill, Battle of (1567) xix, 117, 181
Carey, Robert (Elizabeth's courier to James) 311–12
Carlisle 9, 11, 13–20, 21–31, 32–3, 55
Carlisle Castle 13–15, 16–19, 32, 209; Great Tower (keep) of 18–19; Warden's Tower in 19–20
Carlisle Cathedral 14, 24
Casket Letters 29–30, 42, 43–51, 56, 72, 120, 235; Long Glasgow Letter (Letter II) 45–6; Short Glasgow Letter (Letter I) 45
Castelnau, Michel de, Sieur de la Mauvissière 211, 215, 235, 239, 240, 241, 253, 259; Anjou and Elizabeth, marriage negotiations 203–5; conduit for Mary's letters 182; French ambassador in London, appointment as 181–2; funds for Mary, delivery of 208–09; leaving in disgrace, positivity in doing so 242–3; Mary's communication stratagems 156; putty in hands of Walsingham 232–3; restoration for Mary, renewed hopes for 222, 226–7, 228–9; underground correspondence from Mary, reach of 196–9

Cavendish, Elizabeth 170–1, 173, 222
Cavendish, Sir William 68, 101–02, 140
Cecil, William 49, 56, 66, 68, 70, 90, 104; accusations against Mary, instruction for 28–9; assessment of Mary from Knollys to 22–3, 27; Catholicism, report on support for (Sadler to) 84; dispatching Mary, 'remedy' for 245–6; elevation to Lord Burghley (1571) 115; foreign policy belligerence, Elizabeth's anxiety about 83; incriminating letter intercepted by 110–11; Knollys's report on Mary's treatment to 55; Moray for Regent in Scotland, Mary's denunciation of 50; plans against Mary's claims on England 107–09; power of, Mary's recognition of 107–08; reactions to Mary's arrival in England 21, 24–5; restoration for Mary, assurances of bar on 30, 41; risk of poisoning for Elizabeth, alert to 119; steadfastly protective of Elizabeth xx; sycophancy towards, Mary's exercise of 26; visit to Chatsworth 107–08 See also Burghley, William Cecil, 1st Baron

Charles IX of France 115, 116–17, 124, 175, 201–02
Charles V, Holy Roman Emperor 191–2
Chartley Manor 161, 243, 248–51, 255, 257, 258, 269, 271, 272–3
Châteauneuf, Guillaume de l'Aubespine de 155, 156, 169, 241, 291, 292, 311; Babington plot and 253, 255, 257, 259, 260–1; conduit for Mary's letters 182; description of Sadler as implacable 244–5; residential permanence, Mary's plea of need for 250
Châtelherault, James Hamilton, Duke of 80, 99, 108
Chatsworth House 67–8, 101–11, 133–4, 161, 170, 176, 179, 223, 236; Hunting Tower at 105, 106, 134–5
Cherelles (Walsingham spy in French embassy) 253, 258
Chesterfield 56, 102
Cockermouth 10–11, 13
Confederate Lords xix, 2, 8
Coventry 85, 87–98
Coventry Castle 88, 93–4
Coventry Tapestry 90
Crichton, William (Scottish Jesuit) 217, 228, 232
Cromwell, Thomas 139
Cromwell, Treasurer Ralph 75
Cryptiana (website) 196–7
cryptography 153, 154–5, 160, 196–7 See also Phelippes, Thomas
Cumbria 1–2, 17, 20, 33–4
Curle, Elizabeth 183, 273, 305, 306, 313, 316
Curle, Gilbert 153, 183–5, 263, 265, 269, 278, 282–3, 287, 351

Curwen, Henry 5–6, 9
Curwen (Culwen), Gilbert III de 8
Curwen Castle (Workington Hall) 5–6, 7–8, 9, 10, 13

Dacre, Leonard 77–8, 85
Dacre, Thomas 17, 77
Darnley, Henry Stuart, Lord 4, 72, 92, 100, 117, 170, 177, 201, 288; accusations against Mary in murder of 27, 28–9, 30, 127; Bothwell's deathbed confession concerning 180; Casket Letters and murder of 45–6, 47, 49, 51; Confederate Lords accused of murder of 8–9; Mary's alibi (and hopes of being cleared in murder of) 22, 25; murder of, sensational nature of 3; Scottish Act declaring Mary guilty of murder of (1567) 2
David I of Scotland 15, 19, 275
Davison, William 288, 295–6, 297–8, 310, 312
DECRYPT Project 196
Detection of the Actions of Mary Queen of Scots (Buchanan, G.) 119–20
Diego Guzmán de Silva, Spanish Ambassador 27
Don Juan of Austria 188, 192
Dorset, Frances Grey, Marchioness of 67–8
Dorset, Henry Grey, Marquess of 67
Douglas, Willie 22, 67, 96, 165
Dove, River 55, 58, 60
Dragsholm Castle 179, 181
Drury, Drue 288, 294, 297–8, 301
Dudley, Robert, Earl of Leicester see Leicester

Dumbarton Castle 42, 116
Dunbar 47, 180
Dunn, Jane 25, 204
Durham, James Pilkington, Bishop of 56

Edensor 102, 105
Edinburgh Castle 45, 116, 127, 129
Edward II 60, 299
Edward III 59
Edward VI 107, 118
Elizabeth I 63, 88, 98, 245, 306, 316; Anjou, courtship and romance with 201–02, 203–06; Anjou, Elizabeth and, excitement of Mary at 204–05; Anjou, negotiations for proposed marriage to 115–16; appointment of Shrewsbury as Mary's custodian 65–6; barrenness of, Mary's claims and 93; Bess, favour for 67–8; Bess and Mary, concern at closeness of 103, 176; Bond of Association and Act for Queen's Safety (March, 1585) 233, 237–9, 254, 288, 297; Buchanan and James, Mary's hope of intervention by 119; burial of Mary in France, refusal of 301; Buxton Spa, Mary's permission to visit from 143–5; Buxton Spa, social venue for court of 141; Casket Letters, Mary's denial of knowledge of 56; Catholic conspiracy, anxiety about spas and 143–4; Catholic mission to Scotland, alarm at 195; Cecil's plans against Mary's claims on England 107–09; coldness towards Mary 26; complaints from Mary on tightening of security to 120–1; condolences to Mary from 21–2; cost of Mary's funeral bourne in sop to James 313; curt letter to Mary from (11 October 1586) 278–9; custodianship of Mary, parsimony on costs of 66, 95, 178; Darnley's murder, silence on Mary's innocence plea 180; death sentence on Mary, public proclamation of (4 December 1586) 291; demands on James in Scotland 207–08, 210–11; distrust of rebels, innate nature of 188; downfall of, openness of Mary about wish for 214; Dudley, Earl of Leicester, affection for 92; duplicity of, witnesses to 27–30; evidence in York Commission, change of heart about 48–52; excommunication of (May 1570) 109; fear of civil war on presence of Mary in England 24–5; forcible removal from Bolton, Mary's complaint about 56; freedom for Mary not on agenda of 32–3; good nature of, Mary's overconfidence in 74; grounds for holding Mary, recognition of paucity of 107; health concerns, Mary's petitions about 142–3; hopes for 'good end' to York Commission 44; incandescent at Mary's duplicity 234; injunction that Mary's 'head should never rest' 99; insanitary and inhumane conditions, complaints to 118; intransigence over Mary's claim to

English throne 150–1; James, calculated cruelty towards 100–01; James and Mary, Bond of Association with 233, 237–9, 254, 288, 297; James's preference for, abandonment of Mary and 187; James's eagerness for France as ally, anger at 224–5; letter to James following Mary's execution 310–11; Mary's access to Bess, instructions about 68–9; Mary's arrival in England, Lowther's warning of 11–12; Mary's expectation of regaining Scots throne through 2, 4–5; Mary's gift of falcons to, security arrangements and 40–1; Mary's imprisonment at Bolton Castle, complaints to 32–3, 38–9; Mary's misplaced faith and belief in 41–2; Mary's plea for retiral to 'solitary place' to 239–40; Mary's rightful claim to England, reminder about (1580) 209; mending bridges with James, Mary executed against wishes of 311; Moray's assassination, stricken by news of 99–100; Nau and, perfidy in relationship 184–5; 'never intention to put Mary to death,' Châteauneuf informed 311; Northern Rising and 83–6; nuptial plans of Mary and Norfolk, reaction to 80–81, 82–3; Oath of Supremacy (1559) 139; opprobrium for executing Mary, fears of 297–8; options to Scottish Parliament regarding Mary 79–80; Paulet's protectiveness towards 294–5; penultimate letter from Mary to 292–3; 'pitiable condition,' entreaty from Mary to 8–9; plot to liberate Mary, Shrewsbury's concerns about 135–6; plots against life of 182–3, 228–31, 232, 234, 237, 254, 261–2, 284, 295; preparations for Fotheringhay trial 278–80, 280–1; probity of, Mary's lack of illusion about 116–17; proposal of Norfolk as Mary's spouse 72–3; reaction to news of Mary's execution 310; refusal to meet with Mary 27–8; relations with Mary, serious straining of 122–3; religious and political unease, threats to 139–40; reports to, favourable expressions of Mary in 22–3; request for Mary's burial in France 'beside queens' 316–17; Ridolfi plot and 110; secret murder of Mary, Paulet's defence on 299; Shrewsbury and Mary, concerns about relationship 176–7; Shrewsbury's absence from Wingfield, displeasure at 77; Shrewsbury's removal as Mary's custodian by 235–6; spa centres across England, promotion of 140–1, 144; St Bartholomew's Day Massacre and 124–7; Stuart-Cavendish marriage, ramifications for 170–1, 179; suspicions about Mary, growth of 53–5; swithering over Mary's sentence 288, 290–1; sycophancy in Mary's messages to 26–7; tricked by council into consenting to Mary's execution

311; trouble in Scotland, accusations of stirring up 198–200; Walsingham's appointment as principal secretary 157–8
Elliots of Liddesdale 14, 15–16
Erskine of Gogar, Alexander 166, 167, 193
El Escorial (residence of Philip II) 190–2; Royal Pantheon in 191–2
Essex, Robert Devereaux, Earl of 249–50
Essex and Leicester, Lettice, Countess of 203, 205
executioner Bull, incompetence of 298–9, 307

Ferniehurst 85, 86
Fleming, John, 5th Lord 3, 20, 22, 26, 31
Fletcher, Master Henry 10, 11
Flodden, Battle of (1513) 17, 225
Forster, John, Middle March Warden 227–8
Fotheringhay Castle 33, 93, 274–8, 287–9, 297–308, 309–10, 313; Great Hall at 275, 303, 304, 305–08; sorrow, fog-like, after Mary's execution at 310
Francis II of France (Mary's husband) xviii, 3, 117, 175, 208, 316
Fraser, Antonia 5, 30, 48–9, 100, 180, 184, 185, 223–4, 239, 292
Frederic II of Norway and Denmark 179, 181

Gaunt, John of 59–60, 61
Gifford, Gilbert (agent of Walsingham) 250, 254, 255–8, 259, 261, 262, 266
Glencairn 218–19
Gorges, Thomas 269, 274
Gowrie, William Ruthven, Earl of 218–19, 219–20, 226
Gray, Patrick, Master of 219, 238–9, 291–2
Grey, Lady Jane 68, 102
Guise, Henry of Lorraine, Duke of 124, 217, 224, 228–30, 232, 235, 280, 290, 316
Guise, House of 195, 198, 210–11
Guise, Marie of xviii, 71
Guy, John 46, 110–11, 180, 233, 237, 273, 288

Hadrian's Wall 14, 15
Hamilton, James of Bothwellhaugh 99–100
Hamilton, John, Archbishop of St Andrews 2–3, 99–100, 116, 117
Hampton Court 51, 56
Hardwick Hall 67, 101, 106, 135, 223
Hatton, Sir Christopher (Lord Chancellor) 278, 280, 282
Henri III of France 153–4, 176, 199, 202, 219, 226, 292, 302, 312–13
Henry VI 61, 87, 90
Henry VII 87, 90, 170
Henry VIII xx, 5, 36, 65, 82, 109, 118, 132, 158, 235–6, 314
Heron, George, Deputy Keeper of Tyndale 40
Herries, John Maxwell, 4th Baron 3, 5–6, 9, 26, 27, 41, 44, 48, 53, 80
Howard, Thomas, Duke of Norfolk see Norfolk
Huntingdon, Henry Hastings, Earl of 55, 80, 88, 92, 197, 200, 205

Huntly, George Gordon, Earl of 80, 108, 127–8, 219
hygiene, cleanliness and 132–3
illness and death, Elizabethan attitudes to 173–5; issues of Mary's time, echoes today of xx-i; reinterpretation and reassessment, lifeblood of xvii

James VI and I 50, 117, 171, 205, 206, 275–6, 290, 301; alienation from Mary, machinations towards 169; association between Mary and 210–11, 212, 217–18, 221, 224, 227; Bond of Association with Elizabeth and Mary 233, 237–9, 254, 288, 297; Buchanan's views on monarchy, refutation of 167; Casket Letters, destruction by 45, 47–8; Cecil's plan for 108–09; delicate game-playing of xxi; Elizabeth, mending bridges with 311; emotional needs of, neglect of 168; escape and restoration to power of 220–1; ever-present threat of sudden, violent death for 169; feast for (1604), roasting spits used for 94–5; France, eagerness for alliance with 224–5; gift of pony from Mary (which never arrived) 100–01; hard headed and ambitious, ties with England and 311; indoctrination to think worst of Mary 167; information about, Mary's frequent pleas for 173; intellectual gifts of, Mitchison's perspective on 168; library of (1570s), priceless nature of 167; Mary's illusion of mutual love, unfounded nature of 166; Mary's thoughts, James in forefront of 207–08, 209–10, 212–13; Mary's trial and execution, reaction to 291–2; Moray's demand for James to be King of Scotland 80; official speech to Parliament (August 1571) 168–9; portrait by van Bronckorst of 166; power in Scotland, rebuilding of 224–5; Protestantism of, Mary's reaction to 186–7; raised by Annabella, Countess of Mar 101, 166; revenge for captivity from, Mary's belief in 150; rigorous classical and humanist education by Buchanan for 166–7; Ruthven Castle, captive under heavy guard at 218–20; toddler son left in Scotland 2; uncontested ruler of Scotland, Reid's perspective 109; violent death of grandfather, presence at 169; visit to Mary, refusal of plea for 107; vulnerability to those around him, Mary's concerns 192–5, 198–9; Walsingham, chastisement by 225–6; Walsingham, disrespectful treatment of 226; warning to Carey (Elizabeth's courier) not to cross border 312; Westminster Abbey, removal of Mary's remains to (1612) 316

Jedburgh 16, 34, 78; Mary, Queen of Scots House in 181
Jonson, Ben 144, 287

Kahn, David 154–5, 160
Kennedy, Jane 183, 303, 313; tragic

death by drowning at Leith (1589) 315–16
Kent, Henry Grey, Earl of 298, 300, 301, 307
Kirkcaldy of Grange, Captain of Edinburgh Castle 32–3, 80, 116, 117, 127, 199–200
Knollys, Lady Catherine 56, 70–1
Knollys, Sir Francis 21, 25, 33, 37, 38, 40, 42, 56–7, 71; assessment of Mary to Cecil 22–3, 27; report to Cecil, unease about Mary's treatment in 55; security for Mary, anxiety about 23–4
Knox, John 177

Langside, Battle of (1568) xix, 2, 8
Leader, J.D. 73–4, 111, 160
Leicester, Robert Dudley, Earl of 50, 64, 126, 144, 149, 188, 294; death of first wife, suspicions about 203; Elizabeth and Anjou, concerns about 204, 205, 206; Elizabeth's long-time favourite 141; Fotheringhay, arrival for Mary's final act at 278; marriage between Mary and, proposal for 92; Mary's fears about 197–8; part of Elizabeth's faithful triumvirate 157–8; Walsingham's trap for Mary, knowledge of 257
Lennox, Mary Douglas, Countess of 170–1, 180
Lennox, Matthew Stuart, Earl of 28–9, 100, 116, 117, 118, 168–9, 194
Leslie, John, Bishop of Ross 22, 44, 53, 71, 78–9, 184, 185, 229
Liddesdale 14, 15–16, 85

Lincoln, Bishop of 313, 315
Lindsay, Patrick (Lord Lindsay of the Byres) 44, 48, 218–19
Livingston, Alexander, 5th Lord 3, 44
Livingston, Lady Agnes (Queen Mary's Lady of the chamber) 22, 56, 68–9
Lochleven Castle 3, 22, 25, 46, 77, 79, 85, 123, 165, 228; escape to France from, Mary's rejection of 4–5; imprisonment in, Mary's enforced abdication and xix, 2, 44; Mary's miscarriage of twins in 4, 181
Lorraine, Charles, Cardinal of 31, 175
Lovell, Mary S. 68, 102, 103, 171, 178–9
Lowther, Sir Richard of Lowther Hall 9, 10, 11–12, 13, 19, 24–5, 33

Maitland of Lethington 32–3, 44–5, 48, 49, 72, 80, 127, 180
Mar, Annabella Murray, Countess of 101, 166
Mar, John Erskine, Earl of xix, 52, 101, 117, 127, 168, 169, 193, 219–19
Margaret Tudor xx, 77
Mary Stuart, Queen of Scotland 60–1, 203; abdication calls for, refusal to accept 53–6; aftermath of execution 307–08; alienation of James from, machinations towards 169; Anglo-French treaty (1571) with no provision for 115–16; Arbella Stuart and Lennox title, Mary and 171–3; association suggestion with son James 210–11, 212, 217–18, 221, 224, 227;

Babington Plot, life-changing letters and 262–6; Bess of Hardwick, relationship with (and cooling of) 68–70, 123; Bessie de Pierrepoint and 169–70; body of, disposal of 309; Bond of Association with James and Elizabeth 233, 237–9, 254, 288, 297; Bothwell's deathbed confession and 180–1; Bothwell's imprisonment in Denmark and 179; brutality and horror of final hours 300–01; burial for, arrangement of 313; burial in France, refusal of possibility 301; Buxton spa and Mary's visit to 142–5; Carlisle Castle, arrival at 13–14; Carlisle Castle, as Mary knew it 17–18; Casket Letters, destructive powers against 45–9; Catholic figurehead and mortal threat to Elizabeth xx; Catholic Queen in Protestant Scotland xviii; Cecil's power, recognition of 107–08; character shifts witnessed by those around her xviii; charges at York Commission, no opportunity to answer to 50–1; Chatsworth House, move to 101–02; Chesterfield en route to Tutbury, pains and collapse caused by stress 56–7; clandestine existence 160–1; cloth of state, Paulet's order for pre-execution removal of 289; Cockermouth Castle, on guard against Moray at 11–12; comforts of confinement for, modern reflection on 93–5; Commission at York, agreement to conditions of 41–2; conditions for restoration, discussions on 108–09; Confederate Lords, behaviour towards 8–9; confinement at Tutbury, chafing miserably at 62–3; constant shuttling between residences for 138; contact with James and 'people in France' denied 120–2; correspondence, imperious tone of 164; correspondence, voluminous nature of 161–2; coup in Scotland by Argyll and Atholl, effect of failure on 192–4; curt but ameliorative letter from Elizabeth to (11 October 1586) 278–9; Dacre's plan for escape from Wingfield for 77–8; darkening days for 276–7; Dean of Peterborough, Mary's Catholicism in challenge to 306; death of devoted Raulet, effect on 183; death of Morton, satisfaction at 201; death sentence on, public proclamation of (4 December 1586) 291; deterioration in health at Tutbury 73, 75–6; directness of tone and clarity of expression 31; disrobing before execution, anguish of ladies at 306; distrust and loathing for Buchanan 119–20; dogs, devotion to 164–5; dread of poisoning 119; dressing for Catholic martyrdom 303; duel with Elizabeth, thread running throughout imprisonment xxi–ii; duplicity during imprisonment, undercurrent of xxii; 'dying for her faith,' parting gift from enemies 301; Elizabeth's options to Scottish

Parliament for 79–80; Elizabeth's probity, lack of illusion about 116–17; Elizabeth's reaction to news of execution of 310; Elizabeth's refusal to meet with, effects of 27–8; escape from Scotland 1–2; Esmé Stuart, Mary's fears of influence on James 194–5; *Essay on Adversity*, writing of (1580) 206–07; events in Scotland, lack of full awareness of xxi; everyday life in confinement for, reality of 66–8, 70–1; execution of, aftermath of 309–17; expectations of death, lack of fear about 289–90; fascination with life of, perpetual nature of xvi; favourable impressions from all in contact with 21–3; fears of Spanish invasion 192; final embrace of attendants 306–07; final letters in expectation of imminent death 289–90; final minutes in Scotland 2–3; flight to England, fate sealed in xv; forced abdication and humiliating treatment of, unacceptability to many xix; forces against, gathering pace of 28–9; foreignness of England for, yet no moves to escape 97–8; forever beyond our reach xxiii; formidability in most difficult of conditions xvii; happy days in life of, Bolton and last of 43–4; hardship and heartache, well versed in xviii; health at Chartley, fluctuations in 250; hopes of Anglo-French marriage faltering and lost 205–06, 208; horror of executioner's misjudgment in death of 307; housebound confinement in Coventry 90–2; household, trauma post-execution for 310; household expansion at Carlisle 22, 33; household obligations, final performance of 301–02; ill health, shadow of 163–4; imprisonment at Tutbury, detestation of 64–5; incarceration at Bolton, luxury and indulgence of 34–40; injunction that Mary's 'head should never rest' 99; inner circle of, significant changes in 181–5; innocence, sublime conviction of 236–7; James, eagerness for contact with 100–01; James, thundering denunciation of 239–40; James at forefront of thoughts again (1580) 207–08; jury of inferiors, disdain for, 'theatre of world' warning and 279–80; lack of definitive biography of xvi; landing in Workington (1568) xviii; last letter to Henri III of France 302–03; last scene of tragedy of 277–8; 'laughing with the angels' on final morning 279–308; Leicester as spouse, Huntingdon's proposal for 92; Leslie's statement on Ridolfi plot (and Mary's involvement) 117; *Letter-books* on custodianship by Paulet 245–7; liberty for, loss of last chance for 238–9; life at Wingfield Manor, ups and downs of 73–9; loving, kind and maternal nature of 169; marriage to Darnley, chaos following xviii–ix; marriage to Norfolk, Elizabeth's displeasure at prospect 82–3;

marriage to Norfolk, possibilities (and encouragement) for 48, 50, 72–3, 78–9, 80–1, 92–3; material existence, gilded nature of 95–6; messages from Buxton, unhappiness and despair in 149–51; mind and spirit, strength of 277–8; misplaced faith in James, personal ramifications of 209–10, 212–13; Moray's assassination, welcome news of 99–100; mordant humour, retention of 248; morning prayers on execution day 303; Mothe-Fénelon, kindness in ear of 123–4; mounting scaffold, Paulet's 'agreeable service' on 305; move to Bolton, unwillingness to accept 32–3; news of execution, curtailment of 309–10; nineteen years of imprisonment, weariness of 277; Northern Rising, effects on Mary's captivity 84–6, 87–8; Old Hall Hotel in Buxton, Mary's Bower at 146–9; Paulet's custodianship in Mary's final weeks 289, 293–5; perfidy of, mounting evidence of 229–31; personal and political statement in penultimate letter to Elizabeth 292–3; personality change from 12 years captivity 207; personality in captivity, gradual change in xvii; Philip II of Spain and 187–90; plea to Elizabeth for retiral to 'solitary place' 239–40; pleas for clemency on behalf of 291–2; pleas for James to visit, refusal of 107; position of, grave problems undermining (1570) 109–10;

post-trial exhaustion 285; prayer before dying 307; precipitous flight from Scotland xix; progress to Great Hall on execution day 304–05; prospect of Anjou's marriage to Elizabeth, excitement at 204–05; public anger in France, Mary as martyr to Catholic cause 313; Queen Mary's Tower in Carlisle Castle 19–20; redoubtable and unfathomable individual 3; reign in Scotland, catastrophic decisions during xix, 5; relations with Elizabeth, serious straining of 122–3; release, slimness of chances of 30; request to Elizabeth for burial in France 'beside other queens' 316–17; Requiem Mass in Notre Dame for 312; resilience against captivity and health issues 159–60; restraints on, defiance against 27; return to Scotland (1561) xviii; revisiting life of, rationale for xvi–vii; Ridolfo plot, questions of involvement in 110–11; rightful claim to English succession, reminder to Elizabeth about (1580) 209; rightful queen, implacable belief in being xv; Scotland in uproar about treatment of 311–12; Scottish return, end of possibility for 233–4; secret coded letters 152–60; secret letters from, discovery of (2022) 195–200; security around, tightening at Sheffield Castle 120–1; security for, Knollys's anxiety about 23–4; separation from son James, concerns about 166–9; servant's grief for (and belated release of) 315; Sheffield Castle, dangerous illness (again) for 117–18; Sheffield Castle, lodgement in 112–13; Sheffield Manor Lodge, life at 129–32, 136–7; sheriff's calls on execution day 304; Shrewsbury and Kent as witnesses to execution of 305–06; Shrewsbury's appointment as custodian for 65–6; Shrewsbury's command over, relief of 122; Shrewsbury's marriage breakdown, Mary and 176–9; size of rooms in Fotheringhay, complaints about 276; Skye terrier, faithful to the last 307–08; Spanish Armada, direct consequence of death of 313; splendid show of grief in France for 312; St Bartholomew's Day Massacre, reverberations for 124–8; state of soul and final resting place, concerns about 316–17; strict Catholic regimen of praying 123; sycophancy in messages to Elizabeth from 26–7; tableau of scaffold, demeanour in facing 305; terms of imprisonment, relaxation post-Northern Rising 104; thaw in relations with Westminster 107; threat and prize to England in person of 24–5; timing of execution, inflexibility on 301; torchlight procession and funeral of 313–15; trial at Fotheringhay 281–5; Tutbury again, relationship with Paulet and 245–9; vexations at Sheffield Castle 119–20; vulnerability of, secret communications and 157–8; wake and feast following funeral of 315; Walsingham's agents and Mary's battle against 158–60; wardrobe, extent and richness of 162–3; warrant for execution read to 300–01; Westminster Abbey, removal of remains to (1612) 316; white marble tomb commissioned in Westminster Abbey for 316; will drafted in 1577, provisions of 186–7; wit of, retention to last of xxii–iii; Workington Hall and poignant what-if for 9–10; years as prisoner, hopes and fears of xv–vi

Mary Tudor xx, 68, 102, 109, 126, 187, 191, 192

Medici, Catherine de' 31, 55, 120, 121, 137, 202, 203

Melville, Andrew (theologian) 218, 269, 277, 281, 299, 313, 316

Mendoza, Bernardino de (Spanish Ambassador) 217, 228, 229, 230, 258–9, 260, 277, 289–90

Mildmay, Walter (Chancellor) 108, 278–9, 279–80, 298

Moray, James Stewart, Earl of 1, 2, 4, 21, 25–6, 31, 54, 84–5, 180; assassination of (January 1570) xix, 99–100; capture of Mary, eagerness for 86; Casket Letters, incriminatory use of xix, 50–1, 54; Darnley's murder, machinations around 41–2; Mary at Cockermouth Castle, on guard against 11–12; Mary's accusations of high treason against 27; Norfolk's marriage to Mary,

support for 72; persecution of
Mary's supporters in Scotland by
79–80; Regency of Scotland for
xix, 44, 48–9, 50; wrongdoing by
Mary, counter-accusations by
28–30; York Commission, evidence
to 44, 48–9, 50; zealotry and
ambition of xix
Morgan, Thomas 230–1, 254–7, 262,
294
Morris, John 245, 294
Morton, James Douglas, Earl of 169,
220; arrest of, James' skill in
political manoeuvring and 207–08;
arrest of, steller rise of Esmé Stuart
and 210–11; Bothwell's deathbed
confession and 180; coup against
(March 1578), success of 192–3;
denunciation of 201; English
protest at treatment of 217;
execution of, sore point for
Walsingham 225; fracture of anti-
Morton faction 217; implacable
enemy of Mary 44; malign
interference of, end of 210;
Morton–Mar faction, Lennox as
counterweight to 195; pitiless and
self-serving as Regent 127–8;
refusal to consider Mary's
restoration 108
Morton, John (Mary's secret chaplain)
252
Mothe-Fénelon, Bertrand de Salignac
de La 116, 119, 121, 123–4,
161–2, 163–4, 181, 182, 219

Nau, Claude 28, 149, 153, 164, 268,
269, 273, 301, 302; Châteauneuf's
letters to, writing between lines in
156–7; confession of, inevitability
of Mary's trial and 278; loyalty of
Nau to Mary, Shrewsbury's
questions about 184; perfidy in
relationship with Elizabeth 183–5;
sent to Scottish Court with gifts for
James 206; testimony, fate of Mary
and 287; turned Judas in the hands
of Walsingham 183–5;
Walsingham's plot to destroy Mary,
part in 257, 262–3, 265, 282–3
New Hall, Buxton 141, 142, 144
Norfolk, Thomas Howard, Duke of:
association with Mary 21–2;
chairman of English commissioners
at York 44; disappearance from
court 82, 83; marriage to Mary,
considerations of 48–9, 72–4,
78–81; marriage to Mary,
Elizabeth's reaction to 60, 82–3;
meeting with Mary at Bolton,
controversy about 43–4, 78; release
from Tower and house arrest for
109–10; Ridolfi plan and 110–11,
117; trial and execution of 122–3
Northern Rising (Dacre's Raid) 78,
82–8, 95–6, 104, 111, 117, 123,
126, 140, 230
Northumberland, Anne Somerset,
Countess of 77–8, 140
Northumberland, Thomas Percy, Earl
of 24, 77, 81, 82–3, 85, 86, 123,
229, 230

Oath of Supremacy (1559) 139

Pages, Bastian 22, 69, 78, 96, 251,
277
Paget, Charles 229–30, 256, 258, 260

Parker, Geoffrey 189, 190
Paulet, Sir Amias 242, 278–9, 299–300, 304, 309, 310; Babington plot and 253, 255, 257–8; custodianship in Mary's final weeks 289, 293–5; 'dainty and precise,' Elizabeth's view of 298; 'dead woman without dignity' accusation by 289; death and burial of 316; destruction of Mary's effects by 309; last days at Chartley, Mary's money and 272–4; *Letter-books* on Mary's custodianship 245–7; limbo at Fotheringhay accompanied by 286, 287–8, 293–5; Mary at Tixell Hall and 268, 269–72; Mary's final keeper 244–51; mounting scaffold, 'agreeable service' to Mary on 305; preparations for Mary's execution, part in 297–8; protectiveness towards Elizabeth 294–5; secret murder of Mary, defence against possibility of 299; trial at Fotheringhay, Mary informed by 276–7; Tutbury again, relationship with Mary at 245–9
Persons, Robert 216, 217, 260
Peterborough, Dean of 300–01, 307, 313
Peterborough Cathedral, Mary's burial in 313–15
Phelippes, Thomas (cryptographer) 254–5, 258, 262, 265, 266
Philip II of Spain 109, 110, 155, 238, 258, 284, 290; ambition to invade England, Mary as focus of 182–3; collusion between Mary and, Elizabeth's battle against xx–i; El Escorial (residence of) 190–92; international plan for invasion of England, part in 229; Norfolk project with Mary, interest in 80–81; relationship with Mary 186–92; support of Mary for actions of 214, 215–16, 217
Pierrepoint, Bessie de 169, 183, 269
Plough Inn, London 260, 261
Poley, Robert 256, 261, 265
Pontefract Castle 56, 57, 299
Poor Laws (1563) 97
Pope Gregory XIII 185, 215, 216
Pope Pius V 80, 83, 90, 109, 110, 179, 190, 228, 289–90
Préau, Camille du (Mary's secret chaplain) 251–2, 299, 301, 302, 310, 313
Privy Council in England 51, 54, 64, 86, 142, 197, 287, 299; Babington's plan to murder 260; Bess of Hardwick and sons before (1584) 177, 235; desire to send Mary to the scaffold 234; Elizabeth and Cecil, disagreement on dealing with Mary 21–2; Knollys's searching questions to Cecil about Mary 37; Mary's execution, Burghley's demand for secrecy from 298; reassurance on security of Mary for 136
Privy Council in Scotland 193, 220, 239

Raulet, Pierre 153, 175, 183, 184
Regnans in Excelsis (Papal Bull, 1570) 109
Rerum Scoticarum Historia (Buchanan, G.) 29

Richard III 37, 275, 276
Ridolfi, Roberto (and Ridolfi Plot) 110–11, 117, 119, 188
Rizzio, David 51, 153
Romans (and Roman times) 6, 14–15
Ross, John Leslie, Bishop of 110, 117
Ruthven Lords 225, 226
Ruthven Raid 198, 220

Sadler, Ralph 44, 84, 86, 235–6, 244, 278
St Ann's Well in Buxton 139, 144–5, 147
St Bartholomew's Day Massacre 124–5, 126–7, 135, 157, 175, 204
St Loe, William 68, 118
St Mary's Guildhall, Coventry xvi, 88–97
Savage, John 261, 265
Scotland, Dialogue Concerning Government in Kingdom of (Buchanan, G.)
Scrope, Henry, Baron Scrope of Bolton 17, 36, 37–8, 53–4, 55; ancestral home fit for Mary's confinement 33; Bolton's defences, preparations for attack against 34–5; Elizabeth not having sent Mary, soothing words about 25; envoy from Elizabeth at Carlisle 21–2, 24; stringency of Mary's imprisonment under 27
Scrope, Lady Mary 21–2, 34, 36, 37, 43–4, 78
Seaton, Mary (Queen Mary's Lady of the chamber) 22, 69, 219, 223–4, 307
Sheffield 112–15, 122, 165; Castlegate in 113; mood in, modernity of 115; Old Queens Head in 114–15; Town Hall
Sheffield Castle 64–5, 112–21, 125, 151, 161, 173, 194, 211, 214, 236
Sheffield Daily Telegraph 114
Sheffield Manor Lodge 65, 113–15, 129–33, 134–7, 161, 173, 179, 194, 222, 236, 316; Apothecary Garden at 133, 134; Discovery Centre at 130–1; Long Gallery at 131–2, 137; Turret House at 129, 130, 131, 134–7
Shrewsbury, George Talbot, 6th Earl of 64–7, 68, 73, 76, 78, 137, 148, 149, 165, 316; absence from Wingfield, Queen's displeasure at 77; appointment as custodian for Mary 65–6; Babington and 260; breakdown of marriage 176–9, 222–3, 234–5; building projects, lavishing time and money on 240–1; Buxton, eagerness to develop spa at 140–5; Chatsworth, custody of Mary at 101, 104, 106; command over Mary, relief from 122; Coventry, custody of Mary at 87, 88, 90, 95, 96; family of, Mary's involvement with 169–70, 173–4; fighting with Bess, erratic behaviour and 234–5; frailty of Mary considered ruse for smuggling messages 212; health and finance problems for 222–3; intimidation of Mary by 121; judgement on Mary 282; libel and animosity against Mary, communication of 123–4; loyalty of Nau to Mary, questions about

184; Mary and, Elizabeth's concerns about relationship 176–7; Mary in Sheffield in custody of, state of mind of 196–8; Mary's covert correspondence, warning about 159; Mary's trial, enforced attendance at 278; melancholy nature of xvii; Northern Rising, alarm at proximity of 84–5; oversight by, rigour of 251–2; plot to liberate Mary, concerns about 135–6; removal as Mary's custodian by Elizabeth 235–6; signal to Mary's executioner to swing axe 307; St Bartholomew's Day Massacre, emergency response following 125–8, 129; warrant for Mary's execution, delivery of 298, 300; witnesses to execution of Mary 305–6
Shrewsbury, Gilbert Talbot, 5th Earl of 114–15, 136
Shrewsbury, Gilbert Talbot, 7th Earl of 136, 205, 223
Siddick, Cumbria 3, 6–7
Sidney, Sir Philip 30, 256
Solway Firth 1, 6, 7, 10, 14
Somers, John 236, 245
Spanish Armada 189, 313
Stallenge, Nicholas 274, 278–9, 279–80, 288
Stewart, James, Earl of Moray see Moray
Stirling Castle xix, 117, 166, 168–9, 193, 218
Strickland, Agnes 30, 178, 184, 185
Stuart, Arbella 170–3, 178, 186, 194, 205, 222

Stuart, Charles 170–1, 173, 179
Stuart d'Aubigny, Esmé, Duke of Lennox 194–5, 201, 210–11, 217, 218–19
Sussex, Thomas Radcliffe, Earl of 44, 83, 116

Talbot, Francis (Shrewsbury's eldest son) 222–3
Talbot, George, 6th Earl of Shrewsbury see Shrewsbury
Throckmorton, Francis 228–30, 232, 233–4, 235, 254, 258
Tixall Hall 268–72
Tower of London 65, 67, 90, 117, 171, 229, 274, 310
Tutbury 57–63, 97–8
Tutbury Castle 54–5, 59–61, 68–71, 79, 80–81, 99, 101, 112, 118, 151; arrival for Mary at 57–8; confinement at, Mary chafing miserably about 62–3; deepening woes for Mary on return to 240–2; deterioration in Mary's health at 73, 75–6; en route to, Mary's pains caused by stress 56–7; graffiti and carvings on walls of 61; Great Hall and King's Lodgings at 61–2; Healing Herbery at 62; Mary's detestation of imprisonment at 64–5; Mary's hated prison, return under Sadler's watch to 240–2; Mary's life at, gilded nature of 93–6; Northern Rising target 84; Queen's Garden at 61; Receiver's Lodging at 62; return of Mary to, relationship with Paulet and 244–9;

Walsingham's powers over Mary at 245, 246, 247, 250, 251

Valois, Elizabeth de 110, 187

Walsingham, Sir Francis (principal secretary to Elizabeth) 175, 182, 196, 197, 219, 243, 278, 282, 284, 297; antics of Elizabeth's spymaster xxi–ii; appointment as Elizabeth's secretary (May 1573) 157–8; Babington plot and 256–62, 265–6; Beale's report on Mary's health to 211–12; Castelnau, putty in hands of 232–3; characteristics of, Puritan convictions and 126; chastisement of James (in difficult conditions) by 224–6; coups by, many and various 227–30; double-dealing by Mary, expectations of 214–15; execution for Mary, petitioning for 288; fears for life of Elizabeth, promulgation of 124–7; instructions concerning display of Mary's coffin 310; Machiavellian scheme against Mary 253–4; malign spymaster 110; Mary and, communications, confidences and warnings 198–200; national panic, stoking of 294–5; Nau turned Judas in hands of 183–4, 184–5; painful health of 224–5;

Parry plot, recognition of threat to Elizabeth in 230–1; tampering with Mary's letters, accusation of 283; Tutbury and Chartley, powers over Mary at 245, 246, 247, 250, 251; unscrupulousness of 159

Weir, Alison 28, 46, 53, 216–17

Westminster 21, 29, 38, 103, 107; Star Chamber in Palace of 285, 286–8; York Commission relocation to (November, 1568, and aftermath) 49–50, 72–3, 79–80, 99, 235–6

Westmorland, Charles Neville, 6th Earl of 81, 83, 85, 86, 140

Windsor Castle 232, 266

Wingfield, Sir Robert 78–80, 94, 298, 307, 308

Wingfield Manor 57, 65, 73–7, 236

Wolsey, Cardinal Thomas (and Wolsey's Toilet) 131–2

Wood, John 28, 29

Workington, Cumbria 5–6, 7–8, 9–10

Worksop 223, 235

Wyatt's Rebellion (1554) 68

York Commission (October 1568) 41, 44, 48; relocation to Westminster (November 1568 and aftermath) 49–50, 72–3, 79–80, 99, 235–6